The State, France
and the
Sixteenth Century

EARLY MODERN EUROPE TODAY

Editor: Professor J. H. Shennan

The State, France and the Sixteenth Century

HOWELL A. LLOYD
Department of History, The University of Hull

London
GEORGE ALLEN & UNWIN
Boston   Sydney

© Howell A. Lloyd, 1983
This book is copyright under the Berne Convention. No reproduction
without permission. All rights reserved.

George Allen & Unwin (Publishers) Ltd,
40 Museum Street, London WC1A 1LU, UK

George Allen & Unwin (Publishers) Ltd,
Park Lane, Hemel Hempstead, Herts HP2 4TE, UK

Allen & Unwin, Inc.,
9 Winchester Terrace, Winchester, Mass 01890, USA

George Allen & Unwin Australia Pty Ltd,
8 Napier Street, North Sydney, NSW 2060, Australia

First published in 1983

British Library Cataloguing in Publication Data

Lloyd, Howell A.
    The state, France and the sixteenth century.—
(Early modern Europe today)
1. France—History—16th century
I. Title   II. Series
944′.028   DC111

ISBN 0-04-940066-5

Library of Congress Cataloging in Publication Data

Lloyd, Howell A.
    The State, France, and the sixteenth century.
(Early modern Europe today)
Bibliography: p.
Includes index.
1. Political science—France—History.   2. France—
Politics and government—16th century.   I. Title.
II. Series.

JA84.F8L56 1983   320.1′01′0944   82-16471
ISBN 0-04-940066-5

Set in 10 on 11 point Linotron Times by
Rowland Phototypesetting Ltd
and printed in Great Britain
by Biddles Ltd, Guildford, Surrey

Early Modern Europe Today

In introducing a new historical series it is difficult not to begin by offering some justification for its appearance. Yet if we accept that history is ultimately unknowable in the sense that our perception of the past as distinct from the past itself is forever changing, then no apologia is required. That is certainly the premiss on which this series is posited. In the last several decades the changes have been particularly rapid, reflecting fundamental shifts in social and political attitudes, and informed by the growth of new related disciplines and by new approaches to the subject itself. The volumes contained within this series will seek to provide the present generation of students and readers with up-to-date history; with judgements and interpretations which will no doubt in turn form part of the synthesis of future scholarly revisions. Some of the books will concentrate on previously neglected or unconsidered material to reach conclusions likely to challenge conventional orthodoxies in more established areas of study; others will re-examine some of these conventional orthodoxies to discover whether, in the light of contemporary scholarly opinion, they retain their validity or require more or less drastic reassessment. Each in its own way, therefore, will seek to define and illumine some of the contours of early modern Europe, a coherent period at once remote from our own world, yet crucial to an understanding of it. Each will combine considerable chronological range with thematic precision and each, finally, will be completed by a significant bibliographical chapter. It is hoped that this last, prominent feature, which will make the series especially distinctive, will be of value not only to readers curious to explore the particular topic further but also to those seeking information on a wide range of themes associated with it.

Contents

Acknowledgements

I wish to thank in general the many persons, libraries and other institutions that have helped me in the course of my researches, and in particular the Nuffield Foundation for a grant that enabled me to spend a summer in Paris in preparation for writing this book; the staff of the Brynmor Jones Library, University of Hull, for their co-operation and resourcefulness in obtaining materials for me; Professor J. H. Shennan for his interest in my work and his considerate dealing as General Editor of the series; two friends and colleagues at the University of Hull – Professors K. R. Andrews and Gordon Connell-Smith – for their encouragement and support; and, above all, my wife Gaynor for tolerance far beyond the deserts of a humoursome husband.

H.A.Ll.

for
BECKY

Introduction

In this book I wish to explore some features of the history of France in relation to an important ideological development. This development is the emergence of a new concept of the state as a substantive entity and the source of the ruler's authority over his subjects. I shall maintain that such a concept emerged in French political thought of the sixteenth century, and also that it was promptly assimilated to existing systems of ideas. But in arriving at an account of this development I intend to range far beyond the sphere of political thought as such; for it is equally my aim to shed light upon those selected features of France's history that I shall consider along the way. They include aspects of the kingdom's social formation, means of government, economic condition and religious experience, both prior to and during the sixteenth century itself. In the course of discussing each of these I shall endeavour to indicate how they illuminate and are illuminated by the consciousness which underlies the ideological development that is my ultimate concern.

Let us at once identify that development more plainly. At the beginning of the sixteenth century France was widely regarded as the most flourishing monarchy in Europe. Populous and wealthy, the kingdom had political institutions that were the pride of its royal servants and the envy of neighbouring rulers. Pope and Holy Roman Emperor might still pretend to arbitratorship over Christendom, but in France king and people together constituted a self-sufficient 'body politic', an organic whole. That body was perfect as long as no member of it departed from his proper function. Its head was the king, whose mystical person[1] embraced the principal institutions of government. As such he exercised 'royal authority in its entirety',[2] and in particular judicial sovereignty – though this did not entitle him arbitrarily to override the rightful functions of the body politic's other members. He derived his authority from God – though arguments had been heard, and would be heard again, that the people had immediately conferred it upon the ruler. Even so, such was the extent of the king's authority – to dispense justice, to command the instruments of armed force, to levy taxes whereby those instruments were maintained – that of all monarchies the French was 'the most firmly established' and the most powerful, 'a model to monarchists everywhere'.[3]

But in the course of the century Frenchmen were impelled to debate afresh the source of that authority. From their debates the concept emerged that the authority in question sprang from an entity with distinguishing characteristics and properties of its own: an entity other than God, king or people, and certainly other than Emperor or Pope. This entity was 'the state'. No neologism, the term (*status, état*) had been extensively used by earlier political writers. They had used it in effect adjectivally, and in particular to denote the 'condition' of a body politic as a whole, or even of its several members. Such a meaning, as this book will show, persisted strongly and significantly in France throughout the sixteenth century. Yet it was then and there that the term also acquired its new, substantive connotation: that of a distinct entity from which supreme political authority was derived. Thereafter the entity in question would be recognised in various forms and credited with various roles, and would affect very greatly the lives of peoples throughout Europe and the world.

This, then, is the development that by the end of this book I intend to have examined more fully in relation to its sixteenth-century French context. But before we proceed I must enter two caveats. First, the proposition that the state emerged in sixteenth-century France, itself a controversial field of study, is not agreed by all historians. On the one hand, it has been held that the concept of the state as an entity distinct from ruler and ruled was beyond the grasp of even the most able contemporary thinkers.[4] While I reject that view from the outset, I shall reserve for this book's sixth chapter my attempt to demonstrate that the emergence of the concept is plainly apparent in French political thought of that time. On the other hand, it has been contended that in later-medieval Europe 'states' already existed within 'clearly-defined boundaries' or 'frontiers', the necessary conditions for a state's existence being simply that there should occur 'upon a territory, a people obedient to a government'.[5] The contention refers to the 'territorial state', a construct analytically distinct from the concept that I have identified. I shall in fact comment in the course of this book, and particularly in its second chapter, upon the relation between boundaries, territory, people and government in the case of later-medieval and sixteenth-century France. However, as 'government' is an important term in the foregoing contention, and as the terms 'government' and 'state' are often used interchangeably, I must emphasise at the outset that throughout the following discussion 'government' is to be understood as the means of exercising authority, not as its source. Although it may reasonably be held that prior to the sixteenth century there was a territory, a government and a people of France, prior to that century there was no state in the sense of an entity other than ruler and ruled.

Secondly, in relation to that people I must again distinguish the 'state' from another concept with which it has frequently been coupled or confused: the concept of the 'nation'. While 'nation' has notoriously defied definition in other than tautologous terms, the concept plainly refers to a collectivity of people, however defined, and therefore cannot properly refer to a distinct entity from which authority over such a people may be derived. It may be that the French are one of the oldest nations in Europe. It can certainly be argued that attitudes suggestive of 'national consciousness' spread apace in some quarters of sixteenth-century France – a century remarkable for the development of the French language, and for earnest appeals to patriotic sentiment at a time of foreign interventions and foreign threats.[6] But, although this discussion will stress that the state, too, was a phenomenon of consciousness, 'nation' and 'state' remain distinct terms that refer, again, to analytically distinct phenomena. In my judgement, to identify the one with the other is obfuscating, and to intermingle observations upon them is tendentious.[7] This book is concerned with the emergence and the form not of the nation but of the state, and with some – not all – features of France's history that bear upon the question how that emergence came about.

But, if it be agreed that the state did emerge in sixteenth-century France, is not the question easily answered? At the beginning of the century the kings of France were strong and relatively successful rulers, and the people of France were relatively prosperous and content to obey. Apart from encouraging arguments for a still more powerful royal authority, conditions at that time were not such as to excite fundamental reappraisals of constitutional principles. But by the second half of the century conditions had altered. The last three Valois kings, we are told, were personally weak and politically inept. Their insufficiencies were partially offset by the developing 'formation of a strong royal bureaucracy', a feature of that process whereby Renaissance France experienced a 'depersonalisation and institutionalisation of the exercise of power'.[8] Yet it seems that the people's prosperity was waning; that the kingdom's inhabitants were becoming too numerous for even France's natural resources to support without strain; that a 'price revolution'[9] was gathering pace, bringing opportunities for inflated profits to some and leaving many more in distress and impoverishment. Disruptive in their effects upon traditional communities, these conditions were exacerbated by recurrent warfare as 'revolutionary'[10] Protestants confronted obdurate Catholics, great noblemen contended afresh for political power, and every faction sought assistance from abroad and held, as occasion served, that the king was answerable to the people. In these conditions of 'crisis'[11] a new constitutional theory was devised by thinkers who preferred that the kingdom be conserved than that committed exponents of either religious doctrine, or self-serving leaders of any political faction, should triumph at its expense. So they derived the monarch's authority from the state, and thereby buttressed that authority with an entity that was at once impersonal, secular, and beyond dictation by the king's critics and would-be controllers.

Of course, much of this is relevant to the question of the state's emergence and will be considered – often critically – in the chapters that follow. But as an answer to that question it will not do, for reasons that are fundamental to historical explanation and perspective. Such an answer would seem to imply that between environmental and intellectual developments there is a straightforward correlation, such that changes in the conditions in which men live simply induce corresponding degrees of change in their ideas. Further, it favours too limited a chronological perspective, thereby seeking to explain developments of the sixteenth century largely by reference to developments of that century alone. In that perspective, change is abruptly magnified to the proportions of 'crisis' and 'revolution', and perception of vital continuities is blurred. In this book I shall endeavour to find a less distorting perspective. I shall regularly take account of the medieval background to those features of sixteenth-century France's history with which I shall be concerned. And I shall stress that for interpreting these, as well as in relation to the question of the state, continuity is no less significant than change – above all, the continuity of consciousness.[12] I shall take this phrase to mean the broad persistence of traditional beliefs, sentiments and values, however variously expressed by contemporaries and however modified in detail with the passage of time. The complexity of the interaction between change and continuity, and of the interrelation of conditions and consciousness, is a theme of this discussion, and a premiss from which it begins.

A further premiss concerns the consciousness in question, which embraces far more than the ideas expressed by members of an intellectual élite. Such ideas remain its most coherent testimony, and I shall consider them at length in this book. But the dimensions of consciousness embrace beliefs, sentiments and values apparent at every cultural and social level, and evident not only from men's words but also from their behaviour. The evidence ranges from the symbols and ceremonies of church and court to the traditional rituals, season by season, of country dwellers, by far the majority of the kingdom's inhabitants. Moreover, the evidence extends, beyond overtly ritualistic behaviour, to the ways in which men implicitly sanctioned their forms of social and political organisation. It extends even to their material environment, shaped at least partly by men's behaviour and reciprocally conditioning their sentiments in turn. Complex, variable and so often obscure, the many facets of contemporary consciousness are reducible to no simple formula.

Yet the consciousness of late-medieval and sixteenth-century Frenchmen exhibits two paramount traits. On the one hand, it was markedly metaphysical in its orientation. Beliefs were widespread and intense in immutable influences that animated the universe, were present in men themselves, and furnished criteria for evaluating men's actions and their institutions. These influences were uncertainly perceived, variously identified, and provoked disagreements among the learned. Aristotelians described them as 'qualities' and held that they must be present in a substance before they could be held strictly to exist. For neoplatonists they were 'emanations' that 'proceeded' from a superterrestrial source. In popular beliefs they were personalised by the spirits of the dead, still present among the living and requiring regular recognition of their animating power.[13] Even so, the metaphysical sphere of qualities, emanations, ancestral souls, constituted a perpetual model to which men should continually refer and by which they were, in any case, unavoidably affected. On the other hand, contemporary consciousness was profoundly impressed by a sense of the mutability and instability of human affairs and the conditions in which men lived. Human affairs were continually in flux; human institutions were always imperfect. Even in so favoured a kingdom as that of France there was no earthly prospect that men could order their affairs and their institutions wholly in accordance with the metaphysical model – though some institutions approximated more closely than others to the ideal and might even be said to 'represent' it on earth. Nevertheless, the influences that informed the metaphysical sphere ought always to be exemplified, as far as was humanly possible, in the institutions that controlled men's lives, in the leadership and authority to which men were required to defer, and even in the groups to which men belonged. The metaphysical was thus intimately linked with the ethical; and the state – a term that itself implies stability – emerged as a response to ethical exigencies at a time when the contemporary sense of insecurity had grown acute.

The discussion presented in this book follows from these premisses. It is developed in six main chapters. Two chapters are specifically devoted to aspects of intellectual history. The first aims chiefly to illustrate the significance and variety of meanings that sixteenth-century historians attached to what they termed 'the state', a principal focus of their thought; and the sixth deals directly with the emergence of the idea of the state as a development in the sphere of political thought, dwelling particularly upon two major contemporary participants in the long-standing legal and philosophical debate on the nature and limitations of political authority. The remaining chapters consider in turn questions concerning France's socio-political composition, the exercise and distribution of governmental power, responses to changing conditions of material life, and the organisation of the French Protestant movement together with its main opponents, the Catholic leagues. In relation to the book's main theme, these four chapters highlight from different angles the general persistence and implications of attitudes consistent with a conception of France as a 'body politic'. They also identify some indications of the arrival of the 'state'-idea as an element in royal political calculation. Even so, and although they cover a wide range of related topics, the book's six chapters are not intended collectively to constitute a rounded explanatory model of France's development at the opening of the so-called 'modern' era. What they are intended to provide is a contribution towards understanding political attitudes in a past society by way of a broader contextual approach than is normally to be found in the works of specialist historians of ideas. An epilogue looks forward briefly at France's experience in the seventeenth century; and extensive notes together with a substantial bibliography are appended for the benefit of readers who may wish to embark upon further exploration of topics discussed in the course of the book.

CHAPTER 1

Historical Writing

In September 1494, King Charles VIII of France led his army down to Asti in the Tanaro valley. He had crossed the Alps by the Mont Genèvre pass used, centuries earlier, by Pompey the Great. But Charles was no Pompey. According to the Florentine historian Guicciardini he was sickly and ill-proportioned, 'more like a monster than a man'. In Asti he went down with smallpox. Later in the campaign, as he himself explained defensively to his cousin of Bourbon, he contracted measles. Within four years of his descent into Italy he lay dying on a terrace at his castle of Amboise, after putting his foot through a rotten floorboard and hitting his head against a lintel. He had had, as his would-be adviser Commynes declared, 'neither sense, nor money, nor anything else necessary for such an enterprise' as his Italian venture.[1]

Yet prophets had acclaimed Charles's coming. Men of religion and men of learning had hailed him along the way. The terrible friar Savonarola had harangued him in Pisa. The neoplatonic philosopher Marsilio Ficino had welcomed him to Florence. Charles was an envoy of God, a man of destiny. It was his mission to restore: justice to Italy, purity to the church, Jerusalem to Christendom, peace to the world. And, although none of that was accomplished by his Italian venture, Charles's expedition continued long afterwards to be seen as a portentous event, for Europe and for France. In the nineteenth century it gripped the imaginations of both the young Leopold von Ranke and the mature Jules Michelet. For Ranke, Charles's generation was 'one of the most remarkable that ever existed; its political work was the foundation of a European system of states'. For Michelet, Charles by his expedition brought about 'a great revolution', a 'general change', when 'two great electric currents began in the world: Renaissance and Reformation' – those movements that together gave life to 'modern liberties'.[2]

Like the prophets who acclaimed Charles's coming, Ranke and Michelet did not shrink from explaining events ultimately by reference to universal principles and final causes. The event of Charles's coming into Italy occurred at a particular moment in time; but that moment was universally significant. Its significance was apparent from its place within a temporal whole – a whole shaped by a destiny that lay beyond time. For contemporaries the shape of that whole was cyclical: they looked for a restoration of what had been. For their successors, centuries later, the shape was linear: it led from point to point to what must become. It led, in Ranke's view, to the states of Europe – those 'thoughts of God' that historians pondered as 'priests'. As for Michelet, who had looked the sixteenth century 'in the face', the events of 1494 were linked inexorably with those of 1789, and so with the final cause of liberty.

In the nineteenth century such teleological conclusions were widely acceptable. But few of the great masters' associates could match their historical vision and historiographical power in interpreting events. 'The state', guarantor of liberties, was for most of them primarily a matter of institutions. Nineteenth-century historical scholarship, in Germany and in France, was dominated by institutional inquiries. It was the century of Mommsen, Pertz and Waitz, of Fustel de Coulanges, Delisle and Luchaire: the century of the *Monumenta Germaniae Historica*, and of the cartularies published by Guérard of the newly founded École des Chartes. Technically brilliant, indefatigable, such inquiries had their teleological dimension, too. Was it not in charters, laws and related materials that the origins of public liberties were to be found? Citizens joined in seeking them, forming innumerable historical societies whose efforts, in France, were co-ordinated by the Minister of Public Instruction, Guizot, and his Comité des Travaux Historiques.[3] In the conduct of historical investigation governmental agencies of the state, that major product of the historical process, must have their role to play. Yet the lion's share of such investigation was attracted by the medieval centuries; and, although the sixteenth century might mark an important – even a key – phase in the state's emergence, the precise contribution of that problematical era to its formation remained obscure.

The history of sixteenth-century France in relation to the question of the state remains problematical and obscure to this day. One explanation of this lies in the extent and nature of source-materials for the study of relevant aspects of that period. Applauding the achievements of his nineteenth-century predecessors in the field of medieval French institutions, Doucet observed in 1948 how his task, by comparison with theirs, presented 'new difficulties: an inexhaustible documentation, archives of such immensity as to discourage attempts at even the narrowest detailed study'. There were too many manuscripts; they were 'dispersed' in too many repositories; and, with the decline of medieval standards of calligraphy, they were often very hard to read. 'Difficulties of handwriting', according to a leading historian of seventeenth-century France, have helped to 'make French *seizièmistes* such rare birds'. The invention of printing and the subsequent 'shift from script to print' that allegedly 'revolutionised Western culture' had done little to alleviate and much to augment historians' difficulties. While governmental and private business at every level was still almost entirely recorded in manuscript, the spread of literacy that accompanied the spread of printing fuelled the inflation of source-materials. While five volumes sufficed for Molinier and Polain to describe the *Sources de l'histoire de France des origines à 1494*, Hauser needed four for the sixteenth century alone.[4] And, in that century of strident pamphleteering and energetic memorialising, governmental legislation multiplied apace. The ordinances of France's kings from the eleventh to the sixteenth centuries were collected in twenty-one volumes between 1723 and 1849. By 1960 a further seven volumes had covered only twenty years of the reign of Francis I.

Yet the funereal progress of that collection in the present century is itself an indication that source-difficulties are not enough to account for historians' relative neglect of the question of the state in relation to sixteenth-century France. So noticeable was that neglect by the 1960s that Lapeyre felt bound to upbraid his fellow-countrymen. 'The political history of the French sixteenth century', he wrote, 'was practically abandoned' to Anglo-Saxon scholars; and this was owing to French historians' 'infatuation, undoubtedly excessive, with other fields of study'. The allusion was clear enough. The fault lay with the influence of the 'school of *Annales*'. Studies bearing upon the sixteenth-century state, their development already retarded, had suffered further setbacks through the attacks of the *Annalistes* upon the history of 'events', a category that for them embraced political occurrences and institutions alike. The history of events, 'l'histoire événementielle', was 'capricious' and 'deceitful', according to the *Annalistes'* distinguished leaders, Febvre and Braudel. It was capricious in its selectivity, deceitful in its inherent tendency to approach unilinearly the multi-spatial and multi-temporal problems of the past, to dwell upon specific episodes and to explain them with 'eyes only for Kings, Princes, Leaders of Peoples and of Armies – the "men who make History", *Menschen die Geschichte machen*'. That kind of history could be regarded only with a lively distrust. The distrust was lively enough for one of Febvre's followers to depart so far from precedent as to study the French sixteenth century with scant reference to institutions and none whatsoever to Charles VIII.[5]

And yet for the historical writings of Febvre and Braudel the sixteenth century supplied a temporal focus, and indeed commanded pride of place. They found in it ample scope for pursuing a historiographical vision of their own, a vision that was socio-philosophical in kind. While French problems figured prominently in that pursuit, its concerns were with what were termed 'total', 'global' realities. A total reality was a 'functional' whole: what mattered were relations between its component parts, rather than the parts – such as particular institutions – themselves and their discrete development through time. And, thus approached, the sixteenth century emerged afresh as a century of 'rapid and fundamental transformation'. Dynamism then suffused relations of consciousness and material life, at every level of human association. It was especially manifest in the accelerated communication and circulation of ideas through the media of vernacular languages and the printed book, of currency as the medium of economic exchange, even of men themselves as, multiplying in numbers, they traversed the water-routes of Europe and the world. But it was also manifest in political relations; and their distrust of political history did not warrant banishment of political associations from the *Annalistes'* holistic purview. Even in the 1930s, as he and his colleagues struggled to establish their 'new kind of history', what Bloch contested was the practice of seeking 'to describe a state without having first tried to analyse the society on which it rests'. The *Annalistes* deliberately overthrew that practice, but they did so too decisively. By the 1970s they themselves were acknowledging as much. 'A modern society makes no sense without the State; it is indecipherable,' announced Chaunu; and he admitted that 'the history of the state has suffered a setback in France'.[6]

The setback has been especially severe in respect of the sixteenth century. I have specified three main modes of historical writing: the event-centred, the institutional and the socio-philosophical. All three modes are relevant to the question of the state; yet by modern exponents of all three that question in relation to sixteenth-century France has been inadequately treated, the object here of teleological distortion, there of neglect. It is therefore paradoxical that all three modes are traceable to that same sixteenth century, and to the concern with what they termed 'the state' evinced by students of history at that time. In that century, partly under the influence of classical antiquity and partly in response to contemporary developments, scholars in France studied history as never before. In doing so, it has been claimed, they laid the foundations of modern historical scholarship. Although that claim may be questioned, what those historians wrote undoubtedly persists – perhaps excessively[7] – in present knowledge: for history is a cumulative science. But they did not merely supply precedents and information for their successors. They contributed to the development of the state itself as a phenomenon of contemporary consciousness.

In what follows I shall explore facets of that consciousness as evinced in historical writings by members of sixteenth-century France's intellectual élite. In distinct but interacting modes they surveyed past and contemporary events (as 'exemplarists'), their institutions (as philologists and jurists), and their society (as political philosophers). For exponents of all three modes, philosophical considerations were of first importance. It was by reference to universal ethical principles that they vindicated their study of history, and by the same token that they made what they termed 'the state' a principal object of their thought. Yet they interpreted that term in different ways. Thinkers in the 'exemplar' mode, which evolved from an older historiographical tradition, continued to associate it with its long-established meaning: the condition of a body politic, and in particular that of France. The contribution of exponents of the second mode was to promote and to substantiate an awareness of the historical distinctiveness and intrinsic worth of France's legal institutions. It is in the third, or socio-philosophical, mode that a concept becomes discernible of the state as a substantive entity, the purest form of which on earth was the French monarchy. The major exponent of that mode was Jean Bodin, to whose political ideas I shall return in the final chapter. The present chapter concludes with a brief outline of the course of French historical writing in subsequent centuries.

At the beginning of the sixteenth century historical writing in France was still dominated by the medieval chronicle tradition, with recently acquired humanist overtones. That tradition led directly to the event-centred historiography of the exemplarists. In France the tradition's chief exponents had been the chivalrous chroniclers, who had found their favourite subject-matter in military events, *gestae*, heroic deeds – as Froissart, an idiosyncratic exponent of the genre, frankly put it in the fourteenth century, 'so that great marvels and noble feats of arms . . . may be recorded and made known'. Such a record, for the chroniclers, meant a presentation of events in chronological order, punctuated with anecdotes. Affirming the reliability of their sources of information, they were none the less happy to rely upon hearsay testimony, or upon myths – most notably, that longeval myth of the Trojan ancestry of the French – as evidence for earlier epochs. Avowing their own impartiality and concern for truth, they were none the less eager to praise their patrons and to commend their patrons' aims, especially when the latter could in return designate them official chroniclers. Under Charles VIII and his successor the tradition continued to flourish: in the *Vergier d'honneur* of André de La Vigne, secretary to their queen Anne of Brittany, in the *Croniques* of Jean d'Auton, another of her protégés – even in the *Compendium* of Robert Gaguin, rhetorician, diplomat and Erasmus's friend, who applied unsuccessfully for the post of royal historiographer on the strength of the excellence of his Latin style. What such writers derived from Renaissance humanism was means to embellish the tradition, not to supplant it.[8]

An individual note within that tradition was struck by the 'memoirs' – at first entitled *Cronique et hystoire* – of Philippe de Commynes, King Charles's disenchanted counsellor. Critical and didactic in his attitude towards his masters, Commynes evinced concern with general issues of government as distinct from particular deeds or events; and myths, Trojan or otherwise, held little appeal for him. Yet when Commynes accounted for the outcome of the Italian expedition his explanation invoked alternatives that were unmistakably traditional in kind. According to him, what the expedition achieved was owing rather to providence than to its leaders' wisdom, a quality that they signally lacked. On the one hand, the plainly metaphysical; on the other, the apparently personal – these were explanations of the very kind that had satisfied the chroniclers. In the sixteenth century, under humanist influence, men continued to find them satisfactory. While would-be historians responded to Cicero's admonitions in respect of style, they also responded to his admonition 'ut causae explicentur omnes, vel casus, vel sapientae, vel temeritatis'. In historical discourse all contributory causes were to be adduced: causes reducible, it seemed, to chance on the one hand, and men's wisdom or foolhardiness on the other.[9]

Now, the role of chance in human affairs was not random. It had its own, superhuman logic: the logic of Fortune and Necessity. Something of that logic might be read in metaphysical and prophetic texts, or even in the stars, especially with the aid of numerology. But few were competent to carry out such readings; and even those who claimed competence were disconcertingly prone to disagree. Generally, the logic of the higher powers was beyond the direct grasp of human intelligence. It followed that 'necessity leads men in respect of many matters where reason does not', and that 'men may second fortune, but cannot oppose her'. Despite their disavowals of what they took to be his ethics, Frenchmen throughout the century echoed these maxims of Machiavelli's. In the judgement of the magistrate Michel de Montaigne, Louis XII's brilliant general Gaston de Foix 'would not have marred the day by his death' when he charged the retreating enemy at the Battle of Ravenna, had he not chosen 'to throw victory back into the lap of fortune . . . which will not conform nor subject itself to our reason and foresight'. According to the soldier Blaise de Monluc,

Francis I was defeated and captured at Pavia because he 'expected to find fortune as favourable as at the day of the Swiss [at Marignano]; but she turned her back on him'. To act on the basis of past experience was 'very dangerous', as the historian Guicciardini had warned, 'if the same conditions do not apply not only in general but in every particular, if the matter is not managed with the same prudence and if, in addition to everything else, one does not have the same fortune on one's side'.[10] Was it not evident that conditions altered, prudence varied and fortune was unpredictable? What purpose, therefore, could there be in studying history? Above all, on what ground could it be claimed that history was a storehouse of 'examples'?

And yet throughout the century all sorts of writers insisted not merely that there was such a purpose, but upon that very 'exemplar' claim. It was implicit in the introductory remarks of the royal and *parlement* archivist Jean du Tillet to his *Recueil des Roys de France*, dedicated to Charles IX: 'Writings on past things, even on domestic affairs, are (Sire) not only very useful but very necessary as much for kings and sovereign Princes as for their subjects. For (as Polybius says) men have no easier way to good instruction for life than by knowledge of precedent.' The claim was explicit in the opening words of the *Chronicon Carionis*, by the extraordinarily influential German Protestant theologian Philip Melanchthon: 'Histories are read in all ages and by all peoples because thereby knowledge is attained and many reminders are set forth in examples both of the duties of private life and why disasters occur there, and of how public affairs are managed and the causes of many terrifying changes in governments.' Still bolder was the statement of the claim by the Huguenot soldier Henri de La Popelinière in his *Histoire de France*: since history was 'a true narration of many particular examples, these are much fitter for stimulating and educating people than are the arguments, rules, precepts and other kinds of imperious forms of instruction of the Philosophers'.[11]

Given the classical heritage of history, perhaps the exemplar claim was simply conventional – like du Tillet's reference to Polybius, to whom Melanchthon also alluded at the opening of his *Chronicon*. Less simply, perhaps that claim offered a special consolation for Protestants, denied by their theology from aspiring to direct rational understanding of divine intentions. According to the French legal humanist François Baudouin, who delivered lectures on the theme of universal history at Heidelberg where Melanchthon had founded an appropriate chair, history was 'the only way and means by which we can ascend to that knowledge of divine and human things'.[12] Yet Protestants had no monopoly of the 'exemplar' mode. Less simply still, the assertions of Baudouin and the rest are compatible with another explanation of that mode, philosophical in kind for all that La Popelinière chose to disparage philosophy: an explanation of the vital *rapprochement* between human affairs and the metaphysical that history alone could expose for men's instruction.

Contemporary notions of time have a bearing upon this explanation. The events in which men ceaselessly engaged were ceaselessly in flux; but that flux occurred within a system that in its entirety was shaped, determined, fixed. Men had their transient being, and pursued their fluctuating affairs, within a universal whole that imposed limits upon the possibilities of change. Even Guicciardini admitted as much: 'the world has always been the same as it now is. . . . Things accordingly repeat themselves, but under changed names and colours.' The view was crudely restated by Bernard du Haillan, historiographer of France under the last Valois king and the first Bourbon: 'although persons change, the world nevertheless does not change at all'. Time was cyclical; its revolutions imposed constancy. Du Haillan described the process in accordance with what were, again, Polybian ideas: to see, through history, the link of 'past centuries with the present' was 'to see the beginnings, the institutions, the births and the growths, the grandeurs, the diminutions, the declines and the ruins of great Empires and States'. 'Empires and States' were the concerns of princes who, accordingly, should 'consider the examples by which they can be instructed'; and 'Princes who read and ought to read Histories ought to take care that similar *accidens* do not sweep down upon them'.[13]

But du Haillan, a blatant plagiarist, was also a trivialiser, at whose hands the underlying philosophy of exemplar history drifted towards a naïve supposition that situations might repeat themselves. The concepts of 'example' and '*accidens*' with which he toyed involved far more than he was able to convey. Profound philosophical and ethical significance attached to those concepts. Detached from what they signified, '*accidens*', like 'events', were mere happenings, meaningless particulars. History, as La Popelinière put it, ought not to be a 'simple Narration of *accidens*'.[14] But, properly viewed, they were *phenomena*; and their significance consisted in what they disclosed of the reality to which they related. That reality, far beyond any momentary interaction of particular individuals or circumstances, consisted in the continuing interaction of abiding qualities. And it was through its demonstration of those qualities in action that history fulfilled its exemplar function: a function that, for Baudouin, furnished knowledge of a kind that could not otherwise be obtained. It was also through such a demonstration that historical explanation itself was achieved.

Much of this is apparent from the formula proposed by La Popelinière for explaining '*accidens*':

There are four kinds of cause, material, formal, efficient and final: as much to be considered by the Historian as by the Philosopher. The material is that which the actor undertakes in peace or war, and which the Historian recounts. The formal is the means which he has to carry it out or execute it. The efficient is the actor himself who undertakes it. The final proceeds from his qualities of feeling which he aims to satisfy in carrying out his plans: such as love, hate, spite, vengeance, ambition, avarice and other good and evil passions.[15]

The formula is an obvious application of Aristotelian theory of causes – that explanatory apparatus to familiarity with which all educated Frenchmen were schooled.[16] Less obvious – though unquestionably not to them – in that formula is the implicit presence of other Aristotelian principles. In Aristotelian logic, members of the category of 'quality', unlike those of the category of 'substance', did not exist independently. Qualities must be present in a subject.[17] For La Popelinière they were evidently present in the human actors who took part in the events of which they were the final cause. Accordingly, history furnished the means whereby qualities, whether those of the intellect – wisdom or lack of it, as Cicero and Commynes had specified – or those of the passions such as interested La Popelinière, could be observed. And it was here that history performed its exemplar function. History was not a record of recurring situations, even though it was admissible that situations might recur. History was not merely a series of illustrations of superhuman interventions in human affairs, even though such interventions undoubtedly took place and must be acknowledged. History, and history alone, was above all a storehouse of examples that men ought to ponder for their ethical value – examples of the universal qualities exhibited by their ancestors and present in themselves as they engaged in the events of their time.

Small wonder, then, that French historians in the later sixteenth century should have professed a high sense of ethical purpose. Opinionated, eclectic, they none the less proclaimed with assurance their unfailing devotion to truth. Truth was 'the eye of history' for du Haillan, 'the first law of history' for Jacques-Auguste de Thou. Greatest of contemporary historians of the civil wars, de Thou unhesitatingly declared 'before God that I have written without favour or enmity towards persons, I have love only for virtue and hatred only for viciousness'. But de Thou went farther and declared another love. Writing at the close of the century, he explained how he had been

always a Frenchman and servant of kings, and of the Royal House; and never a pensionary nor a partisan of others. Everything that was contrary to them was contrary to my affection. To the loss of my goods and at the risk of my life I followed them in the armies and everywhere else during these calamitous wars. I nevertheless yielded nothing to favour nor to hatred in writing the History, but I dared more freely to tell the truth, and to preserve its memory for posterity, than anyone who feared envy or odium would have done. I don't doubt that I have thereby seemed to write too freely, even too boldly, on certain matters; but such boldness, and such affection for the state, was eminently necessary, in order to conserve the state.[18]

'To tell the truth' was 'to conserve the state', principal object of de Thou's concern in writing history, that meeting-ground of the universal and the particular.

De Thou's concern as a historian for 'the state' was, like his devotion to 'truth', fervently affirmed by others. For La Popelinière, 'the state' was 'the true subject of history'; for du Haillan it was 'the true point of history'; and Henry IV's historiographer Jean de Serres adopted the epigraph 'for the greatness and strength of the state' for his best-selling *Inventaire général de l'histoire de France*. How were these historians to reconcile their devotion to what they termed 'the state' with the concepts that informed their exemplar mode, and the ethical aims that they so ostentatiously professed? In his writings and other activities de Serres showed himself committed to an irenic purpose, to doctrinal reconciliation among the Christian churches and to peace among secular governments.[19] Was not such a commitment contradicted by his dedication of his work to the greatness of the particular 'state' of France? And yet, for historians who sought in particular events examples of universal qualities, no such contradiction arose; and in devoting their writings, and themselves, to 'the state' they did not deviate from the values of the exemplar mode.

There were Aristotelians who assigned 'the state' explicitly to the category of 'qualities'. The jurist Charles Loyseau, generous in his use of historical materials in his writings, derived the term 'from the Latin *status* . . . [which] signifies a permanent quality or condition of some thing'; and so 'we call the Kingdom itself State'. Many historians were also jurists by training, and all were in some measure logicians. Although few were as rigorous or as openly categorical as Loyseau in their thinking, their concern with 'the state' was fully tenable upon philosophical grounds. On the one hand, the concept signified for them an ethical system composed of universals. Such a signification was rooted in the political doctrines of the Greek philosophical masters. Plato had defined the Greek *polis* in terms of four cardinal 'virtues of wisdom, courage, discipline and justice'; and according to Aristotle 'virtue must be the care of a *polis* that is properly so called'.

Of course, those masters and their successors had disagreed over whether universals had a real existence, an absolute form. But the disagreement constituted no difficulty for historians in Renaissance France. A realist philosophical position was not a prerequisite of commitment to 'the state'. For, on the other hand, the term had long since signified the 'condition' of actual bodies politic – perhaps an optimum condition, but certainly one that occurred, variously, at particular times and in particular places, through the interactions of men in institutionalised groups. Thus 'the state' was at once a universal and a particular phenomenon. And, if historical truth was the meeting-ground of the universal and the particular, by no case within its purview was that encounter better exemplified than by the state – none better, indeed, than by the state of France, for de Serres 'the true pattern of a perfect state, such as the wise politicians in former times used to discourse of in their Academy'.[20]

Now, in his successive discourses upon the *polis* the founder of the Athenian Academy had placed increasing emphasis upon law, which gave the *polis* its unity and animated it as the material universe was informed and ordered by the soul.[21] Plato's ideas were echoed by France's finest exemplar historian. 'Be persuaded', de Thou urged his king, 'that the intelligence and soul and sagacity and judgement of a state lie in laws; and just as our body cannot function without intelligence, so without law the state cannot be used by its parts and sinews, its blood and members'.[22] Doubtless the laws of every body politic were, or ought to be, manifestations within the particular sphere of universal principles of justice and reason. Yet it was apparent that the laws of states varied with time and place; and, although the variation was itself a universal verity and the principles as such were the concern of moral philosophers, it was a valid concern for historians to examine the distinctive features of institutions as they were actually to be found in particular political cases. From examining the case they might proceed to demonstrate how particular institutions exemplified law and order, justice and reason, to a greater or a lesser degree. There were institutional historians who hurried eagerly on to such demonstrations. Others contented themselves largely with the prior examination – and some, even, with collecting materials for it.

For their inquiries the institutional historians were both stimulated and equipped by humanist scholarship. Stimulus and equipment – the techniques of philological and jurisprudential criticism – were closely linked. Philological analysis sharpened awareness of temporal change. Time 'transformed' the meanings of 'many words of good and ancient coinage', 'multiplied' the meanings of others, and brought 'into currency' many more: thus Francis I's librarian, Guillaume Budé, hailed as 'the greatest Greek in Europe', in his commentaries upon the laws of ancient Rome. Words were the stuff of laws; and semantic adjustments were indicators of alterations in laws themselves. 'It is impossible', observed Étienne Pasquier, barrister of the Paris *parlement*, 'to say how many faces the laws of Rome have taken according to the diversity of the times'.[23] And, since laws informed institutions, awareness of change in the *minutiae* of laws brought recognition of time's effects upon entire governmental systems. In criticising the editor of Justinian's lawbooks, the jurist François Hotman could pronounce, with characteristic over-emphasis: 'the study of the Roman *respublica* can be of no value to the government of France, because the forms of those two governments are not in any way alike'. Yet even the immoderate Hotman did not hesitate to evaluate the French constitution, as he discovered it, by reference to universal principles. In his notorious *Francogallia*, devoted to demonstrating on historical grounds that France's institutions were distinctively Germanic in origin and had been corrupted by subsequent rulers, that original constitution was affirmed to be 'the best and most excellent form of *respublica* according to the judgements of Plato, Aristotle, Polybius and Cicero'. A constitution was justified by reference not to what had become of it by its particular passage through time, but, beyond that, to its fundamental consistency with universal principles of reason and equity, principles that Hotman unfailingly evoked.[24]

The affinity is plain between a demonstration such as Hotman's and the exemplar mode of historical writing. Yet the distinctive contribution of the institutionalists to the development of both history and the concept of the state amounted to more than an introduction of more sophisticated subject-matter and techniques of inquiry in the service of what they took for historical truth. Moreover, despite the continued prevalence of cyclical conceptions of time, they did not suppose that the wheel could be brought full circle in every particular – that their search for the origins of France's institutions would enable every detail of a pristine constitution simply to be recovered and reinstated in their own day. If they had ever entertained it, their historical inquiries educated them out of so naïve a supposition. Those inquiries nevertheless led them to a fresh belief, held specifically on historical grounds, though again redolent of ethics. It was the belief that France's constitution was informed – as, doubtless, were other enduring constitutions – by a distinctive genius; and that its continuing perfection depended upon its remaining true to that genius of its own. As Pasquier argued, the genius of the French was manifest in 'the civility of the laws'. Unlike, for instance, the laws of Rome, the laws of France subordinated individual interests to 'the common duty of us all'. The vehicle of their 'civility' in former times had been the kingdom's 'aristocracy' and 'honourable personages'. They had maintained a '*commune police* that was as a mean between the king and the people'. That *police*, an accumulation of constitutional laws, was now guaranteed by 'many honourable personages formally established for the purpose' as the Paris *parlement*. That institution was therefore 'the foundation stone of the conservation of our State'. But the 'state' itself was implicitly identified not with any particular institution nor with king and people as such, whether severally or together. It consisted in the laws themselves, to conserve which was thereby to conserve 'all the greatness of France' and its 'liberty'.[25]

All this, however, was not to formulate a concept of the state as an entity distinct from ruler and ruled, so much as to define the 'condition' of the kingdom and of its preservation in specifically legal terms. The political role of an 'aristocracy' and of 'honourable personages' would be otherwise interpreted by contemporaries of Pasquier's, as we shall see.[26] Yet in developing his view Pasquier enjoyed the support of a circle of scholarly friends, even though their opinions upon France's constitution might differ in detail from his. Pierre Pithou, Antoine Loisel, Claude Fauchet, Louis Charondas le Caron – the circle was large with, on its periphery, younger men such as de Thou himself, admirer of Pithou and cousin of Fauchet, who was royal historiographer under Henry IV. The circle's members were all moderate in religion, all trained and practising lawyers, all office-holders. Their appetites were omnivorous for antiquarian learning. But the impact of their studies was greatest through their publications in the field of law: le Caron's *Pandectes*, Loisel's *Institutions coutumières*, Pithou's *Libertés de l'Église gallicane*. If such 'learned and excellent persons', wrote the exemplarist du Haillan, 'whose heads and libraries are full of so many fine things concerning the history of France would spend their time in writing it, we should see it better written than any history ever was'. They spent their time instead upon a mode of historiography that substantiated their firm belief in the historical distinctiveness and intrinsic worth of France's legal institutions. Their inquiries, prosecuted in an era of civil wars, showed the monarchy of France to be justified by its own foundations. They enabled le Caron to declare: 'This kingdom (by the grace of God) is of all others the first and best endowed with all things: also, it has generally been at all times better ruled and governed than any other monarchy, in justice.' Conversely, disaster struck when those foundations were disturbed: for 'in a State already grown old', as Jean Bodin put it, 'if the foundations that uphold it are removed, however slightly, there is great danger of its ruin'.[27]

However, Bodin neither belonged to Pasquier's circle nor associated himself with the methods of its members, although he knew them well enough. Intellectually more akin to Baudouin and La Popelinière than to the institutional inquirers, he differed from them, too, in his view of history, and surpassed them by far in his practice of it. While Baudouin hankered after 'universal history', 'the history of the world', grandly conceived, he contributed very little to its writing; and La Popelinière finalised his conception of 'perfect history' too late in his career to do more than commend to others the history of France as a suitable subject. With aims as ambitious and a method as fertile as either of these entertained, Bodin practised what he preached. He preached it in his *Methodus ad facilem historiarum cognitionem*: 'history for the most part deals with the state and with the changes taking place within it', and so 'to achieve an understanding of the subject we must explain briefly the origins, developed form and ends of principalities'.[28] He practised it in his *Six livres de la République*, a key work in the history of European thought, and the major instance of sixteenth-century France's third historiographical mode.

Upon Bodin's socio-philosophical mode the influence of classical philosophy was very marked. Plato and Aristotle were ever present in his thinking. Although he criticised Aristotle at every opportunity, it was the Stagyrite who furnished the Angevin with his models. They were models not only for discerning the several forms of states and 'for what kinds of nation the various kinds of constitution are suited', but also for constructing arguments by apparently inductive means. One such means was the use of 'examples'. 'You must give a large number,' Aristotle had advised[29] – a precept observed by Bodin to the point of tedium, as he drew upon his vast store of historical learning. Yet both in his mode and in his view of the state Bodin differed categorically from the exemplarists. He explicitly held it an error in dealing with the state to dwell upon 'the accidental quality'. His concern was with what was 'essential and formal' in the nature of states. Even so, 'we have no wish to describe a State as an Idea without effect, in the manner of Plato and Sir Thomas More'. For Bodin, the state was substantial: it was an absolute entity, 'the state in itself' which, unlike all 'qualities', 'experiences no comparison of more or less'.[30] That substance was largely discernible by reference to history; and, robbed of such reference, the forms indicated by philosophy were merely nominal, and empty.

States differed from each other: 'it is not enough to know which is the best state, one must also know the means to maintain every one of them'. That knowledge was to be sought by way of the fullest comparative examination, of states as such and of the societies to which they related. Bodin's examination ranged over geographical conditions, economic resources, social organisations, political institutions, as well as historical events in all 'the most flourishing cities and states'. How circumscribed – indeed, how trifling – the institutionalists' selective inquiries into France's past, by comparison with his holistic quest! Bodin deliberately distinguished his mode from theirs. The great jurist Jacques Cujas, whom Pasquier and his circle devoutly admired, was singled out for special stricture, his celebrated philological methods dismissed as 'childish disputations about words and insubstantial matters'. Opinions, put about by Pasquier in particular, as to the Paris *parlement*'s constitutional role, were rejected by Bodin as 'not only absurd, but also capital', verging upon the 'crime of *lèse-majesté*'. The French might be well enough endowed with 'civility'; but the power to make law was an essential property of the state. And of all the forms of state 'a monarchy is the most sure'; it was the form best suited to the French; and the state of France 'is a pure monarchy'.[31]

Thus writers of history in each of these three modes made what they termed 'the state' a principal object of their thought. They interpreted that term differently; and, taken together, their writings scarcely presented their contemporaries with a coherent view of the source of political authority. The differences persisted throughout the sixteenth century, and beyond. If Bodin conceived of the state as a distinct entity, long after the publication of his *République* the term continued to be associated in de Thou's work with the composition of a body politic, and to figure in Pasquier's in an institutional sense. Yet all of these writers shared a consciousness schooled in classical philosophy and trained in law, and strove to rationalise accordingly France's historical experience and its political structure. Whether or not they conceived of the state as such as an entity subsisting in its own right, conceptions that may seem abstruse to modern minds were immediately accessible to all of them: conceptions of the political entity that was France as a unique association of the universal and the particular, enduring in its just institutions, an actualisation of principles that were as old as the Greeks.

How far their writings appealed to their contemporaries is another matter. Certainly these historians were a tiny minority among sixteenth-century Frenchmen, and their works no more than a few drops in the flood of print that issued from the presses. For readers eager to immerse themselves in history, those presses poured forth a stream of historical writings quite other than works in the exemplar, institutional and socio-philosophical modes. In popularity those works could not compete with chronicles, such as Gaguin's *Compendium*, reissued nineteen times in Latin between 1494 and 1586 as well as in the vernacular. Still less could they compete with medieval romances, such as the *Roman de la Rose*, reissued fourteen times in the first forty years of the century. Even in the market for contemporary history, high-minded exemplarists had to compete with an upsurge of self-serving memoirs written, as Blaise de Monluc said unashamedly of his own

Commentaires, for 'the defence of my honour and reputation', and so that 'little Monlucs' might 'admire their reflection' in their grand-father's life. As for the institutionalists, their political message did not commend itself even to sober-minded readers in the provinces of France. Parisian doctrines of the kingdom's institutional unity scarcely appealed to men whose interest lay in the defence of provincial, feudal, customary rights. Such sentiments were expressed rather in provincial histories: Bertrand d'Argentré's *Annales de Bretagne*, or Guy Coquille's *Histoire du pays et duché de Nivernais*.[32]

And yet those same defences of provincial liberties and the rights of particular members of the body politic were essentially works of history in the institutional mode. Moreover, during the sixteenth century a significant shift was taking place in France in the production of historical writing. Production of the traditional modes was in decline. The nine 'editions' of Froissart that appeared between 1495 and 1550 were followed in the second half of the century by only two more, with two Latin translations. Conversely, of 271 new historical titles published between 1550 and 1610 almost one-fifth were recognisably works in the institutional mode. Who bought such works, who read them, and how did they interpret what they read? There can be no certain answers to these questions. But the likelihood is strong that historical views of 'the state' in any of its senses appealed especially to men who were directly involved in the practice of government, whether at the centre or in the provinces. It was with participants in the former that the historiographical initiative increasingly lay – with royal protégés better equipped than formerly to 'know the truth about the past' and nevertheless still willing, like the Socrates of Plato's *Republic* and with purposes not dissimilar from his in view, to 'invent a fiction as like it as may be'. From the sixteenth to the eighteenth centuries almost all *historiographes du roi* and *historiographes de France* belonged by birth to the families of royal *officiers*.[33] Members of such families, it may be assumed, also supplied historians with the core of their potential readership. And in the sixteenth century that reader-ship shared with writers who endeavoured to rationalise France's history in terms of 'the state' a consciousness attuned to the philo-sophical and legal concepts that informed their writings.

Now, during the centuries that followed, the divergence between historiographical modes persisted. The seventeenth-century success-ors to exemplar history were the court historians, not the learned institutionalists to whom du Haillan had appealed. Court historians might not lack scholarly equipment and independence of mind and manners. François Eudes de Mézeray, royal historiographer under Louis XIV, had enough philological expertise to play a leading part in the lexicographical researches of a French Academy intent upon promoting cultural uniformity, as well as enough indiscretion to offend his patrons by his criticisms of French governments in his best-selling *Histoire de France*. But, a self-declared admirer of de Thou's 'immortal works' and 'zeal for the greatness of the state', Mézeray himself recognised how his own *Histoire*, replete with myths and invented speeches, stood in direct line of descent from Gaguin and du Haillan. Scholarship was no doubt admirable – a historian of France ought no doubt to study all aspects of Europe, past and present, as well as 'all the archives' – but 'I ask you', protested Mézeray, 'who could possibly put together all of those things?'[34]

So the historians of events went lightly their way, while the institutionalists went more weightily theirs. Prominent among the latter were members of religious orders – most notably, the Congregation of St Maurus whose work, at first devoted to monastic history, culminated in that mighty enterprise the *Gallia Christiana*, an account of all the kingdom's dioceses and abbeys, undertaken at the behest of the Assembly of the Clergy of France. And, like the leaders of the church, political leaders were aware of the uses of institutionalists, and did not confine their patronage to court historians. Early in the seventeenth century a fresh circle of scholars, the *académie putéane*, formed around the brothers Dupuy, friends and helpers of de Thou. Its members entertained unorthodox opinions; but this was no bar to enjoyment of Richelieu's patronage by Pierre Dupuy and his associate Théodore Godefroy, both official historiographers. As royal librarian Dupuy was set to work on an inventory of the confused mass of documents stored in an annexe to the Sainte-Chapelle that constituted the Trésor des Chartes. Although the inventorial work was imperfectly done, it revealed important evidence concerning royal rights both within France and to territories abroad. It also yielded materials for Dupuy's *Traité des droits du Roy* and his *Traité des droits de l'Eglise gallicane*.[35] The latter recalled Pierre Pithou's publication; and among his many activities Pithou had helped the barrister Antoine Fontanon with his collection of royal *Edicts et ordonnances*, one of several such collections undertaken in the later sixteenth century. It was an undertaking that came directly under the aegis of state institutions in the early eighteenth century, when the Académie des Inscriptions et Belles-Lettres, recognised by royal charter in 1701 after its initial foundation by Colbert, began in 1723 to publish its series of *Ordonnances des rois de France* – the series that has continued to inch interruptedly forwards to this day.

A major interruption to all such institutional endeavours came with the Revolution, suppressing religious orders and academies alike, banning whatever appeared to vindicate the monarchical state. But there were revolutionary minds, and even features of revolutionary constitutions, that owed inspiration to a practitioner of the socio-philosophical mode. That practitioner was Montesquieu, far more a successor to Bodin than he cared openly to admit. Both derived from Aristotle a typology of states. Neither was content to ponder a formal typology, to consider as a philosopher *tout court* what Bodin had dismissed as states' 'imaginary form'. Both found it 'necessary', as Montesquieu put it, 'to explain history by the laws and the laws by history'.[36] Laws had in any case to be explained: according to Bodin they were 'dumb' without magistrates[37] – the 'mouth', in Montesquieu's phrase, 'that pronounces the words of the law'. But the words of laws were less than their 'spirit'. That 'general spirit is formed', in Montesquieu's view, by the interaction of many elements – religion, social customs, above all 'climate' – as well as by the influence of past 'examples'. The form of that spirit varied, from case to case, state to state; within every case the interaction was ceaseless; and so every state, by Montesquieu's argument, was 'a moving but pregnant totality',[38] moving through time, pregnant with possibilities engendered through the dynamic relation between its elements.

There is an obvious affinity between Montesquieu's holistic approach and the holism professed by present-day *Annalistes*. But modern historians of events and institutions are disposed to look more kindly upon their respective progenitors than are the followers of Febvre to look upon Montesquieu. For his argument foundered at a key juncture into determinism of a kind that the *Annalistes* have sought sedulously to avoid. Montesquieu ascribed the most powerful function in relation to the 'spirit of the laws' to what he termed 'climate', meaning in effect the natural environment. The lead was again Aristotelian; it was a lead that Bodin, too, had followed. But Bodin had fought shy of the deterministic conclusions reached, long before his time, by 'Polybius and Galen, who held that the country and nature of places have inescapable effects upon men's way of life'. Montesquieu was less circumspect, and pronounced without reservation that 'The influence of climate is the first of all influences'. Even in the eighteenth century so baldly naturalistic an assertion provoked surprise. In the twentieth it was roundly rejected by Febvre, who devoted an early work to an attack upon geographical determinism as espoused by the fateful Germanic school of 'Anthropogeography' – an attack that included strictures upon Montesquieu himself.[39]

Yet in denouncing determinism the *Annalistes* had no intention of denying the importance of the problem upon which the unsatisfactory and dangerous cogitations of anthropogeographers bore. It was that central problem of social and political philosophy: the relation between consciousness and conditions of material life. The problem now demands our attention in respect of France. A decade before Febvre wrote, the doyen of French geographers, Paul Vidal de La Blache, himself a fervent critic of the Germanic school, formulated his particular version of the problem and made it the theme of his contribution to what, remarkably, is still the standard political history of France. 'How', asked Vidal, 'did a fragment of the earth's surface which is neither a peninsula nor an island, and whose physical geography should hardly be thought to constitute a whole, attain the status of a political country?'[40] France had long enjoyed that status, longer than almost any other European country. Historians had helped to promote it in the consciousness of members of their society. For them, the 'state of France' was a phenomenon demonstrable by reference to the events of France's past and its distinctive institutions. The events had been examined and recounted often enough – too often, as some contended. The institutions, too, had been earnestly examined, even though their sixteenth-century development had relatively been neglected. But such examinations did not provide, and even the more alert inquiries of philosophical historians had failed adequately to furnish, solutions to the problem of the state's relation with its territory – and, therefore, with the society materially supported by that territory. Accordingly, the nature of the state itself remained in vital respects obscure. In respect of France, Vidal proposed his own influential solution to that problem. As we turn from the historiography to the society of France, it is reasonable to begin with what he had to say.

CHAPTER 2

Men
in Groups

According to Vidal de La Blache, the key to the problem of France's political formation lay in the *genre de vie* of the French people.[1] They lived – as Michelet had long since described – in a country made up of a great variety of regions, unlike their continental neighbours who occupied territories that were physically far more uniform. Each of France's many regions exhibited a peculiar combination of natural elements. Its varied resources, its own internal diversity, made possible a high degree of regional self-sufficiency. In every case the region's inhabitants had responded distinctively to its possibilities; and in human terms each region was a product of that response, of the relation between men and their environment, rather than simply of the environment's 'natural' character. The unity of every such region was further enhanced by its differences from the many other regional unities that lay around it and within France. Clearly, France as a whole was not to be interpreted merely as an assemblage of regions: indeed, to focus upon these in turn was to highlight the diversity of that whole, rather than its unity. Yet every region was constituted by a similar structure of possibilities and responses. What mattered for the formation of France as a whole were the structural consistencies of so many regional *genres de vie*. These in combination, and not simply in sum, endowed France with a 'personality' that was itself distinctive. That personality was reinforced by France's position in relation to the continental and maritime masses that converged upon its territory. In Vidal's composite vision, regional and global perspectives revealed how the French 'isthmus' uniquely possessed 'unity in diversity'. Hence the possibility of France's 'status' as a 'political country' – a status that had none the less to be realised through political history, and was not the necessary outcome of geographical possibilities alone.

Vidal's influence was great upon French regional geographers – a school distinguished by an acute sense of history – and also upon many French historians, among them leading members of the school of *Annales*. Yet his followers often lacked the sweep and subtlety of their master's vision. Metaphors characterising France as a 'mosaic' and a 'crossroads' became commonplace in both geographical and historical writing.[2] But it was the parts of the mosaic that attracted keenest attention. Regional monographs proliferated. Their proliferation provoked misgivings. Geographers warned French regional researchers that their 'numerous monographs . . . have not cleared the way for any systematic effort at generalisation'. Among historians, Braudel himself greeted yet another regional monograph with a stern reminder that what mattered was not the region but 'the problem'. In relation to any problem that might be mooted, it was an error to suppose that local and general explanations were interchangeable – and especially so in relation to France. 'Young French historians', urged Braudel, ought not to 'throw themselves headlong into enterprises like those of the prestigious disciples of Vidal de La Blache, studying the divers regions of the French mosaic one after another'. Such enterprises seemed almost to suggest that France was a 'machine' to be 'dismantled and explained piece by piece' – an approach, and with it yet another metaphor, against which Vidal himself had explicitly warned.[3]

Meanwhile, the composition of French society under the *ancien régime* was examined in other works where the unity of the region found a counterpart in the unity of the social group. Soon after Michelet compiled his famous description of France's regions, de Tocqueville was observing how in pre-Revolutionary France 'there was no individual who did not belong to a group', one of the 'thousand little groups of which French society was composed'.[4] Twentieth-century scholars developed the observation, resorting as they did so to functionalist terminology and also to biological metaphor. Under the *ancien régime*, when French society was 'largely formed' of an 'astonishing variety of *corps*', the place of every individual, or *personne physique*, was determined by the 'function' he performed; and 'persons performing the same functions . . . voluntarily grouped themselves into associations'. No doubt, as natural-law theorists had long since argued, the individual was prior to the association to which he none the less surrendered much of his original freedom. No doubt, too, voluntary associations that might at any time be dissolved were not to be equated with corporate entities that were formally constituted and enjoyed in law the status of 'moral persons'. Yet all such groups sprang from a prevailing tendency rooted in the very nature of society and the functions that sustained it. Moreover, they included the constituent 'cells' of French society – chief among them the family and the rural community.[5] And when historians turned their attention to the relation between society and the state it transpired that the state itself was a group-entity, the supreme expression of that same tendency in the political sphere. Thus, according to Mousnier, in the last two centuries of the *ancien régime* France was 'essentially a society of *corps* and communities'; and 'from the social groups constituting the society emerges a public corporation or collectivity, willing and acting on behalf of society and in its name. This public corporation, this moral and judicial person, is the State, an organisation that realises the unity of a plurality of individuals.'[6]

Images of the 'personality' of France as seen by geographers and the 'person' of the state as seen by social and political historians, and indeed by lawyers, bear an obvious resemblance to the organological analogy, the image of the 'body politic' so favoured by later-medieval and Renaissance thinkers. The resemblance is significant: all such images convey in some degree an impression of a people's political unity as a product of 'natural' groupings and their spontaneous inter-action. However, in European thought from the seventeenth century onwards the state as *persona moralis* was endowed with attributes that distinguished it increasingly, and categorically, from the *corpus mysticum reipublicae* of organological tradition. The state, for modern political thinkers, was not simply composed of members who together gave it substance. Conceptually, juridically, it was an entity transcending the 'individuals' that, whether as single persons or as groups, were subject to its will. Yet the relation between the supreme entity and those lesser beings remained problematical. Nineteenth-century Romantic theorists offered systematic accounts of that relation. Now every individual was specified as a 'part-unity' of a higher 'group-unity'; every group had a real existence and a personality; and all groups were integrated in and articulated by the state, the highest group-unity of all. No 'mere conglomeration of individuals', far more than the sum of its parts, the state was reality in its most developed form, the supreme 'unity of universal and particular'. Such a concept of the state as a distinct entity and its relation to 'civil society' was far removed from the analogy of the body politic to which earlier thinkers had clung. Nevertheless, as we have seen, strong features of its metaphysical postulates, as well as of the historical sense that informed Hegelian philosophy, were present in sixteenth-century thought. Moreover, for expressing the modern concept of the state political philosophers continued to call upon the services of metaphor: 'group-person' and 'organism', 'body' and 'soul'.[7]

But, whatever its role in Teutonic and other philosophical accounts of the relation between state and society, the role of metaphor has been far more pronounced in historical accounts of France's political and social composition. Indeed, reliance by modern writers upon metaphors of the French 'mosaic' or of France's 'cellular' structure has disguised, as with the followers of Vidal de La Blache, an evasion of 'the problem'. It has served to suggest a correlation, between the country's territorial, social and political composition, that has notoriously defied definition and expression in other than figurative language. The first part of this chapter will illustrate the difficulties of demonstrating such a correlation in objective terms, for the period when France was becoming politically unified. As we shall see, the later-medieval and sixteenth-century kingdom lacked clear territorial limits. The boundaries of its major administrative circumscriptions, notably the *élections* and the *bailliages*, were unstable and uncertain, especially when viewed from the standpoint of central government. Those divisions in any case scarcely corresponded to regional 'unities'. Below the regional level, the hand of government nevertheless fell ever more heavily upon the people through the local institutions of parish and village *communauté*, modifying their roles in relation to the elemental groups of France's overwhelmingly rural society. Yet the modification took place at a time when the structures of such groups, chief among them the 'family', and their landed foundations were apparently in flux. In sum, there is much to suggest that the alleged correlation amounted at that time to no more than an assimilation of certain key institutions to an otherwise arbitrary system of government over a society that was disintegrating from within.

The remainder of the chapter attempts to suggest otherwise, by taking account of features of contemporary consciousness. It considers indications of how later-medieval and sixteenth-century Frenchmen maintained a sense of social and political continuity amid conditions of change. Metaphors figure among such indications; but these are not the plastic images of later writings. Rather, they are terms through which contemporaries at every social level rationalised relationships within groups that were voluntarily formed. They include terms expressive of familial relations, adopted for their legal and ethical significance and applied to 'fraternal' groups of various kinds, as well as to associations of patrons, clients and alliesmen. While such groups could present obstacles to the exercise of royal authority, kings viewed them with disfavour rather when their mode of organisation was overtly 'democratic' than when they were dominated oligarchically by élites. Meanwhile, that authority was exercised increasingly through the medium of men of legal training whose influence, indeed, was becoming all-pervasive in the conduct not only of public but also of private affairs. Contemporary critics denounced their influence as divisive; yet they themselves shared with lawyers and with members of élites a view of how the realm's cohesion and continuity were maintained. That view was expressed through a further metaphor: the metaphor of 'orders' – a description not of society as it actually was, but of an ethical system by which it was ideally informed. The description specified qualities that were, or ought to be, exemplified by men who occupied positions of social and political leadership. And when such men assembled with the monarch as the Estates of the realm, they could be seen as the actual 'embodiment' of France and its political virtues.

The west Frankish kingdom assigned to Charlemagne's grandson, Charles the Bald, in 843 by the Treaty of Verdun disintegrated during the centuries that followed. By the end of the twelfth century the Capetian king was penned in the Ile-de-France. To the west lay the territories of the Plantagenets, whose Angevin empire straddled the English Channel. To the south, control over the territories of the Mediterranean littoral was disputed by the king of Aragon from beyond the Pyrenees. By dint of victories over both John of England and Pedro II of Aragon in the opening decades of the thirteenth century, Philip Augustus established the power of the king of France over virtually all of those territories. In retrospect his victories have appeared decisive.[8] France, it seemed, had taken permanent shape, a shape that would survive short-lived encroachments by Englishmen and others during the Hundred Years War. It would delight later theorists with its natural geometry, and would help persuade historians that the state was 'territorial', with 'clearly-defined boundaries' or 'frontiers'.[9]

But the territorial limits of their power were far from clear to the Valois kings of France. That power was a variable commodity. Kings might exercise it directly over the royal *domaine*, but the term *domaine* signified rights as much as territory. In so far as it was identifiable with the former, the royal claim to power over the *domaine* was merely tautologous. In so far as it was identifiable with the latter, it exposed the limitations of royal power. However defined in territorial terms, the *domaine* was not co-extensive with the kingdom. Much of the kingdom consisted of districts whose occupants' relation to the king varied in accordance with particular contracts and agreements. Those territories in turn merged, especially to north and east, with a penumbra of adjacent lands, of indeterminate limits and under indeterminate control, at once enticing and potentially menacing to royal power.

While it could be argued that the kingdom was bounded to the west by the sea-coast and to the east by rivers, the latter were a hazardous guide. Did France extend eastwards to the Rhine, as Louis XI insisted? Did its limits lie, as others indicated more prudently, along the line of the four rivers, Rhône, Sâone, Meuse and Scheldt? Yet that line scarcely formed an irrefrangible boundary, as was evident from the series of fortresses erected by Louis himself along the Sâone, from Mâcon to Auxonne. Fortresses were necessary, for Burgundy was virtually an open door; and, as Francis I noted in 1527, to hold Burgundy was to dominate the eastern and central provinces of the realm.[10] As for the Meuse, the German emperor claimed many lands to its west – a claim advanced with alarming effectiveness in 1535 before the Paris *parlement* itself, by the advocate Longueval.[11] According to him, if any river marked France's eastern limits it was not the Meuse but the Seine. The suggestion was arresting enough to dissuade loyal Frenchmen from pressing political arguments from river geography too far. In any case, rivers that facilitated as often as they thwarted the movements of ordinary persons were not simply to be accounted barriers to royal power. Rather, they were considerations that kings and their agents might invoke or might dismiss as their political convenience dictated and as they chose to interpret their rights in law.

Rights in law turned rather upon abstract considerations of precedent and title than upon concrete geographical features. When Longueval argued further that 'the high forests of Thiérache and Argonne', fringing Champagne to the east, 'have always been the limits of this kingdom', it was the terms of the historic Verdun treaty that he had in mind. Later anthropogeographers might recognise forests as natural frontier zones, rising 'between cultivated lands like the sea between the continents', and populated by men akin to the savages of sylvan myth; but for Longueval's contemporaries forests were not inhospitable, still less unserviceable, to civilised cultivators such as the men of France. According to Jean Chaumeau, sixteenth-century historian of Berry, in the very heart of the kingdom stood 'a beautiful and great forest called the forest of Châteauroux, covering about five or six square leagues', full of deer, boar, wild creatures of all kinds – 'in brief, it is the most commodious and suitable place for men to live in that can be found in the whole of Berry'. Haunts from time to time of brigands and renegades, forests nevertheless furnished at all times resources and materials that were indispensable to rural and urban dwellers alike. 'There isn't a single art', declared Bernard Palissy, author of *How to Get Rich*, 'that can be practised without wood.'[12] When their subjects continually encroached upon them, when at least one-quarter of the Ile-de-France itself consisted in 1550 of land that law and custom adjudged afforested, kings were not likely to recognise in forests natural and necessary limits to their power. Forest and field, river and settlement were not mutually exclusive but interacting and interpenetrating zones. As such, whatever their possibilities for the composition of Vidalian regions, they did not either severally or together present the rulers of medieval and Renaissance France with ready means of tracing the territorial limits of their realm.

They could trace its governmental divisions no more readily. Within the realm lay a tangle of administrative and judicial circumscriptions, each a quasi-reticulated system, but with interstices that were at once grossly unequal and uncertainly perceived from the centre. One such system was that of the *élections*, fiscal districts formed in the middle of the fourteenth century for administering the *tailles*. Another was the *bailliages* or *sénéchaussées*, stamping-grounds in the later thirteenth century for peripatetic royal agents, and subsequently developed as districts for purposes that included the administration of the king's 'ordinary' revenues.[13] Reckonings of the areas of *élections* varied from seventeen parishes in the case of Beaufort in Champagne to 720 parishes in the case of Poitiers. But such reckonings were unreliable. At first the limits of *élections* had corresponded to diocesan boundaries. They had soon ceased to do so. New *élections* were pieced together from existing ones; sub-divisions of dioceses were assigned now to one *élection*, now to another. Pasquier despaired of describing 'the confusion and chaos precipitated by Henry III . . . through new creations of *élections* and *élus*'. As for *bailliages* and *sénéchaussées*, these again were composed of sub-districts: *châtellenies*, made up in turn of seigneuries, their territories intermeshed in patterns of great, and growing, complexity – and, at bottom, parishes once more. The *bailliage* of Senlis, thirty miles to the north of Paris, comprised ten *châtellenies* in 1300, and the same ten 200 years later. But such an appearance of stability was quite illusory, at least from the standpoint of the central government. Its records showed that the Senlis *bailliage* contained at once fewer than five hundred and more than seven hundred parishes.[14]

Bereft of sound data, lacking reliable cartographical aids as well, kings and their central *officiers* may nevertheless have assumed that these major administrative circumscriptions must correlate with homogeneous regions of territory and people. If so, they were mistaken. The *bailliage* of Senlis, we are assured, was 'merely a marqueterie', a district 'without centre, without unity, made up of bits and pieces taken from neighbouring countries, like an assemblage of *pays* bound to, but turning their backs upon, each other'. Of course, the celebrated *pays* of France were assemblages in their turn. North-west from Senlis lay the '*pays*' of the Beauvaisis, characterised by 'geographical contrast'. To the south of Paris lay Hurepoix, a '*pays* . . . juxtaposing very different geographical features'. In both cases, the unity of the *pays* consisted, it seems, in 'a kind of popular consciousness', in a 'notion of a *pays*' that was 'relatively clear in the minds of sixteenth-century people'.[15] Certainly such a notion was real enough in the experience of John Calvin. As that child of northern France observed, when he and his followers urged men to transform their way of life many responded: 'My condition is that of my *pays*. If I abandon it, what will become of me, and how shall I be fed?'[16] What is equally clear is that neither the Beauvaisis nor the Hurepoix of popular consciousness tallied with the divisions of secular or of ecclesiastical government, for those divisions seamed and sundered each of them. Conversely, in south-eastern France lay the county of Forez, attached from the middle of the fifteenth century to the *sénéchaussée* of Lyon, yet persisting as a distinct administrative district throughout the period of the *ancien régime*. According to the seventeenth-century novelist Honoré d'Urfé, one of its most successful literary sons, the '*pays* named Forez . . . contains within its small compass what is rarest in the rest of France'. Among its contents was a stretch of the Loire, evidently no obstacle to the Forez's administrative formation and survival even though the river flowed through the centre of the district. No less evidently, the Forez preserved by administrators and lauded by *literati* did not derive its unity from popular consciousness. The *paysans* who lived on either side of the Loire sought neither land nor bride on its opposite side, and even differed linguistically from those who dwelt across the water.[17]

If an objective correlation is to be found between France's territorial, governmental and social composition, it is scarcely at the level of the kingdom's major administrative districts. Yet there is no reason to suppose that royal *officiers* at work within those districts shared the uncertainty that afflicted their superiors at the centre – however much they may have contributed to that uncertainty through falsifying their reports and their accounts. Answerable to the king for the realm as a whole, those superiors concerned themselves with divisions of it that were from their standpoint poorly, even arbitrarily, defined. Answerable for such divisions, district *officiers* had to do with sub-divisions that were ultimately specific enough. These were the parishes of France; and the parish, it would appear, was an 'indestructible cell' from its medieval origins to beyond the Revolution when, amid the destruction of so many ancient institutions, it was simply renamed the commune, and so survived.[18] Moreover, the parish was surely from its origins a genuine cadre of socio-economic activity and popular consciousness. Its shape, so often irregular, was conditioned by topography, and by the need of the group of settlers for whom it was initially founded to have access to water and to woodland, indispensable adjuncts to the cultivable lands that lay at the heart of their concerns. Its size was conditioned by the pattern of settlement: parishes were large where settlements were dispersed, small where they were concentrated in nucleated villages. As for group-consciousness, this was never more potently expressed and reinvigorated than at festivals held under the aegis of the parish. Such festivals punctuated the church's calendar and the cycle of the rural year: Easter and springtime, the feast of St John the Baptist and midsummer, the Assumption and the harvest season, All Saints and the approach of winter, harbinger of death. At these climactic moments, Christian observance fused with popular rites of pagan origin, to celebrate and to placate the spiritual beings that animated the local world of the participants, thereby recharging 'the sentiment of belonging to the group' that they composed.[19]

All this is easily exaggerated. In many instances during the medieval centuries, foundations of new churches and interventions by seigneurs 'broke apart the ancient framework of rural settlement' and resulted here in reshaping, there in fragmentation of ancient parishes. Bibulous popular festivals could as easily promote dissension, violence and feud as renewals of group solidarity. Nevertheless, the parish presented royal government with a fundamental unit that exhibited to a relatively high degree both territorial and social coherence and continuity. Its boundaries were marked on the ground; and it seems – though the evidence prior to the sixteenth century is poor – that men born within those boundaries generally found their brides within them, too, and so perpetuated the social group by endogamy.[20] And the parochial unit contained institutions that were immediately exploitable for governmental purposes. Chief among them was the *communauté d'habitants*, the assembly of heads of households, that existed to administer those households' collective affairs. The correlation between parish and *communauté* was by no means everywhere exact. It was closest in parts of northern France: elsewhere, 'the numbers, the centres, the circumscriptions' of parishes and *communautés* were often 'not the same'.[21] Yet, whether the *communauté* coincided with part of a parish or encompassed several parishes, it could certainly be applied to the parish as an instrument of royal fiscality. The collective affairs that were historically its concern involved it in assessing every household's contribution to those affairs. In that sense, the *communauté* as an instrument of public revenue long antedated its assimilation to the royal fiscal system. Once assimilated, its role was vital. Thus, in the all-important matter of taxation the *élu*[22] assigned to every parish its portion of the tax imposed upon his district; and the *communauté* saw to it that a 'just' share of the parochial burden was apportioned to every household that ought to pay.

Taken together, then, parish and *communauté* were the unit of correlation between the framework of government on the one hand and the collective life of the social group on the other. In so far as the demands of the former were moderated through that unit, their arbitrary character was leavened. Such a function was part of the *communauté*'s historic role. Long before royal taxes were regularly imposed, *communautés* had moderated the impact of *tailles* imposed by seigneurs upon rural households. But the *communauté*'s role had extended far beyond matters of taxation. Especially in northern France, it had supervised collective agrarian usages. It had administered common lands; it had issued social and economic regulations that time had hallowed into custom – custom that varied from *communauté* to *communauté*, group to group. Above all, in its medieval heyday it had defended and asserted with *éclat* the collective interests of the members of the rural group *vis-à-vis* their seigneur. It had done so, from time to time, with the support of judgements pronounced in royal courts of law; and in procuring such judgements *communautés* had obtained some measure of recognition that they could possess in law corporate status as 'moral and judicial persons'. The development of regular royal taxation from the middle of the fourteenth century coincided with the abolition of seigneurial *tailles*. So seigneurial power was in process of diminution, royal power of extension; and these twin processes were bound up, it would appear, with a consolidation of that 'organic' institution, the rural *communauté d'habitants*.[23]

And yet, while the *communauté* was assimilated to the system of royal government as the fundamental component of that system, its role in relation to rural households' collective affairs was itself in process of modification. The process accelerated during the sixteenth century – a century when the weight of royal taxation seemed greatly to increase, and when governmental surveillance over its local administration was certainly intensified.[24] Central to the role in question was the maintenance of usages that enabled each household to survive as a unit of subsistence. Its survival might depend upon access to common lands, or upon enjoyment of common pasture after harvest upon the cultivated fields; and such rights depended in turn upon maintaining recognition on the part of every party concerned, seigneur and commoners alike, that the area which any household might cultivate was limited, and that the normal cycle of cultivation must be observed. Although the nature and importance of *droits d'usage* varied widely throughout France, and despite later-medieval changes in patterns of landholding, *communautés* continued at the beginning of the sixteenth century purposefully to maintain collective rights.[25] But their capacity to do so diminished as that century wore on. Common lands were eroded as *communautés* disposed of assets in order to reduce debts that were often the legacy of war. Grazing rights were challenged by individualistically minded proprietors, accumulators of lands – men, moreover, whose influence upon *communauté* assemblies outweighed that of their poorer neighbours.[26] Local customary regulations were reduced through the efforts of royal commissioners to sets of rules applicable throughout entire *bailliages*.[27] What did not diminish was the *communauté*'s task of satisfying the agents of royal fiscality. Charged with this, as well as with maintaining the church's fabric, it was becoming primarily an institution for administering funds extracted from above.

From all this it does not follow that the modification of the *communauté*'s role was either sudden or uniform, nor that the structures of rural society were 'revolutionised' in sixteenth-century France. In parts of the south collective agrarian practices had long since been undermined; elsewhere, in the north and centre of the realm, they persisted under *communauté* aegis to the end of the *ancien régime*. Nevertheless, the contrast is sharp between that institution's modified role, and its role during its medieval heyday as extractor of collective rights from the seigneur. Still sharper is a further contrast to which sixteenth-century developments contributed decisively. It concerns the relation of the parish itself to the spiritual life of the social group. Associated with the *communauté* in the sphere of material affairs, the parish was also, as we have seen, a cadre of popular consciousness expressed in traditional rites. But in the wake of the Counter-Reformation ecclesiastical authority would set its face against the heterodox practices and local idiosyncrasies of popular religion. To an unprecedented degree, the church would impose upon the laity a uniform religious discipline. It would also subject their marital conduct to far more rigorous institutional control. From the sixteenth century onwards the French parish priest, equipped with registers that both ecclesiastical and secular authority required him to keep, would enforce attendance by parishioners at mass each Sunday, would invalidate their marriages if they should fail to take their vows publicly and in proper form before him, would insist that all infants be presented for Christian baptism within days of their birth. The Counter-Reformation church aimed to submerge popular systems of belief and behaviour beneath 'a code of uniform parochial practice'.[28] How rapidly and how widely it did so, and with what precise effects, remain debated questions. Yet, as with the *communauté*, so, too, with the parish: both were being modified in ways whereby they increasingly enabled the hand of superior authority to lay onerous duties and obligations upon local households.

Duties and obligations were owed by those households to other groups, from which they had traditionally derived a measure of protection and security. They were conjoined in seigneurial and kinship systems – systems that again varied throughout France, as did the influence that they exerted upon individual households. Their influence was profound in northern provinces, far less so in the Midi. In general and in principle, however, both systems functioned to preserve social in conjunction with territorial stability. Thus, seigneurial and kin conventions alike restricted the householder's freedom to dispose of his lands: for by exercising such a freedom the individual might damage the interests and the continuity of the group as a whole. Let the *laboureur* content himself with a holding that could be worked by a single plough-team, yielding enough to support his household and to pay the lord his dues. Such a holding, we are assured, was the 'fundamental unit of production' in the 'feudal' society of later-medieval France.[29] It was also the unit that rules of inheritance informed by considerations of kinship were suited to maintain. But by the sixteenth century both systems were manifestly in flux and disarray.

It was largely through its relation to the seigneurie that the rural *communauté* had formerly developed and flourished. That relation was by no means simply one of confrontation with the seigneur. *Communauté* regulation of collective agrarian usages was enforced in the seigneurial court, for the *communauté* lacked judicial powers of its own.[30] That court also enforced payment to the seigneur of dues from the tenants of his landed fief, and exercised a civil and a criminal jurisdiction, too. In theory, therefore, the seigneurie correlated economic and judicial functions over a monolithic territory where the seigneur was his people's arbiter, and also their military protector. But practice everywhere diverged from theory, and diverged even further with the passage of time. Seigneuries were disrupted from within. Seigneurs enlarged their *réserves*, lands kept in their own hands as distinct from their tenants' holdings. They might exploit those lands directly – or, more likely, farm them to capable *laboureurs*, who in turn might thereby accumulate large holdings or find themselves burdened with insupportable commitments. Demographic fluctuations and oscillations in commercial opportunities conditioned such developments, which gathered pace from the fourteenth to the sixteenth centuries. Population-growth contributed to drive prices upwards and the rural group outwards upon lands that thitherto lay beyond the margin of cultivation, and yet were vulnerable to seigneurial demands. Population-decline served to reverse these movements without reversing the seigneur's emergence as primarily a *rentier* landlord. By the middle of the sixteenth century, while seigneurial habitudes 'continued solidly to encompass peasant life' in northern France, seigneurs seemed 'interested no longer in stable tenancies, but in expelling tenants so as to aggrandise [the] "*réserve*" and draw the maximum profit from it'.[31]

Meanwhile, for all the persistence of the seigneurie in peasant life and the consciousness of the rural world, its territorial 'solidity' was also undermined. Seigneuries multiplied: and with them opportunities to hold seigneurial courts, to extract seigneurial dues, even to enact the role of seigneurial arbiter and protector. For it was argued that seigneurial qualities attached to land;[32] and custom assigned, in varying forms and to varying degrees, rights of landed inheritance to offspring other than eldest sons. Those rights were restricted by the ancient feudal rule that fiefs ought not to be divided or alienated. But in practice that rule was modified out of much of its effect, and with the active connivance of royal authority. As early as 1209 Philip Augustus had ordained for the Paris region that when inheritances in vassalage were shared among brothers each should hold his share not as a sub-enfeoffment from the eldest, but as a fief directly from his and their superior lord. Division of inheritances was also restricted through the ability of titled noblemen to preserve at least the bulk of their lands intact by means of various forms of entail. But their success was only partial; and, as sixteenth-century legislation confirmed, the monarch did not favour unlimited entails, and neither did his courts.[33] By that century, fragmentation as well as regrouping of fiefs had become extreme. Around La Ferté-Alais, thirty miles to the south of Paris, there lay three times as many fiefs as parishes. In Brittany, Burgundy, Provence alike, fiefs might encompass a dozen villages or only a couple of holdings in a single village.[34]

Villages consisted of households and so of families, each, for modern writers, a constituent 'atom' or 'cell' of French society,[35] and for earlier thinkers a prototype of its political cohesion. 'The family', wrote Bodin, 'is the true source and origin of every state', the proof of Aristotle's error in attempting to 'divide *oeconomie* from *police*'. As Bodin defined it, by reference to Roman law, the 'family' consisted of children and servants – a minimum of three persons – with the head of the household and his wife: a head whose 'natural' authority over his *familia* was consistent with the monarch's over his people. But the cohesion of the social group to which each family belonged was not simply a matter of paternal authority multiplied many times over. Ties of kinship bound every *ménage* to the other households of its neighbourhood. Indeed, *voisinage* was virtually tantamount to kinship, the social group to a familial community, its structure extremely intricate owing to generations of intermarriage:

> Nous sommes vos voisins, nos filles sont vos femmes,
> Et l'hymen nous a joint par tant et tant des nœuds
> Qu'il y a peu de nos fils qui ne soient vos neveux.

The implications of kinship ties in the composition of rural society were recognised by the church, which in the thirteenth century reduced the canon law proscription against marriage between consanguineous partners from the seventh to the fourth degree. Those ties were reinforced by folk custom, penalising with ridicule, forfeits, even ostracism, women of the group who married 'strangers'.[36] And in much of France customs of inheritance emphasised the rights and obligations at least of close and often of distant kinsfolk in relation to the family's landed holding.[37] Should the head of a household seek to alienate lands which he and his wife respectively had inherited, what he sold was recoverable by his kin or by hers, as the case might be, from the purchaser. Should husband and wife die childless, what they had held by inheritance as a conjugal pair must revert, on either side, to the lineage from which each of them had sprung. Further, when marriage partners had children who ceased to live with the rest in the conjugal household, the outsiders forfeited their rights of inheritance. Restrictions such as these differed widely in their form and application, from region to region and from noble to commoner families. In general they did not apply to *acquêts*, assets that the conjugal pair acquired for themselves otherwise than by inheritance. Yet such acquisitions were unlikely to include much by way of land if customary rules of inheritance were strictly observed, in conjunction with other customs that governed land occupied and cultivated by rural dwellers or held in common by the group as a whole. Taken together, these customs aimed to ensure that the group's relation to its territory remain stable, and that the households within it remain economically viable. They were aims that often depended for their fulfilment upon continuing deference to considerations of kinship.

Considerations of kinship bore less heavily upon inheritance practices in southern France, where custom harmonised with concepts of 'ownership' in Roman law, strongly renascent from the thirteenth century onwards. By comparison with his counterparts to north and west, the *paterfamilias* of the Midi enjoyed to a far greater degree exclusive rights over his lands, and so freedom to favour a single heir, or several heirs, at his own discretion. There are clear signs that, as the sixteenth century approached, a growing measure of that freedom was being extended to heads of households well beyond the traditional zone of the *droit écrit*. Thus by 1510, the year when the extremely influential custom of Paris was officially published in consolidated form, conjugal partners in that region were recognised as free to endow a child who left the household during their own lifetimes, without thereby excluding him or her from the company of their right heirs. When the time for inheriting came, the *enfant doté* could opt to return the endowment and so resume his or her rights of inheritance on an equal footing with offspring who had stayed at home. Of course, the option was worth exercising only when the endowment was lower in value than the share to be expected through inheritance by customary rules. This might not be so. Heads of households were increasingly finding ways of treating inherited assets as if they were *acquêts*. Thereby they reduced the proportion of their holdings that was subject to the control of the familial community as a whole.

Such developments were gradual, modifications of prevailing

practices, not radical innovations. Yet they rendered the stability of landholdings more vulnerable than before to accidents of parental disposition. Of course, it did not follow that the rural group as a whole would be invaded by landholders from outside. Marriage-partners continued to be found largely from within the same neighbourhood: to that extent the continuity of the group itself remained assured. Again, holdings might yet have persisted more or less intact as long as relatively few children survived their parents, and as long as the survivors continued to cohabit. But the stability in question was also vulnerable to demographic change. From the middle decades of the fifteenth century the French population increased markedly once more. Although, as we shall see,[38] the rate of increase is problematical, the fact of increase is well enough established. In these conditions, holdings that could not support inflated numbers were rapidly fragmented when heirs claimed equal shares and retained them in several. Alternatively, when parental discretion was exercised in favour of a particular heir or beneficiary the remaining offspring could not hope to subsist upon what remained to them. Perhaps the aims of heads of households who sacrificed those offspring upon the altar of perpetuating their holdings were not incompatible with the stabilising aims of customary traditions. But pride in the *ménage*, given a free rein, was likely to disrupt the pattern of landholding. Men driven by that motive welcomed opportunities to augment their holdings at their neighbours' expense. Sixteenth-century developments in law concerning landed 'property' facilitated acquisition, and loss, of land, as again we shall see.[39] A complex of legal, demographic and customary changes was inducing fragmentation as well as concentration of lands in individual hands. With the diminishing effectiveness of considerations and institutions aimed at safeguarding its territorial stability, differences multiplied within the social group.

Varying from place to place, unfolding over centuries of time, the processes that we have reviewed thus far gathered pace in the sixteenth century. In the course of this book we shall evaluate many of that century's developments more closely. Taken together, however, they appear to constitute a major conjuncture of significant changes, social, economic, institutional. This was a century of intensified population-pressure upon material resources, of price-inflation, of modified property-relations – a century, too, when customary laws were being consolidated and local institutions assimilated more rigorously to systems of authority directed from above. Upon a society that was apparently disintegrating from within, governmental authority was being brought to bear more immediately and more onerously than ever before. And yet amid conditions of change later-medieval and sixteenth-century Frenchmen maintained in their conduct of social and political affairs a powerful sense of continuity. In the remainder of this chapter we shall consider some indications of how they did so.

In the Roman *familia*, to which Jean Bodin alluded when he defined the 'family', ties other than those of blood or marriage bound slaves to their master, who as *paterfamilias* might also add by adoption (*adoptio*) to the number of his natural-born children. In canon law, godparents and their godchildren were bound together, even in the absence of natural ties, by a 'spiritual kinship' (*cognatio spiritualis*). These relationships were ratified on the one hand by the civil law, on the other by the sacrament of baptism. They furnished distinguished precedents for the 'artificial families' that proliferated, in numerous forms, in later-medieval and sixteenth-century France. All such families are instances of kinship as a social metaphor rather than as a physical connection: a metaphor that conveyed how, 'between the members of the same group, there exists a solidarity – of name, of thought, of interests – which has as its necessary corollary hostility towards the stranger'.[40]

One form of 'artificial family' took shape when two or more persons decided to live 'as brothers', in a fraternal community (*frérage, frérèche, affrèrement*).[41] The members of the community, as described by the sixteenth-century historian Guy Coquille, shared the same house, the same cooking-pot, the same 'hunk of bread'. The community might be enlarged by the arrivals of children, or of adult recruits. It might remain a consociation of two men – as in the case of Jean Rey of Alès, in eastern Languedoc, and his 'great friend Colrat', who formed their community in 1446 when Rey's wife, a 'bad woman', left him. Such accidents of passion are not enough to account for the frequency with which fraternal communities appeared, especially during the fifteenth century but in the sixteenth, too. Scattered throughout the Midi, from Provence to Guyenne, and as far north as the Orléanais, they occurred chiefly in the zone of the *droit écrit*. There, while the absence of customary restraints that elsewhere bridled the power of the *paterfamilias* did not prevent reduction of holdings to uneconomic dimensions, it did facilitate voluntary pooling of resources. In effect, the resultant community gave each of its members access to more land than he would otherwise have enjoyed. It might also lessen the burden of taxes assessed upon single holdings. It might even impede seigneurial claims to occasional dues: how far, for instance, must *droits de mutation*, payments due when holdings changed hands, be rendered if those holdings belonged to an entity other than the individuals who composed it, an entity that continued although its component individuals changed? Above all, however, fraternal communities, formed mainly among the poorer and more vulnerable members of rural society, are explicable as a defensive reaction to the upheavals of the time, by men in need of psychological and material support and protection.[42]

Better-placed Frenchmen sought fraternal support in analogous ways. When professional soldiers of the *compagnies d'ordonnance*[43] declared themselves 'brothers in arms' to other soldiers, they created a 'sort of artificial family bond' to emulate, or to supplement, the natural ties of kinship that often enough linked captains of companies with their followers. Other fraternal declarations suggested more overtly that a quasi-legal as well as an ethical bond was being forged. In the year before Rey and Colrat formed their fraternal community, Pierre de Brézé, Count of Maulévrier and political careerist, declared himself bound 'in so far as one brother *adoptive* and in arms can oblige himself by right to the other', to Gaston, Count of Foix, whose power and alliances in the south-west posed a challenge to royal authority.[44] That declaration, with its allusion to the ancient concept of *adoptio*, was a variant of the 'non-feudal' contracts to which prospective clients, patrons and alliesmen committed themselves as feudal institutions decayed. Relations of allegiance between lords and their followers were ceasing to be cemented by land. Yet they were still reinforced by pledges, formal and informal, in which the terminology of kinship performed an important function. To use the terminology was to declare mutual obligation in elevated form. The usage might be metaphorical, the obligation might lack tangible basis in territory or in blood, and yet the terminology of kinship not only implied that the relationship between the parties was stable and binding, but also endowed it with a quality above that of their increasingly venal expectations from it.

For the expectations of alliesmen and clients went beyond protection to advancement. The larger his group of associates and dependants, the more powerful their 'cousin' and 'patron', the lord. Yet the group swelled or shrank in accordance with his ability to satisfy them, who in turn had to satisfy alliesmen and clients of their own. Ties of kinship might be less dissoluble than bald ties of coadjuvancy, but neither tie need bind those who acknowledged it exclusively to a sole kinsman or a single benefactor. Alliesmen and clients moved, horizontally, from group to group, while the groups themselves extended vertically, deep into society; for protection and advancement, ward and reward, were considerations to be sought at every social level. They were especially valuable in the sixteenth century. In that century, ideological intransigence and civil wars made protection an urgent necessity on either side of the religious divide, as Catholics and Protestants contended violently to impose their beliefs upon other believers whose errors they abhorred, and who abhorred theirs in return. As for advancement, in the sixtenth century it was increasingly identified with offices, and their distribution with brokers from whom only kinsfolk and protégés might expect to gain. Such groups intensified rivalries and bred conflicts of loyalties, ultimately at the expense of the royal authority that *officiers* purported to serve. On the eve of the civil wars the greatest brokers of all were the Catholic leaders 'Messieurs de Guise' who, 'able when they were in favour to give all vacant offices to their dependants, gained such credit among the *officiers* that the latter acknowledged them more than the king, and this was what most enabled them to form the League'.[45]

That 'Holy League', however, was a confederacy that lacked the cohesion and the continuity of many of its component parts, as we shall see.[46] Among those components were religious confraternities, 'artificial families' in yet another form, explicitly designated in kinship terms.[47] Dedicated to spiritual purposes, confraternal groups had ancient antecedents. Such groups pre-dated not merely the religious conflicts signalled by Renaissance humanism and precipitated by the Protestant Reformation, but even the formation of the church itself in the long-distant past. Even so, confraternities multiplied in fifteenth- and sixteenth-century France. They ranged from élite companies such as the Parisian confraternity of St Nicolas, which comprised the barristers and solicitors of the *parlement*, to associations of humble rural parishioners. But, however humble its members, the confraternal organisation was distinct from that of the parish. Confraternities had their own statutes, their own offices, their own material assets. Whether richly or poorly endowed, they assured their particular *confrères* of decent burials, at least a measure of material assistance in time of need, as well as a share in the spiritual credit accumulated through their collective rituals and charitable acts. In return, the *confrères* pledged themselves to regular religious observance, especially of their tutelary saint's festival. They also pledged themselves to mutual protection. As the statutes of the Breton confraternity of St Nicolas of Guérande put it, 'the said brothers must protect and defend each other, and live and die for one another, against all strangers, excepting seigneurie and lineage'.[48] The reservation was important: notwithstanding modifications, seigneurie and lineage continued to command obligations that were binding in custom and in law. Those obligations were complemented rather than displaced by confraternal ties. 'Strangers', however, included members of other confraternities, as eager as their rivals to assert their solidarity. Like the latter, they did so through ostentatious processions, convivial feasts, the standard ingredients of confraternal festivals. Like their rivals, they found such behaviour offensive when other confraternities indulged in it. Sworn *confrères* must surely protect each other from the impact of self-assertiveness by neighbouring groups upon their own consciousness and persons. So confraternal festivals readily erupted into violence. They erupted far too often for the liking of secular and ecclesiastical authorities.

Yet 'artificial families' in all their forms involved hostility towards strangers, despite their members' undeniable ties with other kinds of group. And in all of them assurances of material support and protection were enjoyed by persons who had entered voluntarily into durable relationships that transcended such mundane considerations. Other forms of *societas*, as when partners combined for a commercial venture and terminated their partnership at the venture's end, existed solely for material purposes and only for a time. But when persons modelled their relations upon the 'ancient ideal of fraternity',[49] they dignified their association on ethical as well as on quasi-legal grounds, and gained from it a powerful sense of continuity. The continuity was twofold. The participants affected to behave in accordance with abiding, universal values. They also committed themselves to a group that was patently intended to endure, beyond even their own time. Even so, such 'artificial families' scarcely commended themselves to external authorities. But the degree of suspicion that they aroused, and the response of royal authority in particular to their pervasive presence within the realm, differed markedly from case to case.

The fraternal communities formed by commoners who pooled their resources were relatively innocuous. Such groups might hinder seigneurial rights and confuse royal tax-gatherers, but governmental records for tax-assessment were unreliable for a host of other reasons, or were geared to 'hearth'-units (the *feux fiscals*) that were not equivalent to actual households. Pledges of loyalty to military brotherhoods or to patrons were potentially far more dangerous. They complicated the allegiance owed to the monarch by members of such groups, who might all too easily range themselves against his authority. Not for nothing had Charles VII required captains of his *compagnies d'ordonnance* to swear that they would serve him 'against all, without excepting either their natural seigneur or any other whatsoever'. Yet the king could channel to his own advantage the fraternal inclinations of military men. He did so by himself creating military fraternities, such as the Order of St Michael, whose members, leaders of lesser groups, pledged themselves to each other and above all to him.[50] As for clientage groups, the king could exploit them, too – as long as he disposed of means of patronage beyond what any other source could offer. Great patrons and their clients were in the last resort his dependants; notwithstanding incidental loyalties, the complex of groups that they composed was in effect an informal hierarchy for distributing offices and favours that emanated, ultimately, from above. But religious confraternities had few redeeming features. Quite apart from the physical disturbances that they provoked, their very mode of organisation was antithetical to superior authority, and potentially subversive. Confraternal members devised their own ceremonies, framed and amended their own statutes, elected their own *officiers*. Confraternities were cradles of heterodoxy – worse, of democracy, and capable of political agitation. Sixteenth-century synods of the church in France repeatedly pronounced against them. So, too, did the *parlement* of Paris, *pace* the confraternity of St Nicolas. And these weighty pronouncements echoed the animadversions of successive kings.

Royal disapproval was registered most strongly against confraternities that were linked with urban occupational *corps*, or gilds. 'All confraternities of *gens de métier* and artisans throughout our kingdom', ordained Francis I in 1539, 'shall be cast down, forbidden and prohibited, in accordance with our ancient ordinances and decrees of our sovereign courts.' A generation earlier his predecessor had denounced the 'abuses, conspiracies and monopolies' to which gilds allegedly gave rise.[51] And yet royal denunciations of gild abuses and royal ordinances, however ancient, against gild confraternities did not amount to condemnations of gilds as such. On the contrary: gilds in France had long since developed with royal approval. They had done so in Paris itself, where since the thirteenth century gildsmen had sworn to observe the statutes of the corporate groups that they composed. Incorporation, however, did not entail self-administration, still less self-constitution, in the unacceptable manner of confraternities. Whether or not their members swore a corporate oath, gilds were subject to external review of their statutes, and external supervision of how they managed their affairs. Authority over them might lie directly in royal, or otherwise in municipal or in seigneurial, hands. In any case, it originated in a seigneurial obligation: an obligation that combined the right to judge whether a trade was desirable and legitimate with the duty to protect it and to oversee its practice, once allowed. As the furriers of Nantes in 1498 reminded their duchess Anne, Queen of France, the incompetent must be prevented from trading and thereby injuring the *chose publique*.[52] All this did not mean that tradesmanship must be regarded as simply a matter for public intervention and regulation.[53] Trades involved mysteries, esoteric arts; moreover, men had a natural right to maintain themselves and their families through their skills. But there was a point where how they did so became a matter of public concern. Gilds occurred at that point of intersection. They were, at once, associations of private tradesmen and public institutions, vehicles of *police* administration. Hence, in principle, their endorsement by royal authority.[54] Even so, that endorsement tended in practice to reinforce the oligarchic character of gild organisation.

Their statutes empowered gild *officiers* to admit – or to exclude – aspirant masters, to raise – or to remit – fees for admission, and so to determine who should practise their trade within their particular area of jurisdiction. That they should favour their own kinsfolk and protégés was only to be expected.[55] The *officiers* themselves were chosen by electoral procedures that involved at least some of their fellow-masters, but in which retiring *officiers* had a powerful voice.[56] Gild-direction was largely in the hands of self-perpetuating élites, under external surveillance. And when the surveillance in question was exercised by municipalities, their authority in turn resided in oligarchic hands. Municipal constitutions might differ; municipal liberties might have originated, variously, here in stands that *communes* had taken vis-à vis their seigneurs, there in charters of enfranchisement granted for other reasons.[57] What is clear is that by the sixteenth century the *bonnes villes* of France were administered by minuscule groups of men. Four *échevins* in Paris, eight *capitouls* in Toulouse, twelve *consuls* in Lyon, supported by a dozen or two of councillors and an assortment of judicial and administrative functionaries, were charged with the *police* of their respective towns. These executives were chosen by small, élite colleges whose active membership was smaller still. In Rouen, with an urban population of some fifty thousand, the 'general assembly' of the townspeople numbered potentially a few hundred; and in 1535 it was an assembly of merely sixty-seven councillors and notables that chose the executive. In Aurillac, in the Auvergne, the full complement of the electoral college consisted of the six retiring *consuls* and twenty-four councillors, a nobleman, a *bourgeois*, a cleric and a notary, together with the eleven *bailes* of the town's gilds.[58]

Whether or not gild leaders participated *ex officio* in elections to municipal offices, the oligarchs who held those offices did so with royal approval. Many-headed assemblies of townspeople were un-desirable.[59] Like confraternities, such assemblies excited disturbances and smacked of democracy. Royal interests – and, arguably, municipal interests, too – were better served when the king could conduct his affairs in relation to his towns by dealing with élite minorities, and they in turn with gild and other élites within their charge. Of these several élites, the latter were more dispensable than the former: should the king have to choose between them he was likely to prefer municipal to gild oligarchies. In Lyon, attempts by tradesmen to gain corporate recognition as sworn gildsmen (*jurandes*) were terminated in 1512 by royal letters patent, issued in favour of the *consuls* who had resisted those attempts. The town, with its thriving involvement in international commerce, should remain a home for 'free' trades – subject always to their surveillance by masters whom the *consuls* would appoint. However keen or cursory that surveillance, the masters in question certainly served to perpetuate the consular oligarchy. Every December the *consuls* appointed *maîtres des métiers*; and eight days later the *maîtres* appointed six new *consuls* for a two-year term. *Maîtrises* and *consulat* alike were in the hands of a merchant patriciate, concerned rather with maintaining the commercial prosperity brought by the Lyon fairs than with attending to indigenous manufactures. But even in towns such as Aurillac, where gilds flourished and figured strongly in municipal constitutions, the members of municipal executives were drawn from the ranks far less of manufacturing masters than of long-established merchant dynasties.[60] It was they who commanded egregious status. Rooted in generations of local prominence, their status seemed to entitle them to office and was confirmed, reciprocally, by their governing role. They also commanded wealth that might be mercantile in origin, but was increasingly secured as much by landed and other investments as by commercial enterprises. In the sixteenth century such investments included more and more offices created by the king himself.

Oligarchs, then, presided over municipalities through constitutional arrangements that royal authority endorsed, and also through considerations of social esteem and economic capacity that royal policies helped them to enhance. Their presence brought continuity to municipal administration, and made it contiguous with the greater sphere of royal government itself. Surely the king could with satisfaction underwrite constitutions that consigned municipal authority to men akin to those by means of whom he himself governed. And yet, even though municipal oligarchs and royal *officiers* were so often recruited from the same élite groups, it did not follow that towns would simply subordinate their interests to royal demands and their liberties to the royal will. Rather, the *officiers* concerned had to choose between conflicting loyalties, as royal pressures upon the towns intensified in the sixteenth century. Towns were required to surrender their financial accounts to inspection by the king's *chambres des comptes*, to abandon their powers of civil jurisdiction to his courts, to place their revenues and their creditworthiness at his disposal.[61] But such pressures were brought immediately to bear through the agency of *officiers* who resided in those same towns, were associated with their leaders, and even, in many instances, held municipal offices simultaneously with royal ones. Clearly, such functions were increasingly difficult to reconcile with one another: hence Henry II's edict of 1547, which ruled that men who held royal offices were ineligible for municipal charges.[62] But there was still no certainty that those men would elevate their roles as agents of royal authority decisively and unfailingly above their personal ties with oligarchs who owed at least some of their own prestige to traditions of service to their municipalities.[63] Did not the men in question function within a system of royal government that itself continued extensively to rely upon exploiting various forms of kinship ties? Yet such ties must give way before a sense of impersonal official duty on the part of royal agents, if towns were to be subordinated effectively to the royal will.

The requisite sense was cultivated when royal *officiers* were products of a legal training and, moreover, were disposed to identify with the royal will the laws that they existed to apply.[64] But a legal training was not the exclusive preserve of royal *officiers*. Its products were available, in increasing numbers,[65] to occupy the municipal places from which the king in 1547 sought to debar their royal counterparts. If lawyers and their ethos were serviceable to the monarch, they were no less serviceable to municipal oligarchs. Notwithstanding considerations of status, tenure of municipal office entailed duties that were often burdensome and even baffling to laymen. In the 1540s the *consuls* of Aubusson had to call in a priest 'to read to them some deeds and charters relevant to an action brought against them before the *maître des eaux et forêts* concerning usages claimed by the inhabitants in royal woods and forests near this town'. For such services lawyers had more expertise to offer than had priests. In important respects they had more to offer than even the influential patrons upon whose assistance municipalities were no less willing than other groups and individual clients to call when occasion warranted. Such patrons, as lay and ecclesiastical seigneurs, had long since been accustomed to retain lawyers for their advice on administrative and economic matters as well as for lawsuits. Municipal oligarchs followed suit. Not content simply to rely upon the services of municipal *procureurs*, they admitted the legally proficient more and more fully into the management of their towns' affairs.[66] Apart from occasions of actual litigation, apart even from dealings with royal government, it was wise to have available associates as versed in the complexities of laws as were the agents of the king himself.

For the conduct of public business in later-medieval and sixteenth-century France was characterised by a spreading legalism that also characterised the conduct of private affairs upon which public authority increasingly impinged. Far down the social scale, urban businessmen and rural *laboureurs* alike were more and more frequently putting their signatures or their marks to documents drafted for them by legal practitioners. The omnipresence of lawyers was becoming a byword.[67] In agreements to sell or to settle, to borrow or to repay, to perform or to forbear from acts of all descriptions, the language of the law must be employed. It was a specialised language – for *patois*-speaking

Frenchmen, scarcely less so after the royal ordinance of 1539 that instead of Latin the *langage maternel françois* be used in all documents to do with matters of law.[68] Specialists abounded, at once the carriers of legalism and the symptoms of its spread. In the course of their business dealings in 1521 the brothers Hugues and Jean Boysset, modest merchants of St-Antonin in the Rouergue, employed no fewer than nineteen different notaries. A score of notaries were practising in Aubenas in Vivarais at the end of the fifteenth century.[69] Scarcely anyone, it seemed, could pursue his social and economic concerns without their services, without the protection afforded by the laws. Without their formal assurance, the protection variously afforded by natural or artificial kinsfolk, by patron or confraternity, even by occupational or municipal *corps*, was not enough. Despite the importance of personal ties, such groups in any case owed their cohesion and their continuity at least partly to considerations of a legal nature. But in an overtly legalistic and litigious France, where legislation mounted and the business of lawcourts swelled, the potency of legal considerations, impersonal and distinct, was growing all-pervasive and overriding. And with them grew the significance of the roles fulfilled by men of legal training, in the public and private spheres alike – and so in the relation between government and society.

In the composition of that society, how far did these men in turn constitute a distinct and homogeneous group? Did they, perhaps, form a social 'class', specifically distinguishable from all other groups to which its members might belong? In fifteenth-century Lyon, we are told, before the re-emergence of the merchant patriciate to control that city, municipal authority was in the hands of a 'class of lawyers – an economic class, but still more a social and political class'.[70] Yet that portentous term seems scarcely applicable as a description of the multifarious practitioners of law in sixteenth-century France. Between, on the one hand, the scholarly jurists, the magistrates, the *avocats* of the sovereign courts and, on the other, the notaries feed by the Boyssets and their kind, the gulf was profound. *Avocats* of the Paris *parlement* were graduates in both civil and canon law; from 1499 candidates for magisterial office in that court, including *avocats* of many years' standing, were formally required to submit themselves to examination by a commission of established magistrates. In contrast, even an apprentice carpenter served a longer term than the two years' initiation into notarial mysteries begun in 1521 by young Claude Monier of Cannes, whose master agreed to allow him time off for fishing in return for whatever the apprentice might catch.[71] Parisian counsel and provincial notary stood at opposite poles of occupational proficiency and social rank, the one challenging for noble status, the other barely distinguishable from neighbouring artisans. Between these extremes lay a medley of *praticiens*, as varied in their competence as in their prospects and their means. What these men had in common was a peculiar function: the function of bringing legal rules to bear upon the conduct of the persons with whom they dealt. To that extent, the relation of even the meanest part-time notary to the neighbours who sought his services was identical with that of the most eminent legal counsel to his clients. Yet such identity of function was scarcely enough to constitute that 'coalescence of occupational and economic bonds plus the bond of belonging to the same social stratum', upon which 'class'-formation allegedly depends.[72] Moreover, the functions of legal practitioners were as often divisive as cohering in their effects, upon the *praticiens* themselves and upon the society in which they served. Laws and their agents institutionalised conflicts that might otherwise have been resolved by less formal means,[73] and added conflicts of their own making. Conflicts of jurisdiction were endemic. They eternalised litigation; they were meat and drink to lawyers; they sprang as much from the varieties of lawyer as from the varieties of the laws themselves. Despite efforts at redaction,[74] customary laws remained diversified; and lawyers contended from locality to locality, court to court, while suits lay undetermined and litigants remained in discord.

And yet lawyers were conspicuous among those who appeared to insist that the place of every man was determinate within a harmonious France. In so far as he performed a specific function he belonged to an order that occupied a distinct position within an all-embracing hierarchy of estates or orders. Every order occurred within one of three categories: *orare, bellare, laborare*, respectively the functions of clergy, nobility and common laymen. In that categoric form the schema of orders was nothing new. Lawyers, theologians, moral philosophers had disseminated it in France from the eleventh century onwards. Sixteenth-century commentators continued to canvass it, despite their wide disagreements over the details of the hierarchy. Its very exponents were difficult to place in one of the three categories. For lawyers there ought perhaps to be a fourth, the *estat des gens de pratique*. But what of university doctors, many of them laymen who nevertheless gained their degrees and performed their functions at institutions that were essentially ecclesiastical, as was evident from their chief offices and privileges?[75] As for *laborantes*, many more of them defied tidy ordering by reference to specific functions. There were prosperous *laboureurs* who acquired town houses and thereby claimed to rank as *bourgeois* and to enjoy privileged exemption from the *tailles*. There were townsmen who combined tavern-keeping with the function of printer, surgeon, even notary.[76] There were peasants who were also manufacturers of textiles and retailers of their own produce in local markets. If the schema of orders was intended as a literal description of how men in fact behaved in their society, small wonder that commentators not only disagreed, but also dealt summarily and evasively with the complexities of the Third Estate.[77]

But such literal description was not the intention of the schema's exponents, and they were not evasive in relation to their main concern. For them, the schema was metaphorical in its application to human behaviour and human institutions. It described a system of universal qualities by which, none the less, France's institutions ought as far as possible to be informed. Chief among those qualities was virtue; and virtue was rewarded by honour.[78] Virtue was exemplified, and honour gained, by men who performed their function well. Conversely, to safeguard the performance of a function was to safeguard honour and virtue. The principle was applicable to the Third Estate: it was a potential justification of the gilds. But virtue was exemplified more fully by functions other, and more honourable, than those of *laborantes*.[79] Commentators accordingly dilated not upon that order, but upon nobility. For nobility was overtly honourable, and 'ought to be obtained by virtue'.[80] It had historically been gained by *bellatores*, though not all men of war were noble[81] – however advantageous kinship with noble captains might be to *compagnons d'ordonnance*. But nobility was not simply an honour: to be noble, to 'live nobly',[82] was itself a function, and other high functions, of government and particularly of justice, ought to be associated with it, not it with them. The viewpoint seemed to favour men who could claim nobility by virtue of their birth, and was firmly adopted by their spokesmen.[83] Yet it was also tenable by critics of hereditary noblemen. Nobility, as they interpreted it, was not 'a difference of essence', but 'an excellence of quality'.[84] It could be gained – for instance, by acquiring learning; it belonged to 'the order of having and not of being'.[85] Nobility was a gift, divine rather than genetic in its origin, and its possession was made manifest through performance of virtuous actions. But, whether proved by ancestry or otherwise demonstrated, nobility qualified those who had it for places of leadership in the French body politic. For, as the historian du Haillan affirmed, 'virtue, without which nothing great can be undertaken, engendered France' itself.[86] Indeed, from such a premiss it could reasonably be argued not only that a body politic so engendered was best led by men who exemplified that quality, but also that it was given actual corporeal existence when they gathered together.

They gathered together, at the end of the fifteenth century and again from the middle of the sixteenth, as the Estates-General of the kingdom. The divisions of that assembly did correspond precisely to the three orders – though according to François Hotman, leading advocate of the Estates-General's supreme authority, 'this division into three parts is related not to the system of ordinary life, but to the public council of the people'.[87] Ordinary people, preoccupied with mundane affairs, deviated remorselessly in their behaviour from the principles of an ideal schema. But those principles ought firmly to inform the 'council' which was the embodiment of the realm. Its membership in the sixteenth century was drawn from the ranks of men who could claim either nobility by birth or a measure of it by function. The higher clergy were largely noble-born; members of the Second Estate were noble by definition; and deputies of the Third Estate were predominantly *officiers* and lawyers, many of them members of municipal oligarchies, who designated themselves *noble homme* or *honorable homme*.[88] Within the kingdom other 'public councils' occurred when men of comparable standing gathered together in assemblies of Estates at the level of province or *bailliage*. Such assemblies were bodies politic in miniature; so, too, were the lesser assemblies of urban and rural communities, where the influence of *notables*, men of *honneur* and *honnêteté*, the *maior et sanior pars*, prevailed.[89] Yet the body politic of France as a whole was not simply the sum of these many gatherings. Rather, it took the form of the *corpus mysticum reipublicae* that was made actual when the Estates-General met in the presence of the king.

The authority of the king himself was scarcely enhanced by such an application of the metaphor of orders to France's political institutions. Other groups within the realm derived legal and ethical validity from analogous principles. The urge to propagate and to protect one's kind, the place of every created being within an ordered whole – each was sanctioned by universal natural reason and divine law. Further, the principles were rooted in a consciousness that was profoundly metaphysical in its orientation. Amid far-reaching conditions of change, Frenchmen gained a sense of continuity through their membership of groups that were so validated. The existence of such groups presented obstacles to the assertion of superior royal authority, even when they were dominated by oligarchs. Those obstacles were not insurmountable; but a far greater impediment to the superior authority of the king alone was presented by the existence of an institution, itself oligarchically composed, that could be held to actualise the entire mystical body of the French *respublica*. That institution, where the pristine and metaphysical 'condition' of France, its 'state' in the traditional sense, was embodied by its qualified and assembled leaders, surely took precedence over the king and, as his critics would maintain in the course of the sixteenth century, constituted the source of his authority.

The 'state' in this sense may thus be said to 'emerge' from the 'social groups constituting the society' of Renaissance France, a product of the consciousness that informed both it and them. It is contemporary consciousness that furnishes the factor of correlation between France's social and political composition. Plainly, however, this was not yet the 'state' of modern political thought: a distinct, impersonal entity, other than king or people, with distinguishing characteristics and properties of its own. Later in this book we shall see how such an entity came to be perceived at a time when individual critics of the king and assemblies of Estates were presenting positive and formidable challenges to monarchical rule. Yet the new concept of the state is not to be interpreted as a justification of that rule upon grounds quite other than those occupied by challengers of monarchy – as a rationalisation from different premises of an authority arbitrarily imposed upon a disintegrating society whose members clung to a traditional system of beliefs, sentiments and values. On the contrary – the emergence of the state itself may be taken as a proof that unless political authority over a society is asserted purely by force of arms its assertion must be validated in accordance with legal and ethical considerations of the kind that prevails in the consciousness of that society.

But first we must consider how in France monarchical rule itself was exercised in practice. This chapter has already noted the relevance to its effective exercise of a sense of impersonal official duty on the part of royal agents. We may take the development of such a sense to be part and parcel of the 'bureaucratisation', the 'centralisation', the 'depersonalisation and institutionalisation of the exercise of power' that have been widely held to characterise the emergence of the modern state. To what extent does the practice of government in sixteenth-century France exhibit such developed characteristics? How far was the effectiveness of monarchical rule limited by conflicts of authority, contradictory allegiances and continuity of traditional attitudes within the governmental system itself? These are the questions to which we now turn.

CHAPTER 3

The Practice of Government

The origins of France's major governmental institutions lay in the personal entourage of the medieval ruler – his kinsfolk, his principal household attendants – who gave him political advice and ministered to his domestic and spiritual needs. The chief *officiers* of the realm in the sixteenth century continued to be designated by titles derived from those of ancient household functionaries: the constable from the Capetian keeper of the stables, the chancellor from the head of the sanctum of the Chapel Royal. Around them and their office-holding colleagues, around the king himself, personal favourites continued as before to jostle for position and to attract the disparagement of the excluded, as they engaged in the 'magnified, formalised family life of the court' and snatched at opportunities to influence the decisions of the powerful.[1] Nevertheless, with the kingdom's territorial growth and the expansion of monarchical rule the apparatus of royal government had long since become more systematic and also more complex. Yet that apparatus, too, remained the king's, in principle an extension of his person, in practice subject to his personal intervention and control.

Royal government in later-medieval France centred upon the king's council. From the thirteenth century onwards that institution repeatedly exhibited at its core a group of hand-picked men, pledged by oath to serve the king and to maintain secrecy about their deliberations.[2] Fluid in its composition and in its functions, however, the council also embraced a much wider circle of dignitaries who from time to time asserted claims to be consulted as of right. Thus augmented, the council might be deemed an institution not simply advisory in its purpose, but also 'representative' of the kingdom at large. Yet its active membership, whether in restricted or in augmented form, continued to consist of those whom the king chose to summon, and the council's business of what he chose to put before them. Its senior member, the chancellor, installed in his office by the king[3] and dismissable only by him, kept the seals whereby royal decisions and directives were authenticated, and headed the chancery from where they were dispatched. Although strict protocol might suggest that among royal *officiers* the chancellor was outranked by the constable as the king's military lieutenant, it was the former alone who enjoyed the right to display at his residence tapestries bearing the *fleurs-de-lis* and the arms of France – overt symbols of the chancellor's standing as the monarch's personal representative. Hence his leading role in international diplomacy, his surveillance over appointments and the conduct of royal fiscal *officiers* – and, above all, his headship over the royal judiciary. For the king was primarily the distributor of justice to his people; and his chancellor, erstwhile an ecclesiastic, was from the end of the fourteenth century recruited almost invariably from the ranks of men of law.[4]

Meanwhile other potentates had emerged to carry the king's authority from his court and his council to the provinces at large. The *baillis* were at first itinerant commissioners, charged with supervising the activities of agents already in the field: *prévôts*, *châtelains* and their equivalents, who existed to assert the rights of the Capetian rulers over the parts of the territory of the royal *domaine*. In due course, groups of *prévôtés* and *châtellenies* came to constitute the administrative districts – the *bailliages* and their counterparts in the Midi, the *sénéchaussées* – that lay intermediately between the centre and the localities of France. But in his heyday of the later thirteenth century the *bailli*'s role could scarcely be defined in terms of particular functions which an *officier* of intermediate rank might discharge within a stable administrative system. Over his *bailliage* he exercised what were tantamount to vice-regal powers, so extensive as to render him virtually an embodiment of kingship itself.[5] Fiscal and judicial, military and political affairs fell indiscriminately within those powers' comprehensive scope. The *bailli* received domainal revenues and made payments from them. He dispensed justice upon appeal from lower courts of law. He commanded military levies and saw to the maintenance of fortifications. And leading members of the communities of the *bailliage* were members of his council – an institution that exemplified in microcosm the unity of the head with the members of the realm, through their respective representatives.

Of course, continuity of government even on a far lesser scale than that of France was not to be achieved simply through reliance upon personal initiatives and personal allegiances. In the later medieval centuries governmental practice became more and more the business of depersonalised institutions. At the centre, for all the continued importance of councillors and chancellor under the king,[6] it was effectively under the aegis of the *parlement* of Paris and the *chambre des comptes* that royal justice was dispensed and royal revenues were administered. Each of these institutions had originated as an offshoot of the council. Each remained, technically, an extension of it. Neither controlled recruitment of its own members.[7] Yet both of these institutions were permanently constituted by the fourteenth century, and rapidly developed quasi-'bureaucratic' characteristics.[8] The *parlement* was staffed by professional judges and lawyers of proven competence. Their offices were hierarchically ordered. Their particular functions were performed in particular chambers and in accordance with set procedures. Their business and decisions were recorded in registers which also contained the definitive record of the king's enactments, scrutinised and published on his behalf by his councillors of the *parlement*. They maintained their own archives; their letters were sealed with their own seal and dispatched from their own chancery. Likewise, the *chambre des comptes* had its hierarchy of presidents, masters and clerks, its accumulation of documentary evidences, its right to review financial directives that issued from the royal chancery itself, and its penal jurisdiction over receivers of royal dues, bound regularly to render their accounts upon its *bure*-covered table. In each institution such characteristics contributed to shape its members' ideological awareness of its constitutional significance. But that awareness was also shaped by a continuing sense that monarchical rule had personal and metaphysical properties, and that these informed its leading agencies as well. Thus the *parlement* described itself in 1489 as a '*corps mystique* . . . representing the person of the king, for it is [the court] of final resort and sovereign justice of the kingdom of France, the true seat, authority, magnificence and majesty of the king'.[9]

From the beginning of the fourteenth century both the *parlement* and the *chambre des comptes* were located in the palace rebuilt by Philip IV at Paris's Ile de la Cité. While the royal council itself continued to attend upon the peripatetic king, other governmental institutions soon settled at the same location: the *chambre des monnaies* with its jurisdiction over currency matters, the masters of the royal forests at the marble table in the Great Hall of the palace, the *cour du trésor* that dealt with litigation stemming from administration of the *domaine*, even though the royal treasury itself found its home at the Louvre. With so many tribunals placed close to one another and discharging functions that plainly overlapped, conflicts of jurisdiction inevitably arose. The frequency of such conflicts was limited by the capacity of the *parlement* and, to a lesser degree, of the *chambre des comptes* to vindicate their pretensions to sovereign authority, competent to determine all differences upon appeal. But deference to the *parlement* was less readily forthcoming from the *cour des aides*, which was also established at the palace from the end of the fourteenth century. That court determined disputes that stemmed from the

administration of extraordinary revenues: *tailles* and *aides*, *gabelles*
and various *impositions*. These were taxes upon what the people
themselves possessed, or upon what they bought and sold. They were
categorically distinct from dues that traditionally accrued to the king as
lord of his *domaine*, possessor of land and other perquisites in his own
indefeasible right. Unlike those dues, taxes were accorded him by the
goodwill and volition of his people, or at least of their representatives.
As sixteenth-century commentators supposed, the origin of the *cour
des aides* lay in the machinery erected by the Estates-General in the
1350s to organise collection of these voluntary subsidies, necessitated
in time of war and political emergency.[10] Its nucleus was the members
of the *généraux* who wielded judicial powers by commission, while the
college of *généraux* exercised surveillance over the *élus* charged, in
turn, with apportioning the *tailles* among the parishes. In principle,
therefore, the court could be held to have derived its powers rather
from the assembled body of the realm than simply from the ruler's
fiat.

In practice, however, during the next eighty years of recurrent
warfare the Valois kings repeatedly appropriated taxes without first
obtaining consent. From 1439 their power to do so was established *de
facto* if not *de jure*.[11] By then the *cour des aides* had become part of the
permanent apparatus of central government; and throughout much of
France the system of *élections* associated with that court constituted a
permanent and specialised sector of provincial government, com-
plementing the *bailliages* but distinct from them. As for the *bailliages*
themselves, in the course of the fourteenth and fifteenth centuries the
substance of the *bailli*'s role came to be distributed among a variety of
particular functionaries. Receivers, answerable to the *chambre des
comptes*, handled the revenues of the *domaine*. Lieutenants dealt with
civil litigation and judged criminal offences, subject ultimately to the
jurisdiction of the *parlement*. Even the *bailli*'s military role was passing
into the hands of captains-general, and his council into those of
office-holders, predominantly lawyers.[12] Such developments were consistent with the tendency evinced by central government institutions
towards specialisation of functions. Both at the centre and in the
provinces institutions that had originated as extensions of, on the one
hand, the king's own person and, on the other, corporate assemblies of
members of the realm were becoming for practical purposes the
preserves of professional administrators. Governmental functions, it
seemed, were settling into distinct channels, each a conduit along
which authority could course hierarchically from the centre to the
provinces at large.

And yet the structure of government in France by the opening of the
sixteenth century remained remote from any model of bureaucratic

centralisation. While the kingdom's rulers might pronounce it to be 'governed under a sole king and monarch' from 'the seat of the royal dignity and majesty in our good town and city of Paris',[13] this did not deter them from erecting duplicates of central institutions elsewhere. Even the Paris *parlement* had its duplicates: provincial *parlements*, formally constituted in the middle decades of the fifteenth century in Toulouse, Grenoble and Bordeaux, and joined thereafter by those of Dijon and Rouen, Aix and Rennes. Resembling the sovereign court of Paris in the *style* of their judicial deliberations, they were nevertheless fabricated from provincial antecedents. In most of the provinces that these *parlements* served, provincial *chambres des comptes* and *cours des aides* also appeared. Those provinces fringed the kingdom. Most of them were geographically remote from the capital. In all of them, governmental institutions were already well developed under their dukes and counts prior to their assimilation to the realm itself. In them, too, forms of law and fiscal provisions differed radically from those that obtained elsewhere. But such considerations also applied in some degree to the other parts of France. If a fortnight's journey separated Toulouse with its *parlement* from the capital, places that came within the *ressort* of the Paris *parlement* lay a week or more away from there.[14] In all parts of the realm great diversity of customary laws, fiscal obligations and governmental traditions prevailed. While major governmental institutions in outlying provinces claimed sovereign jurisdictions, lesser institutions duplicated one another throughout the kingdom. Moreover, they performed, as did the sovereign courts, a comprehensive range of governmental functions. They did so as agencies of royal authority, and for reasons that had only partly to do with conditions of geography and local idiosyncrasy.

The comprehensiveness of the functions performed by each of the multiple components of France's government derived from the very nature of authority as contemporaries interpreted it. Unlike modern theorists, they drew no distinction between the administrative and the judicial sides of government.[15] For them, authority comprehended both *gubernatio* and *jurisdictio*. Indeed, the 'sole king and monarch' in whom royal authority as such resided, and from whom royal administrators derived their powers, had primarily to distribute justice to his people. Likewise, the institutions that he headed, whatever their immediate administrative concerns and at whatever level they occurred within his realm, involved means to adjudicate between disputants and to impose penalties upon malefactors. Jurisdictions distinct from the structure of the ordinary lawcourts were 'attributed' to a host of administrative agencies, from major fiscal offices to minor keeperships of fairs. Conversely, the ordinary lawcourts in their turn combined judicial with administrative functions. The courts of *parlement*, *bailliage, prévôté* alike were comprehensive organs not only of civil and criminal justice, but also of *police*.

However, the comprehensiveness that characterised the organs of royal government also characterised the institutions that they overlaid. For all the late-medieval efflorescence of the former, it was with seigneurial institutions that most Frenchmen at large still had immediately to do.[16] Seigneurial courts had cognisance of criminal prosecutions and suits between parties, dispensing justice by reference to local custom. They also maintained seigneurial rights and dues; and they issued *police* directives in relation to highways, weights and measures, and a profusion of other common affairs. Divisions of landed fiefs added to the number of such jurisdictions, especially in regions of the west where custom declared that 'fief and justice are wholly one'.[17] Farmers of seigneurial functions multiplied, too. They exercised those functions in the seigneur's name, enjoyed their fruits in return for paying him a predetermined sum,[18] and so were strongly motivated, as was he, to preserve his accustomed and patrimonial authority in each and all of its several aspects from royal encroachment – whatever they might lack by way of professional expertise in comparison with agents of the latter. As for municipalities, in general their governmental powers were again comprehensive. There were important towns[19] whose charters of enfranchisement had always reserved judicial rights to the grantor – a lay or ecclesiastical seigneur, or the king himself; and, although the *communes* of France 'had always regarded the right of justice as their most precious prerogative', royal *officiers* had steadily encroached upon that right from the thirteenth century onwards. Nevertheless, the principle broadly persisted that a municipality's existence as a distinct governmental unit necessarily entailed not only *police* functions, but also some measure both of judicial privilege for its denizens and of judicial power for its administrative *corps*.[20]

All this dictated that France was scarcely to be governed uniformly from a single centre by bureaucratic means. Perhaps decentralisation and duplication of comprehensive governmental powers were compatible with political unity, as long as Frenchmen ultimately deferred to the overriding authority of their king. Such deference was modified by the active existence within the realm of forms of authority that might be derived from other sources. But, apart from considerations of constitutional principle, the institutional hierarchy that did exist could itself be seen as functioning to the detriment of just and efficient government. Thus, in the vital sphere of justice itself, a litigant ordinarily justiciable before a certain judge might choose instead to bring his suit before another, who would then claim prior cognisance of it. Higher courts, where costs were greater and procedures more elaborate and leisurely, might first arbitrate between the judges and eventually review the judgement upon appeal, only to be overruled in turn at still higher levels. So justice was 'immortalised'; and the better-off litigant might all too easily succeed less through the merits of his suit in law than through his means to pursue the protracted litigation that the judicial hierarchy seemed positively to invite.[21] As for fiscal matters, the global sum, varying from year to year, that central authority demanded of France as a whole by way of *tailles* was divided and redivided by regional and local agencies among revenue-districts of diminishing size, down to the level of the parish.[22] The system of 'repartition' readily fostered disputes over the equitable distribution of the tax, together with claims for exemption and allegations of favouritism and fraud. Meanwhile, the amount of revenue collected for the king and his multitude of paid servitors continually fell short of what they had anticipated.

At the opening of the sixteenth century even admirers of French monarchical rule denounced the 'abuses, wrongs and violences' that afflicted the administration of taxes. Further, observed Claude de Seyssel, 'many people of all estates are destroyed and impoverished by the way in which justice drags on, and many who have good cause abandon its pursuit'.[23] Reformers reiterated such strictures as the century wore on. Justice and sound government were indissociable from one another, as the distinguished chancellor L'Hôpital continued to insist. A ruler who failed to provide them courted danger: this was because, 'as the head of the state, he is so united and joined to its members that there can be no offence nor injury which he himself will not feel sooner or later'. The difficulty was that the appointed instruments of unity – judges, lawyers, *officiers* of various kinds – were themselves major perpetrators of offences and harmful promoters of litigiousness. There was much to be said for that 'simplicity and ancient wisdom' whereby affairs had formerly been regulated in village, municipal and occupational communities by local leaders, 'true physicians of the body politic'.[24] Many Frenchmen less devoted than L'Hôpital to the unity of France would endorse such corporatist sentiments and willingly account themselves physicians. But baldly to invoke time-honoured analogies was rather to compound than to resolve the difficulties that beset the practice of royal government.

In the remainder of this chapter we shall consider sixteenth-century attempts to ameliorate that practice. Impinging upon every area and every level of government, those attempts included modifications of the royal council itself, the emergence at the centre of new functionaries such as the *secrétaires d'état*, and an assortment of reforming measures relating to military, fiscal and judicial administration throughout the realm. In some respects these developments are indicative of change in the direction of 'bureaucratisation', centralisation, the exercise of power by 'depersonalised' means. Yet they and their outcome are also strongly indicative of the continuity of traditional attitudes and structures. A principal outcome of these developments was to consolidate the system of royal government at intermediate levels of the institutional hierarchy – notably, at the levels of the *bureaux des finances* of the *généralités*, and the *bailliage* courts. There, and elsewhere, too, power was distributed among a plurality of élite, collegiate and corporate groups, whose roles were consistent with conceptions of government as the concern of members of a body politic. We shall see how royal fiscal and judicial policies encouraged *officiers* to treat their functions patrimonially and to view them as their own esoteric preserves. We shall also see how those policies provoked questions concerning the scope of the king's authority and its nature. Such questions became pressing upon the death of Henry II, and urgent during the century's later decades, when successive kings faced in the provinces resistance from associations headed, in many instances, by their own *officiers*. But a means of countering such resistance lay in enlarging the use of royal commissioners; and these arrived in the midst of recalcitrant groups as agents at once of the monarchical person, of the laws that he promulgated – and also of the impersonal state, a basis and a justification of the obedience that the ruler demanded from all his subjects.

Throughout the sixteenth century select groups of royal councillors took part in deliberations with the monarch upon major political affairs. The king's regular meetings with such groups, which might number as few as two or three councillors or as many as a score, constituted sessions of his *conseil des affaires*. Its sessions were sessions of the royal council at its highest political level. Other sessions of the council took other forms, for particular kinds of governmental business. Councillors assisted by high-ranking fiscal *officiers* and sitting from time to time as the *conseil des finances* exercised surveillance over the administration of royal revenues. Councillors assisted by professional lawyers and sitting from the 1530s as the *conseil des parties* dealt with petitions to the king for justice. All of these councillors were recruited from the royal council as such, the full membership of which fluctuated during the century from some eighteen at the beginning of Francis I's reign to an allegedly 'boundless number' in the 1590s.[25] A wide range of administrative business continued to reach those who attended the plenary sessions of the council. Omnicompetent in principle, the council in that form was designated from 1578 the *conseil d'état.*[26] But in practice its concerns were limited by the very formation of its own sections. Acting in the council's name and yet without the participation of most of its members, those sections have seemed to typify the formal distribution of business among specialist institutions that is one of the distinguishing characteristics of bureaucratic government.

However, this internal distribution of conciliar functions remained unstable, while the relation of the council both to its parts and to other central institutions remained uncertain. Meetings of the *conseil des affaires* were neither constrained by formal procedures nor confined to high questions of international and domestic policy. Summoned to the royal bedchamber or to an adjacent *cabinet*, its members for the time being might concern themselves with matters as general and momentous as the making of war and peace, or as particular and partial as their own clients' advancement, or as mundane as provincial appeals for tax exemption. Meanwhile, the composition and the role of the *conseil des finances* were repeatedly redefined. A predilection of Francis I's from the mid-1520s for entrusting 'the total administration, superintendence and government of finances'[27] to a single senior councillor, supported by four or five of his colleagues, gave way by 1563 to a royal preference for dealing with such business in what amounted to weekly sessions of the *conseil des affaires*. There followed three decades of experimentation with various forms of financial council. At times such a council took clear institutional shape as a select committee appointed to meet on several days each week. At others it was virtually denuded of its functions through spasmodic resurgences of the plenary council into the field of fiscal management. As for the *conseil des parties*, its very existence provoked objections from the sovereign courts which, for all that they had originated as offshoots of the royal council, now exhibited far better-defined institutional characteristics. Doubtless the king had every right to dispense justice in person, as well as to seek political advice from his councillors and to oversee his revenues through them as he might think fit. But objectors insisted that those councillors had no right to erect themselves into a court of law unwarranted by any edict, still less to trespass at random and at will upon the ordinary jurisdictions of the *parlements* and to controvert the latter's judicial decrees.[28]

One response to such objections was to revive a conception of the council as embracing the sovereign courts themselves as well as other branches of government. In 1557 Henry II directed that 'all the king's councillors shall sit in the sovereign courts and in inferior jurisdictions' – and, conversely, that in addition to its conciliar members the *conseil des parties* should include administrative and fiscal *officiers* of various kinds.[29] These directives were scarcely calculated to clarify the council's specific functions and to distribute them more precisely among its component parts. But ten years earlier the same king had issued other directives which have indeed appeared to constitute a landmark in the development of bureaucratic government. By letters patent of September 1547 he 'made choice of four of our beloved and faithful councillors and secretaries' to take charge of 'despatches of state', each for one of four 'departments'.[30] The departments consisted in every case of a group of outlying French provinces, together with the foreign kingdoms and principalities which lay beyond that group. The patentees were the immediate forerunners of the *secrétaires d'état*, titles that figured explicitly in fresh letters patent of 1558. Evidently, the chosen secretaries were already fully accredited councillors. They had emerged from among the *secrétaires des finances*, élite members of the long-established college of sixty 'clerks, notaries and secretaries of the king'. The members of that college served not only in the king's entourage and his chancery, but also in the sovereign courts. As Louis XI had ordained in 1482, all royal commands and all letters from royal chanceries, councils and *parlements* must pass through their hands.[31] The royal secretaries had also proved their worth, well before their further recognition by Henry II, in conducting diplomatic missions and in managing financial affairs. Whatever the importance of sections of the council in both those spheres of government, it was upon his secretaries that the king could primarily rely to see that his wishes were carried into effect. They attended those sections' meetings; they also attended upon the royal person; they were his creatures and could be expected to disdain conciliar patrons and the factions that the latter so readily formed.[32] Certainly it would seem from Henry II's directives, taken together, that the king expected to assert his authority to greater effect by consolidating the roles of such executive personnel in relation to conciliar and other institutions, rather than by striving further to 'bureaucratise' the council itself.

The *secrétaires d'état* and their roles have been widely interpreted as forerunners of the later bureaucratic ministries that would absorb so many of the functions of council and chancery alike.[33] Their creation was indeed intended to achieve greater 'order' in the handling of 'despatches' – and, by implication, to ensure that sensitive information should not be intercepted by interested councillors. Principal repositories of such information, the *secrétaires* kept confidential registers and supplementary records of the papers that they handled. They were assisted in doing so by small clerical staffs on which, prior to their own appointments to the secretarial office, all of the sixteenth-century *secrétaires d'état* had served, and so had received some professional training. Yet it was to kinship with existing *secrétaires* that they owed their entry into the profession, and often through their superiors'

resignations in their favour that they advanced to secretarial appointments in their turn. Those appointments remained markedly patrimonial in character,[34] while the bureaucratic characteristics of the secretarial office were embryonic in additional respects. Classification of
secretarial business was rudimentary, to judge from extant registers in
which instructions to ambassadors, confidential letters, patents, warrants and miscellaneous memoranda kept indiscriminate company
with one another. Nor did *secrétaires* confine their attention to their
own 'departments', whether as described in 1547 or as revised in
subsequent regulations.[35] In any case, as those regulations showed,
division of business between the *secrétaires* was conceived essentially
in topographical terms rather than in terms of functional specialisation. And yet the topographical division itself made the *secrétaires'*
prime function abundantly plain. Their major concern was with the
defence of the realm and with political matters that related to its
maintenance. Moreover, the defence of the realm depended, always in
principle and frequently enough in practice, upon availability of armed
forces under royal control. Thus the business of the *secrétaires* extended into the field of military administration. And in that field, so
important for the kingdom's subsequent government under the *ancien
régime*, they and other royal executive personnel exhibited both their
potential and their limitations.

Continuous availability of armed forces as a monopoly of royal
authority was not characteristic of medieval forms of rule. Feudal
arrangements had placed intermittently at the ruler's disposal forces
that were otherwise his vassals' to exploit. They were succeeded by
contractual arrangements whereby rulers retained the services of
fighting men who might equally contract their services to others. In the
sixteenth century French kings continued to rely heavily upon *ad hoc*
hiring of foreign mercenaries for campaigns abroad and even for
domestic purposes.[36] Like other European governments, they over-
hauled their means of financial management partly in order to pay the
high *soldes* that mercenaries demanded. However, the desirability of
native forces on a permanent footing and at lower cost had long been
recognised. Claude de Seyssel's recommendation of 1515, that local
infantry bands be maintained under local captains supervised by noble
baillis and *châtelains*, amounted to little more than an endorsement of
time-worn arrangements.[37] Apart from the traditional roles of the
nobles in question, such bands had existed since 1448 in the form of the
francs-archers, instituted as part of Charles VII's military reforms.
Their record was uninspiring; suppressed in the 1530s, they were
succeeded by Francis I's provincial *légions*, ostentatiously introduced
but scarcely more effective as a means of maintaining commoners in
arms to serve wherever they might be needed. Yet those same

fifteenth-century reforms had also produced the nucleus of a permanent and mobile royal army: the *compagnies d'ordonnance*, composed of units of mounted men-at-arms and archers. Captained by noblemen, the companies came collectively under the monarch's direct command. It was exercised simply by his fiat, and needed none of the processing by chancery and registering by sovereign courts that attended so many of his other royal acts. Even so, the civilian population had good reason to look askance at these companies. Their members constituted a 'military society', virtually detached from civilian life and potentially hazardous to it. Moreover, permanent companies had regularly to be paid: unpaid, they became an active and immediate danger to civil peace. Revenues for their pay had to be extracted from commoners, whose natural disinclination to contribute was overcome by the coercive threat implicit in the presence of the forces themselves.[38] And yet in order to be paid those forces had surely to submit to at least some measure of civilian control.

The immediate source of the pay in question, the *ordinaire des guerres*, was funded mainly from 'extraordinary' revenues, and in particular from the *tailles*.[39] In effect permanent taxes from the 1440s onwards, but none the less levied upon the private possessions of the people, the *tailles* were subject to constitutional safeguards. Whatever the constitutional origins of the *officiers* who administered them, those *officiers* were accountable for all assessments, receipts and disbursements ultimately to the sovereign courts and the royal council in one or other of its forms. Deployment of funds for military purposes was scarcely dissociable from a system that existed principally to deliver those funds. Their deployment might none the less be deemed a particular function of that system – a function sufficiently important and sufficiently distinct to engender specific institutions for its performance. From the 1470s a royal secretary was appointed to supervise musters, reviews and payment of the *compagnies*. From the 1530s the 'office' of *contrôleur-général des guerres* was assigned to one of the *secrétaires des finances*, and from 1570 to the senior *secrétaire d'état*.[40] Treasurers, controllers and commissioners for wars clustered beneath that office. 'Do not permit your soldiers to annoy them', advised a mid-century handbook for company captains, 'for commissioners, controllers and treasurers can do them plenty of injury in return.'[41] Their functions extended to logistical arrangements, described in detail in an ordinance of 1549 that stressed their importance as intermediaries between municipal *officiers* and troops needing victuals and quarters *en route*.[42] Royal executive personnel were penetrating the 'military society'. It was they who formed the essential links between the components of that society, the resources of the people, the system that made those resources available to the king, and the authority of the king himself.

And yet in the sixteenth century the personnel in question did not form a stable bureaucratic department. Even at the very centre of government, the *contrôleur général des guerres* had by virtue of his secretarial office an ample range of other duties to perform. Secretaries other than he continued even after 1570 to sign directives concerning the armed forces. Those charged with implementing such directives, nominally his subordinates, did so as often by virtue of an *ad hoc* commission as of holding an established office for the purpose. And, while the number of subordinate positions multiplied, commissions were issued well-nigh indiscriminately not only to civilian administrators, but also to members of the military establishment itself. In relation to the latter, the status of civilian administrators remained unclear in principle and often negligible in practice. 'God's death!' exclaimed Armand de Biron, marshal of France and commander of men in the field in 1574, 'we don't want any commissioners or clerks of the victuals here, we've made our own arrangements.'[43] Changes might take place in martial organisation – the value of mounted men-at-arms as combatants diminished, light horsemen came into vogue, tactical units were reformed[44] – but the military retained their consciousness of themselves as a socially distinct and self-regulating body, under the king, who continued to underwrite the institutions that reinforced their belief. In the year of the creation of the *secrétaires d'état*, royal edicts still described the constable and marshals of France as a 'college' for the 'general superintendence' of the armed forces and equipped with judicial powers for the purpose.[45]

Moreover, the existence of the military as a distinct institutionalised *corps* carried with it the possibility that in their relation with civilian administrators the direction of control would be reversed. Among the captains of the *compagnies* were high-ranking noblemen whom the king also designated *gouverneurs* of provinces.[46] Since the thirteenth century he had commissioned such dignitaries ostensibly as his plenipotentiaries, over and above the *baillis*, to supervise the practice of government within the regions of their charge.[47] Through these *gouverneurs* kings could bring political pressure to bear upon the provinces, while localities within the *gouvernements* could deal through their gubernatorial patron with the king. But *gouverneurs* of the early sixteenth century were largely absentee, and royal directives repeatedly stressed that theirs was essentially a military role.[48] They were 'gros personnages' whom the king was careful to keep 'near us', and whose chief responsibilities were for companies stationed in garrison towns 'in the *pays* and provinces of our kingdom which are *en frontiére*',[49] key zones for the defence of the realm and the launching of campaigns abroad. Despite their social eminence, their élite status in the structure of France's military establishment, the deference shown them by lesser men, they were subject to the discipline of the constable and were even dismissable by him.[50] Yet the *gouverneurs* retained a potentially wider role. Over and above their specifically military functions, their royal letters of provision continued to allude imprecisely to their concern for 'whatever may need to be done for the good of ourself, our affairs and the utility of the public weal'.[51] In the decades of civil war the utility of the public weal seemed to require that that role be activated, and that *gouverneurs* and their lieutenants, exemplars of a military and aristocratic ethos, take the reins of provincial government comprehensively into their own hands.[52]

In the meantime, however, successive governmental attempts were made to improve not merely administrative vigilance over disbursement of funds to the military, but also the efficiency of the fiscal system itself and its yield in terms of cash revenues. Historians of late-medieval and early-modern Europe have interpreted such developments as profoundly significant for the formation of the state.[53] Fundamental political and social changes, we are told, were precipitated by the efforts of aggressive European rulers in inflationary times to appropriate from their peoples ever-increasing amounts of cash for purposes of war. Governmental bureaucracies were enlarged. Circulation of money accelerated, and its use came to pervade economic activity at every social level. This, together with the unequal distribution of the tax burden, served to polarise wealth and to exacerbate and widen social divisions. Meanwhile rulers had to deal with querulous 'representative' assemblies. The seeds were sown of violent confrontations between princely régimes and commoners harassed by fiscal demands, between 'court' and 'country', between 'state' and 'society'. While these confrontations would culminate in the seventeenth century their origins, it seems, are discernible long before. Some of the economic and social questions that arise from such interpretations as this are considered elsewhere in this book. As to the practice of government, it is clear that in sixteenth-century France the apparatus of royal fiscality was indeed magnified and modified, and primarily in response to military exigencies. But far less clear are the degree of bureaucratic centralisation that resulted from these changes, their success in augmenting the flow of revenues to royal coffers, and the significance of these changes for the formation of the state.

Already in 1515 more than one-third of all royal *officiers* were specifically concerned with fiscal administration. Their numbers grew throughout the century. For the single *élection* of Étampes there were five officiers in 1543, seventeen in 1587. The number of *élections* also grew: by 1600 there were some fifty more of these revenue-districts than the ninety-five that existed at the end of the fifteenth century.[54] Their growth stemmed mainly from divisions of existing districts as the ruler tried to impose the *tailles* more rigorously upon local communities,[55] and partly from attempts at extending the *élection* system to fresh parts of the realm. The attempts met with local resistance. Provinces such as Languedoc or Burgundy retained distinctive forms both of taxes and of institutions for administering them, under their provincial Estates. It did not follow that such provinces would escape their share of the general increase in the tax burden.[56] In any case, *élections* covered most of the kingdom by the opening of the sixteenth century, including parts of it that were nominally *pays d'états*. From this administrative level the *élus* with their councils, the members of which included receivers, clerks, sergeants and perhaps some local notables, brought judicial power and coercive pressure to bear in concert upon the parishes. They judged disputes in their peripatetic courts of first instance. Their sergeants were at hand to support local constables in executing penalties of seizure or incarceration upon unwilling taxpayers or collectors who failed to deliver.[57] In sum, both the taxpayer's prospects of equitable dealing and the monarch's of getting in his extraordinary revenues were effectively in the custody of the *élus* and their associates. But *quis custodiet ipsos custodes?*

Ultimate custodianship lay with the royal council, communicating its directives through the *secrétaires des finances*, and with its offshoot the *chambre des comptes* which verified *élection officiers'* accounts, together with the *cour des aides* before which those *officiers* were justiciable. But wide discretionary powers in relation to royal fiscal policy and administration rested at the opening of the sixteenth century with a distinct collegiate group of councillors. These, the king's *gens des finances*, consisted of the *généraux des finances* and the *trésoriers de France*. They headed the four *généralités* which contained the *élections* under the *généraux* together with the *bailliages* as administrative districts for 'ordinary' domanial revenues that were the *trésoriers'* concern. The *gens des finances* were collectively charged with establishing annual budgets for the *généralités* as a whole; each of them was to tour his particular *généralité* with this object in view. Yet their estimates depended largely upon reports from the *officiers* of the *élections*. Further, the *gens des finances* were also charged with ensuring that money be available when and where the king should need it; yet they disposed only of the sums that remained after accustomed disbursements had been made within the *élections* and by the general receiver of each *généralité*.[58] Thus, despite their conciliar standing and collegiate weight, the *gens des finances* were heavily reliant upon their subordinates for the means to perform their own functions. In 1523 the king himself denounced them for lack of efficiency and probity, and so called in question the working of the entire system that they headed.

Chafing under military and diplomatic reversals, threatened by his rival the Habsburg emperor, betrayed by his own constable Charles of Bourbon, Francis I stood in urgent need of funds for the defence of his kingdom and the pursuance of his Italian aims, and discovered that ever since his accession he had been 'continually robbed by the *gens des finances*'.[59] The solution lay in demoting them and reforming the system. Henceforth[60] all royal revenues should be controlled by a single executive agent of the royal council, the *trésorier* of the *Epargne*. He should not himself be a member of that council and should exercise no initiative in respect of fiscal policy, over which the council itself, and in particular the chancellor, reassumed direct control. The *trésorier*'s function was simply to register all receipts and disbursements. Receipts were to reach him in the shape of the cash collected in the localities, delivered to *élection* receivers, docketed and handed on by them to the receivers-general, and transmitted by these in turn, together with the dockets, to the *Epargne*, where the *trésorier* would give his quittance. All disbursements along the way must tally either with accustomed issues as set out in the overall budget for the kingdom, or with warrants given under the great seal by the *secrétaires des finances*. Such authorisations were again to be recorded by the *trésorier* who, by referring to his registers, should be able at any time to tell the council precisely how much money was available to the king for his affairs. As for the *gens des finances*, they lost both their conciliar and their collegiate standing, and were reduced severally to the level of mere supervisors over the *élus*.[61]

The essence of these reforms was administrative unification, simplification and centralisation on bureaucratic lines. But they were not definitive. Even at the centre, supplementary repositories were soon set up for particular receipts. While the *trésorier* of the *Epargne* gained entry *ex officio* to the royal council, his administrative performance was subjected to checks by commissioners among whom figured *maîtres* of the *chambre des comptes*. In 1547 two controllers-general, in fact foreshadowed within a very few years of the *trésorier*'s creation, were directed to countersign all his quittances and to keep a further register of his receipts and disbursements.[62] Yet to ingeminate functions at the centre, whether through commissioners or through conciliar institutions, was not to ensure arrivals of adequate funds from the provinces at large. Their inadequacy became apparent afresh in 1542, again with the renewal of war. Now the number of *généralités* was quadrupled. A commissioner for the otherwise still-emasculated *généraux* and *trésoriers de France* was placed alongside each receiver-general to monitor his dealings. But still more was needed by way of regional control. In January 1552, as Henry II prepared to campaign in Germany, the offices of the *trésoriers de France* and the *généraux* were simultaneously conflated, multiplied and redeployed for the purpose. A single *trésorier-général* for both ordinary and extraordinary revenues was henceforth to reside in each of the seventeen *généralités* and was charged with preparing an annual budgetary statement of its revenue-value for the council, the *trésorier* of the *Épargne*, and for his own receiver-general whose dockets for all receipts he must also countersign, reporting accordingly to the council every quarter.[63]

The re-emergence of the *trésoriers-généraux*, descendants of the powerful *gens des finances* and still endowed with impressive privileges, at strategic points throughout most of the kingdom was a major recognition of the need for decentralised controls. Fiscal custodianship still lay ultimately with the royal council; for its weekly deliberations on financial business two *intendants des finances* sat on the *conseil des affaires* of 1563[64] to furnish its channels of communication with the *généralités*. But what mattered was the practice of government within the *généralités* themselves. Functionaries who jostled and scrutinised one another at the centre and surveyed the regions from afar were no substitute for the immediate and weighty presence of governmental authority in the midst of district and local administrators. The redeployment of the *trésoriers-généraux* was consolidated under Henry III.[65] In 1577 their number in every *généralité* was increased to five. Each of them should annually conduct a tour of one-fifth of the region, so that by the end of every quinquennium they would each have inspected the whole of it. Reports on these tours were to be delivered to the *chambre des comptes* of which, and of the *cour des aides*, all *trésoriers-généraux* were members *ex officio*, 'just as the four ancient *trésoriers de France*' and 'the four ancient *généraux des finances* used to be'. But a feature of their reformed functions no less significant than their renewed standing in relation to the sovereign courts was the revival of their collegiate character. Except when on tour, all five *trésoriers-généraux* were to assemble three times a week in their *bureau*, there 'to prepare their general statements of the values of our finances and to verify the statements of our accounting *officiers*' throughout their *généralité*. Joint counter-signatories of all divisional receivers' dockets for moneys delivered, they were also to negotiate collectively all farms of royal taxes and *domaines*. Further, all commissions concerning *généralité* fiscal affairs were to be addressed exclusively to them and executed by them, 'conferring together' in their *bureau*. And, pledged by oath to exercise in due form the powers that they monopolised in their *généralités*, the *trésoriers-généraux* had also a corporate status as a collective body for the whole of France. The king agreed in 1586 that as such they should 'sometimes consult together in person or by deputies of their *corps*'; and he assented to their accrediting 'at their own expense' one or two deputies 'elected and chosen from their *corps* to inform us and our council of the affairs of their charge'.[66]

The *bureaux des finances* of the *généralités* have been seen as the sixteenth-century 'master-work' of French provincial administration, the 'vital links in the financial system' upon which so much depended.[67] Certainly their formation marks an important stage in the extension of bureaucratic practices at the level of regional government. Specialists in fiscal affairs, bound to observe detailed procedures and to display them at their *bureau*, the *trésoriers-généraux* were essentially administrators.[68] Thus their powers did not include jurisdiction over suits between parties such as the *élus*, their subordinates, still retained. But the formation of their *bureaux* also confirmed the failure of the reforms of the 1520s, which had attempted administrative unification by concentrating power at the centre of government. That failure was soon apparent at the centre itself, in the continued instability of fiscal institutions and the persistent use of commissioners to control the conduct of established *officiers*. Meanwhile in the kingdom at large, where fiscal provisions continued to vary so markedly from place to place, power and responsibility were redistributed as if inexorably among a plurality of regional agencies, the *bureaux des finances*. Administrative unification, in the fiscal as in other spheres of French government, remained at least in part a function of such agencies' capacity to operate as collegiate bodies and to make representations accordingly to the monarch. As for central controls over the *généralités*, they, too, were to be implemented increasingly by commissioners whose significance as instruments of monarchical rule we shall consider in due course.[69]

Nevertheless, there are some grounds for attributing to the formation of the *bureaux des finances* a rapid and dramatic improvement in royal tax-revenues. An estimate for 1576, immediately prior to that formation, indicates that the sum of ordinary and extraordinary revenues in that year was 15.9 million *livres tournois*, of which 7.1 million (approximately 45 per cent) came from the *tailles*. Further estimates suggest that by 1580 the sum of those revenues was approaching 28 million *livres tournois* and was to remain at this level for the next eight years. The *tailles*, at 18 million in 1588, were by far the largest single component of the increase and very nearly accounted for the whole of it.[70] Moreover, the apparent achievement of the reformed revenue system in appropriating direct taxes during the last decade of Valois rule seems to compare favourably with the system's performance earlier in the sixteenth century. At around 1500 tax-revenues were amounting annually to some 2.5 million *livres tournois*, to which the *tailles* contributed 1.8 million (72 per cent). In 1523, on the eve of the creation of the *Épargne*, the *tailles* were contributing 3.2 million (62 per cent) to the total of 5.2 million. The *tailles* alone frequently exceeded 5 million *livres tournois* per annum during the remainder of the 1520s, as Francis I pressed vigorously for funds to support his strenuous foreign policy and to ransom his sons after the Treaty of Madrid. That level of direct taxation was not sustained. In 1547 total tax-revenues stood at 7.4 million: the *tailles*, averaging 4.4 million per annum from 1542 to 1547, constituted 58 per cent of that total. They averaged 5.8 million per annum under Henry II, 43 per cent of his annual tax-revenues of 13.5 million, and in absolute terms scarcely more than his predecessor had managed to appropriate from time to time in the later 1520s. Over the next sixteen years the mean of the *tailles* was some 7 million *livres tournois* per annum, approximately one-half of total tax-revenues each year. From all these estimates, therefore, it would seem that Henry III's administration after 1577 contrived virtually to double those revenues and also to make direct taxes once more as proportionally significant a component of them as in the century's opening decades.

But the estimates in question are profoundly unsatisfactory. Final-ised accounts of actual tax-receipts by the French central government in any year of the sixteenth century are in fact almost entirely lacking.[71] This is partly owing to the subsequent destruction of central fiscal records, in particular those of the Paris *chambre des comptes*.[72] The surviving data consist largely of interim budget estimates, or state-ments by interested *officiers* and other partially informed witnesses. But the lack of definitive accounts such as would yield reliable impres-sions of the kingdom's tax history is also owing to the conservatism of contemporary accounting methods.[73] Government *officiers* from the *Épargne* downwards disdained to use double-entry techniques, de-veloped in Italy and increasingly adopted by private *commerçants*, whereby a balance between credit and debit could be struck with every entry. They continued to rely upon single-entry methods, simply recording receipts and disbursements in chronological sequence and eventually compiling their totals and analytical abbreviates from these accumulated records. The methods made errors hard to trace, omis-sions and malversations easy to disguise. Above all, they rendered final auditing of multiple accounts by central controllers an infinitely laborious task. As long as such methods prevailed, no amount of administrative reorganisation could enable rulers to ascertain with certainty the funds at their disposal when they needed to know that basic fact. That very uncertainty stimulated the repeated exercises in reorganisation and the ceaseless allegations that fiscal *officiers* were congenitally dishonest. As for the data that do survive, their interpretation in respect both of the real value of royal tax-revenues and of the impact of sixteenth-century taxation upon the French economy and the French people is beset with difficulties. The upwards movement of revenues expressed in nominal terms is utterly misleading. In the course of the century the *livre tournois* was progressively devalued and corresponded as a monetary unit to an ever-diminishing quantity of precious metal.[74] Adjusted in relation to price-inflation provoked by monetary and other factors, the value of royal tax-revenues, it has been claimed, was in real terms lower in the 1580s than in Francis I's reign. Perhaps the impact of royal taxation was greatest under Henry II; perhaps it was never as great, throughout the sixteenth century, as under Louis XI. In any case, the true measure of that impact surely lies in the relation of appropriated taxes to the volume of agricultural production, or to the *per capita* incomes of taxpayers.[75] As we shall see, the volume of production and the number of taxpayers are even more problematical than is the real value of the taxes in question. In sum, the effects of organisational changes in revenue administration, like so much else in France's sixteenth-century history, defy statistical measurement.

What is clear, however, is that neither the formation of the *bureaux des finances* nor any other of those changes enabled the revenue administration to gather enough taxes for the monarch's financial needs. The king must borrow. His medieval predecessors had frequently employed agents to negotiate short-term loans on their behalf from foreign bankers. The practice diminished in the later fifteenth century, following the arrival of permanent direct taxation. Yet French kings continued to raise loans by other means, using their other revenues as security. Financially 'capable' individuals and groups paid over substantial sums in consideration of the short-term right either to collect *aides* or *traites* as farmers, or simply to have the yields of specific revenues assigned to them. More simply still, kings demanded 'loans' from towns which normally were free from direct taxes. Unlikely to be repaid, such sums earned their corporate donors no monetary interest. What they did earn was continuance, and possibly extension, of municipal liberties – in a sense, a perpetual interest in the form of rights that included fiscal immunities and the exercise of a measure of governmental power. But to these expedients sixteenth-century rulers, their financial needs continually growing, added fresh methods of long-term borrowing. Conspicuous among these methods were the *rentes sur l'hôtel de ville*, modelled upon mortgage techniques that had evolved in France since the thirteenth century, but adapted by Francis I in 1522 to form a relatively new departure for the French monarchy. The method combined the familiar contrivance of assigning royal revenues with exploitation of municipal credit. In return for his subscription, paid as a lump sum, an investor in the *rentes* of 1522 received an annuity guaranteed by their administrator, the Paris *hôtel de ville*, to which the king assigned a number of local indirect taxes. The annuity was equivalent to interest at a rate of 8⅓ per cent per annum, payable in perpetuity or until the king should cancel the entire arrangement by repaying the whole of the 200,000 *livres tournois* advanced him at the outset.[76]

Parisians viewed the arrangement with grave misgivings: the price of the *rentes* was extortionate, and 'the said sum was furnished more through fear and dread than through friendship and liberality, and not without great murmurings against the king's council'.[77] *Pace* such emotions, Francis I raised money by these means on three further occasions, while his successor did so in almost every year of his reign, and on a far larger scale. The arrangement has been interpreted as heralding developments in the sphere of 'public credit' that were of major constitutional significance. It would seem that, in marked contrast to the short-term expedients upon which earlier monarchs had had to rely, permanent loans were being lawfully negotiated in six-teenth-century France on behalf of the 'civil personality of the State, of indefinite duration',[78] and on the security of its assets. Now, in relation to the particular case of the *rentes* it is clear that such an interpretation goes much too far. The juridical personalities involved in their issue were those of municipal corporations: Paris in 1522 and subsequently, in company with other towns as the *rentes* multiplied and became a major source of royal funds. Nevertheless, in the course of the century attempts at large-scale and long-term borrowing were indeed essayed without formal recourse to corporate municipal intermediaries; and a consequence of these attempts was to draw attention to the realm as a distinct political entity chargeable with obligations that the ruler could not and the ruled would not honour from their own resources.

By 1555 royal commissioners had made on their principal's behalf short-term borrowings that amounted to almost 5 million *livres tour-nois*, by means of repeated dealings with foreign merchant-bankers in Lyon who used their clients' deposits for the purpose.[79] In March of that year 3.5 million of these debts, together with a further loan of some 1.2 million, were consolidated into a unified sum that the king contracted to repay with interest at a rate of 4 per cent in forty-one quarterly instalments, from the receipts of the Lyon *généralité*. This was the 'Grand Parti' of Lyon: in effect, a debt secured by assigned revenues, but directly administered by agents of the bankers and of Henry II. Although the scheduled repayments would have amortised the initial debt within eleven years, no term for amortisation was explicitly fixed; and, in any case, that debt was soon augmented by fresh borrowings. The resources made available to service it proved insufficient, even when those of other *généralités* were brought into play. Repayments were suspended at the end of 1557. Early in 1559 the king's council concluded with his creditors a new contract for 3 million *livres* of his debts. This was the 'Petit Parti', an arrangement geared to issues of *rentes* on the Lyon municipality covered by assigned royal revenues from Languedoc. The agreement marked a return to better-tried borrowing techniques. It was followed almost immediately by Henry II's death. Taken together, his commitments in Lyon and elsewhere amounted in all to a debt of 43 million *livres*.

How far were the king's successors bound by the contracts which he had made? Was it not the late monarch's personal credit that had been engaged? Or were royal obligations binding upon his people, even upon 'the State, distinct from the person of the king'?[80] With the royal council rent by faction and the kingdom succumbing to religious and civil disorder, the post-Henrician government had little leisure to formulate and settle such questions systematically. Its tergiversations and the trepidations of the creditors suggested the possibility that the late ruler's debts would simply be renounced. But a government that habitually borrowed could scarcely afford to cold-shoulder international bankers and their interests. To do so would be to disrupt at a stroke their businesses, the king's remaining financial and political credit, and – especially in view of the terms of the Petit Parti – Lyon's role as a centre for international finance. And so the Estates-General were summoned. The deputies were convoked, as Chancellor L'Hôpital stressed in his opening address to them, with the explicit aim of furnishing the king with means to escape from the 'financial poverty' created by 'twelve long years of war'. In such circumstances kings were entitled to expect the support of their 'subjects' whose goods 'belong to them by sovereign authority (*imperio*)', though not proprietorially (*'non dominio et proprietate'*).[81] This was tantamount to treating Henry II's liabilities as a charge upon one of a set of specific rights which together constituted the supreme political function – a function now actualised through his successors and to which, regardless of all other rights, the members of the body politic must defer.

The deputies saw matters differently. For them, the assembly's prime purpose had altered between the time when they were summoned, in the lifetime of Francis II, and the time when they met, in December 1560, a week after his death. That purpose was now to appoint a regent and a council for the minority of Charles IX. They must therefore seek fresh mandates from their constituents – and still more so in relation to royal financial demands, the magnitude of which was only now made clear to them. The point was reluctantly conceded. In August 1561, simultaneously with the ecclesiastical colloquy meeting in Poissy, a quorum of deputies reassembled in Pontoise, ten miles away.[82] Eager to pronounce on matters of religion as well as on the composition of the regency government, they none the less proposed a solution to the financial problem. It steered between the Scylla of repudiating the debts in question and the Charybdis of accepting that they be charged in effect upon the people at large. Those debts were first and foremost the responsibility of the king himself and his administrators, who must find means of settling them by exercising economies and better management. But they were also the responsibility of the kingdom as a whole, and chargeable upon its assets. This, however, was not to concede that those assets included the sovereign's overriding right to tax. They did include the royal *domaine*, which plainly had been maladministered and was insufficient to resolve the present predicament. They also included the church's wealth, 'the property of which belongs *en corps* to the common wealth of the kingdom, and the clergy have only its usufruct'.[83] The kingdom, then, had capital assets other than those traditionally enjoyed by the ruler or possessed by the ruled; and it was upon these that the king might now draw, with the approval of the Second and Third Estates.

Debates over taxation powers as a feature of 'sovereign authority', attacks upon clerical wealth and fiscal immunities, were nothing new. Yet despite their differing standpoints the chancellor's and the deputies' arguments, taken together, pointed implicitly to the presence of the state as a distinct entity with immaterial and material attributes. The clergy's reaction promptly obscured that implication. They had ample experience of royal pressure upon their temporalities. Since the twelfth century they had contributed funds to the king in the form of clerical tenths. But such contributions were designated 'charitable gifts' and, in principle at least, were freely given. It was true that the principle had been steadily eroded, that kings had demanded their gifts with mounting frequency, that Francis I had demanded them several times a year and had even declared that 'the property of his clergy's tenths was exclusively his own'.[84] Nevertheless, their collection had continued to require clerical consent at diocesan assemblies, and clerical administration. In any case, declarations that the tenths were the king's fell far short of pronouncements that all of the church's temporalities were the kingdom's as a whole. The clergy resisted such pronouncements. In the Contract of Poissy of September 1561 they agreed to render the king tenths totalling 9.6 million *livres* over the next six years, with a further 13 million over the following ten years to be paid directly to the Paris *hôtel de ville* for the redemption of *rentes* underwritten by royal revenues. In terms of annual subventions, these sums were comparable with the tenths rendered since 1547, and with the 'free gift' voted by the clergy to Francis I twenty years earlier towards his sons' ransom. They would be collected by the clergy 'as they themselves shall think best' and through 'such personages as they may wish to choose'.[85] Moreover, the king gave assurances that he would demand of them no further gifts for the period covered by the Contract.

In fact the king's assurances proved empty. During the next quarter-century he not only demanded additional subventions, but also ordained on six occasions that ecclesiastical temporalities be sold outright, using the proceeds to launch new *rentes* rather than to redeem existing ones.[86] While the Pope connived at most of these alienations, they did not depend upon his prior consent – nor, indeed, upon the Estates' endorsement and the position outlined by the deputies in Pontoise. Careless of constitutional niceties, L'Hôpital's successor as chancellor, René de Birague, affirmed in 1575 that 'everything [the clergy] possess belongs to the king', who could sell whenever and as much as he chose 'without even telling them about it'.[87] Yet the king's actions indicated otherwise. The edicts of alienation were regularly followed by provisions for clerical repurchase. And, although sales consequent upon the first of these edicts were handled by royal appointees, thereafter the clergy themselves and their agents were increasingly involved in administering such transactions, and above all in recovering what had been sold. As for the Contract of Poissy, its provisions and subsequent royal demands served decisively to promote the corporate organisation of the Gallican church. A comprehensive revenue system took shape specifically to administer the now continuous clerical tenths. Financial negotiations with the royal government were conducted by the church's representatives, almost as 'equals with equals'.[88] These developments led directly to the establishing of permanent representative institutions that dealt with a wide range of ecclesiastical affairs. The General Assembly of the clergy of France was convened from 1579 at stated intervals, punctuated by *petites assemblées* to handle financial business. Composed of provincial and diocesan deputies, the Assembly was distinct both from the Estates-General and from ecumenical councils of the Roman church. Its existence testified to the clergy's corporate identity within the structure of the body politic – no matter where ultimate rights over ecclesiastical wealth might lie.

Meanwhile the head of that body faced the spiralling costs of his household, his court, his wars. Patrons and clients competed around him for largesse; disappointed, they turned upon their rivals, and even upon him. The wealth of his more affluent subjects, clerical and noble alike, eluded his direct grasp. His direct taxes, administered by *officiers* whose conduct was hard to control, fell mainly upon subjects whose ability to pay was limited. Driven to borrow, he had so often to rely upon the services of corporate intermediaries, and to secure his borrowings with tariffs and tolls that allegedly impeded the trade from which they accrued. The implications of his financial embarrassment were far-reaching, while his resources and room for manœuvre were circumscribed in almost all respects. Yet one resource was virtually inexhaustible – a resource which the monarch generated by the authority he wielded. Funds could be raised and clients satisfied through vending governmental power in the form of offices.

The practice of office-selling was no innovation. It was traceable to St Louis himself, and beyond. What was new in the sixteenth century was the scale of the practice, together with monarchs' open acknowledgement of how lavishly they engaged in it. By 1600 one-sixth of total receipts registered at the *Épargne* derived from the sale of offices. 'This kingdom', expostulated Cardin Le Bret, a high-ranking member of the *cour des aides*, in 1593, 'has become quasi-monstrous through the excessive number of *officiers* that have been multiplied prodigiously'.[89] Their multiplication, kings might argue, was warranted by the need to improve administrative efficiency. In his notorious edict of October 1554 that made almost all 'our account-keeping *officiers* alternative from year to year' and so doubled their number at a stroke, Henry II threatened with suspension those of them who did not use the sabbatical year to prepare satisfactory accounts.[90] But, while there was certainly ample room for such improvement, few doubted that kings created more offices mainly in order to obtain more money. Venal offices not only yielded the sums that purchasers paid immediately for them, but were also exploitable as a borrowing device. In the latter respect they were analogous to assigning powers and privileges, including fiscal immunities, to municipal corporations. *Officiers* enjoyed comparable benefits; and they were likewise expected to advance their ruler funds when he should need them. A prime qualification for fiscal office, therefore, was that the aspirant be himself 'solvable et capable'[91] – a capacity proved in the first instance by his paying the purchase price. Yet did not the king dissipate his own capacity to verify purchasers' credentials, and with it his very means of governing, when he allowed holders of venal offices to treat them as heritable, and even to transfer them to third parties? The fiction that denied such rights was dispelled with Henry III's unambiguous ruling in 1586 that such holders in many instances might 'dispose of [their offices] as of their own property and acquisitions'.[92] Offices were patrimonial; and their tenure, as well as advancement within the governmental system, thus depended upon quite other than bureaucratic considerations. Even so, it was more and more firmly into the hands of prosperous families that 'public functions' passed. Prosperous, they disposed of financial resources upon which the king could indeed continue to draw. Moreover, by their ties of kinship and marriage, friendship and interest, they consolidated the corporate and collegiate character of institutions that was still so pronounced a feature of government itself. And, 'veritable associations for the conquest of social advantages, tribes or, better, clans',[93] these office-holding families, natural and artificial, also consolidated the structural correlation between the composition of government and of French society.

For all that, strong arguments could be and were advanced on ethical grounds against making 'public power' the object of pecuniary transactions and private interest. These arguments were strongest in relation to judicial offices. Persons who sold such offices, fulminated L'Hôpital, 'sell the most sacred thing in the world, which is justice. They sell the *république*, the subjects' blood'. Almost – though not quite – verbatim, Bodin repeated the stricture,[94] which was widely endorsed by other jurists and by laymen. The sentiment figured in royal ordinances as well. No one, declared Louis XII, 'may buy a judicial office' – a declaration repeated eighty years later, on the prompting of the Estates-General, by Henry III with the rider that purchasers of such offices 'shall be declared unworthy and incapable of ever holding royal offices' of any kind.[95] The declarations were disingenuous. They were grossly belied by royal actions, and amounted, as Pasquier gloomily observed, to no more than 'edicts for show and without effect'.[96] Yet their ineffectuality hinged as much upon the attitudes of judges and lawyers as upon rulers' ceaseless quest for funds. No less eagerly than other *officiers*, judicial *officiers* from the members of the Paris *parlement* downwards grasped at opportunities to ensure that their kinsfolk and protégés should succeed them, and were willing to pay for that assurance. And, although at first opportunities for new men to break into the judicial world sprang from the creation of offices for sale, as the sixteenth century unfolded that world at its several levels became more and more the preserve of entrenched social groups.[97]

Nepotism infected not only the tenure of judicial offices, but also the quality of justice distributed in the courts. Time and again royal judges had to be directed not to hear cases where their own close kinsfolk were parties, and even to absent themselves from court when parties to whom they themselves were heirs had litigation to conduct there.[98] Other kinds of corruption, too, were commonly supposed to infect the practice of justice at every level. Were not judges and lawyers notoriously rapacious? Did they not retard and prolong judicial process for the sake of their own *épices*? Yet these were the allegations of the untutored. The sluggard progress of civil suits and criminal prosecutions alike through the royal lawcourts, and the multiplicity of court *officiers*, were at least partly functions of the procedural system with its built-in safeguards against summary and biased conduct by its operators.[99] Derived from Roman and canon law procedures, its mode was to establish facts through having parties and witnesses examined not in the presence of lay juries, but by professional magistrates. This mode of proof involved submissions and resubmissions of statements and interrogatories, as well as of oral testimony given under oath and again recorded. Criminal prosecutions relied upon building up by these means a comprehensive dossier that was ultimately reported to the court to form the basis of its judgement, and of such a judgement's review by a higher court upon appeal. The procedure was essentially bureaucratic. It was also comprehensive in that civil plaintiffs were associated with criminal prosecutors as joint complainants in actions where the former had damages to claim against the accused. Ever more exhaustive in the upper reaches of the judicial hierarchy, the system as it developed in France from the thirteenth century onwards could not be operated without large numbers of professional administrators. Pressure upon it intensified intolerably in the sixteenth century as litigiousness swelled apace. Small wonder that impatient civil litigants should berate 'the dragging on of process', that criminal suspects should be 'long detained in the prisons and crimes unpunished'.[100] If justice fell into disrepute, it was the victim as much of its own meticulousness as of its exploitation at the hands of self-interested professional individuals and groups.

Nevertheless, the situation excited genuine concern and a great deal of reforming legislation. In addition to seeking to ameliorate the conduct of judicial personnel, these reforms aimed specifically to expedite procedure by separating forms of action, streamlining discovery of facts, and placing still greater emphasis upon written records. Threatened with severe penalties if they should neglect or retard criminal prosecutions for the sake of other business, royal judges were enjoined to proceed with the former as their first priority, and without waiting for 'the complaint of civil and interested parties'. Further to obviate delays arising from 'confusion' of 'civil and criminal justice', a judge was established in every *bailliage* court to specialise in dealing with crimes and explicitly debarred from having to do with civil actions. As to the latter, specific measures sought to discourage courts from permitting repeated adjournments for respondents to collect evidence, to take advice or simply to put in an appearance, and from admitting discursive pleadings that dwelt upon points of law as well as upon matters of fact.[101] Material facts were in any case hard enough to ascertain. Two of the French kings' most celebrated reforming measures of the century – the requirement that registers of baptisms, marriages and burials be kept by parish clergy and deposited annually at the nearest *bailliage* court, and the ruling that formal documents be written not in Latin but in French[102] – were manifestly designed to disarm time-consuming debate over when key events had occurred, and over the comprehensibility or otherwise of recorded statements to those concerned.

These and similar measures tended to enhance the bureaucratic characteristics long since evinced by the French judicial system. But their results were largely disappointing. Procedural delays continued to be diagnosed as 'the most frequent cause of the dragging on of process'. The special criminal judgeships suffered a typical fate: other judges soon contrived 'to hold and to exercise the said offices . . . with their civil offices'.[103] More significant than their immediate practical effects were these measures' repeated focus upon a particular level of the jurisdictional hierarchy. It was the level of the *bailliages*. Below that level, the number and scope of inferior jurisdictions was reduced. Municipalities lost their powers in relation to civil litigation. *Prévôtal* courts were made fewer, and the competence was diminished of those that remained. At selected *bailliages*, *sièges présidiaux* were created to determine a wide range of civil and criminal causes 'without appeal, and as sovereign judges and of final jurisdiction'. And, although within the hierarchy of courts the status of the *présidiaux* remained anomalous, the key stratum for bringing royal justice to bear upon the provinces, not least in relation to privileged and corporate groups, was the *bailliage* courts themselves. It was they that should oversee the conduct of municipal elections and the keeping of municipal accounts, they that had cognisance in the first instance of civil and criminal cases involving noblemen, they that accommodated royal *procureurs* for ensuring that ecclesiastical diocesan judges should not encroach beyond their restricted sphere.[104] Above all, it was mainly at the level of the *bailliages* that redaction of the kingdom's profusion of customary laws was carried through.[105]

Customary laws, pronounced Charles VII's ordinance of 1454 that initiated the work of redaction, 'are divers according to the diversity of the *pays* of our kingdom'. Further, they were uncertain; and litigants often 'adopt contrary customs in one and the same *pays*'. If they were 'put in writing', then 'judges would judge them more certainly', for no demonstration of relevant law would be needed 'other than that which shall be written'.[106] The allusion was to the need to consult juries of laymen who gave oral testimony concerning local rules in inquests known unflatteringly to lawyers as *enquêtes par turbe*.[107] Yet when in the sixteenth century the work of preparing and publishing written records of customary laws at last got seriously under way it was ostensibly conducted by consultative means. Constitutional convention dictated as much. Whatever the scope of royal authority in relation to the affairs of the kingdom as a whole, it did not extend to promulgating law unilaterally in relation to the people's private affairs. The customs that governed those affairs had been made by the people themselves, in their local communities, time out of mind. If the king wished to remedy the delays and inconsistencies that undoubtedly arose from unrecorded customs, he must send his agents to discover from those communities once and for all what their customs were. He did so by commissioning *parlement* magistrates to meet with the three Estates of the *bailliages*, together with lawyers of the district as an additional category of deputies at these assemblies. But as the work proceeded it became increasingly clear that the end of redaction was not simply to record existent rules.

The king directed his commissioners 'wherever there shall be need to reform the customs and adjudicate upon them by decree'.[108] Professional lawyers dominated the proceedings, especially when rules were disputed and required jurisprudential expertise for their determination.[109] In theory it could still be held that 'custom finds its source and foundation in the consent of the three Estates' – that it 'passes by the harmony of the three Estates'[110] – but such 'consent' fell far short of the positive and immediate affirmations of custom that members of local communities had traditionally given by those communities' authority. It amounted to little more than acts of concurrence by members of the body politic on behalf of those communities in formulations that, subject to interpretation by the professionals who had helped to prepare them, would thereafter be binding upon all and sundry. As for the authority in question, the *Traité du droit des coutumes de France* explained how 'it is from the king alone that the principle of legislation comes'. The explanation was grounded in metaphysics, so influential upon the thinking of the jurists of the time. What happened in the work of redaction was that a rational 'principle' informed the 'matter' of the customs. While the matter was furnished by the people themselves, it was 'form which determines'; and that form was 'reserved to the king and his power'.[111]

Pursuing such conceptions to their logical conclusion, distinguished jurists urged perseverance with the work of redaction until a unified code of customary law for the entire kingdom were produced. 'Nothing could be more worthy nor more useful and desirable for the whole *république*', wrote Charles Du Moulin, 'than to reduce all the unsystematised and often futile variations of this kingdom's customs to a single concise, clear and equitable harmony.'[112] His own contributions towards achieving that end included his magisterial *Commentarii* on the extremely important custom of Paris, which he launched with the assistance of his secretary François Baudouin, and his annotated compilation of all the customs of France, the *Grand coutumier*. But, while Du Moulin's learned enterprises influenced Charondas le Caron,

Loisel and other jurists in their attempts at comparative analyses of French laws and institutions,[113] none of these endeavours approximated to a unified code. No such code emerged from the sixteenth-century redaction. While that operation has its significance for doctrines – to which we shall return – concerning the monarch's authority as supreme legislator, it left France still with dozens of *coutumes générales* and some hundreds of local variants. Its practical achievement was partially to consolidate laws and their administration at the level of the *bailliages*, where justice was dispensed in the king's name by holders of venal offices skilled in the complexities of the French procedural system. If those procedures were notably bureaucratic, the system itself was markedly decentralised. It concentrated judicial power patrimonially in the hands of regional élites. Knit together by familial ties, the members of those élites within their several regions increasingly constituted 'interdependent *corps*', more or less self-contained, and strongly imbued with a sense of their own prerogatives'.[114] Redaction and its outcome confirmed them in that sense. It cast judicial *officiers* as the 'intermediaries between the law and the people'. It rendered law 'less accessible to common intelligences',[115] and yet in no way less intrusive upon the people's affairs. But all this, however perturbing to Chancellor L'Hôpital and others, was not enough to detach the *officiers* in question from their regional and local involvements. Even as administrators of justice, many of them served more than one master. In the Haute-Marche in 1557 a score of judges held between them seventy seigneurial judgeships together with a dozen posts as *avocats* and *procureurs* in the court of the *sénéchaussée*.[116] The royal legislator might repeatedly direct that men who were judges or who practised law in the royal courts should hold no seigneurial office, and should apply themselves solely to seeing that 'our justice be purely and cleanly administered',[117] but the king's control over courts and lawyers was insufficient to generate such thoroughgoing devotion to professional duty. It was insufficient even to ensure their support for particular measures that he deemed vital to the peace of the realm in the closing decades of Valois rule.

Those decades of civil wars amply exposed the centrifugal tendencies of the French governmental system, and the multiplicity of centres of power within it. The immediate background to those wars is well known. The formal cessation of Habsburg–Valois hostilities in 1559 coincided with the death of Henry II and with the consolidation of a Protestant movement that he had been committed to extirpate from his realm. Amid a rapid heightening of religious tensions, the royal council was divided and its capacity to control events weakened by factional struggles between the leaders of vast clienteles. While differences focused upon the religious issue, noble captains of military companies returned homewards with unpaid troops. Burdened with debts, the monarch could not satisfy them. Unrest mounted: it threatened to 'reduce the authority of the king to the mercy of the subject who would give the law to him from whom he ought to receive it'.[118] Now, of all times, that authority needed the wholehearted support of the lawcourts for the immediate and overriding purpose of restoring and maintaining civil concord. For two years from March 1560 that purpose was pursued through a series of royal edicts that offered varying degrees of amnesty to Protestants and sought to ease judicial pressure upon them as long as they did not engage openly in seditious practices. The edicts ran counter to the policy of the late King Henry, and even – it could be argued – to the coronation oath whereby every French monarch pledged himself to preserve the kingdom's catholicity. They were accordingly introduced as 'provisional', intended not definitively 'to approve two religions in our kingdom', but simply to 'make our subjects live and remain in tranquillity and peace'.[119] Even so, the support of the lawcourts was not forthcoming. From the *parlements* downwards they greeted the edicts with resistance, neglect, or 'so many modifications and declarations that, instead of following the king's will and conserving the people in peace, it seems that they wish to correct the said [edicts] or even revise [them] altogether'.[120] Whatever the constitutional grounds for such attitudes and objections, the members of the lawcourts were all too plainly setting an example of defiance to the royal will. It was an example that other members of France's decentralised, patrimonial and collegiate governmental system were not slow to emulate during the following decades.

The characteristic feature of the French civil wars and a principal cause of their duration from the 1560s onwards was the proliferation and interaction of provincial and local leagues. Such leagues took many forms. They might coalesce into pan-French organisations. They might be limited to alienated groups of men roaming within particular districts: spontaneous movements of oppressed and displaced peasantry, alliances of brigands, some exotically named, some straddling the religious divide as if oblivious of it. Politically more significant than any of the latter were associations formed under the leadership of royal and municipal *officiers*, prominent clerics and hereditary noblemen, in conjunction with provincial *gouverneurs* and their lieutenants. From 1560 the monarch repeatedly ordered *gouverneurs* to reside in their *gouvernements*, and greatly increased the numbers of their local lieutenants. If the king's judicial *officiers* and the lawcourts that they manned were unreliable, the instruments of armed force that were directly answerable to him might at least be expected to enforce his will. The expectation was disappointed. As captains of military companies, *gouverneurs* had good reason for disenchantment with a bankrupt ruler. In any case, they were not simply itinerant military commanders concerned solely with keeping the king's peace by force of arms. As their letters of provision indicated, their concerns were potentially comprehensive – as wide-ranging as those of the king himself whose very dignity and presence provincial *gouverneurs* seemed to embody when they arrived ceremonially in the places of their charge. But their concerns also included personal and familial ties and interests, often of very long standing, within their *gouvernements*. Moreover, apart from considerations of clientage, *gouverneurs* could scarcely prosecute their official concerns by riding roughshod over prevailing attitudes among the members of the corporate institutions with which they had to deal. Like their medieval forerunners, they were equipped with councils, sometimes hand-picked from among their own protégés, but more often 'coalitions of the leaders of the judicial, municipal and ecclesiastical institutions'[121] of their *gouvernements*. Together, *gouverneurs* and their councils might indeed function to the furtherance of royal policies. But royal policies were inconsistent and unstable, shifting in response both to domestic and to international pressures. And so *gouverneurs* were drawn more and more to follow policies that satisfied their own and their associates' particular inclinations, in a fashion that struck interested observers as amounting in places to 'a veritable conspiracy of public powers against the royal will'.[122]

In the course of the civil wars leaguer councils, headed by *gouverneurs*, appeared at the principal seats of *bailliages* in virtually every quarter of the realm.[123] Seeking to rechannel the powers possessed by formally constituted governmental institutions, their members grappled with religious and political opponents who, like them, exploited complex alliances of patrons and clients, confraternities or congregations, natural and artificial families of all descriptions. The constituent groups of French government and society wrenched apart, realigned and ruptured again, under the hands of the king's own agents. His edicts of pacification that punctuated the phases of open warfare seemed, like the earlier edicts that had sought to mitigate unrest, exercises at best in futility, at worst in exacerbating the realm's divisions and its ruler's personal discredit. And yet, for all his difficulties, the head of the body politic was not without additional means of applying those edicts and reasserting his monarchical authority. Those means figured in Henry III's own articles of 'association', circulated among the deputies who had assembled at Blois for the Estates-General of 1576.[124] Signatories to the articles thereby swore that, 'beyond the obedience and service which we are bound by all right to render to our said king Henry at present reigning, we promise to employ lives and goods for the maintenance of his state, conservation of his authority, and execution of commandments [given] by him, his lieutenants-general, or others having power by him'. The significance of these terms is twofold. They distinguished explicitly between the monarch's person and the monarchical state, indicating by their phrasing that the latter and the authority associated with it took precedence over the former. They also alluded to agents, other than the king's lieutenants-general or *gouverneurs*, who had 'power by him'. Such agents were not limited to the entrenched multitude of established *officiers*. They also, and especially, included men whom the king himself directly and immediately empowered by commissions that, unlike offices, he could revoke at will.

In general, commissioners had long been a normal feature of royal government.[125] At every level commissions were issued to *officiers* for tasks that supplemented their usual functions or simply overlapped those of other *officiers*.[126] Thus, commissioners figured in the routine conduct of fiscal and military administration, and were continually deployed by lawcourts to take evidence from witnesses or to arbitrate between parties. Beyond such regular activities, commissioners also intervened in exceptional circumstances to amend, extend or even to supersede the ordinary operations of government. They revised taxation-rates; they fixed food-prices at times of scarcity; most exceptionally of all, they dealt with politically sensitive cases that the king chose not to leave to the discretion of the ordinary courts.[127] Yet, while such full-scale judicial commissions excited disquiet, what the monarch asserted through them was in principle no more than the authority to adjudicate that he always retained,[128] no matter how prodigally he might create offices and consign them into purchasers' hands. In that sense, commissioners whom the king himself empowered, whether for judicial, financial or *police* affairs, directly represented the monarchical person and took precedence over his other agents to the extent that the terms of their commissions allowed. Even so, commissions were at their most formidable when the king issued them to *maîtres des requêtes* of his household. The *maîtres des requêtes* were judicial *officiers* of very high standing, entitled, as Charles VIII described in his edict of 1493, to take charge of the seals of provincial *parlements* that they visited, and likewise to preside over *bailliage* courts. Receivers of requests to the king from his subjects, their functions also embraced the power to hear and determine complaints against other royal *officiers*. That power had been acknowledged since the early fourteenth century; it was endorsed by royal edict in 1539, and again in 1582.[129] Further, by an order in council of 1555 that elaborated upon an edict of two years before, Henry II directed each of twenty *maîtres des requêtes* to tour every year a *département* equivalent to one of the *généralités*, specifically in order to inspect the conduct of *officiers* and to prepare reports of alleged abuses.[130] By virtue of their offices alone, the *maîtres des requêtes* were important vehicles of central control. When the king issued his commissions to them, he forged instruments of direct monarchical rule from metal as weighty as any that he could find.

In the decades of civil war *maîtres des requêtes* were among the recipients of commissions specifically to supervise enforcement of the royal edicts of pacification. As the years of discord went by the roles of such commissioners were significantly enlarged. Following the Amboise edict of 1563 their task was essentially to collect information on the response in the provinces to that measure, so that the royal council might deal with offenders. But already some commissioners were being instructed to deal with certain cases themselves and to supervise the conduct of local judges. Following the Saint-Germain edict of 1570 some commissioners, again, received explicit instructions to investigate the general administration of justice and finance and to proceed against culpable *officiers*.[131] The scope of commissions issued in the wake of the 1577 edict of Poitiers was larger still. By 1582 the *maîtres des requêtes* and other 'personages of authority and quality' commissioned for that edict's enforcement were directed to investigate a comprehensive range of administrative matters and to discipline the *officiers* concerned. They should suspend delinquent judges and send them to answer before the royal council. They should seek to restore 'order and *police*' among the military, should inspect the *bureaux des finances*, should replace censurable financial *officiers* and pronounce upon them judgements 'of equal force to those of our privy Council of State'.[132] Plainly, no commissioner, however impressive his credentials, could hope to execute such instructions as these without the active co-operation of agents of government already on the spot – agents whose unwillingness or inability to honour the monarch's will above their other loyalties was the occasion of his sending his commissioners among them. Perhaps they might yet be persuaded to do so, by the presence of the king's own judicial representatives, directly charged with seeing that the law which he promulgated was enforced. Nevertheless, Henry III equipped his commissioners with further arguments. Through them he appealed for co-operation not only to local *officiers* and local Estates, but, beyond the latter, directly to all his subjects. He grounded his appeal upon 'the necessity in which this kingdom stands'.[133] And he associated that necessity explicitly with the state, which absorbed all particular interests, king's and subjects' alike.

The 1582 commissions urged all 'his Majesty's subjects' to assist 'in this universal cause, which concerns the safety of the State in which all have an interest, their well-being and fortune being so conjoined with it that they cannot be separated from it except by its and their entire overthrow'. How far were these words intended to convey a conception of the state as an entity other than the ruler and those whom he ruled? After all, Henry III, like his predecessors, used the phrase 'my state' often enough in the traditional sense of his monarchical condition, his royal as distinct from his natural or private person. Moreover, the phrasing of those same commissions contained familiar echoes of descriptions such as L'Hôpital's of how 'the head of state' was 'united and joined to its members', and so formed with them a 'body politic'.[134] Yet in the following year, addressing an assembly of his councillors and other government functionaries in St-Germain-en-Laye,[135] the king referred repeatedly to 'the state' in a manner which indicated that his was indeed a different conception. He demanded from his listeners and from all men of goodwill full co-operation, and 'not only because this is useful to me'. He demanded it in the name and 'by means' of France, 'which is the representation of the state, the reason for my having empowered commissioners and assembled you all here [being] . . . to re-establish the principal foundations of the state in their pristine strength and vigour'.[136]

Such a conception was not King Henry's alone. At this same time another discourse upon those 'foundations' referred to 'the machine and weight of the state', distinct from 'the prince' himself, though informed by 'essential parts' that were also requisite for his successful rule.[137] Perhaps the mechanical image was prompted by the 'bureaucratic' features of France's governmental institutions as they had developed during the sixteenth century. But those features were not enough to ensure efficient control from the centre over the practice of government and the exercise of power. Power was distributed among a multiplicity of élite, collegiate and corporate groups. Their members showed themselves capable of elevating obedience to other loyalties above their duty to obey the monarch's will – capable even of aspiring to curtail his authority, when they participated in assemblies of the Estates-General that purported to represent the mystical body of the realm. Their attitudes were shared even by potentates whom the king sent as *gouverneurs* to represent his royal person in the provinces, just as the *baillis* had represented it long before. Hence his resort to commissioners. These men were qualified by legal expertise and judicial office. They were also directly empowered by the king. Their task was to penetrate groups of *officiers* and their associates, in *généralité* and *bailliage*, there to demand from Frenchmen obedience to the ruler, and upon fresh grounds. As the king urged his listeners in St-Germain, every man should devote himself to 'the well-being of the state', and 'not to his own advantage nor that of particular persons bound or obligated to him'. In that well-being 'consists your honour, your duty and your proper well-being and prosperity'.[138] The allusions to considerations of material prosperity and property rights were especially well calculated, as we shall see in the next chapter.

CHAPTER 4

Economic
Affairs

Conditions of material life and prospects of material prosperity varied widely throughout France. Stretching from the English Channel to the western Mediterranean, from the *landes* of Gascony to the foothills of the Ardennes, the kingdom's territory embraced pronounced differences of climate, soil, water-availability – the elemental factors of an economy that was overwhelmingly agrarian. These differences entailed conspicuous contrasts in local and in regional systems of production, while opportunities for medium- and long-distance distribution and exchange diverged markedly from place to place. France was 'a collection of economic compartments'.[1] Many of them lay, and continued long after the sixteenth century to lie, relatively remote from outside influences. Others of these 'compartments' fell within the hinterlands of fair-sized towns that lived principally by trade. These were drawn into the ambits of broader economic zones that extended far beyond the limits of the kingdom. Commercial France was pulled at once northwards towards the Netherlands and the Baltic, eastwards towards the continental interior, westwards towards the great oceans – above all, southwards towards the Mediterranean complex: Italy, the Levant, the Iberian realms. Viewed overall, French economic affairs were simultaneously characterised by, on the one hand, conditions and attitudes of 'localised autarky'[2] and, on the other, openness to multiple international movements beyond the capacity of any political authority to control. None of this suggested that the material prosperity of every Frenchman was necessarily bound up with the welfare of the kingdom as a whole – a whole that was scarcely susceptible of coherent economic direction from the centre.

But why should such direction be contemplated at all? Frenchmen and foreigners agreed that of all European countries France was among the most fertile and best endowed. Medieval and sixteenth-century observers alike enthused over its 'beauty, fertility, fecundity and abundance of all excellent things, as if it were the heart, the cream or the yoke of the egg'. To Hieronymus Münzer, a much-travelled

physician of Nuremberg who toured the kingdom in 1494, the profusion of crops and livestock throughout France was 'marvellous to
behold'.[3] While other peoples had to forage abroad for the necessities
of life, Frenchmen could support themselves and should normally be
left in liberty to do so. The same principle applied to commercial
affairs. By virtue of its geographical position France constituted the
axis of Europe's transit trade. By virtue of its natural resources the
kingdom attracted merchants from all over the western world. Münzer, once more, had seen nowhere else on his travels towns so dense
with people, markets so crammed with produce, quaysides so vibrant
with commercial activity. Such activity, according to deputies at the
Estates-General of Tours ten years earlier, was the surest means of
promoting 'the public good. Therefore it seems to the said Estates that
mercantile affairs should be freely and unrestrainedly pursued
throughout this kingdom.'[4]

The desirability of economic freedom, especially in matters of
commerce, could be argued not only from what was particularly
congenial to Frenchmen, but also from the universal teachings of moral
philosophers with their overriding concern for the 'public good'. For
centuries they had taught that in the buying and selling of goods the
'just price' should prevail. Yet that price was not to be dictated by
some extraneous ruling, nor even by reference to some value intrinsic
to the goods themselves – whatever the importance of qualities
inherent to the person in determining the status of their vendors and
prospective purchasers. In normal circumstances the just price was
simply what the members of a community were willing to pay for a
commodity when it was offered openly for sale in their market. Justice
was betrayed when the vendor pursued gain by fraudulent or coercive
means.[5] 'Fraud' and 'coercion' were perpetrated when vendors acted
in collusion with each other. Accordingly, monopoly practices were
ethically reprehensible; and so, too, was the pursuit of gain through
tampering with money and its free availability as the medium of
exchange. Indeed, there were medieval and sixteenth-century commentators who were prepared to argue, with some Aristotelian support, that the 'value of money' or its price, in common with the prices
of other commodities, should depend upon dealings 'among merchants and other persons', as long as those dealings were open and free
from fraud.[6]

And yet, notwithstanding the virtues in principle of economic
freedom, in practice local administrators continually intervened in
market affairs. Everywhere from time to time abnormal circumstances
arose. Harvests failed and necessity accordingly dictated that public
powers, concerned for the public good, take action to conserve and to
acquire essential supplies and to regulate their distribution. Further,

even in normal circumstances the freedom that merchants coveted and the 'just' exchange that moralists urged could flourish only amid conditions that those same powers must promote. Not only must fraud be penalised, but also fairs and markets must be administered, weights and measures standardised, highways and bridges maintained, if vendible commodities were to be brought to the point of sale and equitably traded. These functions formed part of the *police* responsibilities that seigneurs and municipalities traditionally exercised by right and duty. The rights and duties of *police* extended to supervising the activities of gilds. In so far as gilds were associations of tradesmen intent upon their own exclusive interests and prosecuting those interests along monopolistic lines, they could scarcely be objects of ethical approbation. But gilds were justifiable in so far as they served the public good. They did so through safeguarding the quality of workmanship and thereby preventing fraud, through regulating wages and thereby costs, as well as contributing to provide watch, ward and additional public services that would otherwise have constituted direct charges upon local public authorities. As long as gildsmen paid their dues to the latter and were subject to some form of surveillance by them, such corporate groups could be deemed entirely compatible with the well-being of the greater public body within which they occurred. Their compatibility was all the more evident when gild and municipal authorities overlapped.

Even so, and although the activities of gilds embraced processes of production, it was in relation to processes of distribution and exchange that public authorities as such had their role to play. That role extended to the medium of exchange itself: money – the 'balancing instrument for the exchange of natural wealth' as the philosopher Nicholas Oresme described it in the fourteenth century.[7] Here, at least, the need not merely for local surveillance but for coherent central control was palpable. Although coins might be vendible commodities, for obvious reasons their issue could not be left to private dealers, and the activities of *faux-monnayeurs* were universally condemned. Formerly coinage had been treated as a seigneurial function.[8] But from the thirteenth century onwards the right to issue coins was steadily restricted to the royal mints. Provision of money, Philip VI ordained in 1347, 'appertains solely, and for the whole, in our kingdom, to us and to our royal Majesty, and no one can doubt it'.[9] Yet Oresme promptly doubted that matters were quite as simple as the ordinance implied. It was true that in order 'to prevent fraud' coins 'should be made by one or more public persons deputed by the community to that duty. . . . And since the prince is the most public person and of the highest authority, it follows that he should make the money for the community.' But it did not also follow that he was 'the lord or owner of the money current in his principality'; for money, once made, belonged 'to the community and to individuals'.[10] Nor did it follow, despite King Philip's claims to the contrary in that same ordinance, that the ruler could arbitrarily alter the values of coins expressed in terms of 'money of account'.

Money of account – *livre, sol* and *denier* – took the form not of real currency, but of nominal units in which the values of all things could be reckoned and expressed. The temptation to devalue it beckoned all rulers who had too little currency at their disposal, as did the temptation to lower by debasement the precious-metal content of the currency itself. Devaluation – that is, raising the nominal value of real coins – was especially seductive at times when war heightened royal expenditure and, with it, the attractions of short-term financial expedients. Devaluation might also be necessary for broader economic reasons, as a means of boosting the circulating medium when precious metals were in short supply and scarcity of currency impeded trade. Notwithstanding such considerations, arbitrary devaluation was widely agreed to have harmful consequences for 'the community' at large. It verged upon fraud. It coerced vendors into raising prices for the goods they had to sell, or else they must accept fewer coins than formerly in exchange. It confounded obligations contracted in nominal monetary terms; and these included not only commercial contracts, but also rents and other dues payable by commoners to their superiors, clerical, noble and royal alike. Ethically, economically, socially disruptive, monetary mutation ought as far as possible to be avoided, whatever particular rulers might claim. And, even if necessity should drive the king to it, he ought first to take advice from those whom his actions would immediately affect – among them, the public authorities of towns, where commercial activity was concentrated.

Even in the monetary sphere, then, the monarch's capacity to direct at will the economic affairs of France was circumscribed, and not merely in theory. When in the middle decades of the fourteenth century Philip VI resorted to a series of monetary mutations as a means of paying for war, his measures threatened 'the destruction of the kingdom', according to the Estates of Languedoil. In 1356 they gained the right to appoint the king's monetary *officiers*; and four years later John II's introduction of the gold franc as the exact and real equivalent of the *livre tournois* was in response to demands that monetary stability be restored.[11] Further devaluation and debasement by Charles VI, desperate in his closing years for means to recover from military disaster, drew protests from the Languedoc Estates and prompt assurances from the king's successor that he would get rid of 'black money'. Self-advertisingly high-handed, intent upon his struggle with his cousin of Burgundy, Louis XI none the less consulted with assem-

blies of knowledgeable deputies from his towns before essaying
monetary mutations, and modified his measures in deference to their
'good sense'.[12] And, as with monetary, so, too, with broader economic
affairs. Medieval kings might assert that they could 'dispose and order
the estates, trades, crafts and other activities in which our subjects are
engaged day by day, for the common good and their own sustenance',[13]
but in general such ordering took the form of the king's rewriting
municipal charters, reissuing gild statutes, and so, in effect, promoting
oligarchic management of local affairs and endorsing their diversity. It
also took the form of the king's issuing commissions for purposes that
ranged from placing emergency controls upon grain-prices in localities
stricken by dearth and its attendant threat of disorder to longer-term
projects for developing local industries and expanding commercial
enterprises farther afield. But again such commissions were often
enough addressed to members of local oligarchies,[14] upon whose
co-operation their effectiveness in any case largely depended. Even
when Louis XI, once more, made his notorious attempt to repopulate
his rebellious town of Arras with loyal merchants and craftsmen from
other French towns, the operation was put in hand through regional
assemblies of municipal delegates, and by commissioners who included the mayor and *échevins* of Arras itself.[15]

The Arras operation, undertaken 'for the universal well-being of all
the kingdom of France', ended in failure, and the town's *officiers*
formally recovered the powers of *police* that they had temporarily
forfeited. The kingdom's well-being, like its communities' 'common
good', remained indissociable from local corporate bodies and the
functions that they performed. And yet royal courts and royal *officiers*
had *police* jurisdictions, too. In Paris the *parlement* interfered 'inces-
santly' in the management of the capital's affairs. In Toulouse the
parlement of Languedoc subjected its host municipality to a 'constant
tutelage'. In Anjou, in Normandy, during the fifteenth century royal
agents claimed and exercised an overriding competence to issue
'ordinances of *police* in respect of all crafts and other things necessary
for the function [*estat*] of trade'.[16] Immediate political and fiscal
considerations governed their interventions, which varied in accordance with local constitutions and contingencies. But, however piecemeal, his agents' interventions furnished the ruler with ample precedents to exploit in so far as he could conceive of the kingdom's
economic needs as distinct from the interests of its several communities and seek to direct the latter accordingly. Such a conception was
indeed apparent in Louis XI's emergency directive of 1482 that,
regardless of local protests, the subsistence crisis of that year be
combatted by distributing grain 'equally' throughout the kingdom at
prices which his commissioners should fix. It was implicit, too, in more

measured fifteenth-century attempts at commercial and industrial direction. 'The *pays*', observed Charles VII, 'are enriched by fairs and markets', for these attracted foreign merchants and brought in wealth. But the exchange of wealth was 'balanced' by money; and, although foreign trade might bring riches to particular *pays*, the balance was unfavourable to France as a whole when 'strangers' unloaded luxuries within the kingdom and carried excessive quantities of currency away. Hence royally sponsored attempts, again by Louis XI and again despite local reluctance and opposition, to seize a share of the Mediterranean spice trade for French monopoly companies, or to develop silk manufacture in Lyon and in Tours.[17] By such means the balance would in due course be corrected with no diminution of commercial activity; for foreign dealers in such commodities would come into France to buy rather than to sell.

A combination of bullionist thinking with deployment of governmental power, to support protected merchants and manufacturers to the advantage of the kingdom as a whole and at its neighbours' expense, is apparent in these measures. Running counter to arguments for relative economic freedom under local community surveillance, they have seemed to many historians to presage features of the so-called 'mercantile system':[18] a 'system' whereby the state in collaboration with sectional interests would pursue profit and enhancement of its own power as interdependent objectives – and whereby leading countries of early-modern Europe would be transformed from agrarian to industrial societies. That 'system', we are told, took shape in the wake of economic difficulties which became acute in the first half of the seventeenth century. In France at the close of the fifteenth century, however, Frenchmen and foreigners conducted their affairs in a climate of relative prosperity. The kingdom was well launched upon a flood tide of recovery from the material and political misfortunes of that century's earlier decades. While royal measures had aided that recovery, the time was no longer, or not yet, propitious for sustained experiments in royal economic direction. But, as the sixteenth century unfolded, prosperity gave way once more to widespread difficulties accompanied by a redistribution of economic opportunities. In what follows we shall examine these developments, together with some of the problems that arise from historians' attempts to measure and to explain them. We shall see how they stimulated opinions more favourable than formerly to royal attempts at directing economic affairs. We shall assess the nature and limitations of such attempts in the sixteenth century. Finally, we shall consider how French peasants – by far the majority of the kingdom's population – reacted violently to the impact of socio-economic change and political disorder – and invoked traditional values as they did so.

In the sixteenth century eight or nine of every ten French men and women lived in the countryside and derived their livelihood from the soil. The food-producers occupied holdings that in general were devoted primarily to cereal crops. The kingdom's well-being therefore depended first and foremost upon the level of grain production from year to year. Consuming the greater part of their own produce, the producers had to reserve a proportion of the residue for the next sowing and a further proportion for dues and tithes appropriated by their immediate secular and ecclesiastical superiors. The remaining surplus was available for marketing: it was the source of food-supply for town-dwellers, and of the wherewithal for the producers themselves to buy essential manufactured goods and to satisfy the demands of royal tax-gatherers. Urban fairs and markets constituted centres of exchange for other goods, whether manufactured in France or imported from abroad, that were unattainable luxuries for most rural dwellers with their meagre purchasing power. Yet the trade in luxuries did not proceed independently of the agrarian base. Effective demand for them, by nobles and clerics, *officiers* and prosperous *bourgeois*, was ultimately related to the capacity of the rural economy to yield an appropriable and a marketable surplus.

The hallmark of France's recovery from the depression of the fourteenth and early-fifteenth centuries was renewed abundance of grain. By the 1490s, we are assured, its production in the Paris basin and in the Midi alike had virtually doubled in the course of fifty years.[19] Supplies outran domestic consumer-demand: there was grain available for export. Its abundance stimulated diversification in the rural economy. In that cereal-based economy some degree of animal husbandry was always *de rigueur*, for multi-purpose beasts were indispensable to provide manure and heavy traction. But now marginal land that might otherwise have been tilled could be given over to grazing. Diets, though still dominated by carbohydrates, were more widely enriched by meat, and also varied by vegetables for which urban markets exerted a growing demand: spinach and lettuces, cabbages, leeks and garden herbs, the red onions of Corbeil and the spring onions of Sceaux that were eagerly sought for Parisian tables.[20] Cash crops multiplied. From 1500 the olive spread apace along the Mediterranean littoral, in places even supplanting cereals and affording a culinary alternative to animal fats. And the vine spread more widely still in the provinces of the south, the centre and the Atlantic coast.[21] Thin soils, where cereals would grow only reluctantly, could now be devoted to viticulture. Its expansion testified to the revival of plenty, and brought prospects of affluence in its own train.

The rural economy yielded raw materials for manufacturing industry, which prospered in its turn. Textiles took pride of place. Domestic weaving in the countryside supplied the producers' own needs as well as medium-quality woollens for town-based entrepreneurs to take to market. Manufacture of finer fabrics remained dependent upon imported materials: upon Iberian wool brought into Nantes and Rouen, upon silk for processing in Tours and Lyon, or for tapestry-making in Paris and Orléans.[22] Nevertheless, production from local resources was varied: linen from home-grown flax in Maine and around Reims, sailcloth from hemp in the maritime provinces of the north-west, while the spread of pastel culture which the itinerant Münzer observed around Toulouse showed both how local cultivators were ready to invest in a new labour-saving crop and how French clothiers were claiming a share in the market for dyed fabrics.[23] Hides were available for tanning. The leather industry flourished in the Chevreuse valley; the leather goods of Poitiers, Niort, Châtellerault were 'unrivalled' in sixteenth-century France. As the century wore on French vessels, notably from Rouen, became conspicuous interlopers in the Spanish Caribbean, bringing linens and bearing away hides.[24] From Spain itself ore was shipped not only for redistribution via the French Atlantic ports, but also to supply Normandy's long-established iron industry. While Normandy had ample timber for combustion, France in general was well endowed with that resource which facilitated development of such industries as glass-making even in poorer provinces. Yet south-eastern France had ferric deposits of its own, and in places those who exploited them also made use of locally extracted coal: inhabitants of St-Genis-Terrenoire in Forez were so 'blackened' by its use as to astonish strangers.[25] The spread of the blast furnace in France was an outstanding feature of Europe's 'technological transformation' during the half-century from 1470 to 1520. That transformation included the spread of printing. Early in the 1470s printers were established at the Sorbonne and more brought from Germany to Paris's rue St-Jacques. By 1540 there were sixty master-printers in Lyon alone; and during the intervening decades hundreds of master-printers were disseminating their craft and its products in urban centres throughout the realm.[26]

With its flourishing agrarian base, its manifest manufacturing potential, its receptiveness to new technology, France for much of the sixteenth century was also a scene of vigorous and expansive trade. Markets and fairs abounded.[27] In the single archdeaconry of Josas, close to Paris, there were more than a score, some housed in impressive buildings – in Arpajon, 'in three majestic bays, like a wooden church'.[28] If the capital's proximity was a special stimulus, the geographer Nicolas de Nicolai found that in mid-century Berry 'marvellous profit' accrued to the inhabitants through the 'great trade and commerce' conducted at the provincial fairs, which allegedly numbered more than sixty. Upon these and their counterparts throughout the kingdom, local, regional and international dealers converged to strike their mutually interacting bargains. Merchants flocked to Cosne d'Allier where 'in addition to their ordinary provisions the inhabitants sell and distribute their produce to strangers and to their neighbours'. They did so 'by means of large sums of money';[29] and, even when neighbours concluded their transactions without recourse to real coins,[30] money still played its necessary part as the language for balancing the values of dissimilar goods and services. Thus Frenchmen engaged at every level of sophistication in what amounted to a highly monetarised economy of exchange, and were universally affected by the movement of money values. Even so, commercial activity swelled most rapidly in principal towns in the outlying parts of the realm, as the tide of European commerce rose. Lyon and Rouen, Nantes and Bordeaux were major centres of administration, and some of them of learning. Yet it was commerce that dictated their prosperity and their expansion.[31] Owing to its fairs, its role as an entrepôt for Italian silks and Levantine spices, and then its rapid development as a major international banking and financial centre, Lyon grew in the sixteenth century to a size second in France only to that of Paris. Hopes for a comparable development were entertained in Rouen, Normandy's capital, virtually Paris's outer harbour, and a staging-post, with other western ports, for Europe's north–south transit trade. Mariners from those ports, for whom the Iberian connection was commercially of first importance, busied themselves in the Mediterranean and pursued their southern neighbours across the Atlantic. Breton and Norman captains did not hesitate to raid Spanish intercontinental shipping. They went to the Americas on their own account, in search of fish and furs as well as of mineral wealth, and in order to colonise as well as to plunder. There was no reason in law why Spaniards should be left at leisure to claim lands that they had not yet settled; and, in any case, there was ample incentive for French venturers to penetrate existing Spanish settlements, for predatory and for trading purposes.[32]

But in the course of the century the dynamism of French economic activity slowed and gave way – though by no means uniformly – to recession. Intermittent signs of difficulty were apparent in the rural economy even during the prosperous early-century phase. Local subsistence crises continued to occur; the gap between abundance and shortage could be all too abruptly narrowed. It was narrowed more generally, and with depressing frequency, in the 1520s. Instead of abundance, there was sufficiency of grain when conditions were favourable. More and more often, it seemed, conditions were not favourable, and sufficiency subsided rapidly into dearth.[33] Town authorities might stock granaries as a hedge against seasonal fluctuations in

supplies of essential foodstuffs, but their planning was frustrated when
harvests were poor in successive years, or even when supplies in single
years were exceptionally low. Frenchmen were no better equipped
than their neighbours to store large quantities of perishable goods for
more than minimal periods of time. As the century wore on, years of
repeated scarcity seemed regularly to recur: 1543–6, 1551–2, 1556–7,
1560–3. In 1566, following an exceptionally severe winter, the mean
price of wheat in Paris was almost double that of the previous year.[34]
And from that decade onwards Lyon merchants led a mounting chorus
that commerce in manufactured goods was in decline. Complaining in
1560 of falling demand for French woollens at their fairs, they were
claiming in 1576 that cloth manufacture was ceasing in Languedoc,
Dauphiné and Poitou, and in 1580 that they now sold less cloth in a
whole year 'than formerly at a single fair'. Meanwhile Rouen's export
trade in textiles diminished, allegedly as Spanish demand fell away;
and manufacture of Amiens' noted light woollen serges was collapsing
by 1585. As interested parties continually argued, a thriving cloth
trade was vital to France's commercial well-being. While the kingdom
would seem formerly to have enjoyed a favourable balance of trade
with all countries except Italy and the Levant, the balance was no
longer favourable, and currency was apparently seeping away. Rouen
was reportedly so drained of specie by 1587 that 'there is not a sou to be
had which does not cost the eyes from one's head'.[35]

Now, for all the vigour with which merchants joined in lamenting
their misfortunes, it is clear that France's commercial experience in the
later sixteenth century varied widely from place to place, each of which
was powerfully affected by particular circumstances. Thus, the crisis of
1561 in the important trade in pastel in Toulouse derived immediately
from damage done to the crop by that year's heavy springtime rains.[36]
Fortunes in Lyon suffered particular reversals when Henry II's Grand
Parti failed, and then when religious dissidents seized and controlled
the city in 1562.[37] Its economic plight worsened in the 1570s and had
serious repercussions upon many *pays* of eastern France that lay within
Lyon's sphere of influence. Yet Marseille meanwhile escaped from its
northern neighbour's financial tutelage and enjoyed new opportunities
borne by rechannelled eastern trade as war in the Mediterranean
disrupted Venice's links with the Levant. As for Rouen, the difficulties
experienced there in each of the century's last four decades were
checks within boom periods, notably in the aftermath of the 1559
international peace settlement, and again when the sack of Antwerp in
1576 brought an influx of foreign merchants to the Norman capital.
Indeed, for a decade from the mid-1570s trade flourished at the
western ports, with Breton mariners especially active in shipping
essential supplies to Spain and returning laden with specie. Even as the

Rouennais were bewailing their lack of currency in the late-1580s, merchants in La Rochelle were still conducting such 'an almost incredible amount of trade' that 'gold and silver were as abundant as stones'.[38]

These contrasts signify, once more, the fundamental diversity of France and the divergent influences to which the parts of the realm were variously exposed. They are broadly consistent, too, with the well-known westward shift of the European economy in the sixteenth century: the relative growth of Atlantic and decline of Mediterranean trade. While France's western ports would seem well placed to have gained from that expansive movement, the eastern side of the kingdom suffered by it.[39] Further, the incidence of war and peace, both international and civil, had obvious and immediate short-run effects upon the affairs of particular localities; and, in the longer term, as the wars of religion dragged on few regions of France could escape their cumulative ravages. All this is relevant to explaining the difficulties experienced by more and more Frenchmen as the century ran its course. And yet we are assured that the origins of those difficulties lay deeper – and with them the origins of France's failure fully to profit by the shifts and expansion of the European economy. For it is plain enough that, despite the busy engagement of Bretons and Normans in overseas enterprise, despite the flourishing early-century trade of Nantes and Bordeaux, despite even the hopes entertained for Rouen, none of France's western ports came near to rivalling in international importance the great centres of the Netherlands, Portugal, Spain. In seeking to explain that failure by reference to the structure of French commerce itself, historians have deprecated the attitudes of native merchants towards the conduct of business, and the degree to which France's foreign trade was dominated by foreign business houses. We shall consider such matters as these, and their implications, in due course.[40] But first we must assess what appears to have been the underlying economic vulnerability of the kingdom as a whole, and with it that of those western ports. It is the weakness of their rural hinterlands and, beyond them, the condition of the rural economy at large – the all-important agrarian base which, to judge from the recurrences of scarcity that we have already noted, was in difficulties well before the outbreak of the civil wars.

What caused these difficulties? The fate of the Toulousain pastel crop of 1561 is an instance of the obvious link between bad weather and poor harvests. Contemporaries recognised that link resignedly; and modern historians, drawing upon the findings of phenologists, dendrochronologists, xylochronologists, have suggested that the European climate in general and the French in particular deteriorated in the course of the sixteenth century.[41] Some contemporaries – though by no means all – also supposed that France contained more people than her agrarian economy could comfortably support.[42] This view has found remarkable support among modern French historians.[43] By comparison with their forebears of the fourteenth and early-fifteenth centuries, it seems, French men and women at the close of the Middle Ages were better fed, married younger, lived longer and had more children, more of whom in turn survived to work in the labour-intensive economy and to consume its products. The demographic increase slowed within a few generations. Even so, the number of French people had risen by the 1560s from a nadir of perhaps ten million a century before to stabilise at about seventeen million souls.[44] Thus populated, the realm had reached a point of socio-economic equilibrium.[45] But such an equilibrium was intensely vulnerable to short-run difficulties. The abundance of grain that had facilitated population-growth had been obtained by re-extending a cultivated area which had contracted during the earlier phase of demographic regression. Population pressure ensured, however, that the re-extension was accompanied, on the one hand, by morcellation of peasant landholdings and, on the other, by concentration of holdings in the hands of the fortunate few. As a unit of production, neither the diminished nor the multiple holding was as efficient as the traditional 'family farm' of, perhaps, some fifteen hectares.[46] Meanwhile, traditional collective disciplines in respect of crop-rotation and the pasturing of livestock succumbed to decadence. Risks of overcropping were exacerbated. Supplies of animal manure decreased as beasts were squeezed out beyond the margins to forage upon waste and woodland that seigneurs were in any case anxious to reserve for their own profit. What did not decrease, as the sixteenth century wore on, were efforts by seigneurial and other landlords to appropriate peasant surpluses. In parts of France rents climbed for relatively short-term leases of parcels of demesne lands. Elsewhere, landlords contrived to throw holdings together and lease them on onerous sharecropping terms to desperate takers. Such arrangements denied producers both the means and the incentive to accumulate capital and to engage in medium- or long-term improvement programmes. Thereby they served to impose a ceiling upon the level of grain production, to ensure that actual production would frequently fall below that ceiling, and so to place continually, and increasingly, at risk the surplus which the producer might take to market.[47]

This composite picture of the French rural economy is subject to many reservations. Developments varied, as always, from place to place. If noble landlords in Poitou imposed 'draconian' clauses upon their sharecropping lessees, such *métayage* agreements were 'rare' in the Ile-de-France, where rents for land were none the less high by

mid-century – while in Languedoc rents remained 'meagre and station-
ary' until after 1600.[48] Again, factors other than simple population
growth affected the stability of landholdings. They included developments in law and custom: inheritance practices, which we have already
reviewed, and concepts of property, to which we shall shortly return.[49] Nevertheless, French historians have insistently identified,
as the common factor in determining the kingdom's social and
economic condition, demographic pressure upon the means of food
production.[50] And yet numerical estimates of France's sixteenth-
century population, and of its rate of increase, remain problematical
– as does the relation between that overall population and corresponding estimates of the food-producing capacity of the kingdom as a
whole.

All estimates of the total French population are, in effect, projections from fragmentary data contained mainly in parish registers and
taxation records – sources that are notoriously incomplete or otherwise questionable.[51] From 1539 *curés* were required by royal ordinance
to enter particulars of births in their baptismal registers. Some did so;
others were lax; but, above all, they failed to keep adequate records of
deaths, whether pre- or post-baptismal.[52] In consequence their registers have tended to convey inflated impressions of population growth.
As for taxation records, no simple correlation is to be assumed for the
fifteenth and sixteenth centuries between numerical changes in, on the
one hand, 'hearths' or 'households' recorded as units of fiscality and,
on the other, membership of 'families' interpreted as socio-economic
units.[53] In sum, while the evidence is sufficient to show that the period
was demographically one of substantial growth, the rate of increase
remains indeterminate; and estimates of the total French population
by *circa* 1560 have differed by as much as thirty to forty per cent.[54] As
for food, which meant primarily cereals, a principal basis for assessing
its production consists in estimates of the amount of consumable grain
yielded per quantity of seed sown – estimates that again, in the case of
France, are highly controvertible.[55] However, if a standard seed:yield
ratio of 1:5 is assumed, together with an annual sowing of 1.5 hectolitres per hectare, yields of 7.5 hectolitres of grain per hectare would
normally have been obtained. With one-quarter of the crop reserved
for the next sowing, six hectolitres would have been available for
consumption – enough to feed two people, given an average annual
consumption of three hectolitres per head.[56] To supply with cereals a
population of 17–20 million souls would therefore have required an
area of 9–10 million hectares annually under crops – in effect, some
sixteen million hectares cultivated in rotation.[57] Such an area consti-
tutes slightly over one-third of the 45 million hectares covered by the
kingdom – a kingdom whose territory included a much higher propor-

tion of potentially cultivable land than any of its European neighbours enjoyed.

In theory, then, France as a whole had enough capacity and to spare for its inhabitants to obtain the necessities of life. But, of course, in practice much of the land in question was not available to prospective cultivators who, in turn, were not evenly distributed about the surface of the realm. It has been estimated, once more, that in 1550 some eighteen million hectares of that surface were legally classified as forest;[58] and would-be encroachers upon afforested land with its conversion to arable in view fell foul of rural *communautés*, seigneurs and the monarch alike. For the most part, rural families were penned within the areas of traditional cultivation and their margins. Given prevailing levels of productivity, consumption, appropriation and taxation, the minimum size of holding that would support every such family was of the order of five hectares.[59] But during the century the number of holdings which fell below that minimum increased alarmingly. From studies of particular parishes and villages it seems that in Normandy in 1527 41 per cent of holdings already contained fewer than 5 hectares; that by the end of the century 67 per cent in Languedoc contained fewer than 3.5; and that in the Ile-de-France by 1550 nine-tenths of rural families owned fewer than 2.5 hectares of land apiece.[60] Unable to supply even their own needs from their own resources, members of such families must find employment and wages. Driven to at least a measure of dependence upon the fluctuating market for labour in the rural economy, they joined the multiplying ranks of French men and women in town and country whose survival was bound up with the ability of those who controlled the lion's share of land to produce a marketable surplus of grain.

As the pressure of demand upon that surplus intensified, prices rose. Between 1500 and 1598 the nominal price of wheat increased five-fold in Montpellier, six-fold in Toulouse, ten-fold in Paris.[61] In all probability the rate of price-inflation in major towns outran the movement of prices elsewhere. If market trends favoured the substantial producer in the countryside itself, urban demand for what he could supply was exceptionally heavy. By comparison with the apparent growth of France's population as a whole, towns grew markedly more rapidly. In Paris and Lyon, Toulouse and Bordeaux, the numbers of inhabitants doubled or even tripled in the first half of the sixteenth century. Their numbers also swelled in smaller towns, so many of them semi-rural, centres of habitation for cultivators and herdsmen, but no longer assured of supplying their dwellers' basic needs from their immediate hinterlands. Much of the urban increase may be ascribed to immigration from the countryside. Movement abroad accelerated, notably along well-trodden paths from the Midi to the Pyrenees and into

Catalonia. But there is no good reason to suppose that France did not absorb most of its own migrants.[62] Their arrivals in towns and their indigence once there placed impossible strains upon the charitable resources of ecclesiastical foundations. Laymen took a hand; poor relief became a significant municipal concern, administered in Paris from the 1540s by *bureaux des pauvres*, while in Lyon in the 1530s a 'coalition for welfare reform' culminated in the creation of the Aumône-générale.[63] But urban growth also imposed strains upon the mechanisms of the market, the means whereby effective demand was articulated. And those strains were reflected most sharply in the price of the commodity for which demand was least elastic: grain, bulky and perishable, relatively low in unit value and costly to transport.

The fact of inflated grain-prices impressed itself remorselessly upon the consciousness of contemporaries, high and low. However complex its origins, its particular and immediate cause seemed readily identifiable to them. Hoarders of grain and other fraudulent or coercive dealers precipitated both scarcity and dearness, profiting by the latter to the detriment of the public good. And, therefore, public authorities were duty-bound to intervene. They must take steps not only to ensure availability at least of minimum supplies, but also to chase out those 'granary-rats, market-hunters, crop-engrossers, tithe-jobbers, exploiters of peasants, monopolists of foodstuffs who spread high prices wherever they trade' and so exposed the whole kingdom to the curse pronounced by prophets of old upon an Israel where similar bloodsuckers were allowed to prosper.[64] In France's own history there were ample precedents for intervention such as might reduce human misery and avert divine retribution. But what seemed unprecedented, in the sixteenth century, was the sheer scope of price-inflation. In Paris during the century prices of comestibles other than grain, of woollen textiles, of combustible materials, of timber and metals for construction, rose in nominal terms by factors of from four to seven. Rents – the price of living-space – were ten times higher in the century's ninth than in its first decade. Wages – the price of labour – climbed in the case of building-workers to four times their level of 1500.[65] Again, inflation may well have been exceptionally rapid in the capital; its effects were differential, and its origins debatable. But, again, the fact of general inflation commanded contemporary attention and concern. And, for those who discussed it, a principal remedy for so disturbing a phenomenon lay once more in the hands of public – and, this time, firmly of royal – authority.

Of course, it was scarcely the business of royal authority to increase the kingdom's production of food or to reduce its procreation of children. That authority nevertheless performed a key role in relation to prices, in so far as these were a function of the medium of exchange.

Responding in 1566 to the Paris *parlement*'s concern over the high price of grain, Jehan de Malestroit, *maître des comptes*, pronounced periodic scarcity to be in the nature of things. Bad weather brought bad harvests; better weather would bring better harvests; though measures might be taken to ease the effects of the former, such accidents must ultimately be left to the will of God and the equity of nature. Prices, however, had to do not with things but with language, or with names. Their rise was in itself no proof and still less a contributory cause of real scarcity. It was 'merely an empty opinion or illusion of accounting, with no effect nor substance whatsoever'.[66] Even so, royal authority had perpetrated that illusion. Despite long-standing advice to the contrary, kings had repeatedly devalued the *livre tournois*. Owing to its devaluation, vendors had to raise the nominal values, or prices, of whatever they might wish to trade, or else be content to receive smaller amounts of precious metal in the form of currency. Kings therefore could and ought to restore monetary stability, by 'equalising' monetary valuations, tying the accounting unit to its nearest equivalent coin. The argument echoed the thesis developed nineteen years earlier, on philosophical and legal grounds, by the jurist Charles Du Moulin. For him, the form that gave monetary being to the metallic matter of coins was their accounted value. Thus, money of account and real money were in principle indissociable; and, in practice, a 'just and equitable proportion' ought always to be maintained between them.[67] Notwithstanding such distinguished support and plausible reasoning, however, Malestroit's argument was promptly challenged by Jean Bodin. Was there not, in the France of his day, 'abundance of gold and silver', greater than in the previous four hundred years?[68] Were not inflows of precious metals greatly to be desired, potential harbingers of prosperity, intrinsically valuable and facilitating trade? Yet this very abundance was the prime cause of price inflation: the level of prices was a function of the quantity of money in circulation and rose as that quantity increased. High prices were therefore entirely compatible with economic buoyancy – as long as coins contained as much precious metal as minting processes permitted. Unfortunately, royal authority had undermined that condition by debasing real money, actual coins. Via different routes and heated arguments, Bodin and Malestroit reached conclusions that were fundamentally compatible in one important respect. Difficulties induced by price-inflation were traceable to loss of monetary confidence and so to royal authority, which alone could eradicate them.

As Bodin observed, the inflation in question had further causes, and other than purely monetary factors impaired France's economic well-being. In his opinion, although fears of overpopulation were groundless and Frenchmen commanded 'inexhaustible sources' of 'salt, wine and grain', they relied to excess upon those products. They were especially improvident in their willingness, on the one hand, to relieve Spain's chronic 'necessity of foodstuffs and merchandise' in exchange for American silver and, on the other, to lavish funds upon foreign manufactures and luxury goods.[69] The opinion touched upon genuine weaknesses in the structure of French trade. Despite the nascent variety of domestic manufactures, primary products dominated the kingdom's exports, together with wine and the medium-quality textiles upon which Lyon merchants set such store. Exports depended closely upon the agrarian economy and were affected by its problems.[70] Imports continued chiefly to consist in costly items such as silks and spices; and the outflow of specie to south and east accelerated alarmingly whenever the volume of trade increased.[71] Further, while France seemed to occupy an advantageous position in relation to Europe's transit trade, the kingdom's notorious multiplicity of internal tolls and tariff barriers impeded movement of goods and materials upon its territory.[72] Above all, however, wealth from that trade accrued rather to foreigners than to Frenchmen. Large-scale management of long-distance commerce, which generated the greatest profits, and of international finance alike was dominated by foreign business-houses, exclusive – and particularly Italian – family concerns. Busily though French merchants might redistribute goods within France itself and congregate in Antwerp to conduct in person their unspecialised and 'mediocre' dealings, they appeared unable, or disinclined, to emulate foreign business expertise. Their own transactions seemed innocent of the skills in accountancy, in sophisticated use of credit instruments, in gainfully transferring funds by foreign exchange, that Italians had developed over many generations. Control of finance was effectively in the hands of the latter, for whom productive investment in French manufacturing industry ranked as a low priority. Bankers to kings, they retained as the cornerstone of their commercial interests the luxury Mediterranean trades – the very trades whereby currency seeped out of a French economy that seemed inescapably the prisoner of traditional structures and traditional attitudes.[73]

Of course, much of this defies hard-and-fast demonstration. Modern attempts at quantifying the balance of sixteenth-century French trade and its components are projections from data more questionable even than those which relate to population and production.[74] Certainly, neither Bodin nor any of his contemporaries was able to formulate a coherent view of the kingdom's economic weaknesses, still less to devise a thorough-going strategy for remedying them. But, as difficulties spread in the course of the century, awareness of such weaknesses sharpened. It fostered opinions favourable to royal direction of economic affairs. The elements of those opinions had been aired long since.

There was nothing new in Claude de Seyssel's advice to Francis I in 1515 that France should imitate its neighbours' 'laws and statutes . . . to ensure that gold and silver do not leave their territory, and to attract that of foreigners thither'. Even his recommendation that 'Frenchmen in all parts . . . should apply themselves to building and equipping ships for merchandise, in view of the great gain that other people make by sea', had its fifteenth-century precedents.[75] Yet, as the century wore on, piecemeal recommendations by actual and would-be royal advisers were echoed and amplified with mounting conviction by members of the body politic. The activities of foreigners excited especially strong feeling. Third Estate deputies at Orléans in 1560 denounced those who 'enter this kingdom every day with only pen and paper in hand, and in no time make themselves rich'. 'Experience has proved', pronounced the Lyon *consuls* sixteen years later, 'that strangers, specifically Italians, come into this kingdom not for the king's service nor for his subjects' good, but to serve their particular profit, and by their subtle practices, in which they are more skilled than any other people, to extract everything, whether new or old, from the poor French, and then to withdraw with their spoils to their own country.' By then, however, anti-Italian sentiment embraced antipathy specifically towards the associates of the Italian-born Queen Mother, and so towards the royal court where their influence allegedly prevailed. The court, voracious in its appetite for revenues, corrupt in its manners and its morals, was itself a source of many of France's misfortunes.[76] Nevertheless, opinions simultaneously gathered force that alleviations of the economic difficulties which variously afflicted the parts of the realm could no longer be left simply to local public bodies in the country at large. Who but the ruler, with his acknowledged monetary responsibilities, could act on a broader front, in the interests of the kingdom as a whole? Even so, his sphere of action was distinctly circumscribed, as we shall see.

In March 1517, Francis I summoned to Paris an assembly of notables from seventeen major towns to discuss a set of proposals for the kingdom's economic development. The programme included measures for stabilising currency-values, preventing outflows of precious metals, restricting carriage of goods to French vessels, controlling the activities of foreign merchants, and promoting French manufactures. The king intended that these proposals be written into a 'perpetual law and constitution' whereby 'the subjects of the said kingdom may be enriched and sustained in all things'. Evidently, for such an act there must be prior consultation with the representatives of those whom it would immediately affect. Yet legislation of such scope would greatly have enlarged and consolidated the king's role in relation to his kingdom's economic affairs. Not surprisingly, the deputies' responses showed them to be profoundly preoccupied with local interests, and antagonistic towards interference by royal *officiers* in municipal concerns.[77] No 'perpetual law' of general scope was promulgated; and for much of the century piecemeal and relatively short-lived measures continued to characterise the royal approach to economic matters.

Among the proposals mooted in 1517 was a measure to regulate the prices that innkeepers charged. Distrust of innkeepers was nothing new. Two years later a royal ordinance directed that their charges be subject to tariffs which local commissioners should compile and revise every quarter. The ordinance also implied that high charges at inns tended to pull up food-prices in general. Because of this it has been interpreted as envisaging the creation of permanent machinery for general price-review, under royal agents' direct supervision. Now, so ambitious a measure would certainly have marked a major extension of royal interference with the market. But in fact the ordinance – which in any case was 'very badly kept' – envisaged no such development. It amounted to little more than a restatement of a directive issued twenty years earlier by Louis XII, when that itinerant monarch's entourage complained of persistent overcharging.[78] The degree to which sixteenth-century French rulers went beyond medieval precedents in attempting to control the prices of grain and bread was far less than has often been supposed.[79] Like their predecessors they recognised the link between scarcity and popular disturbances, and were especially concerned that such outbreaks should not occur in Paris. But, like their predecessors, they also knew that supplies fluctuated seasonally, chronologically – above all, spatially. Thus, if maximum prices were to be fixed this must surely be a matter for local consultation and resolution rather than for central decree. Certainly, people who abused the market should be punished: hence Francis I's legislation against forestallers and engrossers who forced up prices unjustly to the detriment of the 'public good', or against exporters of grain at times of dearth.[80] Such enactments were hardly innovatory. Again, while the crisis of the mid-1560s evoked an ordinance that indicated the advantages of an assize of bread throughout the kingdom, the king was content to legislate directly for Paris alone. And, although the Third Estate at Blois in 1576 'called for a series of measures to prevent hoarding and shortages of grain', the royal response was essentially to reinforce the powers of local *officiers* to regulate the market – in particular, to direct that they supervise in accordance with 'the ancient ordinances' negotiations between bakers and millers on milling charges, the results of which should then be registered in the sovereign courts.[81]

All this fell far short of the intention to fix grain prices by central decree with which the monarchs of the time have been credited. However, sixteenth-century experts argued, as we have seen, that the underlying causes of price-movements, in relation to foodstuffs and other commodities alike, were monetary. Six months before the 1517 assembly Francis I solicited the advice of 'expert persons from the *bonnes villes* of his kingdom' on the question of currency-stability.[82] He then raised the nominal value of the gold *écu* as an interim measure, before putting the question again to the municipal deputies in the following March. But two years later a further assembly of 'great and notable personages' advised him that for the time being 'it is not possible to put [monetary matters] in order to the extent that is required, without excessive cost and inconvenience to our subjects'. Accordingly, and despite his own heavy expenditure upon foreign affairs, his interest in promoting mining for precious metals within France, or his willingness to raise prices offered at the royal mints so as to attract such metals for coinage, the king's specifically monetary measures remained largely peripheral and piecemeal.[83] Above all, he fought shy of official devaluation. What drove him to it, in 1533 and again in 1541,[84] was recognition that gold and silver were disappearing abroad while 'miserable and bad moneys' flooded into France, and that his own repeated attempts to proscribe the export of the former and the circulation of the latter had failed.

The problems that arose from the complexities of foreign exchange were indeed acute, greater by far than the controls available to France's rulers could solve. Those complexities included the differential effects of American silver imports upon European currencies. In relation to the monetary needs of the continent's expanding economy, silver nevertheless remained scarce, for all Jean Bodin's optimism; and gold became scarcer still in relation to silver as the century wore on.[85] It was not from political choice so much as from necessity dictated by incomprehensible and unmanageable circumstances that King Francis's successors resorted, with mounting frequency, to monetary mutation. Valued at 40 *sols tournois* by the interim measure of 1516, the gold *écu* was set at 46 *sols* in 1550. In 1561 it was raised to 50 *sols*; fourteen years later the official rate was a further ten *sols* higher. The same sixty-year period saw the official rate for the silver *teston* rise from 10 *sols* to 14 *sols* 6 *deniers*. As with the *écu*, this increase accelerated markedly during the fourteen years from 1561, while from mid-century the nominal value of the silver in terms of the gold coin was significantly lower than at the outset of Francis I's reign. More urgently, more persistently than had he, his successors had to keep the monetary situation under review and to legislate accordingly. Successive devaluations of the money of account were forced upon them by the relentless upwards movement of market prices for specie. Like him, they devalued with reluctance. Time and again currency was refused to allegedly overvalued foreign coins that arrived from all points of the compass to circulate in the kingdom while the coins of France escaped abroad. Such refusals promoted recoinage at the royal mints; and those in the west became unprecedentedly active during the decade from the mid-1570s as moneys from abroad flowed into that region's ports. Recoinage yielded some small profit to the monarch. More importantly, it was a counter to his subjects' inveterate tendency to pay their taxes in the lowest grade of specie that came into their hands. Even so, there seemed little room for doubt that monetary instability damaged the interests both of the king and of his people; and the continual interventions of royal authority were intended 'to stop the inflation and maintain stable conditions',[86] or at least to restore them.

The interventions were ineffectual; stable conditions were not restored. And yet, as he pursued them in the course of the century the monarch exhibited an ever firmer conviction that his authority in the monetary sphere was undivided. Circumstances might be intractable and his subjects wilful, but his policies were not governed by constitutional constraints. The men who helped shape them were his technical advisers, royal monetary *officiers*, rather than municipal deputies or other members of the body politic. The status of those *officiers* rose to the eminence of a sovereign court: the *cour des monnaies*, erected in 1552 by royal fiat, with exclusive jurisdiction over all monetary affairs.[87] Recalcitrant theorists might still argue that 'the king has no right of monetary mutation without the authority of the public council', the Estates-General,[88] but the hollowness of the argument was evident from proceedings at the Blois assembly of the Estates in December 1576. The assembly recognised the *écu*'s rating at 60 *sols*. This was merely an acceptance of what the king had already ordained, early in the previous year, when he had also introduced a new silver *franc* at one-third of the value of the principal gold coin.[89] The measure presaged a proposal put to the Estates that accounts should be recorded in terms of that coin and not of the *livre tournois*. By no means novel in its conception,[90] the proposal was none the less wholly in accord with Malestroit's expert advice.[91] It would link prices directly to the circulating medium; and it would eradicate difficulties that arose in relation to contracts made in terms of money of account when the market or the official value of currency altered in the interval between their acceptance and their discharge. Although such a measure had been solicited by Lyon merchants, the Estates rejected the proposal.[92] Nevertheless, it was implemented by royal ordinance in 1577[93] and, despite its disappointing results, remained in force for the next quarter-century.

The other objectives declared at the 1517 assembly also furnished points of reference for subsequent royal enactments. These constituted no orchestrated attempt at economic direction on the part of either Francis I or his successor. Rather, they amounted to a series of conditioned responses to particular contingencies as well as to particular requests from groups within the realm. Improved facilities intended primarily for French shipping were constructed at Le Havre in response to petitions from Rouen merchants for an outport on the Seine estuary. Imports from England were banned in 1534 unless they were carried in French vessels – an act of reprisal solicited by the *jurats* of Bordeaux against a counter-ban by Henry VIII. On no account to be outdone by his English rival, King Francis interested himself in shipbuilding. His *Grand François* of the early 1520s was his answer to the mighty *Harry Grace-à-Dieu*; while at Le Havre ten years later another royally backed vessel took shape, a ship 'of such vast dimensions that she must surely be unnavigable'.[94] Somewhat more realistically – for it was with smaller fighting and merchant ships that the immediate future lay – Henry II took steps to refurbish his Mediterranean galley fleet, especially for service to the Levant.[95] Meanwhile the activities of foreign merchants within France itself excited scrutiny, though less for simply economic than for political and fiscal reasons. Some 'exert themselves to scheme and conspire against us and our kingdom'; some evaded customs dues by trading falsely under the names of compatriots who 'have letters of naturalisation from us'. On the other hand, German merchants from the Imperial cities were welcome to the point of enjoying special privileges in so far as they brought in 'copper, metals, armour and sundry things profitable' in time of war. Considerations of war finance also dictated that foreign bankers in Lyon in 1551 be declared exempt from regulations which, in the interests of monetary uniformity, aimed at imposing the *compte par livres* upon all commercial transactions.[96]

Particular international events stimulated royal measures to promote French manufacturing industry as well. It was in bitter reaction to his desertion by his Genoese allies in Italy that in 1530 the king banned velvet and silk imports from Genoa and set about re-establishing silk manufacture in Lyon. Textiles, however, were an object of perpetual concern. Its expression was partly negative: French monarchs relentlessly re-enacted sumptuary legislation, on the grounds that 'gold and silver, which are the nerve and strength of the public weal, leave our kingdom' owing to people's passion for luxury fabrics and garments 'inappropriate to their condition [*estat*]'.[97] But in relation to woollen cloths, so important for French commerce and for popular employment alike, expression of royal concern had its positive side. An edict of 1540 sought to institute a standard system for measuring cloth

throughout the realm – only to be revoked three years later.[98] Manufacturing practices were administered by gilds, trading practices by
fairs; and kings themselves persisted in underwriting such institutions'
privileges.[99] Thereby they perpetuated diversity in matters that ranged
from the quality of the product to the penalties that applied for
breaches of contract or for debt. Entrenched local practices defied
central efforts at unification, and continued to defy them even in the
sphere of royal finance. Would not administration of export duties be
at once more efficient and less perplexing to all concerned if those
duties were to apply throughout the kingdom at uniform rates, and if
they were collected at the ports instead of at inland places where
merchants had to enter bonds before they could legitimately depart *en
route*? From 1540 onwards came a succession of royal attempts to
introduce such changes. They excited vigorous distrust and opposition; and in 1556 much of the unifying legislation was withdrawn.[100]

Thus, although by the end of Henry II's reign the economic objectives proposed to the municipal deputies of 1517 were reflected in a
certain amount of *ad hoc* legislation, neither in its conception nor in its
effects did that legislation constitute the relatively coherent programme of economic management that seemed to have been envisaged
at that time. By 1560, however, a significant shift of opinion was taking
place among members of the body politic. In contrast to the negative
attitudes of those who attended the 1517 assembly, deputies at the
Estates-General of Orléans, and then of Blois, displayed a much more
positive disposition towards the desirability of royal intervention to
regulate economic affairs in relation to the kingdom as a whole.[101]
Their *cahiers* contained heated complaints against the activities of
foreign bankers and foreign merchants who abused their privileges and
intruded upon retail as distinct from wholesale trade. Some of these
complaints clearly sprang from sectional grievances. But the Third
Estate at Blois transcended sectional interests in calling for general
measures to promote domestic industry by prohibiting export of raw
materials and import of foreign manufactures. Linked with this was the
same Estate's demand, at both assemblies, for legislation to facilitate
movement of commercial goods by ensuring that the proceeds of
internal tolls be used to maintain roads and the navigability of rivers,
and by unifying weights and measures – this last a recommendation to
which all three Estates subscribed. Moreover, in enunciating such
demands the deputies were evidently giving vent to opinion from
within their own ranks and, no doubt, their own localities, rather than
following their convenors' lead. Neither Chancellor L'Hôpital nor
Chancellor de Birague paid more than fleeting attention to specifically
economic questions in their respective keynote addresses to these
assemblies, for all the former's celebrated commitment to judicial and

administrative reform, and the latter's readiness to salute the Third Estate as 'similar to the sinews and veins of the human body, giving it strength and nourishment'.[102]

In the 1560s and 1570s, then, opinions expressed formally on the kingdom's behalf indicated the presence within it of attitudes potentially far more receptive than before to central economic direction. Yet, if the major ordinances that followed these assemblies of Estates are any guide to their direct impact upon royal legislative policy, France's ruler made only a limited response to the opportunity with which he was now apparently presented. The ordinances of Roussillon (1564) and Blois (1579) required foreign bankers to lodge caution moneys and foreign merchants to register with the clerks of the courts in whatever localities they might do business – and, should they be acting as agents, to declare the names of their principals. What inspired these measures was less an antipathy towards foreigners as such than an intention to strengthen the laws governing recovery of debt and prevention of fraud. They tallied with the article whereby the ordinance of Orléans (1561) extended throughout France the liability of all defaulting merchants to physical arrest and to distraint – penalties thitherto enforceable as privileges of certain fairs. The article partially accommodated a demand of the Estates; so, too, did Henry III's ordinances of 1571 and 1577 which revived earlier attempts to lay down standard measurements for woollen cloth and prohibited export of unworked wool; and the Orléans and Blois ordinances alike included articles on using toll-revenues to maintain road and river communications.[103] But the benefits of unifying weights and measures in general, which L'Hôpital himself acknowledged elsewhere,[104] found no place in either of these two main ordinances that followed the Estates' deliberations.[105] Both of them nevertheless amply reflected the deputies' commitment to uphold the functions of the gilds. It was a commitment that heavily qualified the body politic's receptiveness to direction by its head, and plainly limited the ruler's opportunity to attempt it. The deputies deprecated the practice of creating masters by royal *lettres de maîtrise* and craft inspectors by royal appointment. The former should continue to submit masterpieces for inspection by existing masters who had been elected by their peers and so represented the gilds themselves, not the monarch as his *officiers*. Further, gild cohesion should be enhanced by printing statutes 'in intelligible language'. The ordinances of Orléans and Blois conceded all of these demands.[106]

In L'Hôpital's view, 'mercantile activity is the wealth of this kingdom'. But that activity was best left to those who engaged in it. They observed among themselves 'good faith', for breach of which 'the penalty is infamy: whoever fails in good faith loses his credit'. Such a view married concepts from Roman law, in which the humanist chancellor had been schooled, with traditions of commercial freedom.[107] It was also consistent with legislation of the 1560s that created *tribunaux consulaires* in Paris and more than forty other French towns. These tribunals, composed of judges assisted by councillors chosen by the merchants themselves, exercised jurisdiction over disputes between *commerçants* in a manner that dispensed with the formal and time-consuming procedures of the ordinary courts of law.[108] Conferring upon merchants some of that disciplinary franchise which gildsmen already enjoyed, the spread of these tribunals was scarcely consonant with an intention to bring royal direction to bear upon the conduct of economic affairs. And yet, two years after his confirmation of gild franchises by the Blois ordinance, Henry III took deliberate steps to undermine them 'in the interests of our subjects of all conditions'. In towns where there were no gilds, demand for soundly manufactured goods allegedly outran supply; in towns where there were gilds, apprentices had notoriously to bribe their way to masterships. Better for all concerned – apart, perhaps, from established masters – if aspirant craftsmen should simply pay a fee and declare their competence on oath before a judge or one of the royal commissioners whom the king would authorise for the purpose. Hence his ordinance of December 1581, which further ruled that 'all artisans received as masters in our town of Paris' should thereafter be free to practise their crafts anywhere in the kingdom without having to furnish fresh proofs of their skills to local gilds.[109]

Often interpreted as an attempt to extend the gild system throughout France,[110] this measure in fact struck a blow against the exclusive and corporate characteristics of that system. It was promulgated on the eve of the commissions of inquiry that prepared the ground for the St-Germain assembly of 1583. Among the many matters discussed at that assembly were questions of *police* and economic affairs. The questions ranged over all the proposals mooted in 1517, and far beyond them. They included poor relief, food-prices, rents for housing – above all, the perennial problems of how to conserve gold and silver within the realm, and how to boost its manufactures, particularly of textiles. The assembly's members perceived very clearly that these were interconnected problems. They advised that the solution lay in applying selective import and export controls. Foreign manufactures should be either refused entry altogether or, in cases where international treaties prevented their exclusion, 'sold at such low prices that [foreigners] themselves will cease to bring them here'. Raw materials from abroad should be allowed 'free entry'; and France would do better to have commodities such as raw silk brought direct from the Levant by French traders than to rely upon Italian entrepreneurs.

Once available in large quantities, such materials would attract foreign workmen able to train native ones in appropriate skills; and idleness and poverty would in due course be eliminated. All this could be accomplished by central regulation: it fell, obviously, within the compass of royal fiscal administration. But the other questions of *police* could not be dealt with in such a way. In respect of those many and varied questions, the assembly could recommend only that 'his majesty establish and institute local *juges de police* . . . to be elected annually on the same day and in the same manner as mayors and *échevins* of towns' were chosen. They should have jurisdiction over all *police* matters, management of which they might be expected effectively to improve – as long as 'his Majesty (if he should graciously agree) resolve forthwith never to allow the said *juges de police* to be erected into offices, for in that case, instead of guaranteeing the benefits expected through their institution, they will certainly procure the contrary'.[111]

Strictures on venal offices had been aired at the Estates-General, too.[112] Yet the members of the St-Germain assembly were not themselves chosen by electoral procedures, and were not the constitutional equivalent of deputies to the Estates. Although some deputies from provincial Estates were present at the royal court to protest against taxes when the assembly began, and probably attended its opening sessions, its membership in fact consisted of royal functionaries and *officiers*. The assembly was 'a committee of technical experts'; and the information upon which they based their advice to the king was not derived from *cahiers* channelled through Estate deputies as 'representatives' of the body politic. It came from the commissioners whom he had dispatched to collect it directly, among the people in the provinces and localities at large, as 'representatives' of royal authority.[113] They had done so in the interests of the kingdom as a whole – and of the state, as Henry III gave his listeners at St-Germain to understand.[114] This short-circuiting of traditional processes of consultation resulted in a more coherent view than had been formulated thitherto of the kingdom's economic difficulties. Those difficulties had already induced more amenable attitudes than before to the prospect of royal economic intervention. The king had responded only partially to recommendations for such intervention that had reached him through the medium of the Estates-General, and had deferred to that body's insistence upon the roles of specific corporate groups. Since then, however, he had taken significant steps to modify the latter, and now seemed poised for still more far-reaching economic action.

And yet, as his own experts advised him, the field where the ruler might hope effectively to act on his own initiative remained severely circumscribed. The difficulties of the kingdom embraced a host of matters that must be left to the discretion of representatives of local bodies, the *juges de police*. Where the king might act, on his experts' advice and through his own appointed agents, was in the sphere of indirect taxation – an area of economic affairs that abutted on the monetary sphere, where the constitutional initiative was already firmly his. But even in the fiscal sphere the experts at St-Germain took leave to doubt their principal's resolution to make the kingdom's economic well-being his first priority.[115] After all, his interest in economic affairs was ultimately no more than a function of his appetite for revenue. It was an appetite that had long since informed his quest for monetary stability, and was apparent even in his recent legislation concerning the gilds. The economic benefits envisaged at St-Germain would accrue – if they accrued at all – only in the long term. In the short term their pursuit would entail some sacrifice of revenue. It was a sacrifice that the king could not afford. The royal need of revenue was immediate and urgent. The lion's share of the assembly's time was devoted to considering how it might be assuaged. And, willing though the monarch might be to adopt a stance in the name of the state as the potential alleviator of his kingdom's economic difficulties, that need drove him inexorably to exacerbate them. So, at least, it seemed to the people upon whom the burden of taxation fell most heavily: the peasant communities of the realm.

How heavy was that burden? As we have seen, it is not to be assessed simply in terms of the total nominal sum which the king extracted from his subjects – a sum that in any case is so hard to ascertain.[116] However, if the *tailles* are assumed to have yielded 18 million *livres tournois* in 1588, the burden of direct taxation on each contributing household may be estimated at, on average, some six *livres*.[117] In that year the mean price of a *setier* (1.5 hectolitres) of wheat in Paris was 8.75 *livres*.[118] Such a household could therefore have obtained the six *livres* in question by selling in Paris 0.68 *setier* (about 1 hectolitre) – the produce of about one-seventh of a hectare of land.[119] The position in Béziers in Languedoc was much the same.[120] In the Paris region in 1515, with the *taille* at 16 *sols* per household and the mean price of grain at 1.88 *livres* per *setier*, the proceeds from merely two-thirds of a hecto-litre, or one-tenth of a hectare, would have sufficed to satisfy the royal tax-gatherer. Clearly, the king demanded more in real terms in the course of the century; and obviously the market price of grain is not to be equated with the producer's profit. Even so, calculations such as these from the available data do not in themselves suggest that the average burden of direct taxation need have weighed insupportably upon the peasant household. What made taxation burdensome to so many households was the reduction of their landholdings to dimensions too small for them to produce from their own resources any marketable surplus whatsoever.[121] In bringing that reduction about, developments in the laws relating to property were a significant factor.

Customary laws in medieval France had recognised in land a multiplicity of rights which, in any particular case, appertained to several parties. If any of them should abuse or seek to alienate the object of his right, it was reasonable that he should compensate the other parties whose rights he was thereby likely to have impaired. No occupant, therefore, could exploit what appeared to be his land without restriction, nor mortgage or sell it without sanction. The system complicated the work of tax-assessors, too. Land was the major source of the wealth that they endeavoured to tap; and the values of immovable units of land might conveniently be assessed. But how was the party liable to pay to be identified, if no one enjoyed exclusive property rights over such a unit – that is, if there was no outright owner? Surely, then, taxes must be personal rather than real, assessed by reference to the right vested in each party and not simply to the estimated value of the land itself. Broadly, this was indeed so in central and northern France, in the *pays* of *droit coutumier* and the *taille personnelle*. In the south, however, where the customs of the *pays* of *droit écrit* bore the stamp of Roman influence, 'ownership' was less trammelled and more plainly discernible, and land-values furnished the basis for the *taille réelle*. Moreover, it was partly through studies of Roman law that late-medieval jurists developed a theory which helped to clarify the situation elsewhere. According to the theory of 'double domain', all rights in land were classifiable as either 'eminent' or 'of use'. The distinction applied to fiefs and to holdings by commoners in perpetuity (*censives*) alike. Rights 'of use' were enjoyed by the actual exploitant of the land; if he should sublet his holding, then those rights passed to the lessee while the lessor himself became the holder of 'eminent domain' – a position analogous, in the theory, to that of his own lord. As for the king, he might be deemed to hold 'eminent' rights over all the lands of the realm. The position seemed to entitle him to demand as of right his share of the fruits of those lands from the people who occupied them – and especially so at times of 'necessity'.[122]

Although the theory of double domain helped to rationalise an otherwise incoherent tenurial system, restrictions remained, not least upon the use of land as security for credit and upon the redistribution of rights by sale. It remained the case that any act of alienation by the user would prejudice the 'eminent' interest, the holder of which was accordingly entitled to compensation. Such compensation took the form of payment of 'rights of transfer' (*droits de mutation*), chiefly *lods et ventes* – a significant proportion of the proceeds of a mortgage or a sale. Negotiation of credit was further inhibited by the rule that any user who wished to raise a loan through constituting a *rente* upon his holding must designate a specific parcel of land as security, and so became liable to pay transfer-dues as if his intention were simply to sell that parcel.[123] In common with customary laws of inheritance, these principles were geared to a prevailing assumption that the pattern of landholdings, and with it the stability of rural communities, should be maintained. However, their implications were increasingly offset as late-medieval lawyers, impelled both by considerations of practical convenience and by their understanding of Roman law, sought to identify one or other of the interests in question with outright 'owner-ship' or 'property'. They accorded that status to the commoner occupant of a holding who used it in perpetuity and enjoyed its fruits – the *censitaire*. As for fiefs, the authoritative Charles Du Moulin pronounced in the sixteenth century that the same solution in effect should apply to them, so that the vassal rather than his seigneur 'is said to have true domain and property in the object [of his right] (*res*): and him alone we call proprietor'.[124] Ownership carried with it greater freedom than ancient custom had allowed the individual landholder to exploit or to dispose of his land at will. The implication was endorsed by rulings in the royal courts which culminated in the celebrated decree of the *parlement* of Paris in 1557, that *lods et ventes* should no longer be deemed due upon the constitution of a *rente*.[125] Distinguishing more precisely between an intention to secure a monetary loan and an intention to alienate land, these rulings cleared the way for more energetic credit operations on the part of urban and rural dwellers alike.[126]

Features of a movement towards individualisation of property-rights, these changes served to enliven the land-market. Holdings could now be more easily accumulated; so, too, could heavy debts on the part of numerous peasant owners. As for royal tax-gathering, while ownership of rural wealth might now be more certainly established, the king's rights of 'eminent domain' no longer seemed to license him to appropriate his subjects' property. The principle of 'necessity' none the less continued to apply: as Du Moulin put it, even though the ruler must respect his subjects' private property-rights, 'when the common good and the necessity of the public weal requires it, to that extent, and for that purpose only, everything is the king's'.[127] What brought mounting difficulties to so many of those subjects, however, was scarcely the direct burden of taxation that he himself imposed. A complex of demographic, economic, institutional developments – as well, no doubt, as improvidence on the part of individual heads of households – paved the path that peasant families in growing numbers trod towards indebtedness and morcellation of their holdings. Moreover, others than the king imposed burdens of appropriation upon them. Clergy and lay farmers demanded tithes as a proportion of producers' crops – demands that did not lessen in substance as inflation gathered pace,[128] unlike obligations expressed in nominal money-terms. The declining values of traditional dues depleted the incomes of noble landlords. But, at least in parts of France, the rural nobility proved more adaptable than was once supposed to changing economic circumstances, and more successful in exploiting their tenants and their demesnes to commercial advantage and their own economic salvation.[129] Some were not successful, and their fiefs changed hands. It did not follow that such alienated fiefs passed out of noble ownership. In the district of Bayeux, 'on the contrary, nobles, rather than commoners, and within the nobility, old nobles, were the groups that profited from the many changes in ownership taking place in the sixteenth and seventeenth centuries'.[130] There is, however, ample evidence from both northern and southern provinces that town-based merchants and *officiers* were invading the countryside and purchasing seigneurial and commoner holdings alike.[131] Opportunities to foreclose on mortgages were a factor in facilitating that invasion. But rural *laboureurs*, too, were capable of expropriating their neighbours by degrees, of dispensing rural credit and so, in due course, of joining the ranks of *coqs de village*, or better.[132] Meanwhile, the partially dispossessed struggled to survive on the yields of minuscule holdings, supplemented by low wages gained in a buyer's market for labour where underemployment prevailed; while the wholly dispossessed drifted into pauperism and away, miserably, to the towns.

How far advanced, and how general, was this deterioration in the condition of French peasant families by the middle decades of the sixteenth century? There can be no certain answers to these questions. In some respects factors that contributed to precipitate rural commoners' distress served, conversely, to safeguard the peasantry as a whole. Peasant proprietors, their status as owners guaranteed by laws enforced in the royal courts, continued in the seventeenth century to possess almost one half of France's soil.[133] Changing rules of inheritance enabled the head of a household to pass his holding to a single heir.[134] The beneficiary could be seen as 'representing' the family, perpetuating occupancy of the holding in the family's name, even though his next of kin might thereby be displaced. Further, if the 'elements of the peasant crisis'[135] were apparent well before the civil wars, it was these wars with their attendant calamities that aggravated the crisis and enlarged it to a point where the condition of peasant communities *en masse* became intolerable. War exposed their members to physical assault and spoliation by soldiery, while rival politico-religious and military organisations superimposed their fiscal demands upon what the king himself authorised. 'If I had wanted to', recorded Blaise de Monluc, lieutenant-general of Guyenne, with unconvincing self-righteousness,[136]

> I could have had a man of straw go about the towns and villages to whisper to the principal inhabitants that they must give me money in order to be saved, or that otherwise I would ruin them and let the *gens de guerre* eat them to the bone. I could also have said to the huguenots who stayed in their houses under the protection of an edict that unless they spat in the basin I would ruin them all. How much would they have given me to secure their lands and goods! . . . But instead of using all these artifices to make myself rich, I let the captains and the soldiery and the king's servants take everything.

It was such circumstances as these that triggered the phenomenon of mass peasant uprisings in the century's closing decades. As the militant communities of Monluc's own region, the *Tard-Avisés*, declared in 1594, they had been goaded at last to take arms by 'armed men of both parties who have reduced them to starvation, raped their wives and daughters, repeatedly taken their livestock and devastated their crops, while imprisoning still more of them to die of hunger for not being able to pay the great *tailles* and subsidies which both parties have constrained them to disgorge'.[137]

But, although the perpetrators of war and war-taxation were the precipitating cause of revolts and the immediate objects of peasant demands for redress, such protests seemed to many contemporaries to have a deeper significance. According to Monluc, actions by villagers such as those of St-Mézard and Astaffort signified an intention to wage 'open war against the nobility'. In Provence at the century's end, according to Guillaume du Vair, 'the animosities of subjects against their lords is a very widespread malady'. In that same province, much earlier in the century, germs of the malady had seemed active among Lubéron villagers who, in the wake of their seigneurs' imposing upon them more rigorous tenurial agreements, resorted to Protestantism and guerrilla warfare. When seigneurs of Saintonge tried in 1548 to persuade the peasant *Pitaux* to desist from their revolt against the royal *gabelle* and 'the soldiers' oppression of the people', 'the commons threatened to kill them and to sack their houses'. In Brittany in the 1590s the cleric and lawyer Jean Moreau believed that the peasants were 'utterly committed to a revolt against the nobility and the towns, wishing to be subject to no one'. Townsmen had allegedly attracted the

Pitaux's hostility forty years before: the insurgents 'seized merchants and, not content with robbing them, the swine killed them without knowing why nor wherefore'. The *Tard-Avisés* certainly claimed to know why: 'the towns [which], instead of functioning as seats of justice, care nothing for the ruin of the poor people, for our ruin is their prosperity . . . sell to us at whatever price they choose, and make fine *métairies* which are cheap for them while they make us pay rent at twice or three times what we ought to pay and help themselves to "justice" whenever it pleases them'.[138]

Were France's insurgent peasants protesting, then, blindly at first, with greater self-consciousness as the sixteenth century drew disorderly towards its close, against their exploitation not merely by military and political intruders, but by entrenched social classes whose members were permanently in their midst: the classes of nobility and *bourgeois* who commanded economic and governmental power – the power of a system that was becoming an instrument of oppression? Such an interpretation is not to be altogether dismissed. Of course, alarmist reports by hostile observers are scarcely proof of peasant attitudes and intentions. Yet the *Tard-Avisés* were not alone in crying out – perhaps more articulately than other insurgents – against 'the towns' and what they seemed to signify. Peasants of the Dauphiné in 1580, we are told, waged war 'against the expansion of an agrarian capitalism centred on urban rents and urban outlets for agricultural products . . . [that] ruined and undermined the peasant system, which was based on small family-run farms'. Noble landlords were capable enough of adapting to the requirements of the market, and did so, at their tenants' expense. And yet, although peasant insurgents reacted in due course by slaughtering extortionate nobles and those who confronted them in arms, burning *châteaux* and even denouncing privileges such as tax-exemption that noblemen in general enjoyed, these reactions did not entail rejection of nobility as such. On the contrary: even in the Dauphiné the rebels 'remained respectful towards the true nobility'; while the *Tard-Avisés*, for their part, protested 'that the orders of the Church, the nobility and justice ought to be maintained, that without them the State cannot subsist'.[139]

The effects of political disorder drove the peasants to desperate courses. Their sense of collective security was already undermined by a concatenation of changes that seemed to erode the traditional values and structures of rural society. In their revolts they manifested a desire to refurbish those values and, with it, an expectation that the 'true nobility' would protect them against oppressors external to the communities in which they continued to believe themselves and such protectors to be conjoined.[140] The expectation was not unfounded. The old nobility of Saintonge – the barons de Ruffec, de La Force, de Jarnac – 'exculpated as many of their tenants as they could' when the king's councillor, the duc d'Aumale, arrived with troops to wreak retribution upon the *Pitaux*. The *Tard-Avisés* drew comfort and confidence from there being 'in this *pays* a great many seigneurs and gentlemen above reproach . . . who have sworn and promised us every assistance'.[141] But sentiments of trust in the traditional seigneurial role were not enough. It was rather through reviving the power of rural communities themselves, seen as corporate entities, that France's peasants organised for immediate defence and hoped for better security in the future. Doubtless their belief in that power was informed by notions of a past golden age when taxes were low, good lordship prevailed, and men lived in harmony with each other and with natural and divine law – a harmony guaranteed on earth by the institutions of *communauté* and parish. But, however visionary these notions, and despite modifications of those institutions' functions,[142] parish and community could continue to furnish a practical basis for peasant organisation and peasant aspiration.

Contemporary observers noted how peasant insurgents set out in parochial groups to assemble *en masse* under the leadership of syndics of their *communautés*. Those syndics acted as a council of war, deciding what should be done forthwith. They also formulated the assembly's political demands; and the 'most precise' of the *Tard-Avisés*'s demands was for a 'syndic of the inhabitants of the country-side' who would act 'as a tribune of the people, for the purpose of conserving them in their liberties and privileges', and would represent them at the provincial Estates. Had this demand succeeded, the existence of such a syndic would have signified that 'the people' in question enjoyed corporate status in law. The Estates of Périgord rejected it on these very grounds, argued by the king's procurator: it would be tantamount to creating 'a fourth Estate . . . separate from the true Third Estate who are the three principal towns'.[143] Even so, in making that demand the insurgents expressed their understanding of the nature of the 'state' that they declared to be in danger, and their aspiration to be accommodated directly and formally within it. The 'state' was a body politic, consisting of corporate groups. They themselves were no longer content to leave their protection within it in the hands of noble 'representatives', still less of municipal deputies. By virtue of their existence as communities – communities whose existence secular and ecclesiastical authorities were willing enough to exploit for fiscal and other purposes – and through the medium of syndics who emerged in assemblies of those communities, they asserted their claim to corporate recognition in their own right, and so to the political advantages that the recognition must entail. And such a claim was not peculiar to peasant insurgents. In the course of the sixteenth century a case for accommodation within the body politic was made, on analogous grounds, by the leaders of dissident religious groups, to which we now turn.

CHAPTER 5

Heresy
and Aristocracy

Five hundred years before the Protestant Reformation there were outbreaks of heresy in France amid conditions of population increase, heightened market activity, and new social formations. Especially in towns, groups took shape that were less close-knit than those of village and kinsfolk, and more disposed to challenge the authority of seigneurs, who were often ecclesiastics. The rise of the communes may be seen as a political, and outbreaks of heresy as a religious, manifestation of such a disposition. In eleventh-century northern France the church, in association with the secular ruler, possessed enough power to suppress such heretics. It lacked both power and wealth in twelfth-century Languedoc, where secular political authority was also fragmented and unstable. There noblemen, their own resources shrunken through subdivision of inheritances, plundered what the church did possess and meanwhile warred among themselves. In that region the Cathar and Waldensian heresies took root, the one patronised by noblemen but particularly seductive to members of a commercial 'middle class', the other exceptional among medieval heresies both for its appeal to the peasantry and for its survival into the sixteenth century, in frontier valleys of the Dauphiné and Provence.[1] Elsewhere in medieval France as in Europe at large, marginal men and women proved fertile soil for radical and outlandish forms of heresy. Preached by prophetic leaders to listeners never more receptive than at times of dearth and plague, 'revolutionary millenarianism' excited to apocalyptic fervour landless peasants, artisans unprotected by gilds, commoners alienated from traditional communities. And the decline of traditional community responsibilities and loyalties was also, we are told, a condition for the spread of witchcraft or at least of its exposure, which culminated in the witch craze that accompanied the civil and religious wars of the late-sixteenth and early-seventeenth centuries.[2]

Thus the history of heresy, broadly viewed, provides some grounds for postulating a connection between social and political instability and change on the one hand, and religious dissidence and deviance on the other. But, as modern historians rightly insist, the grounds are general and the connection, in so far as it can be demonstrated at all, is far from simple. Too often the behaviour of medieval heretics has been sweepingly explained in terms of their material deprivation or aspirations, when in fact all too little is known about their immediate circumstances. The socio-economic context of heresy is not to be ignored; but heresy itself must be defined as what ecclesiastical authority, and in particular the Pope, decided to stigmatise as such.[3] It follows that explanations of occurrences of heresy are to be sought, at least in the first instance, by reference rather to the condition of orthodoxy than to conditions of material life; and orthodoxy in turn was formed, and re-formed, in a religious and intellectual climate that was far from constant. Such cautious considerations as these have also prompted historians to fight shy of postulating connections between medieval heresies and the Protestant Reformation. Although the great reformers clearly made use of ideas current in medieval thought, we are assured that 'the medieval Church had beaten most of its heretical movements: persecution, the isolation of supporters of heresy from intellectual life, the passage of time, and a changing intellectual climate eliminated them or pushed them to the margin of society'.[4]

And yet attitudes that linger in the margin of society have their relevance for new developments at the centre of affairs. Apart from the uncertainties of their movements' social and political implications, medieval heretics certainly and repeatedly evinced three attitudes that bear upon developments in sixteenth-century France. First, in its negative aspect heresy characteristically involved an antipathy towards the visible church, a denial of the validity of its sacraments, a denunciation of its hierarchy, a rejection of the role of its priests. Secondly, in its positive aspect heresy characteristically involved a search for spiritual satisfaction beyond what the church provided: an internal satisfaction on the part of the believer, initially individualistic therefore, but leading rapidly to the formation of defecting groups and to their multiplication through evangelism. Thirdly, in both its aspects heresy characteristically involved an intellectual dimension, at once capable of embracing extra-Scriptural conceptions and yet fundamentalist in its aversion to doctrinal accretions that obscured the authority of Scripture and distorted the teachings of the early church. Such attitudes challenged the essential functions of the church as it had become, and could scarcely be tolerated by it. Yet all three were fostered by men who, while they dreaded heresy and remained within the church itself, nevertheless found it deficient and sought its reform.

The first part of this chapter indicates how all three of these attitudes are discernible in early sixteenth-century France. They are features of the *préréforme,* the background to the French Protestant Reformation. Thereafter, the chapter's prime concern is to assess the political significance of that religious movement, rather than specifically to correlate its development with socio-economic conditions such as we have already reviewed.[5] For, although those conditions have their contextual relevance for the development in question, French Protestantism, like its medieval forebears, continues to defy explanation in socio-economic terms. Secondly, the chapter considers how that movement, sternly opposed by a monarchy committed to the defence of an ecclesiastical system that reinforced its own authority, was initially 'congregationalist' in character, but was in due course organised and disciplined by leaders who sought its accommodation within the body politic. Their measures will be examined in some detail; and it will be seen how, at the expense of the movement's spontaneous development, the organisation was given shape and the accommodation pursued by reference to an 'aristocratic' principle of 'representation'. Thirdly, in relation to the closing decades of the civil wars the chapter shows how a comparable principle was also espoused by fervent, though disunited, opponents of the Protestant heresy. They exploited it in resisting extensions of monarchical authority as well – the very authority to which Protestant leaders had looked for political concessions that were ultimately granted in the name of the state.

As the sixteenth century opened, Paris rang to denunciations of the highest clergy in the land, by men who themselves were prominent within the church and enjoyed the patronage of its leaders. They included Olivier Maillard, *provincial* of the Franciscans in France, Jean Raulin, principal of the College of Navarre, Jean Standonck, principal of the austere Congregation of Montaigu.[6] No respecters of persons, immoderate in their language, they directed their shafts especially at bishops, whose addiction to pluralism and to worldly pursuits necessarily entailed non-residence – the holding of titles without performance of functions. There were plenty of bishops who were vulnerable to such denunciations; and below them in the hierarchy came clerics eager to act as vicars to these absentees, to collect for themselves benefices by the dozen, and to combine them with academic and judicial offices, too.[7] Since bishoprics were heavily monopolised by members of noble families,[8] episcopal absenteeism in a sense created opportunities for men who could not otherwise have expected to discharge episcopal functions. Whatever of that, those functions remained in effect poorly discharged. In consequence the lower clergy were poorly directed by their superiors. The need for such direction was palpable. The failings of bishops might make spectacular sermon-fodder; but, as would-be reformers knew well enough, it was what happened at parish level that mattered most in relation to the welfare of church and laity alike.

Diocesan synods were the principal source of direction of the lower clergy. Councils of the church had firmly ruled that bishops should regularly hold them. But even when the ruling was observed and direction was forthcoming it could scarcely make up for priests' lamentable lack of training. Standonck's view that 'unlettered, vicious, disreputable' men were admitted to holy orders had a firm basis in fact. Sons of artisans and *laboureurs*, taught at *petites écoles* by men of similar background to their own, presented themselves as candidates with qualifications limited to some elementary acquaintance with Scripture, an ability to chant in Latin, and a rector's recommendation. They presented themselves in enormous numbers, and were admitted with little difficulty. From all over southern France in the early sixteenth century candidates flocked to the province of Avignon, which depended directly upon the Pope, 'there to pass within a few days . . . into the sacerdotal dignity'.[9] So a plethora of ill-directed and ill-trained priests filled France's parishes – at once a symptom and a cause of a devotional and sacramental fever, of which laymen were not only the victims but also the occasion.

For clerics could multiply and still subsist as long as laymen's wills continued to contain clauses stipulating payment 'to each priest up to the number of fifty who will say a mass' for the soul of the departed. So vague a stipulation was readily exploitable. A high mass cost more than a low, just as a *grande* cost more than a *petite litanie* – and what of extreme unction, the vigil of the dead, burial itself, each of which carried its fee in accordance with a regular tariff? Such matters concerned unattached and beneficed clergy alike. The latter, with the connivance of their patrons, farmed their benefices to curates, who in turn farmed the fixed revenues to others again; and all looked, for the major part of their income, to fees for administering sacraments. Small wonder that direction of the ministry should have been so pronounced a feature of Calvin's movement in France. Yet it is clear that what anticlerical sentiment denounced as abuses on the part of the clergy, high and low, were facilitated by religiosity on the part of laymen of every degree. All in effect were parties to transactions of the kind recorded by the nobleman Pierre de Sainte-Feyre in 1508: 'the *curé* agreed that I should found a chapel in the cemetery' of Sainte-Feyre, 'and that he should have two thirds of the offerings, and the vicar whom I placed there should have one third', the chapel's consecration being performed by 'the Bishop of Treguier, by permission of messieurs the vicars of Limoges, *sede vacante*, and he granted for it forty days of pardon every year, and I have letters to that effect sealed by his seal'.[10]

So clerics and laymen collaborated with each other, channelling to private ends the spirit that had induced the mighty reconstruction of France's churches in the wake of the Hundred Years War. Yet no amount of collaboration could conceal the religious confusion of the time. Within and around the places of public worship, sensationalism threatened to swamp religious observance. More and more visual and audial stimuli were pricking the senses of the lay worshipper: stained glass, rood screens, realistic icons relating especially to the cult of the Virgin, tombs bearing the death-masks of the affluent departed, depictions of the Stations of the Cross and of the *danse macabre*, all reverberating to the sounds of bells, instrumental music and the voices of boy choristers.[11] It seemed as if miraculous salvation could be attracted by display, and then sealed by sacramental ritual bought at prescribed rates. But the rates were high, and not only in pecuniary terms. Sacramentalist devotion placed a heavy burden upon the individual conscience. Confession and penance, if fully observed by reference to the multitudinous sins catalogued in *Miroirs de la Confession*, were arduous exercises. Even indulgences depended for their efficacity upon some prior act of contrition. As the use of books of hours and rosaries spread, the exercises of the devout brought them continually into solitary confrontation with a demanding deity.[12] Doubtless the truly devout were a minority, and literate ones an élite – far outnumbered, even in an age of conspicuous religiosity, by the spiritual descendants of Frenchmen of whom a fourteenth-century friar had despaired in doggerel:

> They attend neither mass nor matins . . .
> Drink and eat is all they do,
> To church they never care to go![13]

The devout were further outnumbered, and their individualisation offset, by the convivial groups who attended and participated in processions, performances of mystery plays, festive meetings of confraternities,[14] where communal excitement carried religion easily towards carnival. But men and women to whom such excitement offered no appeal, indifference no escape, and the sensationalism of the visible church no consolation were carried instead towards internalised devotion, and so to mysticism. And, as followed by the misleadingly named Brethren of the Common Life, mysticism included among its precepts, set out in the widely distributed *Imitatio Christi*: 'Whosoever purposeth to come to inward and spiritual things, it behoveth him to decline from the company of people – with Jesu.'[15]

The Protestant Reformation, as it eventually developed in France, was to renounce all of this. In its place it would offer, in due course, a trained and directed ministry, a severe reduction of the sacraments, a rejection of sensationalism and display, a sober discipline of observance – and, above all, a firm emphasis upon the corporate nature of the church. The true church was the body of Christ, and invisible. Yet there was also a visible church on earth; and it consisted neither in the paraphernalia of Roman institutions, nor in a mere agglomeration of individual believers, but in the community of the faithful. Just as St Augustine had insisted long since upon the 'society' of Christians, a society where 'all members co-operate together in one body . . . without severing themselves from it',[16] so the French reformed churches would declare: 'we believe that none should withdraw himself and be alone'.[17] In principle, none of that was peculiar to the French movement. In practice, however, the Reformation in France developed along a peculiar course, more gradual at first than in neighbouring parts of Europe, but rapid, and violent, at last. Its impact upon the kingdom in mid-century – the impact of a movement that simultaneously challenged established institutions and sought accommodation amongst them – coincided with a breakdown of political order precipitated by the death of Henry II and the ensuing confrontation between bitter noble rivals. The condition of the church that the Protestants themselves confronted and the religious aspirations to which they offered an alternative were none the less prior and necessary to their movement's impact. And among those preconditions were the activities of scholars who were no Protestants, but whose work embraced ideas that had a formative bearing upon the movement's outcome.

By the opening of the sixteenth century generations of critics had exposed not only how the accretions and distortions of medieval scholasticism obscured Scriptural and patristic teaching, but also the narrowness and poverty of the scholastic approach. It did not follow that men should look elsewhere for philosophical enrichment of their faith. Did not the author of the *Imitatio Christi* issue a general warning 'against vain and secular knowledge' and 'the subtle sayings of men'?[18] Yet products of the Brethren's own teaching thought differently. They included, in the fifteenth century, Nicholas of Cusa, pluralist, canon lawyer, and advocate in his *De Concordatia Catholica* of a conciliar solution to the problems of church and empire. Cusanus was powerfully influenced in his thinking by neoplatonic metaphysics, notably as expounded by Dionysius the Areopagite and Ramon Lull. Of course, Dionysius had supposedly been a disciple of that authority to whom all must defer, St Paul; and Lull was certainly a thirteenth-century Franciscan. But Cusanus' ideas influenced in their turn thinkers willing to explore philosophy and its relation to Christian theology outside the Christian tradition, beyond even a revivified Aristotle, as far afield as oriental sages. In France the chief amongst them was Jacques Lefèvre d'Étaples, so often designated the 'father' of the Reformation there.[19] When Lefèvre, protégé of a pluralist but reforming bishop, settled at Meaux in 1521 to his commentaries on the four gospels and his translations of the New Testament and the Psalms, he had already published numerous Aristotelian texts and commentaries, and editions of works by Dionysius, by Lull, and by that alleged contemporary of Moses and descendant of Egyptian gods, Hermes Trismegistus.[20] Undertaken primarily for pedagogic purposes, Lefèvre's was the work of a staunchly Christocentric thinker who nevertheless found mutual illumination in profane and in sacred writings. Indeed, for him ancient philosophers were not profane: they were men 'whom God in his own time made his priests and prophets, torches shining even in our own time . . . even though God, who illumines all men, had not yet appeared visibly in the world'.[21] It was a syncretic viewpoint to which French and Italian humanists subscribed in considerable numbers. Their writings contributed to an intellectual storm that raged within and around the church, which pronounced some of them heretics.

The humanist impulse to inquire, correct, collate was an essential feature of the *préréforme*, but that impulse was distrusted by the great reformers. Thus John Calvin, despite his humanist training, would only reluctantly admit that 'since all truth is of God, if any ungodly man has said anything true, we should not reject it'.[22] In particular, Calvin himself had little time for Lefèvre's approach; and Lefèvre, appointed in 1526 by Francis I librarian of his *château* of Blois and tutor to the royal children, did not endorse either the German or the Swiss Reformation. Nevertheless, ideas that Lefèvre helped to communicate to his contemporaries left their mark upon the organisation of the Reformation in France. Among his works was an edition of Cusanus. And among the ideas that Cusanus had influentially discussed and developed as he sought concord between Catholics was a principle of representation:[23] a principle whereby the church was identifiable with the episcopal council, the embodiment of the church as a whole. As we shall see, the French Protestant movement was organised in due course in a manner consistent rather with such a principle than with doctrines of the church as comprehensively the community of the faithful to which all the leading reformers purported to subscribe. Disorderly and persecuted at first, that movement was eventually marshalled under the leadership of Calvin and his immediate followers, who looked to the monarch to recognise its corporate existence, and to concede its accommodation within the body politic.

The first French Protestant martyr, Jean Vallière of Normandy, was burned in Paris in August 1523, followed within four days by a bonfire of Lutheran books. Two years later the regent, Louise of Savoy, published within the kingdom Pope Clement VII's bull against 'lutherans' and commissioned magistrates of the Paris *parlement* to extirpate 'that unhappy and damned sect and heresy'. In December 1530, Francis I ordered all agents of secular justice to assist the judge-delegates appointed for that purpose by his chancellor Duprat in his capacity as cardinal of Sens and papal legate in France. A further royal directive of January 1535 expedited procedure by removing the right of convicted heretics to appeal to the *parlement* as such, empowering judicial commissioners finally to determine all such appeals. Additional measures in the later years of the reign increased the anti-heretical powers of the secular arm.[24] From time to time King Francis might seem ambivalent. Personal and political considerations might intermittently affect his stance: his self-image as a Maecenas of humanist learning; his own sister's association with reforming opinion; his interest in exploiting divisions in the Empire and the embarrassment to his rival, Charles V, that Luther's movement induced. But Protestant leaders deluded themselves in so far as they expected that in general France's 'most Christian king' might be persuaded not to set his face and his power against the development of such movements in his own realm.

His attitude could scarcely have been otherwise. Administratively, socially, politically, the kingdom's secular and ecclesiastical institutions were closely intertwined, from the parish at the base of the governmental system to the cardinalates at the head of the First Estate, dignities reserved either to members of France's princely houses or to the monarch's principal *officiers* such as Duprat himself. As for the king, the aura of sanctity that surrounded the monarchical person and enchanced the ruler's authority bore with it the obligation that he attend to his people's religious welfare. The obligation was the more immediate and pressing since the negotiation of the Concordat of 1516 between Francis and the Pope. That agreement had rendered the king's sense of his duties towards the Gallican church suspect in the eyes of magistrates and clergy alike. In their view, far from contributing to the regeneration that the church so evidently needed, the Concordat had exacerbated its difficulties. The Gallican liberties had been betrayed – and in particular the clergy's corporate rights to elect the holders of high ecclesiastical offices. While those offices were now formally at the king's disposal, in practice they lay more than ever exposed to the intrigues of worldly patrons intent only upon 'the promotion of their friends', as leading members of the Paris *parlement* warned. They also warned, in language reminiscent of the terms of the ruler's coronation oath, that the preservation of the faith and the extirpation of heresies which the church denounced were prime royal duties. King Francis had every intention of demonstrating that he took those duties seriously; and the royal judicial machinery was at the disposal of the Reformation's opponents from an early date.[25]

They faced an obscure enemy that defied specification in terms of numbers, status or creed. What the authorities termed the 'lutheran contagion' was most easily diagnosed in towns, but it struck seemingly at random. Lists of suspects and martyrs in the early 1530s included regular and secular clergy, seigneurs and *officiers*, merchants, common servants and artisans. Members of the book trade were conspicuous among these last; but print, acclaimed by Luther himself as an 'act of divine grace' for spreading the gospel, was scarcely the indentured servant of Protestantism. 'Dissension and tumult' were what Erasmus thought Luther had undammed.[26] Confusion was already present, but it proliferated afresh in the wake of the printed matter that flowed about the kingdom, much of it arriving from abroad. One source was Neuchâtel, early identified by the peripatetic radical Guillaume Farel as a likely place for launching propaganda into France. There, in 1535, partly as a result of an earlier meeting between Farel and Waldensian leaders, the Lyon-born printer Pierre de Vingle produced Pierre-Robert Olivétan's French translation of the Bible with its famous preface by the translator's cousin, John Calvin.[27] But such a semblance of concerted reformist endeavour was misleading. In the previous year Vingle's presses had produced the famous *placards*, which attacked Lutheran as well as Catholic positions; and from those same presses also came works by Erasmus, who professed 'hatred' for Farel, and by John Eck, Luther's arch-adversary. If Luther's writings inspired scores of little handbooks of instruction, these competed for readers with significant numbers of Catholic liturgical and intercessionary manuals: in 1528 the publisher Guillaume Godard had in stock one hundred thousand copies of the latter. Reform-minded editors might introduce heretical propositions into overtly orthodox books of popular piety, but the effect of their subtlety was scarcely to supply readers with unambiguous doctrine. In the 1560s, when battle-lines were more clearly drawn, the enormous production of Huguenot psalters was rapidly countered by production of the revised Catholic breviary under the auspices of the Council of Trent. Print proved, at least over the long term, to be at the service of whoever could pay for it; and, in any case, prior to mid-century the Reformation as it affected France was scarcely capable of coherent propagandist effort. The battle of the books was a promiscuous combat; and the early French Reformation was not a movement so much as an assortment of attitudes and opinions.[28]

Yet its very disunity was an aid to its survival as a distinctive presence. Leading reformers might seek agreement among themselves; distinguished agents of the French ruler, spokesmen for Catholic evangelism, might make overtures to Martin Bucer in Strassburg and Philip Melanchthon in Wittenberg; but high-level negotiations had little bearing upon the activities of such spontaneous and scattered groupings as those of the French reformed. Calvin might repeatedly declare that there were in France 'few indeed who have received a right knowledge' of Christ, and that 'the poor folk are there famished for true doctrine',[29] but 'true doctrine' was still in fundamental respects an open question, to which answers were sought at places other than Geneva. Well before Calvin established his authority in that city they had been sought at Zürich where Zwingli, dismissing any need for a 'representative' *ecclesia*, identified the church with the congregation of 'the whole local community'. They were also sought in Strassburg, where Bucer's teaching reassuringly indicated the congregation to be 'a divine fraternity, community and unity'. Of course, congregations required ministers – and ministers, too, were forthcoming from Strassburg and elsewhere for the embattled companies of the faithful in France. But for those multiplying companies answers and ministers alike were primarily to be found nearer home, within the congregation itself, its own inspiration and its own members. As persecution intensified under Henry II, still 'the faithful were taught only by the reading of good books and as it pleased God to instruct them, without administration by ordinary of preaching or of sacraments, nor consistory'.[30] Informal congregationalism was the hallmark of the first generation of French Protestantism, at once a sign of its heterodoxy and a secret of its strength.

All this was transformed in the course of the 1550s. Frustrated thitherto by the very nature of the heretical enemy and also by local potentates' capacity, and willingness, to protect it, royal and ecclesiastical authorities summoned up means to even more vigorous repression, only to be frustrated afresh by their various agents' mutual antipathy and distrust. In the atmosphere of heat that judges and inquisitors – central and local, secular and clerical, Gallican and papal – helped to generate, Protestantism appeared to grow explosively. The influence of Geneva grew as well. During the decade, of more than four thousand refugees who flocked to Calvin's city two-thirds were Frenchmen, from almost every part of the kingdom. Among them artisans far outnumbered members of all other occupations, but artisans could move their means of livelihood more easily than could most:[31] the social composition of the Geneva refugees is no index to the social composition of the French reformed. In the same period dozens of trained missionaries, with men of noble or *bourgeois* origin disproportionately numerous among them, were sent secretly to minister to French 'churches', under the direction of the Geneva Company of

Pastors. Geneva was a magnet; it was also a driving force. Yet Geneva was not in control of developments in France.

Although the Geneva missionaries established new churches, their pastoral missions were regularly preceded by requests from churches already in existence.[32] The growth, and strength by the 1560s, of French Protestantism[33] is not to be explained simply by reference to the activities of pastors. According to the registers of the Company, admittedly incomplete, seven were sent to the Dauphiné in the seven years from 1555;[34] yet in 1562 the minister of Valence, who thought that a thousand were needed by the faithful of the province, estimated the number of ministers there at 'scarcely forty'. What Geneva supplied was the *régiment d'élite*, not the main host of the ministerial army. Calvin was driven to distraction. Pastors were demanded of him, he wrote in 1561, 'with a desire as great as the sacraments are coveted among papists'; his doors were besieged by suppliants who sought his favours like the clients of 'prostitutes'. The needs of France could not remotely be satisfied from the resources of Geneva. Yet Calvin censured churches that tried to satisfy themselves: 'in what school did you learn that private men could elect a man to their ministry? Such licence was always accursed, for it tends only to disrupt the union of the church.'[35] By then a union had indeed emerged in France. Its emergence, too, had escaped the control of a Calvin filled with trepidation by the tendencies both of France's pullulating congregations and of their impetuous leaders.

The union took shape via a series of deliberations and declarations. In 1557 'political articles' were drawn up at a 'synod' of the Poitou churches held at Poitiers. In that same year Calvin was himself responsible for preparing a confession of faith to be submitted to Henry II, 'so that you can best judge whether we are wrongly or rightly censured'. Two years later the so-called first national synod met at Paris, six weeks before King Henry's fateful death. It adopted a Discipline and a Confession. Calvin viewed the meeting with disfavour, and involved himself in it only at the last moment, sending a belated 'message' by three emissaries, two of whom arrived only in time to attend the closing proceedings, while their leader, owing to illness, did not attend at all.[36] In return Calvin was sent an account of the synod and an admission that 'it was seen fit to add somewhat to your Confession, but in fact to change it very little'. The allusion was to the 1557 confession,[37] to which that of 1559 did indeed make considerable additions.

The additions included six articles (24–9) that dealt with relations between the churches and with their government. Among them was the proposition, which was reaffirmed at the head of the Discipline and in effect repeated the first of the Poitiers articles, 'that no church should pretend to any domination or lordship over another'. The government of any church should be determined 'by election'. That term was indicated in the Confession to mean 'that all Pastors, Overseers and Deacons should possess evidence of being called (*ayent tesmoinages d'estre appellez*) to their offices'. But the Discipline dilated upon this:

> In those places in which Church-Order is not yet established, both Elders and Deacons shall be chosen by the common Suffrage of Pastor and People; but where Discipline is already constituted, it shall be done by the Minister and Church-Council, who shall give them their Charge, and they shall subscribe the Confession of Faith professed and avowed by us, then they shall be presented unto the people; and in case any one should oppose their Election, it shall be debated and determined in the Consistory; but if they cannot agree, it shall be referred unto the Provincial Synod.[38]

Clearly, the hierarchy of institutions that would characterise the organisation of the French reformed churches was already taking shape. Equally clearly, compromises were unavoidable in 1559 with congregational needs and so with congregational power, to a degree that contradicted Calvin's tenets and confused the very concept of 'election'. Compromises and contradictions were also implicit in articles that concerned 'election' of pastors. 'The Church', said the Confession, restating a clause of Calvin's own, 'cannot consist unless there be Pastors';[39] but the Discipline directed that pastors be 'elected at the consistory by the elders and deacons' – and even then 'the people for whom they are ordained' were not obliged to receive them, and had in effect a power of veto.[40] Finally, the concept even of a common Discipline was threatened by the Confession's recognition that, although none should depart from 'what has been ordained for us by our Lord Jesus Christ, this is no impediment to there being some particular statutes in every place as convenience may require'.[41]

Thus in 1559 the French reformed churches were poised between congregationalism on the one hand, and firm consistorial and synodical direction on the other. The former was implicit in the development of the French Reformation thitherto. The latter was urged by Calvin and by his eventual successor at Geneva, the Burgundian Theodore Beza, who explicitly termed it 'the aristocratic principle'[42] of ecclesiastical organisation. By adherents to either alternative, the church could be defined as 'the company of the faithful', and the principle of 'election' could be invoked. But they interpreted definition and principle very differently. The congregationalist tendency was towards a view of that company, nominalist-fashion, as the sum of its parts, and of election as involving an exercise of their suffrage. The tendency favoured and promoted by Calvin and those of his mind was quite otherwise. For them the company of the church was a corporate unity, to be directed, and represented, by those who best exemplified the qualities which as a unity it must possess. Thus, when new pastors or elders were to be chosen recognition of those qualities was the business of men already known to exemplify them. Such a principle was especially to be defended in relation to churches that in France were exposed to heterodox influences and were likely to contain what the Confession bluntly termed 'hypocrites'. Together, the Confession and the Discipline came close to confounding that principle, and to substantiating Calvin's fears. But subsequent synods removed the danger, and set the French Reformation on a decisive course.

The disciplinary powers of consistories and their role in inducting pastors were enhanced. Control over these functions was vested in synods, and certainly not in local congregations. Local conditions notwithstanding, it was ruled that there should not be 'any company which could be termed the council of the church, separated or different from that of the consistory'. Membership of the national synod was restricted to ministers and elders who were already members of provincial synods. Much of this was justifiable by reference to contingencies. Shortage of ministers – a problem exacerbated by 'great lords', patrons of Protestants and protectors of congregations who none the less took ministers 'away with them in their removals or travels abroad with their families' – led to disputes between churches over inviting and retaining pastors. In order to resolve, and to avoid, such disputes, churches must act in concert. They must also act in concert if excommunication, the most powerful instrument of discipline and never to be lightly used, were to be effective. In 'very disturbed and even dangerous' times it made good sense to restrict the numbers who had to travel to synods.[43] Even so, synodical and consistorial élites were in the saddle, ensuring between them that congregations should not be autonomous and that what Beza termed 'most troublesome and seditious democracy'[44] should be kept at bay. Congregationalist aspirations remained troublesome throughout the 1560s. They were expressed most forcefully by the young Henry of Navarre's own tutor, Jean Morély, and by Paris's most controversial teacher and logician, Peter Ramus. Both affirmed the rights of every congregation as a whole in disciplining its own members and in electing – and deposing – its pastors and its elders. Successive synods, culminating at Nîmes in May 1572, rejected their opinions and urged dissident congregations to conform to the general discipline.

But in striving to promote conformity Calvinist leaders were not simply responding to contingencies. They were guided by a fine combination of political sense and of doctrine concerning the nature of the church. They sought to regularise their churches' relation with the secular power, and were committed to a view of how to achieve such regularisation within the body politic of France. In sharp contrast to Geneva, where collaboration between magistracy and church ensured the city's steadfastness in the faith, France was a theatre of the churches' persecution at the hands of magistrates, and volatility characterised religious behaviour. Extreme congregationalism was a recipe for volatility, for encouraging every kind of outlandish doctrine, for abandoning religion in many localities to the whim of lay patrons; and even moderate congregationalism must rob the churches' leaders of credibility, as they publicly defended their beliefs and practices and sought political emancipation. If the status of those leaders were merely that of their churches' 'elected' representatives, if they should be answerable to their constituents like deputies at discordant assemblies of ineffectual Estates-General, what confidence could the secular power repose in them? Of course, were deputies from the churches to be admitted to the Estates, this would itself mark a significant step towards *de facto* emancipation. But, although the possibilities of such a step were indeed explored in 1560, the first priority remained that the churches obtain *de jure* the right to assemble for religious purposes – that 'a kind of Gallican liberty be conceded' them.[45] In order to obtain that 'concession' they must gain the confidence of the secular power: above all, of the king who by his grace could grant corporate recognition to constitutionally acceptable groups within his realm. As Beza wrote, hot from confuting bishops at the Colloquy of Poissy, it was 'official authority' that could 'open the way to our certain victory'; and so 'I never cease to warn and to beg that the rules be observed'.[46] The principle of representation upon which the churches' leaders relied as they strove for political 'concession' was compatible enough with those rules. It was fully consonant with their doctrine of the nature of the church. The church derived its qualities from Christ, not from men. It formed a corporate unity by virtue of His grace, not of its members' worth or discretion. Christ 'elected' the leaders of churches – most notably, pastors who 'should be received as representing the person of he who has ordained them',[47] namely Christ Himself. By virtue of representing His 'person', those leaders necessarily represented 'the union of the Church' as well.

Yet even in the ecclesiastical sphere the control of Calvin, Beza and their associates over the French reformed churches in the early 1560s was far from complete. Likewise in the political sphere they did not control the advance that Protestants were achieving at that time. To the policies of the movement's leadership in relation to the secular power[48] may be credited the Edict of St-Germain of 17 January 1562, one of the two most favourable measures accorded to the reformed churches under the last three Valois kings. It gave them not only freedom of worship outside towns, but also a form of supervision by royal *officiers* that seemed a step on the road towards collaboration. By that edict[49] the monarch empowered his *officiers* to license or to attend consistories and synods, to approve 'regulations for the exercise of the said religion', and to swear in ministers. But the edict was both short-lived and counter-productive. In effect, Protestants were already in breach of it, and specifically of its prohibition against their recruiting armed men for their defence. Such recruitment was under way before 1562, and well before March of that year when Beza himself at last instructed the churches to prepare against 'the forces and threats of our enemies'. The characteristic military organisation of the 'Huguenots' had been taking shape at the latest from November 1561. At the provincial synod of Haute-Guyenne in that month 'it was ordered, among other things, by the gentlemen who were there' that 'provincial protectors' be appointed to command 'the particular captains of churches' grouped in colloquies under 'colonels', thereby co-ordinating 'the forces of the churches'.[50] The declared intention was that such forces, which clearly already existed, should be employed to assist the ruler – an argument used by the Huguenot leaders Coligny and Condé, as well as by Beza himself, in justification of military preparations and activity. But Protestant political advance neither waited upon those leaders nor was confined to measures of a military kind.

Without reference to the former, Protestants had been seeking, and gaining, political power in the municipalities of France. When Condé rode into Orléans and issued his famous Protestation of April 1562 that precipitated the first civil war, towns rallied to his cause in numbers that would be as inexplicable as his military strength, were it not for what had gone before. What had gone before included widespread religious rioting and iconoclasm. It also included political advance into the bastions of municipal government. Popular disturbances might accompany that advance. In Agen in 1561, where Protestant artisans smashed altars and images and argued that 'if one tarried for the Consistory it would never be done', the *sénéchal* directed the *consuls* to 'elect twenty-four good men to give assistance to the law', twelve from a list of Protestant nominees and twelve from among the Catholics. But in Nîmes in the same year the consistory itself founded a Council of Twenty-Four that took over the military functions of the town government which, based on a four-man *consulat*, was by 1562 under Protestant control. Nîmes had a Protestant majority; but neither the pressure of popular disturbance nor the allegiance of a numerical majority of townspeople was a necessary precondition of Protestant political advance. In Troyes, by 1561 three of the eight *échevins* belonged to the town's reformed minority. Election of *capitouls* in Toulouse in November 1561 left Protestants in charge of the city. The given circumstance that favoured Protestant advance was France's pattern of oligarchic municipal government. A minority that recruited members of the oligarchy thereby penetrated the oligarchy itself, and could hope for an urban mastery that its numerical strength among the populace scarcely warranted. In Lyon 'the Reformation had made such progress among the local merchant aristocracy that the reformed could hope, in December 1561, to conquer the *Consulat*'.[51]

It is impossible to gauge how far urban Protestants might have succeeded in advancing by constitutional means, or by means of bringing about local modifications of municipal institutions. So often accompanied by popular disturbance, their advance might well have been arrested by the Catholic backlash that both provoked, in towns as at the royal court. But it was certainly interrupted by Condé's declaration. From the response of towns to his call, it momentarily seemed that urban France was falling wholesale under Protestant control. But the political foundations of the response itself were insecure. It rested, in the event, upon premature attempts at *coups d'état*. The *coups* were precipitated by the actions of the Huguenot leadership, headed now by Condé. Designated 'Protector' by 'the *sanior pars* of the seigneurs, gentlemen and subjects of the king', he 'sent men to the best towns of the kingdom in order to seize them'. Nine days after the Protector issued his Protestation, the Protestants of Agen, aided by 'strangers of their sects', imprisoned the *consuls* and seized the town. They held it for four months, only to be expelled in August by the deputy lieutenant-general of Guyenne supported by his eventual partner in office, Monluc. In the belief that the provincial governor Nevers was a Condé sympathiser, the Protestants of Troyes in mid-April seized the gates of their town and were briefly in control of it. In fact Nevers frustrated their *coup*, and early in August they in turn were either expelled or forcibly reconverted. In Toulouse, following communication with Condé's Orléans headquarters the Protestants launched their *coup* on 12 May. It was countered by the *parlement*, appealing to Monluc and other Catholic seigneurs. Days of fighting ended in a complete Catholic victory and the *parlement*'s condemnation of hundreds of Protestants.[52]

In Nîmes and elsewhere, notably in southern towns, where Protestant advance was more securely based, such reversals were avoided. In Orléans they were at least postponed: in 1563 Protestant control of the seven-member electoral college, and thereby of the twelve-member *échevinage*, was simply counterbalanced by adding twelve Catholic *échevins*, with royal approval. While the experiment, effectively in municipal government by means of parallel councils, was not peculiar to Orléans,[53] it led there in due course to the Protestants' losing their hold on power. It also led, by 1568, to the king's imposing direct control of elections to a degree that severely eroded the town's liberties. Conversely, in Lyon, where the Protestants were in touch with Condé and with the self-styled 'colonel of the legions of the Dauphiné', the baron des Adrets, before their *coup* of April 1562, a dozen Protestant councillors were designated to work alongside the existing twelve-member *consulat*; and by September it was the latter who had abandoned their posts. Protestant dominance lasted until December 1563 when, in accordance with royal wishes, the *consulat* was made up of six Protestants and six Catholics. Again a Protestant *coup* had led to a royal intrusion upon municipal liberties. Further, during the term of Protestant ascendancy the archbishop's powers of secular justice were finally assimilated to the royal *domaine*. Curtailment of those powers had been sought by earlier generations of *consuls*; but other developments under Protestantism were entirely unwelcome to the Lyonnais. They included blockade of the city, sequestration of absent merchants' goods, and direct taxation to supplement municipal revenues now reduced through the interruption of fairs and trade. Plague ravaged Lyon in 1564; by 1567 reprisals against Protestants were ravaging it once more, as a complete restoration of Catholic power took place.[54]

Reprisals culminated, in Lyon and elsewhere, in the bloody massacre of St Bartholomew's Day, ten years after the events of 1562. The correlation between these episodes is significant.[55] Towns where the massacre was especially violent were conspicuous among those where Protestants had earlier attempted their *coups*. Those same towns were also conspicuous, as we shall see, in the pattern of urban declarations for the League in the later stages of the civil wars. Upon all of this the oligarchic structure of municipal government had an important bearing. Protestant activity had exploited that structure and had also led, in several instances, to its modification. The monarch had been presented with opportunities for intervention, and municipal liberties had suffered in consequence.[56] But the monarch was impotent to resolve the religious crisis. What had been resolved was the French Reformation's course of development. It was in the 1560s that the movement, both in its ecclesiastical and in its political aspect, was effectively subjected to the 'aristocratic' principle. Congregationalism had been checked. Municipal oligarchies, their authority buttressed by just such a principle, had been penetrated by Protestants whose advance had been disrupted by the policies and initiatives of their movement's 'aristocratic' leaders. 'Representing' their churches, claiming that the '*sanior pars*' of the realm itself adhered to their cause, those leaders failed in a decade of civil wars to gain a lasting accommodation within the body politic for their followers. Yet in the aftermath of the *Saint-Barthélemy* the aristocratic principle continued to prevail.

During the 1560s Huguenot assemblies had equipped their military 'protectors' with advisory councils and with agents to administer funds, as well as with guidelines for military action. The Languedoc assembly held at Nîmes in November 1562 had been dominated by members of the Third Estate, most of them municipal *consuls* and office-holders.[57] But in subsequent assemblies of that decade the influence of the hereditary nobility had grown. In 1573 further assemblies, at Montauban and at Millau, drew up elaborate articles for managing military, financial and judicial affairs in the territories that the Huguenots now controlled. Applied initially to Languedoc, the Millau articles divided the province into two *généralités*. Each had a noble general; each also had an assembly, which was to meet quarterly.[58] The 'principal noblemen of the said *généralité*', members of its assembly, would 'elect' a nobleman and a member of the Third Estate as deputies to an 'Estates-General' of the entire confederation, together with a magistrate to attend and advise at the latter's six-monthly meetings. The assembly of the *généralité* would also designate, as a council to advise the general on all 'affairs of state' other than strictly military matters, persons of 'sufficient integrity and discretion, experience and fidelity'[59] – a set of terms the last of which had more to do with ties binding alliesmen to their noble leaders than with considerations of religious faith. Further, the articles stipulated that towns and villages should be governed 'in accordance with their ancient customs', and that 'all the privileges and municipal statutes, franchises and liberties of the *corps de villes*' should be observed. Earlier, at Montauban, it had been proposed to the king that towns be 'administered equally by Catholics and those of the Religion';[60] but such a revival of the experiments of the 1560s found no room in the Millau arrangements for Languedoc.

Nor did those arrangements find room for 'democratic' proposals that radical theorists were canvassing in 1573. According to those proposals, set out in the anonymous *Réveille-Matin des françois* and repeated in other tracts,[61] the inhabitants of every town should annually elect by popular suffrage a mayor and a Council of Twenty-Four chosen, regardless of considerations of social status, from 'among the nobles or among the people'. Council and mayor together would constitute an executive; and, with the addition of a further seventy-five councillors, likewise elected, they would also constitute a legislature with an extensive political competence and a criminal jurisdiction as well. The concept of councils of one hundred (25 + 75) was characteristic of municipal constitutions regulated in accordance with the

Établissements de Rouen, that institutional model which had greatly influenced municipal charters in south-western France. In Languedoc, where town deputies had traditionally been a dominant element in the provincial Estates, proposals concerning municipal government might be expected to have excited close attention. But, although the framers of those radical proposals took care to highlight the importance of ecclesiastical discipline and consistories, it was plainly their position that 'political sovereignty rested with the assembly of the people of every city'.[62] Adherents to the aristocratic principle could not, and did not, have anything to do with that.

That principle governed Protestant political thinking. It continued to govern the Huguenot series of constituent assemblies that culminated at Nîmes in January 1575, where Catholics participated for the first time and associated themselves with 'the union'.[63] For political radicals associated with the movement, its development was surely disappointing. That development also disappointed enemies who had warned that Protestantism entailed 'looking boldly at Princes and, instead of them, making God's lieutenants out of the suffering poor of your sect'.[64] French Protestantism as shaped and eventually controlled by its ecclesiastical and political leaders entailed nothing of the kind. Prominent among those leaders was Beza, opponent of congregationalism, exponent of 'aristocratic' control of the churches by consistory and synod, and advocate in his tract of 1573 for the right of 'inferior magistrates' to remedy wrongs perpetrated by a tyrant monarch. Their right was also an obligation, required of them by the 'universal rule of Justice, founded on maxims and common principles, which abide in man, however corrupt he may be'. Yet not all men were qualified to act even against a ruler so tyrannical, and so perfidious in his dealings with subjects who had sought concessions from him, that he had betrayed them savagely in 1572. For such action additional qualities were needed; and they resided in those who held 'estats et charges publiques'. These were 'Dukes, Marquises, Counts, Viscounts, Barons, *Châtelains*', and 'the elective officers of towns, such as Mayors, *Viguiers, Consuls, Capitoux,* Syndics, *Échevins* and the like'.[65] The principle of election, and so of representation, as it applied to them owed nothing to notions of popular sovereignty, in church, municipality, or body politic at large.

To emphasise the significance of that principle for the organisation of the French Protestant movement is not to devalue the importance of other traditions of thought for its adherents' political ideology and aspirations. For its ecclesiastical leaders the authority of Scripture was always paramount – an authority that stressed how 'the powers that be are ordained of God', and yet thereby left room for identifying a plurality of ordained powers competent to restrain the superior magistrate should he betray his trust.[66] Arguments for resistance by 'inferior magistrates' drew, further, upon juridical concepts concerning the duty of legal guardians to safeguard the interests of those committed to their charge.[67] Conversely, such concepts also conditioned the hopes and manœuvres of the 1560s to obtain from the ruler 'concessions' that would imply at least a measure of corporate recognition for the reformed churches.[68] But those hopes were bitterly disappointed; and when at last the churches did gain an enduring political recognition it was justified upon quite other grounds, as we shall see.[69] They gained it, a quarter of a century after Beza published his resistance tract, at the hands of their erstwhile 'protector' Henry of Navarre, now France's ruler by hereditary right and effectively so by force of arms. Even so, in the meantime royal attempts to pacify the kingdom foundered primarily, and repeatedly, upon the intransigence of Catholic leagues – movements that proved incapable of developing an overall organisational coherence such as their Protestant rivals had achieved, and yet were informed by principles analogous to those which the latter had espoused.

Sixteen months after the Nîmes constituent assembly, Henry III granted French Protestants a settlement on the most favourable terms that they were offered during the civil wars. Gained with the assistance of the king's brother and of so-called *politiques*, the edict of Beaulieu extended to those who professed the *religion prétendue réformée* freedom of worship throughout the kingdom except in Paris, authorised the holding of consistories and synods, and enjoined royal *officiers* to assist at them. While Protestants were pronounced capable of holding all offices, the edict created in the *parlements chambres mi-parties*, with Protestant and Catholic judges in equal numbers, fully empowered to hear and determine civil and criminal cases. In effect Protestants, with their distinctive ecclesiastical system and their peculiar needs as litigants, were being accommodated within the realm. Accordingly, they and 'united Catholics' were alike directed to 'desist from all associations' other than what the edict recognised.[70] Neither party complied with this directive.

While the Huguenot organisation persisted, so, too, did the multiplicity of local leagues that since the early 1560s had emerged to oppose its adherents, often in association with Catholic *gouverneurs*. Within a month of the Beaulieu edict's promulgation, the *gouverneur* of Péronne formed a fresh 'holy Catholic association', which developed into the famous League of 1576. All Catholics of town and village corporations were secretly to be summoned to join it, and those who declined to do so would be accounted its enemies. Its members swore to preserve the Catholic church and to obey 'the chief who shall be deputed'. The position of chief was soon claimed for himself by Henry III, who in the following year substituted for that of Beaulieu an edict much less favourable to Protestantism. But the articles of the League also declared as its aim the restoration of their ancient rights and liberties 'to the provinces of this kingdom and its Estates', regardless of the Beaulieu edict's express guarantees of all such liberties to all provinces and towns. As for the Estates-General, which the king had promised in that edict to summon within six months, the League invoked his coronation oath as binding him to observe 'the articles which shall be presented to him' at that assembly.[71]

The opponents of the Protestant heresy were stealing, and embellishing, its political clothes. Protestant organisers and theorists had affirmed the importance of 'representative' assemblies; but the Protestants fought shy of attending the Estates-General that assembled at Blois in November 1576. At Blois all three Estates called for restoration of religious uniformity. They also proposed that twelve members of each Estate should join with twenty-four royal councillors to constitute a council of sixty, charged with compiling legislation based upon the Estates' *cahiers*. Such legislation would be inviolable and irrevocable, except by another assembly of the Estates-General. Since the *cahiers* ranged widely over ecclesiastical and secular affairs, embracing the kingdom's judicial, financial and military organisation as well as detailed matters of law and custom, the constitutional implications of the proposal were extremely far-reaching. It was pressed by Leaguer deputies who wished to bind the king by oath to observe *cahier*-based ordinances. Had it been carried, and had he accepted it, the monarch's status as positor of law would virtually have been transferred to a committee representing the body of the realm. However, the proposal stirred misgivings among Third Estate deputies, who were furnished with arguments from principle by one of their number, Jean Bodin.[72]

Bodin's arguments turned on a view of political authority radically different from the concept of representation that underpinned much of Protestant and Leaguer thought. Observing that at the Estates-General the entire population of France appeared to be reduced to some four hundred deputies, he found it absurd that these deputies should further reduce their own number to thirty-six, and so form 'Estates in miniature'.[73] Affairs concerning the kingdom as a whole should be determined either by its monarch or by a numerical majority of deputies equipped with mandates direct from the people. For France the latter alternative would be dangerous; but the conciliar proposal under consideration would be an absurdity, an attempt flying in the face of all reason to mix monarchy with aristocracy and with democracy all at once.[74] The philosopher-historian's Third Estate colleagues may well have been swayed rather by wariness of accepting a minority position on such a council than by the force of his theoretical reasoning. Even so, the proposal failed; and the assembly, despite its supposed domination by the League, also failed to vote taxes to pay for war against heresy, to recommend removal of royal courts that threatened seigneurial jurisdictions,[75] and otherwise to endorse the League position on a wide range of issues.

Nevertheless, there were issues that gave the League an appearance of widespread support, enabling it to knit together the interests of religion, of its leaders and of its adherents, and to attract the uncommitted. At Blois such an issue was venality of offices. Deputies, among whom office-holders formed the greater part of the Third Estate, demanded that venality be bridled. *Officiers* concerned for the value of their existing investments and men from municipalities resentful of invasions of their liberties by royal appointees could all subscribe to that demand. So, too, could nobles who derived prestige and power from their roles as patrons of extensive clienteles. The patronage of the Guise family, whose head led the League, was paramount in the system of benefices and dignities that constituted the church they defended. It had also been extremely prominent in relation to offices of secular government. Unbridled venality threatened to set patronage at naught, to make power, prestige and profit, too, matters of simple exchanges among those who had the means to buy and sell. Those who had sufficient means could purchase as well the right of succession to offices that were worth the expense. By the same token, ancient families were threatened – as they supposed – with displacement by *nouveaux riches* and *nouveaux venus* who made up in money for what they lacked in lineage, and then proceeded to lay claim to dignities proper to lineage as well. But even such *arrivistes* were threatened by a system that allowed major offices to be taken out of the market only to flood it with minor ones which brought offices in general into disrepute. The threat of venality must be resisted, the monarch educated into recognition of his responsibilities towards ancient values and established rights. The issue was not new, and opinions differed as to the details of what ought to be done; but at least in respect of *parlement* magistracies the concept of election by existing office-holders was strongly canvassed at the Blois assembly.[76]

But, although such issues as venality provided grist for the League's mill, they did not enable it to thrive as a coherent movement. Like the movement it opposed, it sprang initially from spontaneous groupings. Yet its dependence was far greater than that of its opponents upon the charisma of a dominant leader, and its capacity far less to impose upon its adherents a common discipline, and so to curb spontaneity and particularism. The League of 1576 soon disbanded. When it was revived in 1584, amid rapidly deteriorating economic circumstances[77] and fears that a Protestant Bourbon would succeed to the throne, prompt steps were taken to develop its organisation. Henry of Guise, emulating Condé's action of over twenty years before, sent men to selected towns to make sure of their support. As with Condé, his agents were seeking to exploit situations that had developed independently of him. In Paris itself the clandestine society of the Sixteen was already in existence, counting among its members magistrates, merchants, lower clergymen and middling lawyers, and sending 'from town to town and from province to province honest persons of quality and credit, to act as spokesmen and to advise their confederates of what was happening in Paris'. Leaguer cells dimly resembling the Paris model took embryonic shape here and there. But members of *corps de ville* remained as yet less seduced by talk of confederation than preoccupied with the security of their own towns. For military security Guisard forces might be useful; but in their absence towns such as Toulouse simply made their own arrangements with their neighbours. In any case, for the members of *corps de ville*, among them many lawyers whom neither patronage nor venality had satisfied with royal offices, security meant much more than military protection. It embraced what they interpreted as the liberties of their municipal 'républiques'.[78] Those liberties, they could claim in many instances, were now safeguarded through alliances forged between local élites and local *gouverneurs*. Why should they, with their own councils, their 'party' organisations, their practised dismissals even of royal directives, now innocently submit to the tutelage of Paris, or even of Guise himself? Nor did they, until the climactic developments of 1588–9 – and, indeed, not even then.

In May 1588, Guise occupied Paris at the invitation of the Sixteen. The members of the *bureau de ville* were replaced by members of that conspiratorial group. The king was petitioned 'to allow the inhabitants of the city to elect, with liberty and by the customary forms, their *échevins* and their magistrates'. The new *bureau* dispatched letters to the *bureaux* of other towns, inviting them to send deputies 'with whom we may confer', especially about bringing royal financial and judicial agents to heel.[79] Further, a project was mooted for maintaining in Paris permanent deputies from allied towns, 'which will engender a form of Estates in miniature[80] of those towns . . . like pendants to the girdle of Monseigneur of Guise'.[81] But the response was muted. The Paris experience was scarcely enticing to incumbent mayors and *échevins* elsewhere. More heartening to the Sixteen was the response of the king himself to their approach. Now a fugitive from his capital, he was prompt to agree that a fresh Blois assembly of the Estates-General be summoned, and that 'what should be settled there should be inviolably observed and performed'.[82] It seemed that Henry III was bent upon collaborating in principle with his critics, and in practice even to the extent of disallowing elections that returned his own supporters to the Blois assembly.[83] Yet before that assembly could meet he had taken steps to disarm the League. In July he issued his Edict of Union, in which he assented to leading Leaguer demands, but thereby guarded against resigning the monarchy to the tutelage of the Estates. Moreover, although in the absence of Protestant deputies the Blois assembly seemed once again to be dominated by supporters of the League, in fact the latter were still disunited. Even members of the Sixteen bickered amongst themselves as to whether merchants, *corps de métier* and other 'inhabitants' of Paris had the right to participate directly in electing a deputy for the *prévôté* of the capital and its environs.[84]

It was amid the extraordinary wave of reaction to Henry III's assassination of Guise and of his brother, the Cardinal of Guise, at Blois in December 1588, that the League's organisation at last made convincing strides. At once the Sixteen created in Paris a new Council of Forty. In Toulouse a Council of Eighteen was set up in January; in Rouen a Council of Twelve on 7 February 1589. While each council purported to be made up of members of all three Estates, lawyers and *bourgeois* notables, including past and serving members of town corporations, in fact predominated upon them all. While each purported to be authorised by a municipal assembly, in Paris and in Rouen the members of the councils were certainly nominated by reference to ready-made lists. Each council claimed supremacy over both the *bureau* and the *parlement* in its town, in directing municipal affairs; and steps were taken to purge the latter into compliance. The Paris Council of Forty claimed even more. It was the nucleus of the long-heralded 'estates in miniature'. More letters to that purpose were sent to the provincial capitals, and from there to neighbouring towns and communities to win them for the League. Thus an emissary, armed with his Parisian letter, appeared in March at the provincial Estates of Forez, sent from Lyon to invite Forez deputies to the newly reconstituted Leaguer council in that city, the successor to the *gouverneur*'s 'conseil d'état' which had run it since the Protestant *débâcle* over twenty years before. All of these towns, together with Bourges and Troyes, where equivalent councils also appeared,[85] had been scenes both of Protestant *coups* in 1562, and of exceptional violence at the time of the *Saint-Barthélemy*. But while Protestants had long since inspired their opponents to violent courses and the formation of local leagues, proven Valois 'tyranny' now seemed to inspire them to a great deal more. A hierarchy of councils was plainly envisaged: provincial councils, located in principal towns, incorporating representatives from local communities, and represented in turn upon the supreme council in Paris – the whole geared to representation in the form of Estates, but primarily and in effect by reliable notables and men of law,[86] the urban League's equivalent of the elect.

But, as in the earlier experience of the Protestant movement, the development of the urban League was disrupted by actions on the part of hereditary noblemen. In February, Guise's surviving brother, Mayenne, came to Paris and augmented the Forty with his own nominees. Proceeding to Rouen, he added his own nominees to the council there. His tour had begun in Dijon, capital of his own *gouvernement* of Burgundy. There he had gratified the mayor and *échevins* by charging them with 'all régime and government'. But Mayenne had also left, to co-ordinate the province's affairs, a lieutenant-general and a council, analogous to the councils of the urban movement, but answerable to him rather than federated with that of Paris. With Guise gone it was Mayenne whom the Paris council designated lieutenant-general of the kingdom until the Estates-General should meet again. That council could therefore claim to have empowered him. But Paris did not govern Mayenne, nor Mayenne Paris; and neither succeeded in knitting the multiple components of the League into an enduring organisation. Even the king's assassination in August – an event that transformed the prospect of a Protestant succession to the throne into a virtual reality – failed to unite effectively those who had sworn the Catholic Leaguer oath. Differences sharpened between Mayenne and the Sixteen. While he schemed to deprive them of control over the capital, they riposted with subversive committees and a reign of terror in its suburbs.[87] Meanwhile, provincial towns had all too often to be left to their own devices. Agen reconstituted its council in April and associated itself with Toulouse in the prescribed manner. Six months later the Agen Leaguers complained to Mayenne that these actions had received no endorsement whatsoever either from the Paris council or from him.

In the absence of effective co-ordination and central direction, the League fragmented into local associations whose particular struggles distorted its declared aims. It had declared in favour of local liberties, and against their invasion by agencies of the monarch. But among the motives of the Agen *consuls* for aligning themselves with it was news that one such agency, the *siège présidial* with whose judges they had long disputed precedence within the municipality, was to be transferred from Agen to rival Villeneuve.[88] The pan-French system of councils envisaged by the Sixteen foundered upon perennial quarrels between provincial towns – quarrels which included disputes over their jurisdictions among local magistrates, who also figured prominently on the provincial councils. Far from transforming local attitudes, those councils crystallised the long-standing preoccupations of their members. It was too much to expect that deep-seated rivalries between upper and lower Berry, the rivalries of municipal oligarchs and magistracies, could be swept aside simply by establishing a Leaguer provincial council in Bourges. In the Auvergne, where municipal and jurisdictional disputes were endemic between Riom and Clermont, once one town had hesitatingly declared for the League its rival promptly declared itself royalist. But Mayenne's arrangements were ill-fated, too. In Dijon, conflict rapidly developed between the mayor and the *gouverneur*'s lieutenant-general. Mayenne subordinated the latter to his own step-brother, Nemours. But Nemours had ambitions of his own which, with the crown disputed, included partitioning the French Midi with his fellow-Leaguer Scipion de Joyeuse. Small wonder that the war-weary populace should have despaired of their municipal and noble leaders alike. Those leaders had sponsored clerical demagogues to maintain, by means of sermons and processions, popular enthusiasm at boiling-point for Catholicism and the League. But in St-Malo artisans closed the town's gates against 'anyone whomsoever, of whatever party he may be, king, prince, *gouverneur* or any other'. In Amiens it was again artisans who at last precipitated the provincial council's collapse and the town's return to the royalist fold.[89]

There was therefore good reason for the claim expressed by an anonymous member of the Sixteen in the summer of 1593 that the 'poor Catholics' had been 'betrayed by most of their magistrates, royal *officiers* and great families, and furthermore badly served by *gouverneurs* and gentlemen who commanded the party'. These, 'instead of making war against the heretic, conspired with one another, at the people's expense'.[90] The League's leaders, noble, provincial and Parisian, too, had certainly conspired for their particular purposes, and had negotiated with foreign powers as well, to the further confusion of their movement. Meanwhile, the heretic Henry of Navarre made war to far better effect than did they, and ultimately disarmed them altogether by abjuring Protestantism in July of that year. No less certainly, Mayenne made war with aristocratic considerations in mind. He had stated his position in articles which he intended to present in Reims in 1591, to an assembly of the Estates-General that in fact never met. For him, 'the body of this monarchy' was 'indivisible'. Although a Catholic king should be elected by the Estates-General, he should thereafter exercise 'sovereign authority'. But the monarchy could thrive only 'through a very strict liaison of its members'. A council of deputies from every province would enable the king 'to maintain the correspondence, liaison and union that are so necessary for the welfare and safety of the State'. Here was an echo of the Leaguer conciliar proposal at Blois in 1576 – as well as an identification of 'the state' with the unity of the body politic. But also necessary to the welfare of 'the state' in Mayenne's corporatist sense was maintenance 'of the ranks and qualities of persons'. To fail to observe 'distinctions of ranks' was to reduce the kingdom to a 'popular and tumultuous State'.[91] In the hierarchy that he prescribed, mayors and town corporations must defer to the hereditary nobility. How could this be reconciled with the views of the Sixteen?

And yet the Sixteen professed their own version of the aristocratic principle of representation. According to their self-appointed apologist, it was they who 'represent' the people and 'adhere to the general good'. It was they who had established the Paris council. They had done so because 'it was necessary, until the assembly of the Estates, to use an aristocracy to govern'. The king must be elected: what mattered was not that 'he should merely be the next in line in order to succeed, but that he should be of the necessary quality and condition'. The 'necessary quality', in the ruler's case as in the case of 'the general species of the nobility', was 'virtue that one gains for oneself', and not some inherited property.[92] But by whom, and how, might such virtue be recognised? For the Sixteen, it was indissociable from staunchness in the Catholic faith. Yet they had found their aristocracy of virtue among *bourgeois* notables and men of law. Owing partly to noble intervention, but also to entrenched attitudes among those who emerged as the elect, they had failed to integrate such representatives into an effective urban-based confederation. Significantly enough, like the Protestants before them they had also failed to agree upon the question of who should participate directly in exercising the franchise, and so upon broadening the basis of municipal representation.

The narrowness of that basis had enabled Protestants to gain their political advance of the early 1560s. In the wake of their efforts, the monarch to whom their leaders had appealed for political concessions exploited the occasion to invade the liberties of municipal corporations. In the 1570s and subsequently both Protestants and Leaguers had insisted afresh upon the preservation of those liberties. In respect of the kingdom as a whole, their respective apologists had also insisted upon the rights and duties of persons imbued with appropriate qualities to resist a ruler who abused his authority. They should do so as 'representatives' either of the entire body politic, or of its several members. Such arguments, however, variously propagated amid mounting conditions of disruption, seemed calculated rather to hasten that body's dismemberment than to safeguard its union. While 'union and concord' were the prime watchwords stressed in successive edicts of pacification, those royal acts seemed only to exacerbate the contrary, for all the endeavours of king and council to oversee their enforcement by means of commissioners. How was the union of the

body politic to be restored if its head were discredited and its aristocratic members were at loggerheads with one another as well as with
him?

The same watchwords figured afresh in the edict promulgated by
Henry IV at Nantes in 1598. But while that act repeated many of the
provisions of earlier edicts, the first Bourbon king found additional
reasons for requiring its acceptance – and with it submission to his
authority. He had overcome resistance by force of arms – a demonstration of power that had eluded his immediate Valois predecessors. Now
he urged his 'subjects well and truly to understand that in the observation of this our ordinance consists' not only 'the principal foundation of
their union', but also 'the restoration of this entire State to its pristine
splendour, wealth and strength'.[93] None of the earlier pacification
edicts had explicitly adduced 'the state' as a reason either for accom-
modating or for restricting Protestant practices. King Henry adduced
it again, in commending his edict to a Paris *parlement* still reluctant to
countenance the accommodation now proposed. It was true that
'necessity compelled me to make this edict'. Even so, the ruler was
entitled to obedience if 'for no other consideration than that of my
quality'. But there was a further consideration: 'If obedience was due
to my predecessors, as much or more devotion is due to me, especially
as I have established the State . . . I have re-established France',
despite those who had done their utmost 'to ruin the State'.[94] Restored
by a monarch who demanded his subjects' obedience in its name, the
state, it would seem, was distinguishable from any and all of them. To
our specific demonstration that such an idea had indeed emerged in the
political thought of the time – the idea of the state as an entity distinct
from ruler and ruled – we come at last.

CHAPTER 6

The Idea of the State

By what right does a ruler exercise authority? For leading medieval thinkers the answer had lain in their idealisation of Christian society as an all-embracing whole, co-terminous with the church.[1] That society was hierarchically ordered. Within it men harmoniously performed their functions as members of a single corporate body headed by a divinely appointed monarch, the Pope of Rome. Secular rulership was one of those functions. The ruler was God's servant, the appointed guardian of his people, who were, accordingly, his ward. He was duty-bound to combat evil-doing, towards which the people were naturally inclined. They must obey him, for his actions were to their collective benefit. Yet he in turn must act in accordance with the law – the soul of that collectivity, and ultimately to be interpreted by the Pope alone.

Over many centuries, answers consistent with such a model were developed and refined. It accommodated a profusion of principles grounded in Scriptural and patristic teaching, in Platonic and neoplatonic philosophy, in Roman law. The support of general principles was indispensable for thinkers who reasoned deductively, from premiss to conclusion with abundant proofs along the way. But from the same sources other thinkers drew support for significantly different answers. If the secular ruler was God's servant, as much a divine appointee as the Pope himself, it followed that no man could coerce him. If the ruler must act in accordance with the law, this was not because the law confined him, but because he embodied it, animated it, expressed it through his will. The soul of the public collectivity was thus 'what pleases the prince', which 'has the force of law'.[2] The law that he pronounced was the human equivalent of holy writ; and those who administered it in his name were tantamount to priests.[3] Such arguments pointed to a dual authority in Christendom, at the expense of the unitary authority of the Pope. Yet it did not follow that Christendom itself was not a unified entity; for the arguments tended in favour rather of a universal emperor than of particular rulers in particular realms.

Even so, the aspirations of the latter mounted, and were not to be denied. Fresh arguments arose after the thirteenth-century rediscovery of Aristotelian texts which further enriched the sources of European thought. Against the universalist principles of papal monarchy or of papal–imperial dualism, it could now be argued that men lived by nature in discrete communities, and that every self-sufficient political community was an end in itself.[4] French thinkers were conspicuous in putting Aristotle to work in vindication of their monarch's authority.[5] But Aristotle was not to be employed to the exclusion of established sources; and, although these might be interpreted to designate a king emperor in his own kingdom,[6] they readily yielded arguments that were far less congenial to him. For, if the political community was what mattered, the very principle that identified law with the prince's will also indicated how the people themselves had originally conferred authority upon him. Was that authority revocable by the community and, if so, in what circumstances? Did its continued exercise depend upon the continuance of trust? Trust was already implicit in the Roman principle of guardianship, for his exercise of which the ruler was answerable only to God and under His law. But it could also be held to imply the feudal principle of contractual relations between king and people, with rights and obligations on both sides. Further, feudal law was rooted in custom; and custom was made by the people themselves. They made it in their natural communities, for the protection of their private rights. Yet it was also tenable by reference to Justinian's lawbooks that they retained as well a role in positing law for the public community of the realm: that they themselves must approve whatever the ruler might seek to enact if his enactment should affect them all.[7] In sum, such arguments seemed to threaten to undermine not only universalism, but the coherence of law itself, and with it the very keystone of rulership.

However, every thinker could concur in one universal proposition: that the end of all laws, divine or natural, positive or customary, was justice and the common good. The difficulty lay in deciding how those timeless ideals were to be actualised on earth, and how their actualisation might be recognised. The debate, accordingly, had to do with means, and as much with metaphysics as with politics. In the closing medieval centuries some would argue that the common good was indissociable from the good of its parts. Those parts were individuals; and the whole that together they might be held to compose was merely a collective term. In that case, the actualisation of the common good must involve the participation of all individuals, in making laws. Yet they could scarcely participate without some form of representation:

an institution, or set of institutions, in which their collective being was, as it were, embodied. For strict nominalists, if there was such an embodiment it amounted to no more than a convenient fiction. For others, the concept was profoundly significant. The common good was not to be reduced to the mere sum of its parts. Like justice, it existed in its own right, at a level of reality other than that of individual existence. Its actualisation could be instrumented by means only of an institution that was at once terrestrial and superterrestrial. And for that embodiment the obvious candidate was surely the king, whose highest and most sacred office and dignity were perpetual, while their holder himself was mortal.

So the debate continued, and prompted strenuous re-examinations of the sources. Late-medieval biblical exegesis, symbolic and allegorical in its modes, gave way in time to the philological and textual scholarship of the humanists, who revealed important errors in the Vulgate, challenged church teaching at key points of doctrine, and paved the way for the translations and controversies of the sixteenth century.[8] Meanwhile Platonism, overshadowed though never eclipsed by the cult of Aristotle, was reinvigorated in the Italian *quattrocento*. By the later-fifteenth century the name of Ficino, Plato's leading translator and interpreter, was 'loved and extolled in all the colleges of Paris', where disputation raged between Platonist moderns and Aristotelian ancients.[9] But there, as elsewhere, the Master's influence continued paramount; and Aristotelian principles, whether fragmented by the expository methods of scores of scholastic commentators or reintegrated by the textual zeal of humanists, remained the foundation of academic studies and the starting-point for all inquiry and disputation. Further, the medieval texts of Roman law had been annotated and re-annotated by the glossators and postglossators. While humanist scholars derided their efforts and satirists taunted their 'inept opinions', sixteenth-century editions of the *Corpus Iuris Civilis* still carried the *glossa ordinaria* that every student of civil law was required to read. As for customary law, it, too, had attracted the attentions of the glossators, and early compilations of the French *coutumes* were permeated with civilian influences.[10] Yet, for all their limitations and imperfections, such compilations were proofs that custom had a more than merely local application, and prefigured the concept of a consolidated code distinct from that of Rome and common to all Frenchmen.

Frenchmen of the sixteenth century would draw upon all of these sources together with all of the elements of the medieval debates, as they continued to dispute the question of the ruler's right to exercise authority. But in the course of their disputes a fresh answer emerged. The answer was the idea of the state. Earlier thinkers had laid the foundations for that idea, and had even made ample use of its terminology. It was clear enough to them that the state, or condition, of the ruler was different from the state of the ruled. It was also clear to them that every political community as a whole – each of those 'mystical bodies . . . assembled by a civil and political union' – had, like 'human material bodies', an optimum condition of well-being that might be termed its 'state'.[11] What they had lacked was the idea of the state as a distinct entity, subsisting in its own right. Without that idea, they could not derive the ruler's right to exercise authority from a property of such an entity, as distinct from God, from the people, or from their representatives. The idea was decisively formulated in the 1570s, as disputes among Frenchmen, sharpened by religious controversy, by monarchical propaganda, and by the growth of government, reached fever-pitch.

From Origen's in the third century AD to the present day, commentaries upon St Paul's epistle to the Romans have perhaps outnumbered those upon any other historical document or portion of Scripture.[12] For Luther and Calvin alike the epistle supplied the key to biblical understanding. Sixteenth-century Catholic commentators stressed its importance no less firmly. In an age when religious and political considerations were so closely intertwined, Paul's pronouncements on the authority of rulers were invoked on all sides. The epistle's thirteenth chapter furnished sufficient proofs both for thinkers who insisted on the duty to obey and for those who asserted the right to resist. On the one hand, God was the source of all power. The ruler who bore that power was His minister, and could therefore be resisted only at the price of damnation. On the other, that same pronouncement seemed to imply a distinction between the power and the person who bore it. Should that person use the power otherwise than for the promotion of good and the punishment of evil, the duty of obedience must surely lapse and the power be turned against its abuser.

However, such grounds for denying obedience were attenuable in so far as the person of the ruler could be identified with the office of monarchy itself. Indeed, if the identification could be shown to be absolute, would not those grounds disappear altogether? Efforts at projecting such an identification reached a peak in the pageantry of the French Renaissance court. By the opening of the sixteenth century the solemn entries of kings into the towns of their kingdom had developed from relatively simple ceremonies into ornate spectacles, heavy with symbolism. The royal visitor came in triumph, attended by biblical and classical heroes, by alleged founders of the kingdom and better-attested founders of his dynasty, all associating his presence with their own, and so with their sempiternal qualities. Symbolism grew ever more elaborate and esoteric as the century wore on. Increasing use of allegorical sculpture was reinforced by strong infusions of neoplatonic themes. Triumphal arches through which Henry II rode into Rouen in 1550 figured afresh in 1571 when Charles IX entered Paris to banquet amid paintings illustrating the myth of Cadmus, master of magical music and 'saviour of the harmony of the world'. In other forms of court festivity those themes became dominant as Valois rule entered its closing decade. At the marriage festivities of the royal favourite Joyeuse in 1581, blends of music and dance with dramatic spectacle amounted to incantatory rituals, drawing down astral influences upon the household of Henry III, himself depicted as the sun from where all power emanated.[13]

Most striking of all rituals was the royal funeral ceremony with its sixteenth-century centrepiece – a lifelike effigy of the dead king. Honour was done to the effigy and meals served to it until the corpse it represented was interred. The effigy bridged the gap between the ruler's death and his successor's inauguration first at the moment of burial and then at his coronation. While theorists had long since argued that the monarchical office did not die, although its mortal holder must perish, the effigy blurred that distinction. It rendered the office's perpetuation dependent upon the continuous presence of a monarchical person. From there the step was short to a position where transmission of power to his successor was acknowledged to be instantaneous at the moment of a king's death. Now monarchy and monarch were both in effect immortal, and the identification between them was complete. The position was reached by 1610: 'The king is alive, there he is,' exclaimed the chancellor, pointing to the eight-year-old dauphin, almost within the hour of Henry IV's assassination.[14]

But this is to anticipate. Earlier, despite the uses of metaphysics for the image of the monarch that he and his associates endeavoured to propagate, their efforts were potentially counter-productive. If the monarch was identifiable with his office, were not other office-holders likewise identifiable with theirs? In that case, feudal lords, magistrates, heads of corporate bodies, might claim to be as absolute in the exercise of their powers as the monarch in the exercise of his. Of course, those lesser powers varied in degree, and were in many instances exercised specifically by concession or by delegation. But, in so far as power was inherent in the office itself, to seek to distinguish it from the person of the office-holder was to insist upon the very distinction that monarchical propaganda sought to erode. Conversely, not to do so seemed to entail an admission that power was distributed among the office-holding members of the body politic, each of whom exercised his portion of it by unassailable right. Further, that right was arguable not only from metaphysics but also from law, on grounds that

sixteenth-century developments helped to consolidate. Medieval jurists had interpreted it in terms of property, thereby equating a relation
to public authority with a relation to private lands or goods.[15] By selling
offices so vigorously, sixteenth-century French rulers appeared resolved to sanction that equation; and some contemporary jurists, such
as Pierre Rebuffi, continued to maintain that all holders of offices,
once created, 'form part of the established order and have jurisdiction
by proprietary right'.[16] Moreover, they did so at a time when the feudal
concept of *dominium* was succumbing to the concept of unitary
ownership, rooted in Roman law.[17] Rights in what was otherwise
assigned to the user were reserved to the monarch by the former
concept, but denied him by the latter: 'we cannot be deprived of what
is our own', as Rebuffi observed, 'unless we do it ourselves'.[18] All in all,
metaphysics, law and the prodigality of the Valois kings seemed
together to drain power from the monarchy with which those kings
strove to identify their persons.

Yet other jurists had available more legal and philosophical arguments with which to reverse that flow. When the postglossators had
tried to define the nature of public power, they had drawn fine
distinctions in specifying its forms.[19] By reference to these, it was
arguable that office-holders exercised power neither in its highest
forms nor with full proprietary rights. *Merum imperium*, the pure form
of power to command, appertained only to the monarch.[20] Lesser
office-holders had powers, or jurisdictions, which they used. But use
was not tantamount to ownership: so much, at least, was plain enough
in Roman as in feudal law. Precisely what a man acquired when he
purchased an office and identified his status with it remained obscure.[21]
Office as such and the power connected with it were none the less
distinguishable from each other; and so, too, was monarchy specifically different from offices that subjects might hold. And yet, unless
the members of this triad – office, power, monarchy – were to be left
discrete, there must be between them some means of association and
interaction. Means were supplied by the concept of emanation, rooted
in neoplatonism, that figured prominently both in the court
propaganda[22] and in the juristic commentaries of the sixteenth century.
Power emanated from a source which was in no way diminished by its
flow, and to which it must ultimately revert. The source was the
monarchy, the receptacles the offices which were thereby filled with
powers that office-holders were not only enabled but obliged to use.
And, should they neglect to do so, 'their jurisdiction necessarily
reverts to the ordinary and royal abode from which it emanated'; for all
such jurisdictions 'emanate and derive from our supreme king, as from
one very prolific origin, and the source to which they return'.[23]

Thus Charles Du Moulin, perhaps the most distinguished legist of his day, and deeply committed to the view that no source of power, and certainly no allegiance among subject individuals or groups, should intrude upon the uniform relation between the ruler and each of them. Others in the first half of the sixteenth century supported monarchical authority with still more far-reaching philosophical arguments. In a work intended to enable everyone 'to know the order and end of his condition (*status*)', Barthélemi de Chasseneux stressed how, under God, 'majesty, that is, *maior status*' appertained to the ruler alone, from whom, therefore, authority 'shines'. Sole terrestrial source of light and power, the ruler distributed his 'influence' to those who exercised command and gave them their very 'existence' in the public sphere. Public persons moved others to act, and so were more fully existent than private ones. But the ruler alone was the unmoved mover, the absolutely necessary being in a political system: all others were contingent upon him, the *ens per se*. When Aquinas' metaphysical arguments for the existence of God were redeployed in this way, it would seem that justifications of monarchical rule and denials of *officiers'* independent rights could scarcely be taken farther. As for the analogy of the body politic, Chasseneux had no difficulty in maintaining that all 'noble virtues such as imagination, memory, intelligence, common sense and the like are located in the head'. What resided in lesser members was 'only touch'; and, while the intellect doubtless responded to that sensation, it was once more the ruler as 'animated law' who furnished the rational principle whereby they might act coherently.[24]

Even so, difficulties persisted over the question how that 'head' of the body politic was composed, and thereby the nature of the ruler's 'person' to which it seemed to correspond. Here, Chasseneux and his follower Charles de Grassaille admitted that, especially in respect of matters of law, 'the council of senators . . . is deemed part of the prince's person'; indeed, that they 'are the soul of the prince', just as he in his monarchical – though not in his private – persona was *lex animata*.[25] That council, jurists could agree, must include the members of the *parlement* which, in Grassaille's phrase, 'represents the body of the king', in the sense, as Du Moulin expressed it, of his 'intellectual' as distinct from his carnal person.[26] But to admit the representative role of conciliar institutions and their capacity to regulate the legislative proposals of the monarch sole was seriously to modify the position of absolute dominance with which philosophical arguments had appeared to identify him. It was also to leave open the door for counter-arguments. While the instruments of government might owe their existence to the ruler, his laws had still to be measured against the requirements of justice and the common good. Laws, observed Rebuffi, were indeed 'the work of the prince', but they were posited 'for the benefit of the polity': they were 'not good' and 'do not hold' if they 'disturb its good condition (*bonus status*) and peace'. Formerly, good kings had 'proposed laws by the consent of the three Estates, and it would be good if as much were done today. For the three Estates represent the condition of the people'; and, although there were times when they 'cannot assemble together, on account of the people the senate at least should be consulted'.[27]

By the middle of the sixteenth century, then, although theorists had taken significant steps towards reinforcing monarchical authority, most notably upon philosophical grounds, the debate that they had inherited from their medieval predecessors remained inconclusive. That many-sided legal and philosophical debate continued to revolve around the entities of ruler and people, the agents of the former, the representatives of each, and the status that attached severally to them all. As long as these remained its points of reference, the terms of the debate could always be redefined at the expense of the ruler and his supporting jurists. They were redefined very vigorously in the 1570s, by Huguenot advocates of resistance to monarchical rule who turned to their advantage even its supporters' most promising recommendations. Jurists, with Du Moulin once again to the fore, had urged the desirability of eliciting from France's customary laws a unified *droit commun coutumier*, to be applied throughout the realm under the king's aegis.[28] Such a unification would confirm his authority as supreme law-giver – together with that of the lawyers who in practice would apply his laws. But the desirability of unifying the customs was also endorsed by Huguenot resistance theorists, with very different implications in view. Was it not partly owing to the complexities of the customs that so many jurists and legal practitioners were able to flourish in France? And was it not by means of this 'rabble of interpreters of the law' that kings had been able to undermine the authority of the 'public council'?[29] That council was the Estates-General, the 'epitome' of the kingdom. It 'represented' the 'whole body of the people';[30] it made government 'harmonious';[31] and the whole body was prior to and greater than the king, greater though he might be than any individual member of the realm.[32] The king was mortal, the kingdom everlasting:[33] only 'court mountebanks' who would 'call kings gods' presumed to argue otherwise. By their suggestion nothing was 'just in itself', and justice had no 'form' unless the king ordained it. But, although a 'good king' gained 'movement, feeling and life' by the law, as did the body by the soul, it was surely better to obey the soul, which was 'reason or intelligence' and resided in the 'public council', than the body, which, however royal, was also moved by 'passion' and 'appetite'.[34]

Such well-worn postulates, time and again reshuffled, sufficed to counter the metaphysical propositions of the jurists. Without their assistance, monarchist arguments from property rights were easily reversible, too. The king might be owner of his patrimony; but of the *domaine* and revenues of the kingdom it was he who had only the use. These were the property of the kingdom as a whole, and even to term him their 'usufructuary' was an exaggeration.[35] As for things privately owned and used, the king had no right to them:[36] indeed, it was in order to prevent the rich from despoiling the poor that kings had originally been created. Even so, Huguenot theory relied far less upon precise juridical considerations of property than upon historical examples and broad principles of natural law. From the former it was evident that kings were originally elected by the body of the people.[37] From the latter it was plain that men would not voluntarily have surrendered their natural liberties except upon conditions.[38] The relation between king and kingdom could therefore be described in contractual terms. The original contract between king and electing 'council' was reaffirmed at every coronation. Particular contracts, set out in provincial and municipal charters, were reaffirmed when kings made their solemn entries into the parts of the realm.[39] So much for the significance of those ceremonies. As for laws concerning all the people, these were also interpretable as contractual agreements. They were arrived at, as they ought to be, by kings in consultation with the Estates.[40] So every king was bound by the laws.[41] If he should betray the agreements into which he had entered, the co-contracting party, likewise bound to maintain such agreements, had the right to renounce him. The right was primarily the 'public council's'; but should that body not be convened the right devolved upon the 'inferior magistrates', who were both the conservators of provinces and towns and the lesser *officiers* of the kingdom as a whole, so many of them of feudal origin.[42]

As developed by its three main Huguenot exponents – François Hotman, Beza, and the author of the *Vindiciae contra tyrannos*[43] – this theory rested no less heavily upon long-laid foundations than did the monarchical arguments that they opposed. Stressing particular features of it, each theorist invoked propositions of a universal kind. Hotman might emphasise the original role and continuing relevance of the 'public council' in France's history, and might rely to an exceptional degree upon historiographical materials; but classical philosophers, and especially Aristotle, were called upon to bolster his repeated justification of that council as the 'mixed and tempered' form of rule.[44] While Beza drew his citations largely from Scripture, Aristotelian tenets concerning the 'ends' for which actions are performed figured early in his tract, though he took care explicitly to reject the views of 'pagan philosophers' on 'the true end of well-ordered polities'.[45] As for the *Vindiciae*, Aristotelian positions again underpinned its author's contentions that law was reason subduing passion, that kings were protectors of property rights, that tyrants served only their own pleasure.[46] The 'marks' of tyranny, the nature of a people as a corporate body and the source of legislative right – such questions were commonplaces of medieval debate; and the idea of contract that Beza and the author of the *Vindiciae* both placed at the centre of their discussions was treated by them explicitly in the traditional terminology of feudal law. Yet at their hands that idea acquired fresh conceptual overtones, of which Hotman's thinking remained relatively innocent.

In discussing the 'whole' and 'highest administrative authority', Hotman was content to identify it with the 'public council',[47] as opposed to identifying that authority with the king himself. These were the essential alternatives – on the one hand the representative and conciliar, on the other the absolutely monarchical – to be derived from medieval precedent. But Beza and the author of the *Vindiciae* groped, however uncertainly, towards a unified conception of authority that was distinguishable from those alternatives. By that conception, law was linked to 'sovereignty' in a relation that implied the presence of the state as an abstract entity. The author of the *Vindiciae* described law, Aristotelian-fashion, as the 'instrument' for 'conducting men's society to a happy end'. Such was the end sought by the people when they concluded the contract with their king who, in turn, was the 'instrument' of the law. To maintain the laws of a polity was, *ipso facto*, to maintain the 'public benefit' and 'the State of the kingdom'.[48] In that case the 'state' was identifiable with those laws – a view consistent with the position that Pasquier had recently suggested.[49] When the laws were not maintained, the *république* ceased to be, the contract was annulled.[50] In that event 'sovereignty' became identifiable with those who would call its royal administrator to account, namely the 'body of the people'.[51] But between sovereignty and people Beza predicated a firmer distinction. Sovereignty was the contract itself, 'founded on equity and natural reason', or natural law.[52] The king was its administrator,[53] the Estates its protectors: and 'de par la souveraineté' the 'inferior magistrates' received their charge. The people themselves were always subject to the contract and had no right of resistance. But when kings contravened 'what they have sworn to the sovereignty' its other authorised agents, 'maintainers of the sovereignty', could and ought to oppose them, even by force of arms.[54]

So, in the circumstances of the 1570s, Huguenot theorists took significant steps towards formulating an idea of inviolable sovereignty that implied the existence of the secular state as an entity distinct from ruler and people. But the steps were hesitant, and the idea was dimly perceived. It remained for Bodin, in those same circumstances, to carry the development farther. His intention in doing so was partly to refute the thesis of the Huguenot 'monarchomachs'.[55] He challenged them, again partly, on their chosen ground, arguing by reference to historical materials and to considerations of natural law. Major questions from earlier debates figured afresh in his analysis: the nature of legislative authority, the relation of magisterial offices to royal power, the origins and ends of political society, the significance for that society of property rights and contractual undertakings. But in his *Six livres de la République* the focus of Bodin's arguments differed radically from that of his predecessors', as did his utilisation of sources upon which they had drawn. When he turned, as he did, to Scripture, it was rarely to the New Testament[56] in order to assess political authority on the basis of Pauline teaching.[57] When he deployed his academic knowledge and practical experience of jurisprudence,[58] it was seldom in order to interpret rulership in terms of precise analogy with positions such as the guardian's in Roman law.[59] Representation as a metaphysical concept in respect of the 'body politic', or even logical distinctions between office and person,[60] found relatively little place in Bodin's thesis, for all his philosophical expertise. That expertise, however, was essential to his thesis. The thesis sprang from a new marriage of philosophical concepts with examples from ancient and recent history. Even so, that marriage was attended by traditions of thought whose fruitfulness was far from exhausted.

In the opening chapter of the *Six livres* there were signs that Bodin might intend to imitate the Greek masters, in describing the perfect *république*, in identifying its 'happiness' with the happiness of the individual, in urging him to rise by 'contemplation' towards knowledge of the world's 'melodious harmony', the unity of God, and the significance of all of this for men's well-being.[61] But, while that chapter showed the importance of Plato and Aristotle for Bodin's thought, it also announced that he had no intention of simply following their lead. His *Six livres*, as its author claimed, were to examine political actualities as closely as possible.[62] He would approach his task by stating at the outset his definition of his subject, and would then consider each of that definition's component parts.[63] This method of organising a literary composition,[64] allegedly of more practical use than the Aristotelian logic of the university schools, was certainly less rigorous than the latter. Yet Bodin neither followed the method scrupulously nor eschewed the rules of formal logic, when it suited him to apply them.[65] Nevertheless, the approach enabled him to make at once his major contribution to political thought.

The first sentence of the opening chapter declared: 'A *république* is a lawful government of many households or families and of what belongs to them in common, with sovereign power.' The definition had six parts: many families; things in common; government; legality; power; and sovereignty.[66] These parts were distinguishable from each other, but no combination that did not include them all was enough to constitute a *république* in Bodin's sense.[67] A well-managed family – husband, wife, children and servants – might be 'the true model for a *république*'; but the *république* as such was not simply the sum of the families associated with it. While each family had its 'proper goods' or private property, there were also things 'which are either common or public or both together' – markets and thoroughfares, laws, lands and treasure. Without things 'public or common' the *république* could not be; yet 'nothing can be public where nothing is private', and so to seek to make everything common would be to destroy the *république*. Its government should, accordingly, safeguard both forms of property. But that government, in turn, was not the *république* itself: 'the state of a *république*', Bodin repeatedly declared, 'is different from its government and administration'.[68]

By Bodin's reckoning, 'the state of a *république*' could take any one of only three forms. But before examining these he must deal with the remaining parts of his definition. Already the method was breaking down: there were excursions upon slavery and observations upon sovereignty before the famous eighth chapter that defined the latter was reached. Since, in that chapter, sovereignty itself was defined as 'absolute and perpetual power',[69] by adopting the phrase 'sovereign power' in preference to 'sovereignty' for his carefully worded opening definition Bodin would appear to have courted tautology. Further, since the 'first mark' of sovereignty was 'the power to give law',[70] the distinction initially drawn between legality and sovereignty might also seem otiose. But in Bodin's mind both power and law were distinguishable from sovereignty as such. Beyond the 'power and authority to judge or to command' that were proper to sovereignty and combined the *jurisdictio* and *imperium* long since discussed by the postglossators,[71] power had to do with force or coercion. Before arriving at his definition of sovereign power, he proposed coercive power in explanation of how and why *républiques* had originally taken shape: 'reason and the light of nature lead us to believe that force and violence gave to *républiques* their source and origin'.[72] Force in relation to the *république* was prior to sovereignty, and continued separable from it.[73] For, although the 'second mark' of sovereignty was the right to declare war and peace, sovereign power had often given way to force. 'In matters of state', Bodin pronounced, 'it can be taken as an unquestionable rule that he who is master of the armed forces is master of the state.'[74] Sovereign power might lack coercive means, and the consequences of such a lack were likely to be disastrous. So much was apparent in the France of Bodin's own day; and in allotting to

power a distinct place in his definition of the *république* he took
account of that.

As for law, the law-giving 'mark' of sovereignty was again not
equivalent to law as such. That mark was described in seemingly
comprehensive terms: laws were given by the sovereign to 'all [his
subjects] in general and to each of them in particular', and 'without
their consent'. Moreover, laws so given were simply what the
sovereign willed and commanded. They did not bind him; nor was he
bound by laws given by his predecessors. Yet law remained distinguishable from sovereignty, as the definition had indicated. There
were other law-giving agencies: although a magistrate was no sovereign, he might also 'give law', if only to persons 'within the compass of
his jurisdiction'. Further, the sovereign source of laws for each and all
was emphatically not the source of all law. The sovereign power had its
essential place within a system that also comprised 'the laws of God
and of nature' and of nations. Although that power might abrogate the
last of these, divine and natural laws were universally binding. 'Divine
justice', 'natural reason', were the guarantors of universal order and
the yardstick against which the sovereign's commands might reasonably be measured. Owing to them, it was not lawful for the sovereign to
take 'any private man's goods'. Owing to them, too, a sovereign must
honour contracts voluntarily agreed with subjects or with strangers.[75]
The first of these limitations was to condition Bodin's account of the
sovereign's power to levy taxes.[76] The second occasioned him no
embarrassment. Laws might sanction contracts; but there was no
question of following Huguenot theorists in identifying the one with
the other,[77] and still less of reducing sovereignty itself to a contractual
agreement.

Sovereignty, the final part of the *république*'s definition, was its
'absolute and perpetual power' in relation to the 'subject'.[78] Power,
therefore, could not be sovereign if it were held from another party, or
upon express conditions, or for a limited period of time. So much for
the relevance of contract. As for 'subjects', there were varieties of
them. Some might be vassals to lords other than their sovereign –
though the right to receive liege fealty and homage while pledging
them to none was another of the 'marks' of sovereignty. But, in
relation to his 'natural' sovereign, every lord or vassal, free citizen or
slave, was inescapably a subject.[79] Sovereignty had half a dozen further
'marks'. One 'certain sign' concerned the sovereign's power in relation
to magisterial offices. If the sovereign had *imperium*, the power to
command, so, too, did magistrates who were not sovereign. They had
it by virtue of their offices, which were governmental. As such, those
offices were properties of the *république* itself, as it had already been
defined. Further, the power of appointing to those offices was,

directly, or indirectly, a function of sovereignty alone. Two further marks had to do with jurisdiction over litigants and criminals. While such a jurisdiction was obviously exercised by numerous *officiers*, all subjects might appeal from them to their sovereign, and none could appeal beyond that highest power. In addition to that final appellate jurisdiction, only the sovereign could pardon persons whom the law had condemned. Two of the remaining three marks were the power to coin money, and to regulate weights and measures.[80] Both of these plainly concerned the *république*'s 'things in common'. But the last 'mark' was not so easily accommodated. It was the power of levying taxes upon the subjects, which again appertained to the sovereign alone.

Although Bodin's account of sovereignty has generally been given pride of place in assessments of his political thought,[81] such an emphasis is misleading. The concept of highest and absolute power was familiar enough to medieval publicists.[82] Contemporaries of Bodin's had emulated them in compiling lists of monarchs' prerogative powers. A decade before the *Six livres*'s appearance he himself claimed to have discussed such 'marks' of sovereignty in a still earlier work, with a title closely resembling that of a postglossatorial treatise,[83] a possible source for his chapters on sovereignty in the *Six livres* itself. The importance of sovereignty as he interpreted it lies far less in the originality or even the components of the concept itself than in its function in relation to the *république* that he defined. The *république* had its own parts. It was neither the sum of the members of the political community, nor embodied by their representatives or by the monarchical head; nor was it simply the 'condition' of any or all of them. While its parts, of which sovereignty was one, were distinguishable from each other, together they gave being to the *république* as a distinct entity. This was the epoch-making idea that Bodin formulated – in effect, the idea of the state, despite his own inconsistent use of the latter term.[84]

However, of all the parts of the state sovereignty was the most significant. Although its marks could be severally itemised, sovereignty itself was 'always indivisible' and 'wholly one'. The form of a state was determined by the location of its sovereignty. In a monarchy one person had it, in an aristocracy a minority of the citizens, in a 'popular state' a majority of them.[85] No other form of state was possible. Thinkers[86] who accepted the possibility of a 'mixed' form were utterly mistaken, owing chiefly to their failure to comprehend the meaning and the wholeness of sovereignty. In a polity where some of the marks of sovereignty appertained to some of the citizens, and others to others, none would have the highest power. There would therefore be no sovereignty, and so no state. Such a polity would continually experience 'the winds of civil sedition' and 'resort to arms', until sovereignty was 'wholly' with 'one prince', or a minority or 'the whole of the people'. Only then would there be a state, in one of its three possible forms. To insist upon this was not to deny that under any of the three forms there might with advantage be corporations or colleges of citizens, or assemblies of Estates. Corporations consisted of many families; they might have things in common, might discipline their members, might make ordinances and decrees. But corporations were specifically different from states, and were not a part of them. Corporations had no sovereign power: they existed 'under a sovereign power', and without its 'permission' they could not exist at all. As for assemblies of Estates, their advice and assistance were highly advantageous to the sovereign power in the exercise of the functions that were its marks. Their assistance might extend to considerable participation in government. But the form of a government was not the form of a state. A government might be popular while the state itself remained a monarchy or an aristocracy, according to the location of its sovereignty.[87] Conversely, if the assembly of the Estates had sovereignty, then the state was an aristocracy, regardless of how many or how few of its citizens participated in government; for the highest power would be in the hands of a minority of them.[88]

Yet the right of levying taxes, that ninth mark of sovereignty, depended, it seemed, even in a monarchical state upon the consent of the Estates.[89] Was not sovereignty therefore divisible after all, and Bodin trapped in self-contradiction? No such contradiction arose. In a state duly constituted in accordance with every part of its definition, law, sovereignty, family and the rest must each have its function and its place. The right of consent was rooted in natural law, for taxes were levied upon what was privately owned, in which law allowed the sovereign power no proprietary right.[90] If taxation gave rise to a difficulty in Bodin's argument, this was through his admission not of the right of consent, but of the sovereign's capacity to dispense with that right. It was dispensable in circumstances of 'necessity', when the sovereign had to act speedily, and without tarrying for consent, in order to safeguard the 'welfare' of the 'people', and so of the state.[91] The principle that *necessitas* warranted suspension of ordinary rights in the interests of the public welfare was abundantly familiar to medieval publicists.[92] In adopting that principle, Bodin simply identified the public welfare with the preservation of the state, the central pillar of his thought. The same principle underpinned, less firmly, his denial that magistrates might disobey the sovereign power even when they believed its command to contravene the law of nature.[93] Even though that law 'is more resplendent than the splendour of the sun', their belief might be erroneous. But, in any case, it was enough that magisterial disobedience would offer 'an example of rebellion to the subjects' and disrupt 'a well-ordered and constituted state'.[94]

The phrase 'well-ordered state' recurred throughout the *Six livres*. The adjective was essential to Bodin's thesis. He had identified the conditions necessary for the state to exist, and had affirmed that its preservation should take precedence over private rights, proprietary or otherwise, as well as private consciences. He had done so, throughout his work, with heavy reliance upon historical examples, having declared at the outset his intention of dealing with actual constitutions. From these it was clear that states were continually afflicted by changes and imperfections. Monarchies degenerated into tyrannies, aristocracies were vulnerable to faction and popular insurrection, 'popular states' were inherently unstable owing to the 'inconstancy and boldness of a populace'.[95] Why, then, should men submit themselves to the state and accept that to maintain it was to maintain the public welfare? Bodin's answer was dictated by his opinion of the needs of France. It was supplied, however, less by the inconvenient variables of past events than by the alleged constants of philosophy. All states were mutable, but each must ultimately be evaluated against the 'highest' form of state and its 'end'. The ideal form, orderly and harmonious, was a macrocosm of the individual and a microcosm of the universe. It was a royal, or lawful, monarchy with a government that was at once aristocratic and popular. In that form, governmental offices were given to all men, whether base-born or noble, according to their 'merits' and 'virtues', and yet 'with sufficient discretion for nobles to retain some advantage over the commoners'. While the proposition was backed by some rudimentary social psychology, it was founded upon an elaborate number mysticism. Aristocratic government functioned according to 'geometrical proportion'. Popular government operated by 'arithmetical proportion'. To combine them was to achieve 'harmonical proportion'[96] – as long as they were also combined with the lawful rule of one. That last condition was vital. France was a royal monarchy: and, at whatever risk of change towards tyranny, the monarch must not be disobeyed. In passages rich with metaphysical allusions, Bodin came to his conclusion on 'a most beautiful and harmonious form of state: for just as from unity depends the union of all numbers, which have neither being nor power but from it, so, too, is one sovereign prince necessary, from the power of whom all others depend'.[97]

Bodin's definition of the secular state promised to place political analysis upon a fresh footing. It will be seen from what we have examined earlier in this book how many of his arguments ran counter to socio-political attitudes that were widely held in the France of his day. And yet his defence of French monarchical rule amply exhibited principles and values rooted in well-established modes of thought. Moreover, the closing passages of the *Six livres*, linking neoplatonic notions of orderly dependence from the One with Platonic and

Aristotelian accounts of justice in mathematical terms,[98] rehearsed themes introduced in the work's opening chapter, with its observations upon the emanation of virtue from the sun, its implicit borrowings from Plato and its explicit strictures upon Aristotle.[99] These influences permeated the whole work. Extended portions of it amounted almost to a running debate with Aristotle, whose views Bodin repeatedly distorted, but to whose guidance he owed far more than he cared to acknowledge. He himself complained very soon that his critics misunderstood and distorted his own position. He had had, he claimed, no intention of assigning so much 'power to one man' as they pretended.[100] Yet in the event the originality of Bodin's position suffered less from the attacks of avowed opponents than from the support of royalist thinkers and propagandists who saw him as an ally. They seized upon his doctrine of legislative sovereignty – and yet persisted in describing the *république* as 'a kind of unified community . . . that makes, as it were, one body composed of many and divers members under one supreme power as under one head and one spirit'.[101] Post-Bodinian vindicators of royal authority continued, like his predecessors, to describe how in 'the head of the body politic', that 'civil animal', 'intelligence resides'; and, although the 'royal majesty' who 'commands as sovereign' was 'considered as God among men', the 'majesty' in question still appertained to the public as distinct from the private 'person' of the ruler.[102] Meanwhile, counter-theorists continued to maintain that the *corpus mysticum reipublicae* consisted of the Estates as well as the monarch, that the kingdom's laws were essentially contractual, and that in the communites of the realm lay the true origins of France's customs – customs that guaranteed not only private rights of property, but also the jurisdictions possessed and exercised by feudal lords.[103]

But, although Bodin's contribution did not transform the terms of French political theoretical debate, the idea of the state amplified those terms and provided a fresh focus for subsequent attempts at synthesis. The most significant of those attempts was stimulated by developments concerning the long-standing and unresolved question of the relation between authority and property. It was the work of the Parisian advocate and jurist Charles Loyseau, who in the 1590s published distinguished commentaries upon questions of ownership and obligation, and in the following decade added to these a set of major political treatises. Loyseau wrote them amid conditions very different from those that had troubled Bodin. France was now at peace: unlike his predecessors, the king had succeeded in asserting force over his enemies and in settling the kingdom with treaties and laws.[104] But Henry IV also disposed of offices of government with scant regard for other than financial considerations. To sell such offices,

Bodin had exclaimed, was to 'sell the state', of which government was a part, and to admit 'all vices and filth'.[105] Yet the first of the Bourbons institutionalised the practice,[106] and so gave Loyseau an immediate motive for composing his triad of treatises.[107] He was also concerned to discredit the administration of justice by petty feudal lords, of whose 'wrong-doing' he claimed to have had years of experience at first hand.[108] Thus impelled, he applied himself to fundamental political issues; and, drawing upon his wealth of legal and philosophical learning, he constructed a thesis that was abstruse, discursive, but ultimately as coherent as Bodin's own.[109]

Throughout his three treatises Loyseau exhibited a sense of history that enabled him not only to find relevance in Roman and medieval institutions for understanding those of contemporary France, but also to emphasise how times and conditions had changed, so that 'it is an abuse always to ascribe the ways of Rome to our own'.[110] All three incorporated arguments from Scripture, from classical axiom, from grammar, philology or mere semantics,[111] such as so richly characterised humanist scholarship. Even so, Loyseau repeatedly insisted that his was the work not of a historian nor of a humanist, but of a 'jurisconsult', inspired by those jurisconsults of republican and imperial Rome who were accustomed to 'philosophise on the law'.[112] Further, for all his expertise as a civilian he displayed throughout his treatises a wide-ranging familiarity with the *coutumes* and their commentators, true to his own precept that 'Roman law must be linked with our own'.[113] But what gave coherence to his arguments and his materials was the method that he adopted and the philosophies to which he subscribed. Unlike Bodin's, Loyseau's thesis was constructed on the basis of formal logical rules. Those rules, in his case, were predominantly Aristotelian; and a combination of Aristotelian and neoplatonic metaphysical and ethical concepts informed his interpretation of the French monarchical state.

Logic dictated that he begin by placing the topics that concerned him in their correct *category*. These topics furnished the titles of his three treatises: Seigneurie, Office and Order. All three were assigned to the category of 'quality'. It followed that each had in some way to be present in a subject, owing to Aristotle's rule that only members of the category of 'substance' could 'exist independently'.[114] Further, the *genus* of all three was 'dignity', as distinct from the genus of 'condition'. The latter limited a man, as when he was a minor. The former elevated him, making him 'more worthy' of respect by reason of the 'honourable quality' that it attached to him.[115] The genus was *divided* in turn, by the *difference* of 'power'. Power did not attach to 'simple dignities' – forenames, descriptive titles, honorary positions. It did attach to 'true Orders, Offices or Seigneuries'. But within their genus each of these was again differentiated from the other two, and constituted a *species*. So Loyseau arrived at his *definition* in respect of each. Seigneurie was 'Dignity with power in property'; Office was 'Dignity with public function'; and Order was 'Dignity with aptitude for public power'.[116]

In the case of Seigneurie, further division was called for, owing to the presence of 'property' in the definition. Property might be either a right, or the object of that right. Seigneurie, accordingly, could signify either *'in abstracto* every right of property, or proprietary power, that one has in some thing', or *'in concreto* a seigneurial land'. Seigneurie *in abstracto* had 'two species, namely public and private seigneurie'. The latter applied only to lands and not to persons, for there were no slaves in France.[117] There were, however, two 'degrees' of it: the familiar 'direct' and 'useful' seigneuries of late-medieval jurisprudence.[118] But public seigneurie applied to persons. It signified 'public command or power', which 'consists in justice'. Here, again, there were two 'degrees'. One was called 'suzerainty'; and among those who appeared to enjoy it were the petty seigneurs whom Loyseau so heartily disparaged, and whose alleged right to administer justice – a right that impeded its efficient administration by royal agents – he was determined to disprove. The other degree of public power was called 'sovereignty'; and sovereignty remained 'inseparably with the state'.[119]

Loyseau, then, defined sovereignty in terms of proprietary right in public power over persons. Beyond this, he was largely content to follow Bodin's account of the 'marks' of sovereignty and the significance of divine and natural law in relation to that power. But what of the state? Here the concept of seigneurie *in concreto* came into play. Land was where seigneurial power resided, the material object in which that abstraction was present. In the case of suzerainty the land in question was a territorial fief. By no means every fief was a seigneurie – a point of great importance for Loyseau, in his determination to disqualify the petty seigneurs. A fief was seigneurial only when public power, or justice, appertained to it. Given this, 'the fief is the matter and justice is the form, which animates and gives being to the body of the seigneurie'. In the case of sovereignty, the requisite land was the territory of the state. Without sovereign power that territory was inert matter: 'sovereignty is the form which gives being to the state'. Yet proprietary right was also part of the definition. And so, just as 'every seigneurie is communicated to the possessors' of seigneurial fiefs, so in a monarchy sovereignty 'appertains to the person of the monarch, who in consequence is called sovereign or seigneurial prince'. Alternatively, in a 'democracy' sovereignty appertained to 'all the people', and in an aristocracy to some of them. In monarchy, however, it 'shines more perfectly' than in the other two; and Loyseau's concern in his treatises was solely with 'our monarchical France'.[120]

Were France's monarchs with their sovereignty thus no more than superior seigneurs? Loyseau had no intention of leaving his argument there. What seigneurs had was a proprietary right in the public power that attached to their fiefs. Thereby, the fruits of justice – fines, confiscations and the like – certainly accrued to them. Thereby, too, they could appoint '*officiers* and public persons' to administer justice, with power even to condemn men to death. But the rights of seigneur *qua* seigneur did not include the function of actually administering justice.[121] This was abundantly clear from the specific difference between Seigneurie and Office. It was office, not seigneurie, that was 'Dignity with public function'. Conversely, the same difference indicated clearly enough that offices as such had nothing to do with property. By what right, then, were offices in France bought and sold? Loyseau subjected the question to an extended technical examination.[122] There were feudal and domainal offices which were associated with material 'things', consequently were 'at least reckonable' as things themselves, and so might reasonably be objects of purchase and succession. But almost every other office was 'an accident or quality inherent to the person'. No amount of division by jurisconsults nor of legislation by monarchs could endow such offices with a material nature. They were parts of the public power that appertained to the state. To alienate them was 'to deprive the state of what is inseparable from it, and without which the state cannot exist'. The monarch should therefore take their 'entire disposition' into his own hands.[123] So much, at least in principle, for the vexed question of venality of offices. And yet the question still remained whether the monarch as seigneur was himself debarred from public function.

The answer lay, well prepared, to hand. France's ruler was at once a sovereign and seigneurial prince, and an *officier*. And this 'best-established monarchy that ever was' in fact was 'rather an office than a seigneurie'.[124] The debates of medieval theorists yielded plenty of grist to that mill. Was not the monarch's office analogous to the office of a legal guardian, established 'for the benefit of the people entrusted to one's care'?[125] Was not the monarch the '*officier* of God', 'minister Dei' in the Pauline phrase that Loyseau explicitly invoked? Pauline teaching also implicitly underpinned Loyseau's contention that the people were 'bound by divine and human law entirely to obey' their ruler.[126] But the guiding inspiration of his thought remained pre-Christian. As with his sixteenth-century predecessors, neoplatonic influences powerfully informed some of his leading arguments. The 'offices' of 'government, justice and finance . . . these three functions, or divers powers, are the three fleurons of the crown, or the three lilies of the arms of France', he pronounced; and the king, from whom the 'mystic energy and signal power . . . proceeds' had 'alone in his kingdom these three functions combined in his person, and this in all sovereignty'.[127] Yet Loyseau's thought sprang ultimately from the same source as had given him his method. It sprang from an Aristotelian vision of individual and political *télos* in terms of activity, by men performing their functions well, realising their capacities in virtuous action.[128] Seigneurs might be allowed a proprietorship of public power, but that power must be exercised by others than they. Kings were themselves *officiers*. And, although there was still a sense in which their *officiers* in turn 'represent the person of the prince', just as the ruler 'represents' the deity, kings 'perform the principal exercise of their power themselves and in their own persons; and Bodin proves that both conscience and the state oblige them to do it'.[129]

The king of France, then, had as seigneur the property and as *officier* the use of public power that by virtue of sovereignty the state communicated to him. His authority in the public sphere was thereby supreme, over his subjects, over their customs which had legal force only by his approval: the king alone could make 'absolute and immutable laws'.[130] But what, finally, of Order, the third species of 'dignity' in Loyseau's tripartite schema? Earlier commentators had dilated upon the relation between order and function, and had even ascribed to persons of noble quality the function of 'representing' France itself.[131] Once more Loyseau turned for guidance to the propositions of Aristotelian metaphysics, where 'function' was linked with the concepts of 'actuality' and 'potential', or 'capacity'.[132] Elaborating, as with Seigneurie, upon his preliminary definition, he declared Order to be 'an honourable quality which appertains in the same way and with the same name to a number of persons; not in itself attributing to them any public power, but through the rank that it gives them it endows them with a particular aptitude or capacity to attain either to office or to seigneurie'. How was a particular capacity to be discerned? In respect of office, the indications varied from case to case. An advocate, such as Loyseau himself, must prove his capacity by formal graduation in civil and canon law.[133] But, whatever the proof, potential for office could be actualised only by the actual *officier* who was the monarch: 'no one can call himself a king's *officier* unless he has letters of provision from his Majesty', who should accordingly be 'informed' of the candidate's capacity: for 'merit' in 'the highest bidder' in venal terms could certainly not be assumed.[134] There were, however, offices other than royal ones. Holders of public seigneurie ought to be noble. Because their dignity 'resides formally in land' it might seem to be 'communicated' from the fief to the holder. But this was not so. Fiefs had no 'power to ennoble their possessor': they were simply 'assigned to

persons already noble', just as the person to whom the state communicated sovereignty was himself already royal. And it was Loyseau's
'infallible rule' that 'no one other than the king can confer nobility'. He
could do so in three ways: 'either by express letters of ennoblement, or
by conferment of great offices, or by investiture of fiefs of dignity. And
then, of course, it is not the money tendered to obtain letters of
ennoblement, nor yet the office, nor the fief of dignity that ennobles,
but the king by his sovereign power'.[135] As for petty seigneuries held by
commoners, it was an error to suppose that their holders 'bore the right
to justice'. They had no such right: those holders lacked the capacity
for public power, and all such pretended 'landed justices' ought to be
abolished altogether.[136]

The recommendation was nothing new. Du Moulin, and others after
him, had long since urged abrogation of seigneurial jurisdictions.[137] At
this juncture of his thesis, as at others throughout his treatises,
Loyseau's position rested upon long-standing arguments and materials. Still older ones supplied him with his principal points of reference. To discuss monarchy as an office, the relation between power
and its holders in terms of property rights, or human society as a
hierarchy of orders was scarcely to discover fresh grounds for political
debate.[138] Bodin's thesis of the state as a distinct entity had promised to
place such debate upon a fresh footing. Loyseau responded positively
to that thesis. Under God, the state was the source of the ruler's
authority, and its territory the concrete foundation of the sovereignty
that was exclusively his. Yet even that territorial dimension was
suggested by considerations of a feudal kind; and Loyseau accommodated the idea of the state only in so far as he could assimilate it to older
traditions of thought.

Chief among them was the Aristotelian philosophical tradition. Like
clever pupils taking issue with their mentor, sixteenth-century intellec-
tuals might revel in disputing points with Aristotle and in questing after
other philosophical masters. But Aristotelianism was not dislodged
from its central place in educational curricula.[139] For Loyseau's readers, schooled in the same intellectual modes as was he, the rules that he
observed and the concepts that informed his thesis stamped it with the
hallmark of scientific demonstration. That thesis anchored the idea of
the state more firmly to the principle of monarchical power than, by his
own account, the author of the idea had intended. Moreover, it did so
at the very time when another of the traditions that governed both
Bodin's and Loyseau's thought was being seriously modified. In 1583
there appeared a new edition of the *Corpus Iuris Civilis*. Its editor,
father of the historiographer Godefroy,[140] discarded the glossatorial
apparatus that earlier editions had borne.[141] Thereby he discarded a
key to the interpretation of the element of 'law' in Bodin's definition of

the state. Trained, as was Loyseau, in civilian jurisprudence, Bodin had hedged sovereign power about with divine justice and natural reason, or natural law. While the 'natural laws' of medieval jurisprudence might be variously interpreted, they none the less pointed to specific rights, above all in the private sphere. Deprived of such jurisprudential reference, the concept of natural reason stood at the opening of the seventeenth century in danger of reduction to nebulous considerations of ethics and morality. And, as the developments of that century would show, the morality of private dealings had little to do with the reason of a state that was exemplified by an absolute monarch, a sovereignty that was communicated only to him, and a governmental and social order that he alone could actualise.

Epilogue

In the first summer of the seventeenth century French armies were marching once more towards Italy, on territory that commanded the approaches to the Alpine passes. They occupied the marquisate of Saluzzo, lying in the heart of the duchy of Savoy and admirably situated as a place for assembling troops and preparing them to descend upon Milan. But the objectives of Henry IV's campaign were very different from those that had drawn Charles VIII southwards in 1494, and his successors in his wake. Despite the justice of French claims to Saluzzo, despite protests by the king's lieutenant-general in the Dauphiné that the outcome of his campaign was tantamount to abandoning Italy and his prospective allies there to Habsburg domination, the marquisate was exchanged for a group of territories lying on the Rhône to the east of Lyon. The acquisitions strengthened France's eastern frontier. They enabled the French to cut at will Spain's most convenient overland route from northern Italy to the Netherlands. In King Henry's calculations, crusading ideals such as had inspired Charles VIII occupied no place; and even questions of legitimate title were secondary to hard-headed strategic considerations assessed in relation to the interests and the needs of the territorial state.

Frontier-extension and frontier-consolidation to east and north were major themes of France's seventeenth-century history. Within the kingdom they were accompanied by a strengthening of the apparatus of central monarchical rule. While the structure of the royal councils remained remarkably fluid, the king's principal advisers now took the form of ministers who headed specific departments of state: foreign affairs, finance and war. The political role of the sovereign courts was severely restricted, and with it their capacity to obstruct royal legislative acts. Personal experience in the work of those courts remained an important qualification for men pursuing careers that they hoped would culminate in entry to the deliberations of the select and supreme *conseil d'en haut*. But such career-prospects could rarely be entertained other than by members of families already established among the administrative – and especially the judicial – élite. From the ranks of the latter the king commissioned his key agents for enforcing his policies in the realm at large. Like Huguenot fears for their own hard-won immunities, the Huguenot diagnosis of France's government was largely confirmed. Lawyers dominated its workings, to the exclusion of the Estates-General which assembled only once in the entire century. The *intendants*, committed instruments of direct rule, became a permanent feature of provincial administration, displacing in importance the *gouverneurs*. They presided over the *bureaux des finances* and carried taxation to unprecedented heights. They invaded municipal government, proposed modifications of municipal constitutions, and prepared the way for the final submission of French towns to unambiguous royal tutelage. They examined titles to nobility, translating into practice the principle that such dignities derived only from the king. Through them, together with the armies whose administration he put also in their charge, the monarch seemed equipped to ride roughshod over all impediments to his will that might rest upon grounds of ancient or ordained liberties enjoyed by members of the body politic, or even private rights.

Yet the France of the *ancien régime* remained thick with inert obstacles to effective centralised rule. The kingdom preserved as if in aspic its multi-layered administrative system, heavy with venal offices and dense with patronage. Its judicial system still defied attempts at legal unification. Despite Loyseau's strictures, seigneurial justice persisted. Despite Colbert's mercantilist endeavours, agricultural production continued to stagnate, while commercial and manufacturing ventures succumbed to the remorseless imperatives of war finance and investors' unshakeable preference for offices and land. For all the interventionist and regulatory zeal of royal agents, governmental power continued in great measure to be diffused among a multiplicity of entrenched élites, jealous of their status and resistant to reform. From time to time the obstacles became dynamic. Less inclined than formerly to regard themselves as representatives of local communities, members of élites none the less encouraged violent hostility towards intruders whose activities on the ruler's behalf trespassed upon their own concerns. Revolts flared in every decade of Louis XIII's and Louis XIV's reigns. They ranged from noble conspiracies to insurgencies triggered by *parlementaires* to the popular uprisings of *croquants* and *nu-pieds, ormistes, torrébens* and *camisards*. While their causes varied, it was tax-increases and tax-innovations above all else that drove peasant communities repeatedly to desperate courses. But neither they nor more sophisticated rebels proved able to build upon arguments for resistance and constitutionalism such as sixteenth-century French theorists had devised. Those theorists found ingenious seventeenth-century successors in England, the Netherlands, the German empire. They found remarkably few in France itself where the will seemed lacking to formulate political opposition in terms other than the defence of sectional interests or the alleged misdeeds of particular royal servants.

Yet the very frequency of revolts played into the hands of monarchist propagandists.[1] It vindicated assumptions that men were naturally incapable of governing their appetites without the coercive presence of a strong restraining power. For this reason, it could be argued, they had originally surrendered their freedom to a sovereign ruler. In that case the surrender was absolute: it was an act neither of delegation nor of contract. Alternatively, the ruler was simply appointed by a merciful God to ensure that divine reason prevail in the ordering of human affairs. The commands of 'the prince who represents Him' were inherently just and again required absolute obedience. Their justice was not to be evaluated by reference to canons that men ought to observe in their private dealings. There was 'one conscience for affairs of state and another for personal matters'; and, while the latter was expressed in the rules of ordinary justice, the former dictated that 'the safety of the state is the supreme law'. The aphorism modified significantly a time-honoured maxim: *salus populi suprema lex*. It drew attention to an entity distinct from the people, as well as from God, with an overriding interest of its own. This was the interest that the monarch was bound to serve. He was bound by 'the promise made by the sovereign to the state when he assumed direction of it' – a promise that transcended all other obligations. Under God, the state was the source of the ruler's authority, and its interest the justification of the commands that he pronounced. And in the last resort all of his subjects must be compelled – if they would not do so voluntarily – to set aside qualms of private conscience or considerations of personal well-being, in order that the interest of the state be maintained.

Notes

INTRODUCTION

1 On the concept of the king's 'natural' and 'politic' persons, see E. Kantorowicz, *The King's Two Bodies: A Study in Medieval Political Theology* (Princeton, NJ, 1957).

2 Claude de Seyssel, *La Monarchie de France*, ed. J. Poujol (Paris, 1961), p. 115.

3 H. Lapeyre, *Les Monarchies européennes au XVIe siècle: les relations internationales* (Paris, 1967), pp. 59, 74; G. R. Elton (ed.), *The New Cambridge Modern History*, Vol. 2, *The Reformation, 1520–59* (Cambridge, 1958), p. 439.

4 J. H. Shennan, *The Origins of the Modern European State, 1450–1725* (London, 1974), p. 76; H. C. Dowdall, 'The word "state"', *The Law Quarterly Review*, vol. 39 (1923), p. 101; cf. also Q. Skinner, *The Foundations of Modern Political Thought*, Vol. 2 (Cambridge, 1978), p. 353.

5 B. Guenée, *L'Occident aux XIVe et XVe siècles: les États* (Paris, 1971), pp. 63, 79; H. Mitteis, *The State in the Middle Ages* (Oxford, 1975), pp. 5–6; P. Imbart de La Tour, *Les Origines de la Réforme*, Vol. 1 (Paris, 1948), pp. 4–5.

6 See, for instance, M. Yardeni, *La Conscience nationale en France pendant les guerres de religion (1559–1598)* (Paris, 1971). The importance of language as a component of 'national consciousness' is widely recognised. There is, of course, ample evidence that in early-modern France, despite royal legislation that only the 'langage maternel françois' be used in formal transactions, linguistic uniformity was very far from being achieved; and even the significance of that legislation is debatable (see below, p. 43, n. 68). In general, the efforts of legislators, administrators and scholars ensured that Parisian French should monopolise writings in the vernacular; but even by the end of the sixteenth century 'French was as yet spoken only by a tiny minority in the south' (P. Rickard, *A History of the French Language* (London, 1974), p. 88).

7 Thus, claims that the state emerged after the nation imply that the former was in some way a consequence of spontaneous 'national' aspirations; while claims that the state was prior to the nation imply that the latter was in some way created by an exercise of political power. See V. G. Kiernan, 'State and nation in western Europe', *Past & Present*, no. 31 (1965), pp. 20–38; also Yardeni, *Conscience nationale*, pp. 8, 331–2, for some tendentious intermingling of these terms.

8 F. Chabod, 'Y-a-t-il un état de la Renaissance?', *Actes du Colloque sur la Renaissance organisé par la Société d'Histoire Moderne* (Paris, 1958), p. 68; H. G. Koenigsberger, 'Dominium regale or dominium politicum et regale?', *Der moderne Parlamentarismus und seine Grundlagen in der ständischen Repräsentation*, ed. K. Bosl (Berlin, 1977), p. 51, citing N. Elias, *Über den Prozess der Zivilisation*, Vol. 2.

9 As the sixteenth-century rise in price-levels continues to be known: see E. E. Rich and C. H. Wilson (eds), *The Cambridge Economic History of Europe*, Vol. 4, *The Economy of Expanding Europe in the 16th and 17th centuries* (Cambridge, 1967), p. 401.

10 H. G. Koenigsberger, 'The organisation of revolutionary parties in France and the Netherlands during the sixteenth century', *Journal of Modern History*, Vol. 27 (1955), pp. 335–51.

11 J. H. M. Salmon, *Society in Crisis: France in the Sixteenth Century* (London, 1975).

12 The concept derives from Durkheim's famous account of *conscience collective*: see *The Division of Labour in Society* (Glencoe, Ill., 1933), pp. 79 ff. Modern

sociologists and historians have fought shy of such a concept and have devised numerous, and narrower, alternatives. But, for the continuing relevance of the Durkheimian approach, see, for instance, the definition of 'culture' proposed by P. Burke, *Popular Culture in Early Modern Europe* (London, 1978), p. xi.

13 On this characteristic of popular beliefs, see especially R. Muchembled, *Culture populaire et culture des élites* (Paris, 1978), pp. 83–4.

CHAPTER 1

1 F. Guicciardini, *Storia d'Italia* (Bari, 1967), I, ix (p. 68); J. de La Pilorgerie, *Campagne et bulletins de la grande armée d'Italie, commandée par Charles VIII* (Paris, 1866), p. 67; P. de Commynes, *Mémoires*, ed. B. de Mandrot (Paris, 1901), Vol. 2 (1477–98), p. 130.

2 L. von Ranke, *History of the Latin and Teutonic Nations, 1494 to 1514*, trans. G. R. Dennis (London, 1909), p. 387; J. Michelet, *Histoire de France* (Paris, 1879), Vol. 9, pp. 127, 180, and Vol. 12, p. 373.

3 See especially G. P. Gooch, *History and Historians in the Nineteenth Century* (London, 1928); B. Guenée, 'L'histoire de l'état en France à la fin du Moyen Age, vue par les historiens français depuis cent ans', *Revue historique*, Vol. 232 (1964), pp. 331–60; D. Knowles, *Great Historical Enterprises* (London, 1963); G. Monod, 'Du progrès des études historiques en France depuis le XVIᵉ siècle', *Revue historique*, Vol. 1 (1876), pp. 5–38.

4 R. Doucet, *Les Institutions de la France au XVIᵉ siècle* (Paris, 1948), Vol. 1, p. 8; P. Goubert, 'Registres paroissiaux et démographie dans la France du XVIᵉ siècle', *Annales de démographie historique* (1965), p. 47; E. Eisenstein, 'The advent of printing and the problem of the Renaissance', *Past & Present*, no. 45 (1969), p. 19; H. Hauser, *Les Sources de l'histoire de France: XVIᵉ siècle (1494–1610)*, 4 vols (Paris, 1906–15).

5 Lapeyre, *Monarchies européennes*, p. 23; F. Braudel, *Écrits sur l'histoire* (Paris, 1969), p. 46; L. Febvre, *Combats pour l'histoire* (Paris, 1953), pp. 64, 208; R. Mandrou, *Introduction à la France moderne: essai psychologique et historique, 1500–1640* (Paris, 1961).

6 L. Febvre, *A New Kind of History*, ed. P. Burke (London, 1973), p. 88; T. Stoianovich, *French Historical Method: the 'Annales' Paradigm* (London, 1976); M. Bloch, 'La France au XIIIᵉ siècle', *Annales d'histoire économique et sociale*, vol. 6 (1934), p. 307; P. Chaunu, 'L'état', in *Histoire Économique et sociale de la France*, ed. F. Braudel and E. Labrousse, Vol. 1 (Paris, 1977), pt 1, pp. 11–12.

7 See L. Romier, *Le Royaume de Catherine de Médicis*, Vol. 1 (Paris, 1922), p. ix.

8 Quoted in D. Hay, 'History and historians in France and England during the fifteenth century', *Bulletin of the Institute of Historical Research*, Vol. 35 (1962), p. 114; D. Hay, *Annalists and Historians* (London, 1977); P. S. Lewis, 'War propaganda and historiography in fifteenth-century France and England', *Transactions of the Royal Historical Society*, ser. 5, vol. 15 (1965), p. 20; J. Dufournet, *La Destruction des mythes dans les mémoires de Philippe de Commynes* (Geneva, 1966), pp. 14–21; B. Guenée, 'Histories, annales, chroniques: essai sur les genres historiques au Moyen Age', *Annales: Économies, Sociétés, Civilisations*, vol. 28 (1973), p. 1013.

9 W. Bouwsma. 'The politics of Commynes', *Journal of Modern History*, vol. 23 (1951), pp. 315–28; Commynes, *Mémoires*, Vol. 2, p. 130; Cicero, *De Oratore*, II, xv, 63. On the classical origins of 'exemplar' history see G. H. Nadel, 'Philosophy of history before historicism', *History and Theory*, Vol. 3 (1963–4), pp. 291–315.

10 N. Machiavelli, *The Discourses* (New York, 1950), chs vi (p. 129) and xxix (p. 383); M. de Montaigne, *Essais*, ed. M. Rat, 3 vols (Paris, 1958), Vol. 1, pp. 312–19 ('Of

the uncertainty of our judgement'); B. de Monluc, *Commentaires, 1521–76*, ed. P. Courteault (Paris, 1964), p. 44; Guicciardini, *Storia d'Italia*, I, xiv (pp. 83–4).

11 J. du Tillet, *Recueil des Roys de France, leur couronne et maison* (Paris, 1580), sig. Aij; P. Melanchthon, *Chronicon Carionis*, in *Corpus Reformatorum*, ed. C. G. Bertschneider, Vol. 12 (Halle, 1844), col. 712 (the *Chronicon Carionis*, a universal chronicle originally compiled by the German mathematician and astrologer John Carion, was completely reworked by Melanchthon, who was therefore, in effect, its author: ibid., pp. 707 ff.); Henri (alias Lancelot) Voisin de La Popelinière, *Histoire de France depuis l'an 1550 jusques à ce temps*, Vol. 2 (Paris, 1581), first six unnumbered pages.

12 F. Baudouin, *De Institutione historiae universae*, quoted in D. R. Kelley, *Foundations of Modern Historical Scholarship: Language, Law and History in the French Renaissance* (London, 1970), p. 131, n. 30.

13 Quoted in J. R. Hale (ed.), *Guicciardini: History of Italy and History of Florence* (London, 1964), p. xxiv; B. de Girard, seigneur du Haillan, *L'Histoire de France* (Paris, 1576), sigs *ij^{vo}–iij^{vo}

14 La Popelinière, *L'Idée de l'histoire accomplie*, in *L'Histoire des histoires* (Paris, 1599), p. 103.

15 ibid. On 'qualities of feeling' (La Popelinière's term is 'affections'), cf. Aristotle, *Categories*, 9^b 35; Cicero, *De Inventione*, I, xxiv, 35–xxv, 36; Cicero, *Academica*, I, vi, 27–8.

16 Arguably, what they were schooled in was the Thomist version of Aristotelian causation theory (cf. L. W. B. Brockliss, 'Philosophy teaching in France, 1600–1740', *History of Universities*, vol. 1 (1981), p. 139; but this scarcely affects the point at issue here.

17 Aristotle, *Categories*, 2^a 11–34.

18 Du Haillan, *Histoire*, sig. *v^{ro}; J.-A. de Thou, *Historiarum sui temporis* (London, 1973), Vol. 7, pt 1, ff. 16, 7.

19 La Popelinière, *L'Idée*, p. 30; du Haillan, *Histoire*, sig. *iij^{ro}. On de Serres, see especially C. Vivanti, *Lotta politica e pace religiosa in Francia fra cinque e seicento* (Turin, 1963), pp. 249–53.

20 C. Loyseau, *Cinq livres du droit des offices*, in *Les Oeuvres de Maistre Charles Loyseau* (Lyon, 1701), I, i, 29–30; Plato, *The Republic*, s. 427; Aristotle, *Politics*, 1280^b 6 (classical philosophical influences upon contemporary political thought are illustrated more fully below, chapter 6); J. de Serres, *A General Inventorie of the History of France*, trans. E. Grimeston (London, 1607), sig. A1.

21 Plato, *The Laws*, ss. 738, etc.

22 De Thou, *Historiarum*, Vol. 1, f. 17.

23 The foregoing quotations from Budé and from Pasquier will be found in Kelley, *Foundations*, pp. 68, 75, 57, 284.

24 Hotman, *Antitribonian*, quoted in J. Franklin, *Jean Bodin and the Sixteenth-Century Revolution in the Methodology of Law and History* (New York, 1963), p. 148; Hotman, *Francogallia*, ed. R. E. Giesey and J. H. M. Salmon (Cambridge, 1972), p. 148, see also pp. 398–405; R. E. Giesey, 'When and how Hotman wrote the Francogallia', *Bibliothèque d'humanisme et Renaissance*, vol. 29 (1967), pp. 606–7, n. 1.

25 E. Pasquier, *Les Recherches de la France*, in *Les Oeuvres d'Estienne Pasquier*, Vol. 1 (Amsterdam, 1723), cols 143, 45–6, 237.

26 Below, pp. 45–6 and chapter 5 *passim*.

27 Kelley, *Foundations*, pp. 245, 262; du Haillan, quoted in J. G. Espiner-Scott, *Claude Fauchet: sa vie, son œuvre* (Geneva, 1938), p. 69, n. 1; Le Caron, quoted in W. F. Church, *Constitutional Thought in Sixteenth-Century France: A Study in the Evolution of Ideas* (Cambridge, Mass., 1941), p. 200, n. 17; J. Bodin, *Les six livres de la République* (Paris, 1583), p. 575.

28 G. Huppert, *The Idea of Perfect History* (London, 1970), p. 149; Bodin, *Method for the Easy Comprehension of History*, trans. B. Reynolds (New York, 1966), p. 153.

29 Aristotle, *Rhetorica*, 1360ª 33, 1394ª 15.

30 Bodin, *République*, pp. 252, 4, 339.

31 ibid., pp. 574, 4; ibid., dedicatory epistle to Gui du Faur, *président* of the Paris *parlement*; ibid., p. 263 (where the stricture is levelled at Hotman as well as at Pasquier); ibid., pp. 675, cf. 690, 972, 264.

32 L. Febvre and H.-J. Martin, *L'Apparition du livre* (Paris, 1958), pp. 427, 430; Monluc, *Commentaires*, pp. 7, 821, 823; H. Aubépin, 'De l'influence de Du Moulin sur la législation française', *Revue critique de la jurisprudence*, vol. 3 (1853), pp. 622–3; Church, *Constitutional Thought*, pp. 272–302.

33 C. Vivanti, 'Paulus Emilius Gallis condidit historias?', *Annales ESC*, vol. 19 (1964), pp. 1117–24; Plato, *The Republic*, s. 382; F. Fossier, 'La charge d'historiographe du seizième au dix-neuvième siècle', *Revue historique*, vol. 258 (1977), p. 81.

34 F. Eudes de Mézeray, *Histoire de France depuis Faramond jusqu'au règne de Louis le Juste* (Paris, 1685), Vol. 1, 'Préface'; see also de Thou, *Historiarum*, Vol. 7, pt 8, f. 19; O. Ranum, *Artisans of Glory: Writers and Historical Thought in Seventeenth-Century France* (Chapel Hill, NC, 1980), pp. 197–232.

35 Knowles, *Great Historical Enterprises*, p. 55; H. F. Delaborde, 'Les Travaux de Dupuy', *Bibliothèque de l'École des Chartes*, vol. 58 (1897), pp. 126–54; C.-V. Langlois, *Manuel de bibliographie historique* (Paris, 1901–4; repr. 1968), pp. 271–2.

36 C.-L. de Montesquieu, *De l'esprit des lois*, 2 vols (Paris, 1973), xxxi, 2; quotations that follow at xi, 6; ii, 4; xix, 4.

37 Bodin, *République*, p. 430.

38 L. Althusser, *Montesquieu: la politique et l'histoire* (Paris, 1959), p. 47.

39 Aristotle, *Politics*, 1327ᵇ 20 ff., himself following Hippocrates; Bodin, *République*, pp. 547–666; Montesquieu, *Esprit des lois*, xix, 14; L. Febvre, *A Geographical Introduction to History* (London, 1925), esp. pp. 91–8.

40 P. Vidal de La Blache, *Tableau de la géographie de la France* (Paris, 1911), p. 8.

CHAPTER 2

1 See especially the first section (pp. 9–54) of Vidal's *Tableau*. On the widely discussed concept of *genre de vie* see, for example: P. Vidal de La Blache, 'Les genres de vie dans la géographie humaine', *Annales de géographie*, vol. 20 (1911), pp. 193–212, 289–304; M. Sorre, 'La notion de genre de vie et sa valeur actuelle', *Annales de géographie*, vol. 57 (1948), pp. 97–108, 193–204.

2 Examples abound: for instance, P. Pinchemel, *Géographie de la France*, 2 vols (Paris 1964), Vol. 1, p. 19; F. Braudel, *The Mediterranean and the Mediterranean World in the Age of Philip II*, 2 vols (London, 1972), Vol. 1, pp. 216–23; F. C. Spooner, *The International Economy and Monetary Movements in France, 1493 –1725* (Cambridge, Mass., 1972), p. 301; B. Guenée, *Tribunaux et gens de justice dans la bailliage de Senlis à la fin du Moyen Age (vers 1380–vers 1550)* (Paris, 1963), p. 45.

3 J. Labasse, *L'Organisation de l'espace* (Paris, 1966), p. 398; P. Claval, 'Géographie et profondeur social', *Annales ESC*, vol. 22 (1967), pp. 1025–7; F. Braudel, 'Beauvais et le Beauvaisis au XVIIᶜ siècle', *Annales ESC*, vol. 18 (1963), pp. 774, 777–8.

4 A. de Tocqueville, *L'ancien régime* (Oxford, 1904), p. 103.

5 F. Olivier-Martin, *L'Organisation corporative de la France d'ancien régime* (Paris, 1938), p. xii; E. Lousse, *La Société d'ancien régime: organisation et representation*

corporatives (Louvain, 1952), p. 42; M. Bloch, *French Rural Society: An Essay on Its Basic Characteristics* (London, 1966), p. 150.

6 R. Mousnier, *Les Institutions de la France sous l'ancien régime (1598–1789)*, Vol. 1, *Société et état* (Paris, 1974), pp. 496, 8.

7 O. Gierke, *Natural Law and the Theory of Society, 1500 to 1800*, trans. E. Barker (Cambridge, 1958), esp. pp. lxiv–lxxiv, 118–21; G. W. F. Hegel, *The Philosophy of Right*, trans. T. M. Knox (Oxford, 1942), esp. pp. 198, 155, 283.

8 Y. Renouard, '1212–1216: comment les traits durables de l'Europe occidentale moderne se sont définis au début du XIIIᵉ siècle', *Études d'histoire médiévale*, vol. 1 (Paris, 1968), pp. 77–91.

9 N. B. Smith, 'The idea of the French hexagon'. *French Historical Studies*, vol. 6 (1969), pp. 139–55; Mitteis, *The State*, pp. 5–6; Guenée, *Les Etats*, p. 79; Imbart de La Tour, *Origines de la Réforme*, Vol. 1, pp. 4–5; cf. H. Lemonnier, *Les Guerres d'Italie (1492–1547)* (Paris, 1903), p. 134.

10 P. S. Lewis, *Later Medieval France: The Polity* (London, 1968), p. 1; H. Drouot, *Mayenne et la Bourgogne: étude sur la Ligue (1587–1596)*, 2 vols (Paris, 1938), Vol. 1, p. 7; R. Clemenceau, 'Une frontiére ouverte: duché de Bourgogne et Franche-Comté sous le règne de François Iᵉʳ', *Annales de Bourgogne*, vol. 27 (1955), pp. 73–97; J. Petesch, 'Comment on fixait une frontière au XVᵉ siècle', *Les Cahiers haut-marnais*, no. 78 (1964), pp. 117–20; G. Zeller, *La Réunion de Metz à la France* (Paris, 1926), pp. 25–7.

11 J. Rigault, 'La frontière de la Meuse', *Bibliothèque de l'École des Chartes*, vol. 106 (1945–6), pp. 80–99.

12 R. Dion, *Les Frontières de la France* (Paris, 1947), p. 16; cf. G. Hoyois, *L'Ardenne et l'Ardennais: l'évolution économique et sociale d'une région* (Brussels, 1949), p. 84; M. Devèze, *La Vie de la forêt française au XVIᵉ siècle* (Paris, 1961), Vol. 1, p. 261, and Vol. 2, pp. 11, 191.

13 Guenée, *Les États*, p. 188; F. Lot and R. Fawtier, *Histoire des institutions françaises au Moyen Age*, Vol. 2 (Paris, 1958), p. 147.

14 G. Dupont-Ferrier, *Études sur les institutions financières de la France à la fin du Moyen Age*, Vol. 1 (Paris, 1930), pp. 49–51; G. Dupont-Ferrier, 'Ignorances et ractions administratives en France au XIVᵉ et XVᵉ siècles', *Bibliothèque de l'École des Chartes*, vol. 100 (1939), pp. 145–56; B. Guenée, 'La Géographie administrative de la France à la fin du Moyen Age: élections et bailliages', *Le Moyen Age*, vol. 67 (1961), pp. 293–323; Pasquier, *Oeuvres*, Vol. 1, col. 96.

15 Guenée, *Senlis*, p. 45; P. Goubert, *Cent mille provinciaux au XVIIᵉ siècle: Beauvais et le Beauvaisis de 1600 à 1730* (Paris, 1968), pp. 29, 34, 45; J. Jacquart, *La Crise rurale en Ile-de-France, 1550–1670* (Paris, 1974), pp. 9–11.

16 H. Meylan, 'Individualité et communauté: le secret des Réformateurs', *Individu et société à la Renaissance: 3ᵉ colloque international de la fédération internationale des instituts et sociétés pour l'étude de la Renaissance* (Brussels, 1967), p. 69.

17 G. Dupont-Ferrier, *Les Officiers royaux des bailliages et sénéchaussées et les institutions monarchiques locales en France à la fin du Moyen Age* (Paris, 1902), p. 894; C. Lucas, *The Structure of the Terror* (London, 1973), pp. 1–6; C. Longeon, *Une Province française à la Renaissance: la vie intellectuelle en Forez au XVIᵉ siècle* (Saint-Étienne, 1975), p. 12; M. Gonon, 'La Loire, lien ou obstacle en Forez au Moyen Age', *Bulletin de la Diana*, Vol. 30 (1966), pp. 289–301.

18 F. Lot, 'L'État des paroisses et des feux de 1328', *Bibliothèque de l'École des Chartes*, Vol. 90 (1929), p. 60; J. Godechot, *Les Institutions de la France sous la Révolution* (Paris, 1968), pp. 109, 596.

19 Muchembled, *Culture populaire*, pp. 69, 66, 79 ff.; J. Heers, *Fêtes, jeux et joutes dans les sociétés d'Occident à la fin du Moyen Age* (Montreal, 1971), pp. 52–3.

20 G. Fournier, 'Rural churches and rural communities in early medieval Auvergne', in F. L. Cheyette (ed.), *Lordship and Community in Medieval Europe* (New York,

1968), p. 333; Y.-M. Bercé, *Fête et révolte: des mentalités populaires du XVIe au XVIIIe siècle* (Paris, 1976); Jacquart, *Crise rurale*, p. 448; Goubert, *Cent mille provinciaux*, p. 91; P. Goubert, *The Ancien Régime: French Society, 1600–1750* (London, 1973), p. 44.

21 A. Meynier, 'La commune rurale française', *Annales de géographie*, vol. 53–4 (1945), pp. 161–79; cf. Mousnier, *Institutions*, Vol. 1, p. 428; E. Le Roy Ladurie, *Le Territoire de l'historien* (Paris, 1973), p. 149.

22 Or his equivalent, in parts of France outside the system of *élections*; on the kingdom's financial institutions, see below, pp. 61 ff.

23 G. Sivery, *Structures agraires et vie rurale dans le Hainault à la fin du Moyen Age* (Lille, 1977), p. 286; G. Duby, *Rural Economy and Country Life in the Medieval West* (London, 1968), pp. 157–60, 282; R. Fossier, *La Terre et les hommes en Picardie jusqu'à la fin du XIIIe siècle* (Paris, 1968), Vol. 2, pp. 708–30; F. Dumont and P.–C. Timbal, 'Gouvernés et gouvernants en France: périodes du Moyen Age et du XVIe siècle', *Recueils de la société Jean Bodin pour l'histoire comparative des institutions*, Vol. 24 (Brussels, 1966), pp. 231–2; F. Cheyette, 'Procurations by large-scale communities in fourteenth-century France', *Speculum*, vol. 37 (1962), pp. 18–31.

24 These questions are discussed in Chapter 3 below.

25 Examples in the contributions by H. Neveux ('Déclin et repris: la fluctuation biséculaire, 1330–1560') and J. Jacquart ('Immobilisme et catastrophes, 1560–1660') to G. Duby and A. Wallon (eds), *Histoire de la France rurale*, Vol. 2 (Paris, 1975), esp. pp. 117–19, 284. Compare Jacquart's contention that the *communauté* was at its strongest in the first half of the sixteenth century with his account of its functions in his *Crise rurale*, pp. 85–100. Both P. Chaunu ('L'état') and E. Le Roy Ladurie ('Les masses profondes: la paysannerie'), in *Histoire économique et sociale*, Vol. 1, pt 1, pp. 53–7, and pt 2, pp. 648–9, generalise very freely from the Hurepoix case.

26 P. de Saint-Jacob, 'Études sur l'ancienne communauté rurale en Bourgogne, IV: les terres communales', *Annales de Bourgogne*, vol. 25 (1953), p. 235; G. Bois, *Crise du féodalisme* (Paris, 1976), p. 183; Jacquart, *Crise rurale*, pp. 560–1.

27 cf. below, pp. 75–7.

28 J. Bossy, 'The Counter-Reformation and the people of Catholic Europe', *Past & Present*, no. 47 (1970), p. 53; M. Venard, 'Les confréries de penitents à la fin du XVIe siècle dans la province ecclésiastique d'Avignon', *Cahiers d'histoire publiés par les universités de Clermont, Lyon, Grenoble*, vol. 9 (1964), pp. 83–4.

29 Thus Bois, *Crise*, p. 352 and passim, in an analysis that suggests how men with smaller holdings furnished wage-labour for that 'unit' and were essential to its efficiency – as were common lands and collective usages to their survival.

30 But cf. Sivery, *Hainault*, p. 340.

31 Duby, *Rural Economy*, pp. 317–27, 340–1; J. P. Cooper, 'In search of agrarian capitalism', *Past & Present*, no. 80 (1978), pp. 20–65; Jacquart, *Crise rurale*, p. 85; Bois, *Crise*, p. 204.

32 cf. below, p. 164.

33 P. Ourliac and J. de Malafosse, *Histoire du droit privé, Vol. 3, Le Droit familial* (Paris, 1968), p. 406; G. Fourquin, *Lordship and Feudalism in the Middle Ages* (London, 1976), p. 153; M. Petitjean, *Essai sur l'histoire des substitutions du IXe au XVe siècle dans la pratique et la doctrine, spécialement en France méridionale* (Dijon, 1975), p. 519; J. P. Cooper, 'Patterns of inheritance and settlement by great landowners from the fifteenth to the eighteenth centuries', in J. Goody *et al.* (eds), *Family and Inheritance: Rural Society in Western Europe, 1200–1800* (Cambridge, 1976), pp. 252–76; F. A. Isambert *et al.* (eds), *Recueil général des anciennes lois françaises depuis l'an 420 jusqu'à la Révolution*, 29 vols (Paris, 1822–33), Vol. 14, pp. 75, 204.

34 Jacquart, *Crise rurale*, p. 69; H. Sée, *Les Classes rurales en Bretagne du XVIe siècle à la Révolution* (Paris, 1906), pp. 26–49; Drouot, *Mayenne*, Vol. 1, p. 36; R. Pillorget, *Les Mouvements insurrectionnels de Provence entre 1596 et 1715* (Paris, 1975), p. 97.

35 Again, examples abound: for instance, E. Le Roy Ladurie, 'Family structures and inheritance customs in sixteenth-century France', in Goody *et al.* (eds), *Family and Inheritance*, p. 45; Goubert, *Ancien régime*, p. 93; Mandrou, *Introduction à la France moderne*, p. 112.

36 Bodin, *République*, pp. 10–11; P. Corneille, *Horace* (1640), Act I, sc. iii; R. Vaultier, *Le Folklore pendant la guerre de Cent Ans d'après les lettres de rémission du Trésor des Chartes* (Paris, 1965), p. 14; Ourliac and de Malafosse, *Droit privé*, Vol. 3, p. 196; J.-L. Flandrin, *Familles* (Paris, 1976), p. 40. See also P. de Saint-Jacob, 'Études sur l'ancienne communauté rurale en Bourgogne, I: Le village – les conditions juridiques de l'habitat', *Annales de Bourgogne*, Vol. 13 (1941), p. 174.

37 In addition to works already noted, the following discussion of inheritance practices and their implications is based on G. Chevrier, 'Quelques traits du droit familial montbéliardais au XVIe siècle', *Mémoires de la Société pour l'Histoire du Droit et des Institutions des Anciens Pays Bourguignons, Comtais et Romands*, vol. 20 (1958–9), pp. 299–331; J. Gaudemet, *Les Communautés familiales* (Paris, 1963); R. E. Giesey, 'Rules of inheritance and strategies of mobility in pre-Revolutionary France', *American Historical Review*, vol. 82 (1977), pp. 271–89; A. Gouron, 'Coutume et pratique méridionale: une étude du droit des gens mariés', *Bibliothèque de l'École des Chartes*, vol. 116 (1958), pp. 194–209; J. Hamon, 'Un exemple de morcellement du bien censif dû au partage égal préscrit par la coutume du Maine', *Le Pays bas-normand*, année 52 (1959), pp. 16–25; J. Hilaire, 'Les aspects communautaires du droit matrimonial des régions situées autour du Massif Central à la fin du XVe et au début du XVIe siècle', *Recueil de mémoires et travaux publiés par la Société d'Histoire du Droit et des Institutions des Anciens Pays de Droit Écrit*, vol. 4 (1958–60), pp. 99–109; J. Hilaire, *Le Régime des biens entre époux dans la région de Montpellier* (Montpellier, 1957); G. Lepointe, *Droit Romain et ancien droit français: régimes matrimoniaux, libéralités, successions* (Paris, 1958); G. Lepointe, *La Famille dans l'ancien droit* (Paris, 1953); J. Prevault, 'Le régime des biens entre époux dans la coutume d'Anjou (1508–1789): analyse de l'ouvrage de M. Le Calonnec', *Revue des facultés catholiques de l'Ouest*, no. 3 (1963), pp. 31–8; J. Yver, 'L'Etat des études d'histoire du droit privé en France', *Revue historique de droit français et étranger*, sér. 4, année 45 (1967), pp. 708–11; J. Yver, *Essai de géographie coutumière* (Paris, 1966).

38 Below, p. 96.

39 Below, pp. 111–13.

40 W. W. Buckland, *A Textbook of Roman Law from Augustus to Justinian*, 3rd edn, rev. P. Stein (Cambridge, 1975), pp. 121–4, 370–1; W. W. Buckland and A. D. McNair, *Roman Law and Common Law: A Comparison in outline*, 2nd edn, rev. F. H. Lawson (Cambridge, 1952), pp. xiv, 38 ff.; Ourliac and de Malafosse, *Droit privé*, Vol. 3, pp. 29–35, 201 (quotation at p. 31).

41 R. Aubenas, 'Réflexions sur les "fraternités artificielles" au Moyen Age', *Études historiques à la mémoire de Noel Didier, publiées par la faculté de droit et des sciences économiques de Grenoble* (Paris, 1960), pp. 1–10; cf. the *societas universorum bonorum* in Roman law, traceable to the ancient arrangement of *consortium* by which the children might continue to enjoy an inheritance in common after the death of the *paterfamilias*, and which 'could be created artificially between persons not actually brothers or sisters' (Buckland and McNair, *Roman Law and Common Law*, p. 304, n. 1; Buckland, *Textbook*, pp. 513–14).

42 E. Le Roy Ladurie, *Les Paysans de Languedoc* (Paris, 1966), Vol. 1, pp. 166–7;

Gaudemet, *Communautés familiales*, p. 95; J.-L. Gay, *Les Effets pécuniaires du mariage en Nivernais du XIVe au XVIIIe siècle* (Dijon, 1953), pp. 9, 240; Ourliac and de Malafosse, *Droit privé*, Vol. 3, p. 64; Bloch, *Rural Society*, pp. 164–5; Imbart de La Tour, *Origines de la Réforme*, Vol. 1, p. 483.

43 See below, p. 59.

44 P. Contamine, *Guerre, état et société à la fin du Moyen Age: études sur les armées des rois de France, 1337–1494* (Paris, 1972), pp. 429, 482–3; P. S. Lewis, 'Decayed and non-feudalism in later medieval France', *Bulletin of the Institute of Historical Research*, vol. 37 (1964), p. 176.

45 Fontenay-Mareuil, *Mémoires*, quoted in R. Mousnier, *La Vénalité des offices sous Henri IV et Louis XIII*, 2nd edn (Paris, 1971), p. 595. On the extent of Guise 'brokerage' see R. R. Harding, *Anatomy of a Power Élite: The Provincial Governors of Early Modern France* (New Haven, Conn., 1978), p. 35.

46 Below, pp. 137–44.

47 The following account of religious confraternities is based on: G. Le Bras, *Études de sociologie religieuse*, Vol. 2 (Paris, 1956), pp. 418–62; E. Delaruelle *et al.*, *L'Église au temps du Grand Schisme et de la crise conciliaire (1378–1449)*, Pt 2 (Paris, 1964), pp. 666–93; P. Duparc, 'Confraternities of the holy spirit and village communities in the Middle Ages', in Cheyette (ed.), *Lordship and Community*, pp. 341–56; A. N. Galpern, *The Religions of the People in Sixteenth-Century Champagne* (Cambridge, Mass., 1976), pp. 52–72; and J. Toussaert, *Le Sentiment religieux en Flandre à la fin du Moyen Age* (Paris, 1963), pp. 479–81, for comment on views of confraternities as instruments of class struggle and economic warfare.

48 Quoted in P. Adam, *La Vie paroissiale en France au XIVe siècle* (Paris, 1964), p. 56.

49 Aubenas, 'Réflexions', p. 7; cf. Gaudemet, *Communautés familiales*, pp. 101,130.

50 Contamine, *Guerre, état et société*, pp. 402, 427–8.

51 Ordinance of Villers-Cotterets (1539), art. 185; cf. Ordinances of Orléans (1561), art. 10; of Moulins (1566), art. 74; of Blois (1579), art. 37: all in Isambert, *Recueil général*, Vol. 12, p. 638, and Vol. 14, pp. 67, 210, 391. E. Coornaert, *Les Corporations en France avant 1789*, 2nd edn (Paris, 1968), quotes Louis XII's stricture and regrettably obscures the distinction between *confréries* and *corps de métier*. On gilds in general see H. Hauser, *Travailleurs et marchands dans l'ancienne France* (Paris, 1920), pp. 130–216.

52 Olivier-Martin, *Organisation corporative*, pp. 89, 99, cf. 149.

53 cf. below, pp. 85–6, also p. 45.

54 Thus, Vol. 1 (Paris, 1887) alone of P. Marichal (ed.), *Catalogue des actes de François Ier*, contains forty-four separate acts confirming various gild statutes and privileges.

55 But cf. J. P. Sosson, 'La structure sociale de la corporation médiévale: l'exemple des tonneliers de Bruges de 1350 à 1500', *Revue belge de philologie et d'histoire*, vol. 44 (1966), p. 469, for indications that a gild might become more 'open' and 'democratic' even when its statutes favoured the opposite.

56 Olivier-Martin, *Organisation corporative*, pp. 141–2.

57 C. Petit-Dutaillis, *Les Communes françaises: caractères et évolution des origines au XVIIIe siècle* (Paris, 1947); cf. J. Dhont, 'Petit-Dutaillis et les communes françaises', *Annales ESC*, vol. 7 (1952), pp. 378–84. See also Lewis, *Later Medieval France*, pp. 238–9.

58 Doucet, *Institutions*, Vol. 1, pp. 370–1; E. Le Parquier, *Les Élections municipales à Rouen au XVIe siècle* (Rouen, 1925), pp. 2–4; C. Bonis, 'Un année municipale à Aurillac au XVe siècle (1493–1494)', *Revue de la Haute-Auvergne*, vol. 41 (1969), pp. 522–3. My estimate of Rouen's population may well be too conservative: P. Benedict, 'Rouen during the wars of religion: popular disorder, public order and the confessional struggle', Princeton University PhD dissertation, 1975, ff. 3, 247, estimates that town's population by the middle of the sixteenth century at over

70,000, and suggests that the early-century population-increase may have levelled off before the outbreak of the civil wars.

59 B. Chevalier, 'The policy of Louis XI towards the *bonnes villes*: the case of Tours', in P. S. Lewis (ed.), *The Recovery of France in the fifteenth Century* (London, 1972), p. 269.

60 R. Gascon, *Grand commerce et vie urbaine au XVIe siècle: Lyon et ses marchands (environs de 1500–environs de 1580)* (Paris, 1971), pp. 680–3, 720–7, 408–18; Bonis, 'Année municipale'; cf. M. Saint-Eloy, 'Des Échevins de Nevers, 1309–1610: condition sociale, fortune et profession', *Bulletin philologique et historique du Comité des Travaux Historiques et Scientifiques*, vol. 2 (1966), pp. 561–91.

61 See below, pp. 67–8, 75.

62 Doucet, *Institutions*, Vol. 1, pp. 366–7, and 364–92 passim.

63 cf. the account of attitudes in Burgundy, in Drouot, *Mayenne*, Vol. 1, pp. 73–102.

64 For views to the contrary, held by distinguished jurists, see, for instance, below, p. 152–3.

65 While there is ample evidence of the growth in the numbers of lawyers of various kinds, few of them were trained in the law faculty of the University of Paris (see L. W. B. Brockliss, 'Patterns of attendance at the University of Paris, 1400–1800', *Historical Journal*, vol. 21 (1978), pp. 514, 522–3, 540–3); it is conceivable that, had that faculty developed in the later-fifteenth and sixteenth centuries as a major training-ground for French secular lawyers, the latter might have been detached more effectively from their regional and local loyalties.

66 M. Dayras, 'Les privilèges de la ville et franchise d'Aubusson: l'enquête du 6 novembre 1566 et jours suivants', *Mémoires de la Société des Sciences Naturelles et Archéologiques de la Creuse*, vol. 34 (1962), p. 399; G. Fourquin, 'Le droit parisien de la fin du Moyen Age: droit des "notables"', *Etudes d'histoire du droit parisien* (Paris, 1970), p. 381; Imbart de La Tour, *Origines de la Réforme*, Vol. 1, pp. 451–2; Chevalier, 'Policy of Louis XI', pp. 289–93. In Lyon in the 1570s lawyers would again hold more municipal offices than were held by merchant families (Gascon, *Grand commerce*, p. 412).

67 Hotman, *Francogallia*, p. 512, citing Budé's *Annotationes* of 1508; see also below, p. 153.

68 Ordinance of Villers-Cotterets (1539), art. 111 (Isambert, *Recueil général*, vol. 12, pp. 622–3). On the vexed question of this celebrated act's significance see: A. Brun, *Recherches historiques sur l'introduction du français dans les provinces du Midi* (Paris, 1923); H. Peyre, *La Royauté et les langues provinciales* (Paris, 1933), esp. pp. 84 ff.; P. Fiorelli, 'Pour l'interprétation de l'ordonnance de Villers-Cotterets', *Le Français moderne*, vol. 18 (1950), pp. 279–98; A. Brun, '"En langage maternel françois"', *Le Français moderne*, Vol. 19 (1951), pp. 81–6.

69 E. Forestié, 'Les livres de comptes des frères Boysset, marchands de Saint-Antonin de Rouergue au XVIe siècle', *Bulletin archéologique et historique de la Société Archéologique dé Tarn-et-Garonne*, vol. 20 (1892), p. 15; J. Régné, *La Vie économique et les classes sociales en Vivarais au lendemain de la guerre de Cent Ans* (Aubenas, 1926), p. 22.

70 R. Fédou, *Les Hommes de loi lyonnais à la fin du Moyen Age: étude sur les origines de la classe de robe* (Paris, 1964), p. 442.

71 E. Maugis, *Histoire du Parlement de Paris de l'avènement des rois Valois à la mort de Henri IV*, Vol. 1 (Paris, 1913), p. 126; R. Aubenas, 'L'apprentissage à Cannes au XVIe siècle', *Annales de la Société Scientifique et Littéraire de Cannes et de l'Arrondissement de Grasse*, Vol. 21 (1969), pp. 148–9.

72 The 'specific characteristics of the social class', according to P. A. Sorokin, 'What is a social class', in R. Bendix and S. M. Lipset (eds), *Class, Status and Power* (Glencoe, Ill., 1953), p. 88; cf. M. Bouvier-Ajam and G. Mury, *Les Classes sociales en France*, Vol. 1 (Paris, 1963), pp. 180–90, for a critique of Sorokin's position from

the Marxian standpoint of 'class' as determined by 'relationship to the means of production'; and, for rejection of 'class' concepts on grounds of their irrelevance to early-modern French society, R. Mousnier, *Social Hierarchies: 1450 to the Present* (London, 1973).

73 cf. Michel de L'Hôpital's opinion, below, p. 54.

74 Below, pp. 75–7.

75 J. Batany, 'Le vocabulaire des catégories sociales chez quelques moralistes français vers 1200', in D. Roche and C. E. Labrousse (eds), *Ordres et classes: colloque d'histoire sociale, Saint-Cloud, 24–25 mai 1967* (Paris, 1973), pp. 69–70; J. Batany, 'Des *trois fonctions* aux *trois états*', *Annales ESC*, vol. 18 (1963), pp. 933–8; F. Dumont, 'Recherches sur les ordres dans l'opinion française sous l'ancien régime', in *Album Helen Maud Cam: études présentées à la commission internationale pour l'histoire des assemblées d'états*, Vol. 1 (Paris, 1960), pp. 199–200; R. E. Giesey, 'The French estates and the *corpus mysticum regni*', in ibid., pp. 153–171; M. J. Wilks, *The Problem of Sovereignty in the Later Middle Ages* (Cambridge, 1963), pp. 57 ff.; A. Jouanna, 'Recherches sur la notion d'honneur au XVIème siècle', *Revue d'histoire moderne et contemporaine*, vol. 15 (1968), pp. 597–623; P. Michaud-Quantin, 'Le Vocabulaire des catégories sociales chez les canonistes et moralistes du XIIIᵉ siècle', *Ordres et classes*, p. 83.

76 For example, A. Fontaine, 'Conflits à propos de la taille', *Annales de Normandie*, vol. 3 (1953), p. 232; Gascon, *Grand commerce*, p. 383.

77 For example, Barthélemi de Chasseneux, *Catalogus gloriae mundi* (Lyon, 1546), Pt xi (ff. 213–36); cf. C. Loyseau, *Des Ordres et simples dignités* (in *Oeuvres de Loyseau*), i, 39; and cf., too, R. Mousnier, 'Les concepts d'"ordres", d'"états", de "fidélité" et de "monarchie absolue" en France', *Revue historique*, vol. 247 (1972), p. 300. Bodin expressed misgivings over the wisdom of arranging citizens in orders and assembling them accordingly, in bk III, ch. viii, of the Latin edition (1586) of his *République* – a chapter that does not figure in the 1576 and subsequent French editions of that work.

78 cf. Aristotle, *Nicomachean ethics*, 1123ᵇ 35.

79 cf. Jouanna, 'Recherches sur la notion d'honneur', p. 611.

80 Sr de Rochefort, *La Harangue de part la noblesse de toute la France* (1560), quoted in M. A. Devyver, *Le Sang épuré: les préjugés de race chez les gentilshommes français de l'ancien régime, 1560–1720* (Brussels, 1973), p. 82.

81 See especially the discussion by Devyver, *Sang épuré*, ch. 4: 'Naissance du mythe germanique'.

82 cf. E. Dravasa, *'Vivre noblement': recherches sur la dérogeance de la noblesse du XIVᵉ au XVIᵉ siècle* (Bordeaux, 1965).

83 Notably by de Rochefort (above, n. 80); and by François de l'Alouette, *Traicté des nobles et des vertus dont ils sont formés* (1577) – among the most powerful statements of the 'hereditary' case.

84 M. de Launoy, *Remonstrance . . . à la noblesse de France*, quoted in Yardeni, *Conscience nationale*, p. 250. De Launoy was a founder-member of the Paris Sixteen; for the rift between the two views of 'aristocracy' in the climatic phase of the League, see below, pp. 143–4.

85 A. Jouanna, 'Les gentilshommes français et leur rôle politique dans la seconde moitié du XVIᵉ siècle et au début du XVIIᵉ', *Il pensiero politico: Rivista di storia delle idee politiche e sociali*, vol. 10 (1977), p. 30.

86 Du Haillan, *De la fortune et vertu de la France* (Paris, 1570), p. 5ᵛᵒ.

87 Hotman, *Francogallia*, p. 292.

88 J. Russell Major, *The Deputies to the Estates-General in Renaissance France* (Madison, Wis., 1960), pp. 138–9; Mousnier, *Vénalité des offices*, pp. 541–53.

89 Though their influence was not exclusively dominant in assemblies of rural *communautés*: see Jacquart, *Crise rurale*, p. 561, cf. p. 157.

CHAPTER 3

1 Lewis, *Later Medieval France*, p. 103; cf. P. M. Smith, *The Anti-Courtier Trend in Sixteenth-Century French Literature* (Geneva, 1966).

2 Lot and Fawtier, *Histoire des institutions*, Vol. 2, pp. 76 ff.

3 And chosen by him – though on three occasions in the late-fourteenth and early-fifteenth centuries the chancellor was elected by the royal council, as was the constable on two occasions at that time: see ibid., Vol. 2, pp. 64, 53; H. Michaud, *La Grande Chancellerie et les écritures royales au XVIe siècle* (Paris, 1967), p. 34; Doucet, *Institutions*, Vol. 1, p. 108.

4 Michaud, *Grande Chancellerie*, p. 34; Lot and Fawtier, *Histoire des institutions*, Vol. 2, p. 61.

5 cf. Guenée, *Les États*, p. 188.

6 ibid., p. 191.

7 Lot and Fawtier, *Histoire des institutions*, Vol. 2, pp. 349–53; J. H. Shennan, *The Parlement of Paris* (London, 1968), pp. 111–16.

8 The following passage takes account of criteria specified by Max Weber in his classic definition of 'bureaucracy' (*Economy and Society: An Outline of Interpretive Sociology*, ed. G. Roth and C. Wittich, Vol. 3 (New York, 1968), pp. 956–8): essentially, clear specialisation of functions by the particular parts of the system, existence of an official hierarchy, importance of written records, recruitment of personnel on the basis of ability and professional qualifications for the tasks concerned, and development of a professional ideology. In Weberian terms, 'bureaucratic' differs specifically from 'patrimonial' officialdom: cf. ibid., pp. 1028–31.

9 Quoted in E. Maugis, *Histoire du parlement de Paris*, Vol. 1, p. 375.

10 While Gustave Dupont-Ferrier (*Nouvelles études sur les institutions financières de la France à la fin du Moyen Age* (Paris, 1933), pp. 10 ff.) argues persuasively that this view is mistaken, it was certainly current in the sixteenth century. See, for instance, Pasquier's account 'De l'assemblée des trois Estats de la France, Cour des Aydes, sur le faict de la justice, tailles, aides et subsides', in *Oeuvres*, Vol. 1, cols 85–92; and his contention that 'Du commencement les Généraux qui estoient commis pour l'ordination des finances venant des aydes, l'estoient aussi pour le fait de la justice' (ibid., col. 92).

11 cf. M. Wolfe, *The Fiscal System of Renaissance France* (New Haven, Conn., 1972), pp. 33–5.

12 Dupont-Ferrier, *Officiers royaux*, pp. 249–53, 532–3.

13 *Ordonnances des rois de France de la troisième race*, 22 vols (Paris, 1723–1849), Vol. 19, p. 539.

14 On relative distances and travel times see Y. Renouard, 'Information et transmission des nouvelles', in C. Samaran (ed.), *L'Histoire et ses méthodes* (Paris, 1961), p. 113; B. Guenée, 'Espace et état dans la France du bas Moyen Age', *Annales ESC*, Vol. 23 (1968), p. 752.

15 'There was no such distinction in the Middle Ages' (B. Tierney, 'Bracton on government', *Speculum*, Vol. 38 (1963), p. 308, commenting on C. H. McIlwain, *Constitutionalism Ancient and Modern* (New York, 1958), ch. 4); cf. N. Valois, *Inventaire des arrêts du conseil d'état (règne de Henri IV)*, Vol. 1 (Paris, 1886), p. xvi. Nor is it implied by the Roman law distinction between *auctoritas* and *potestas*, to which my next but one sentence alludes.

16 For example, M. T. Lorcin, 'Les paysans et la justice', *Le Moyen Age*, vol. 74 (1968), pp. 269–300.

17 Nor did the contrary principle that prevailed elsewhere – that 'fief and justice have nothing in common' – prevent discrepant morcellations of jurisdictions and feudal lands.

18 See particularly Guenée, *Senlis*, pp. 183–4.
19 For example, Chartres and Orléans: see, for instance, A. Blondel, *Essai sur les institutions municipales de Chartres, spécialement du XIIIe au XVIe siècle* (Chartres, 1903), pp. 128–9.
20 Petit-Dutaillis, *Communes françaises*, p. 256; Dupont-Ferrier, *Officiers royaux*, pp. 862–3; H. Pirenne, *Les Villes au Moyen Age* (Paris, 1971), pp. 149–50.
21 Guenée, *Senlis*, pp. 132–3, 529–31.
22 The system is conveniently described in Wolfe, *Fiscal System*, pp. 304 ff.
23 Seyssel, *Monarchie de France*, pp. 164, 159, 153.
24 Michel de L'Hôpital, *Traicté de la réformation de la justice*, in P. J. S. Duféy (ed.), *Oeuvres complètes de Michel de L'Hôpital*, 5 vols (Paris, 1824–6), Vol. 4, pp. 38, 363, 205, 254 ff., 266, 303, 328–30, 348, 354–5, 343, 315–20, 350. L'Hôpital is generally accepted as the main, though not the only, begetter of this treatise: it is apparent from internal evidence that he cannot have written it all.
25 Du Haillan, *De l'estat et succez des affaires de France*, quoted in Valois, *Inventaire*, p. cv. Much of the material for this account of the council is derived from Valois' 'Introduction' to his *Inventaire* (pp. v–clii). Membership of the council under Francis I is discussed by R. Mousnier, *Le Conseil du roi de Louis XII à la Révolution* (Paris, 1970), pp. 21–2. F. Decrue, *De Consilio regis Francisci Ier* (Paris, 1885), apps IV and V, prints the king's instructions to his council in 1536 and a 'roll' of its members in 1543.
26 Valois, *Inventaire*, p. lviii. Until then the council was often described as the *conseil privé*; by then that description was being applied to the *conseil des parties*. But various terms were used to describe all sections of the council – a further symptom of their instability.
27 Quoted in Valois, *Inventaire*, p. lxiii.
28 Doucet, *Institutions*, Vol. 1, pp. 146–9; Pasquier, *Oeuvres*, Vol. 1, cols 83–4.
29 Valois, *Inventaire*, pp. xiv, xlix, l.
30 Quoted in N. M. Sutherland, *The French Secretaries of State in the Age of Catherine de Medici* (London, 1962), pp. 30–1.
31 Michaud, *Grande Chancellerie*, pp. 91–2, 111.
32 cf. V.-I. Comparato, 'Guillaume Bochetel, secrétaire d'état, ?–1558', in Mousnier, *Conseil du roi*, p. 117.
33 For example, Michaud, *Grande Chancellerie*, pp. 127–64, 396.
34 cf. ibid., pp. 138, 141–2.
35 H. Michaud, 'Le registre de Claude Pinart, secrétaire d'état (1570–1588)', *Bibliothèque de l'École des Chartes*, vol. 120 (1962), pp. 142, 137; Michaud, *Grande Chancellerie*, p. 144; Sutherland, *French Secretaries of State*, pp. 39–52.
36 B. D. Lyon, *From Fief to Indenture: The Transition from Feudal to Non-Feudal Contract in Western Europe* (Cambridge, Mass., 1957); F. Lot, *Recherches sur les effectifs des armées françaises des guerres d'Italie aux guerres de religion* (Paris, 1962).
37 Seyssel, *Monarchie de France*, pp. 171, 194.
38 Contamine, *Guerre, état et société*, pp. 337–64, 278, 399 ff., 542–51; Doucet, *Institutions*, Vol. 2, pp. 630, 638–41; G. Zeller, *Les Institutions de la France au XVIe siècle* (Paris, 1948), pp. 305–6; H. Michaud, 'Les Institutions militaires des guerres d'Italie aux guerres de religion', *Revue historique*, vol. 258 (1977), pp. 31–2; J. B. Henneman, 'The military class and the French monarchy in the late Middle Ages', *American Historical Review*, vol. 83 (1978), pp. 946–65.
39 Doucet, *Institutions*, Vol. 2, p. 648.
40 Contamine, *Guerre, état et société*, pp. 505–7; Michaud, *Grande Chancellerie*, pp. 146–7.
41 Quoted in Michaud, 'Institutions militaires', p. 41, n. 3.
42 Fontanon, *Edicts et ordonnances*, Vol. 3, ff. 97–103.

43 Michaud, 'Institutions militaires', pp. 37–42; Michaud, *Grande Chancellerie*, p. 147.
44 In general, M. Roberts, *The Military Revolution, 1560–1660* (Belfast, 1956); see also A. Karcher, 'L'assemblée des notables de Saint-Germain-en-Laye', *Bibliothèque de l'École des Chartes*, vol. 114 (1956), pp. 160–1. Even so, specifications relating to armour, conditions of recruitment, etc., in ordinances such as Henry III's of 1584 on the *gendarmerie* illustrate how slowly governments departed from established norms (Fontanon, *Edicts et ordonnances*, Vol. 3, ff. 129–39).
45 ibid., Vol. 3, ff. 4–5.
46 All but one of the *gouverneurs* appointed from 1515 to 1560 were captains (Harding, *Anatomy of a Power Élite*, p. 21).
47 Dupont-Ferrier, *Officiers royaux*, pp. 55–70.
48 Harding, *Anatomy of a Power Élite*, p. 26; Dupont-Ferrier, *Officiers royaux*, pp. 233–45. For the sixteenth century see, for instance, the *règlement* of January 1515 (Isambert, *Recueil général*, Vol. 12, pp. 2–18), art. 37, where the *gouverneurs* seem virtually to be equated with 'capitaines et chefs desdits gendarmes'.
49 Isambert, *Recueil général*, Vol. 12, pp. 346–9, 892–3.
50 For example, the *règlement* of January 1515, art. 38; cf. Doucet, *Institutions*, Vol. 1, p. 112, where the constable's powers in this regard are considerably understated.
51 Quoted in Doucet, *Institutions*, Vol. 1, p. 237; cf. Harding, *Anatomy of a Power Élite*, p. 14.
52 See below, pp. 78–80.
53 The classic statement of the thesis outlined in what follows is J. Schumpeter, *Die Krise des Steuerstaates* (Wiesbaden, 1951); other relevant works include the collection of essays on the so-called 'general crisis of the seventeenth century' edited by T. Aston, *Crisis in Europe, 1560–1660* (London, 1965).
54 Mousnier, *Conseil du roi*, pp. 17–18; Mousnier, *Vénalité des offices*, p. 43; Dupont-Ferrier, *Études*, Vol. 1, p. 32; cf. Wolfe, *Fiscal System*, p. 256, and D. Buisseret, *Sully and the Growth of Centralized Government in France, 1598–1610* (London, 1968), p. 58.
55 Guenée, 'Géographie administrative', p. 305.
56 L. Desgraves, 'Aux origines de l'élection d'Agen (1519–1622)', *Recueil de travaux offerts à M. Clovis Brunel*, Vol. 1 (Paris, 1955), pp. 357–65; J. Gay, 'Les exigences de la fiscalité royale en Bourgogne dans la seconde moitié du XVI⁰ siècle (1547–72)', *Revue historique de droit français et étranger*, sér. 4, vol. 44 (1966), pp. 172–4.
57 Wolfe, *Fiscal System*, pp. 44, 256–7, 304 ff.; Doucet, *Institutions*, Vol. 2, p. 564; Dupont-Ferrier, *Études*, Vol. 1, pp. 61–159.
58 ibid., Vol. 1, pp. 57, 167–74; Dupont-Ferrier, *Officiers royaux*, pp. 534 ff.; Mousnier, *Conseil du roi*, p. 21; Wolfe, *Fiscal System*, p. 68.
59 G. Jacqueton, 'Le Trésor de l'Épargne sous François Iᵉʳ (1523–1547)' (2 pts), *Revue historique*, vols 55–6 (1894), pt 1, p. 1.
60 Ordinance of 28 December 1523, in S. Fournival, *Recueil général concernant les fonctions, rangs, dignités et privilèges de présidents, trésoriers de France, etc.* (Paris, 1655), ff. 141–6.
61 Jacqueton, 'Trésor de l'Épargne', pt 1, p. 21; ibid., pt 2, p. 38.
62 J.-P. Charmeil, *Les Trésoriers de France à l'époque de la Fronde* (Paris, 1964), p. 6, n. 23; Decrue, *De consilio*, p. 91; Jacqueton, 'Trésor de l'Épargne', pt 1, pp. 29–30; ibid., pt 2, pp. 1–2, 7–8; Isambert, *Recueil général*, Vol. 13, p. 5.
63 Edicts of Cognac (December 1542) and of Blois (January 1552), in Isambert, *Recueil général*, Vol. 12, pp. 796–806, and Vol. 13, pp. 236–47.
64 Above, p. 56.
65 Edict of Poitiers (July 1577), supplemented by the *règlement* of July 1578, in Fournival, *Recueil général*, ff. 308–15, 319–27.
66 Edict of Paris (January 1586), in Fournival, *Recueil général*, f. 375.

67 Zeller, *Institutions*, p. 286; Buisseret, *Sully*, p. 61. The latter phrase applies despite Sully's strictures in the 1590s upon the 'abuses and malversations' of the *trésoriers-généraux*, and his efforts to ensure that they apportion the *tailles* 'with more intelligence and judgement' (Fournival, *Recueil général*, ff. 406 ff.: *règlement* of 8 April 1600, amply illustrating the continuing importance of these *officiers* for the working of a system which by then the *surintendant des finances* had emerged to dominate in the name of king and council).

68 cf. above, pp. 52–3.

69 Below, pp. 80–2.

70 J.-J. Clamageran, *Histoire de l'impôt en France*, 3 vols (Paris, 1867–76), Vol. 2, pp. 198–244: Clamageran himself stresses the role of indirect taxes in bringing about this increase; cf. Chaunu, 'L'État', pp. 152–77, in respect of the figures that follow. They may also be compared with those prepared at the time of the 1583 Assembly of notables (see below, pp. 82, 108–10), in Bibliothèque Nationale, manuscrits français no. 23050, ff. 50ro–78vo, which gives summary statements of all royal receipts at the central treasury in the last year of the reign of each of Henry III's sixteenth-century predecessors, as follows: 1514–4·9 million *livres tournois*; 1547 – 14.2 million *livres tournois*; 1559 – 12.1 million *livres tournois*; 1560 – 9.1 million *livres tournois*; 1574 – 8·6 million *livres tournois*. To these are added a figure of 10·6 million for the year 1581; this last amount is expressed in *écus*, and would equal 31·8 million *livres tournois*. On the other hand, Henry III's budget estimates for 1585, prepared in December 1584, state total disposable receipts of only 3·5 million *écus*, or 10·5 million *livres tournois*, (ibid., 6413, ff. 112–13).

71 Though at the time 'Nicolas Froumenteau' (probably Nicolas Barnaud, also – as 'Nicolas de Montand' – author of the polemical dialogues *Le Miroir des françois*; see below. p. 98, n. 64) claimed to know in detail how taxes had increased since the time of Louis XI, and published his findings as *Le Secret des finances de France* [1581].

72 By fire, in 1737.

73 The problem is discussed by Mousnier, *Vénalité des offices*, pp. 448–53.

74 The question of price-inflation is discussed more fully below, pp. 97–9.

75 These several alternatives are suggested by Chaunu, 'L'État', and by M. Morineau, 'La conjoncture ou les cernes de la croissance', in *Histoire économique et sociale*, Vol. 1, pt 2, pp. 978–80; the latter's tabulated analyses contain several errors. For further comment on production and population, see below, pp. 95–7.

76 The 1522 issue was cancelled by Henry II in 1547 (P. Cauwès, 'Les commencements du crédit publique en France – les rentes sur l'hôtel de ville au XVIe siècle', *Revue d'économie politique*, vol. 9 (1895), pp. 114–15). A rate of 10 per cent had at first been proposed – significantly higher than the 8⅓ per cent, the normal rate for private credit, that was eventually offered (Cauwès, p. 113; B. Schnapper, *Les Rentes au XVIe siècle* (Paris, 1957), pp. 68 ff.).

77 G. Fagniez (ed.), 'Livre de raison de Me Nicolas Versoris', *Mémoires de la Société de l'Histoire de Paris et de l'Ile de France*, Vol. 12 (1885), p. 119.

78 Cauwès, 'Les commencements', p. 97.

79 For what follows, see especially R. Doucet, 'Le Grand Parti de Lyon au XIVe siècle', *Revue historique*, vol. 171 (1933), pp. 473–513, and vol. 172 (1933), pp. 1–41.

80 Doucet, 'Grand Parti', vol. 172, p. 10.

81 L'Hôpital, *Oeuvres*, Vol. 1, pp. 389, 392.

82 On this assembly see especially: P. Van Dyke, 'The estates of Pontoise', *English Historical Review*, vol. 28 (1913), pp. 472–95; J. Russell Major, 'The Third Estate in the States General of Pontoise, 1561', *Speculum*, vol. 29 (1954), pp. 460–76.

83 *Cahier* of the *noblesse* at Pontoise, quoted in Picot, *Histoire des États-généraux*, Vol. 2, p. 245.

84 Quoted in L. Serbat, *Les Assemblées du clergé de France, 1561–1615* (Paris, 1906), p. 25.
85 [MM. Le Merre (eds)], *Recueil des actes, titres et mémoires concernant les affaires du clergé de France*, Vol. 9 (Paris, 1721), col. 4.
86 The alienations are studied in I. Cloulas, 'Les aliénations du temporel ecclésiastique par les rois Charles IX et Henri III (de 1563 à 1588), particulièrement dans les diocèses de Bourges et Limoges', *Positions des thèses à l'École des Chartes* (1957), pp. 37–46; I. Cloulas, 'Les aliénations du temporel ecclésiastique sous Charles IX et Henri II (1563–1587): résultats généraux des ventes', *Revue d'histoire de l'église de France*, vol. 44 (1958), pp. 5–56.
87 Quoted in I. Cloulas, 'Grégoire XIII et l'aliénation des biens du clergé de France en 1574–1575', *Mélanges d'archéologie et d'histoire: École française de Rome*, vol. 71 (1959), pp. 381–404.
88 J. Coudy, *Les Moyens d'action de l'ordre du clergé au conseil du roi (1561–1715)* (Paris, 1954), p. 10. See also Doucet, *Institutions*, Vol. 2, pp. 838–9.
89 Mousnier, *Vénalité des offices*, pp. 421, 127.
90 Isambert, *Recueil général*, Vol. 13, pp. 406–10.
91 See Wolfe, *Fiscal System*, pp. 63–6, on the 'fiscal sponge'.
92 Quoted in Mousnier, *Vénalité des offices*, p. 52. The ruling was long presaged: cf. Doucet, *Institutions*, Vol. 1, pp. 412 ff. On the distinction between *propres* and *acquêts* see above, pp. 33–4.
93 Mousnier, *Vénalité des offices*, p. 84.
94 L'Hôpital, *Oeuvres*, Vol. 4, p. 303; cf. Bodin, *République*, p. 743, where by his phrasing ('ils vendent la république: ils vendent le sang des subiects') Bodin would seem to imply a distinction lacking in L'Hôpital's statement.
95 *Ordonnances des rois de France*, Vol. 21, p. 185; Isambert, *Recueil général*, Vol. 14, p. 406.
96 Pasquier, *Oeuvres*, Vol. 1, col. 404.
97 Guenée, *Senlis*, p. 84; cf. J. Dewald, *The Formation of a Provincial Nobility: The Magistrates of the Parlement of Rouen, 1499–1610* (Princeton, NJ, 1980), pp. 109–11; but cf., too, Dewald's observations (ibid., pp. 274–5) on the significance of changes in the pattern of *parlementaire* marriage alliances from *circa* 1570.
98 Ordinance of Blois (1499), arts 36–7; of Orléans (1561), arts 52–3; of Blois (1579), arts 118–19, 121–2 (*Ordonnances des rois de France*, Vol. 21, p. 185; Isambert, *Recueil général*, Vol. 14, pp. 78, 411–12).
99 For what follows, see especially J. H. Langbein, *Prosecuting Crime in the Renaissance: England, Germany, France* (Cambridge, Mass., 1974).
100 Edict of May 1552 (Isambert, *Recueil général*, Vol. 13, p. 271).
101 Ordinance of January 1529, art. 10; of Villers-Cotterets (1539), arts 18, 24–5, 34, 42–5; of Orléans (1561), arts 63–4; of Blois (1579), art. 184; edicts of January 1522 and of May 1552 (Isambert, *Recueil général*, Vol. 12, pp. 310, 604–9, and Vol. 14, pp. 81, 424).
102 Ordinance of Villers-Cotterets (1539), arts 50–4, 111; of Blois (1579), art. 181 (Isambert, *Recueil général*, Vol. 12, pp. 610–11, 622–3, and Vol. 14, p. 423).
103 Ordinance of Blois (1579), art. 155; edict of May 1552 (Isambert, *Recueil général*, Vol. 14, p. 418, and vol. 13, p. 272).
104 Ordinance of Moulins (1566), arts 13, 71; Edict of Crémieu (1536), arts 5, 26–7; Ordinance of Orléans (1561), art. 50; Edict of Fontainebleau (1552) (Isambert, *Recueil général*, Vol. 14, pp. 77–8, 193, 208; ibid., Vol. 12, pp. 505–10; ibid., Vol. 13, pp. 248–54).
105 R. Filhol, 'La rédaction des coutumes en France aux XVᵉ et XVIᵉ siècles', in J. Gilissen (ed.), *La Rédaction des coutumes dans le passé et dans le présent* (Brussels, 1962), p. 68.

106 Ordinance of Montilz-lez-Tours, 1453/4, art. 125 (*Ordonnances des rois de France*, Vol. 14, pp. 312–13).

107 Literally, inquiry by the rabble – though even these juries had come to be dominated by local lawyers (J. P. Dawson, *The Oracles of the Law* (Ann Arbor, Mich., 1968), p. 272). The extent to which in the French judicial system professional lawyers took over functions that in some other European countries continued to be left to juries recruited from local communities is, of course, highly significant.

108 Quoted in R. Filhol, *Le premier président Cristofle de Thou et la réformation des coutumes* (Paris, 1937), p. 78.

109 J. P. Dawson, 'The codification of the French customs', *Michigan Law Review*, vol. 38 (1940), p. 779.

110 Quoted in Filhol, *Christofle de Thou*, p. 70.

111 Quoted in Filhol, 'Rédaction des coutumes', p. 74.

112 Du Moulin, *Oratio de concordia et unione consuetudinum Franciae*, quoted in J.-L. Thireau, *Charles Du Moulin (1500–1566)* (Geneva, 1980), p. 115.

113 See above, p. 13.

114 P. Goubert, 'Officiers royaux des présidiaux, bailliages et élections dans la société française du XVIIe siècle', *XVIIe siècle*, vol. 42 (1959), pp. 62–3.

115 Filhol, 'Rédaction des coutumes', p. 84.

116 P. Villard, *Les Justices seigneuriales dans La Marche* (Paris, 1969), pp. 153–4; see also Mousnier, *Vénalité des offices*, pp. 184–92.

117 Ordinance of Orléans (1561), art. 44; of Moulins (1566), arts 14, 19; of Blois (1579), arts 112–13 (Isambert, *Recueil général*, Vol. 14, pp. 76, 193–4, 409).

118 Francis II to the *parlement* of Toulouse, 31 March 1560, in C. Devic and J. Vaissète, *Histoire générale de Languedoc*, 18 vols (Paris, 1872–1904), Vol. 12, cols 562–3.

119 Declaration of 14 February 1562, quoted in N. M. Sutherland, *The Huguenot Struggle for Recognition* (New Haven, Conn., 1980), p. 135; Edict of Saint-Germain (July 1561), in E. and E. Haag, *La France protestante*, 10 vols (Paris, 1846–58), Vol. 10, p. 47; cf. the preamble to the edict of Romorantin (May 1560), and article 3 of the edict of Saint-Germain (January 1562), in Haag, *France protestante*, Vol. 10, pp. 44–50; and cf., too, M. François (ed.), *Lettres de Henri III*, Vol. 3 (Paris, 1972), p. 124, n. 1.

120 Devic, *Histoire générale de Languedoc*, Vol. 12, col. 578.

121 Harding, *Anatomy of a Power Élite*, p. 91; much of the material in this paragraph derives from this source.

122 Thus Beza on the situation in Burgundy, quoted in ibid., p. 58.

123 Almost all of the towns in Harding's list (*Anatomy of a Power Élite*, p. 92) of creations of League councils in 1589 were *chefs-lieux* of *bailliages* or their equivalents. Several of these already had such councils; cf. also the existence of such councils in towns not included in this particular list – for example, at Bourges, *chef-lieu* of the *bailliage* of Berry (below, p. 143). On medieval precedents for *gouverneurs'* councils see Dupont-Ferrier, *Officiers royaux*, p. 68; and on *baillis'* councils, above, pp. 49, 51.

124 François (ed.), *Lettres de Henri III*, Vol. 3, pp. 86–8.

125 A. Petracchi, 'I "Maîtres des Requêtes": genesi dell' amministrazione periferica di tipo moderno nella monarchia francese tardo-medioevale e rinascimentale', *Annali della fondazione italiana par la storia amministrativa*, vol. 1 (1964), pp. 231–2.

126 For some examples, above, pp. 59–60, 63.

127 For some examples see G. Dupont-Ferrier, 'Le rôle des commissaires royaux dans le gouvernement de la France spécialement du XIVe au XVIe siècle', in *Mélanges Paul Fournier* (Paris, 1929), pp. 171–84; see also below, p. 88.

128 i.e., the theory of *justice retenue*: see Dupont-Ferrier, 'Rôle des commissaires royaux', pp. 176–7; also R. Bonney, *Political Change in France under Richelieu and Mazarin, 1624–1661* (Oxford, 1978), p. 442.

129   *Ordonnances des rois de France*, Vol. 1, pp. 680–1, and Vol. 2, p. 216; Isambert, *Recueil général*, Vol. 12, pp. 592–4, and Vol. 14, p. 513. The 1493 edict is printed in part in *Ordonnances des rois de France*, Vol. 20, p. 428; see also Bonney, *Political Change*, p. 102.

130   Petracchi, 'I "Maitres de Requêtes"', pp. 236–7; F. Garrisson, *Essai sur les commissions d'application de l'édit de Nantes* (Montpellier, 1964), p. 41, n. 90, observing mention of *chevauchées* in a *règlement* of 1526; cf. Michaud, *Grande Chancellerie*, p. 79, n. 5.

131   Harding, *Anatomy of a Power Élite*, p. 193; Garrisson, *Essai*, pp. 42–7; Bonney, *Political Change*, pp. 140–1.

132   Quotations from the 1582 commissions are taken from G. Hanotaux, *Origines de l'institution des intendants des provinces* (Paris, 1884), pp. 187 ff.

133   Hanotaux, *Origines*, p. 208, and for the quotation that follows.

134   See above, p. 54.

135   Karcher, 'L'assemblée des notables', p. 135.

136   Bibliothèque Nationale, manuscrits Dupuy 87, f. 151vo.

137   ibid., manuscrits français 23050, f. 107: 'Des fondemens de l'estat et des moyens de regner'. Largely a typical Renaissance handbook for the prince, this anonymous treatise, bound with other papers prepared for the Saint-Germain assembly, nevertheless contains clear echoes of Bodinian ideas on sovereign authority; see below, pp. 158–9.

138   Bibliothèque Nationale, manuscrits Dupuy 87, f. 151ro.

CHAPTER 4

1   Spooner, *International Economy*, p. 248.

2   Goubert, *Ancien régime*, p. 69.

3   Ch. de Figon (1579), quoted in Yardeni, *Conscience nationale*, p. 36; E. P. Goldschmidt, 'Le voyage de Hieronimus Monetarius à travers la France, 17 septembre 1494–14 avril 1495', *Humanisme et Renaissance*, vol. 6 (1939), pp. 71 ff.

4   Quoted in Picot, *Histoire des Etats-généraux*, Vol. 1, p. 506.

5   J. Kirshner, 'Les travaux de Raymond de Roover sur la pensée économique des scholastiques', *Annales ESC*, vol. 30 (1975), pp. 324–5; J. A. Schumpeter, *History of Economic Analysis* (New York, 1954), pp. 93 ff.; R. de Roover, 'The concept of the just price: theory and economic policy', *Journal of Economic History*, vol. 18 (1958), p. 423; R. de Roover, 'Scholastic economics: survival and lasting influence from the sixteenth century to Adam Smith', *Quarterly Journal of Economics*, vol. 69 (1955), p. 169.

6   Quoted in D. Richet, 'Le cours officiel des monnaies étrangères circulant en France au XVI[e] siècle', *Revue historique*, vol. 225 (1961), p. 324; Schumpeter, *History of Economic Analysis*, p. 100, n. 26; cf. Aristotle, *Nicomachean Ethics*, 1133[a] 5–1133[b] 29.

7   C. Johnson (ed.), *The 'De Moneta' of Nicholas Oresme* (London, 1956), p. 10.

8   H. A. Miskimin, *Money, Prices and Foreign Exchange in Fourteenth-Century France* (New Haven, Conn., 1963), pp. 50–2; cf. Spooner, *International Economy*, p. 105.

9   Quoted in R. Cazelles, 'Quelques réflexions à propos des mutations de la monnaie royale française (1295–1360)', *Le Moyen Age*, vol. 72 (1966), p. 96.

10   Johnson (ed.), *'De Moneta'*, pp. 10–11.

11   Cazelles, 'Quelques réflexions', p. 275; Picot, *Histoire des États-généraux*, Vol. 1, p. 166; *Ordonnances des rois de France*, Vol. 3, p. 440; R. Cazelles, 'La stabilisation de la monnaie par la création du franc (décembre 1360) – blocage d'une société',

Traditio, vol. 32 (1976), p. 293. A phase of monetary stability did indeed ensue: Miskimin, *Money, Prices*, pp. 187 ff.

12 Picot, *Histoire des États-généraux*, Vol. 1, p. 307; *Ordonnances des rois de France*, Vol. 13, p. 34; R. Gandilhon, *Politique économique de Louis XI* (Rennes, 1941), pp. 324–41.

13 Thus Charles VI in 1406, quoted in E. Miller, 'The economic policies of governments: France and England', in M. M. Postan *et al.* (eds), *The Cambridge Economic History of Europe*, Vol. 3, *Economic Organization and Policies in the Middle Ages* (Cambridge, 1963), p. 331.

14 For example, *Ordonnances des rois de France*, Vol. 2, pp. 58–9, and Vol. 5, pp. 499–502; Gandilhon, *Politique économique*, pp. 446, 449.

15 ibid., pp. 121–35.

16 Lot and Fawtier, *Histoire des institutions*, Vol. 2, pp. 434–5; H. Sée, *Louis XI et les villes* (Paris, 1891), p. 70; Gandilhon, *Politique économique*, p. 167.

17 ibid., pp. 156–7, 217, 175 ff., 245 ff.

18 The most convenient introduction to debate over the meaning and significance of 'mercantilism' is D. C. Coleman (ed.), *Revisions in Mercantilism* (London, 1969); and to discussion of the so-called seventeenth-century 'crisis' G. Parker and L. M. Smith (eds), *The General Crisis of the Seventeenth Century* (London, 1978). On pre-seventeenth-century precedents for 'mercantilist' postures in France, see the opening chapters of C. W. Cole, *Colbert and a Century of French Mercantilism* (New York, 1964).

19 E. Le Roy Ladurie, 'Les masses profondes: la paysannerie', in *Histoire économique et sociale*, Vol. 1, pt 2, pp. 506 ff.

20 Y. Bézard, *La Vie rurale dans le sud de la région parisienne de 1450 à 1560* (Paris, 1929), p. 159.

21 Ladurie, *Paysans de Languedoc*, Vol. 1, pp. 201–4; R. Dion, *Histoire de la vigne et du vin en France* (Paris, 1959), pp. 417 ff.

22 R. Gascon, 'La France du mouvement: les commerces et les villes', in *Histoire économique et sociale*, Vol. 1, pt 1, pp. 251–2; Gascon, *Grand commerce*, pp. 308–13.

23 A. Bouton, *Le Maine: histoire économique et sociale, XIVe, XVe et XVIe siècles* (Le Mans, 1970), p. 268; G. Caster, *Le Commerce du pastel et de l'épicerie à Toulouse, 1450–1561* (Toulouse, 1962), p. 383; Ladurie, 'Masses profondes', pp. 586–7.

24 Bézard, *Vie rurale*, pp. 175–7; P. Raveau, *Essai sur la situation économique et l'état social en Poitou au XVIe siècle* (Paris, 1931), p. 42; K. R. Andrews, *The Spanish Caribbean: Trade and Plunder, 1530–1630* (New Haven, Conn., 1978), p. 181.

25 R. H. Bautier, 'Notes sur la commerce du fer en Europe occidentale du XIIIe au XVIe siècle', *Revue d'histoire de la sidérurgie*, vol. 1, no. 4 (1960), pp. 7–35; B. Gille, 'L'organisation de la production du fer au Moyen Age', *Revue d'histoire de la sidérurgie*, vol. 9, no. 2 (1968), p. 103; H. Polge, 'Les techniques pré-industrielles en Gascogne gersoise', *Bulletin de la Société Archéologique, Historique, Littéraire et Scientifique du Gers*, année 66 (1965), p. 389, and année 67 (1966), pp. 195, 197; P.-M. Bondois, 'Le développement de l'industrie verrière dans la région parisienne de 1515 à 1665', *Revue d'histoire économique et sociale*, vol. 23 (1936–7), pp. 45–68; L. Trenard, 'Le charbon avant l'ère industrielle', *Charbon et sciences humaines: actes du colloque organisé par la faculté des lettres de l'université de Lille* (Paris, 1966), p. 54.

26 B. Gille, 'Contribution à une histoire de la civilisation technique, ii: L'évolution des techniques au XVIe siècle', *Techniques et civilisations*, vol. 2 (1953), p. 120; E. L. Eisenstein, *The Printing Press as an Agent of Change: Communications and Cultural Transformations in Early-Modern Europe*, 2 vols (Cambridge, 1979), Vol. 1, p. 399; Gascon, *Grand commerce*, pp. 389, 904; Febvre and Martin,

L'Apparition du livre, ch. 6; R. Hirsch, *Printing, Selling and Reading, 1450–1550* (Wiesbaden, 1974), pp. 19–20.

27   And even more so under Francis I: see below, p. 194, n. 99.

28   Bézard, *Vie rurale*, p. 195.

29   Quoted in Morineau, 'La conjoncture', p. 895.

30   Thus J. Meuvret, 'Circulation monétaire et utilisation économique de la monnaie dans la France du XVIᵉ siècle et du XVIIᵉ siècle', *Études d'histoire moderne et contemporaine*, vol. 1 (1947), pp. 14–28; and Y.-M. Bercé, *Histoire des Croquants: étude des soulèvements populaires au XVIIᵉ siècle dans le sud-ouest de la France* (Paris, 1974), Vol. 1, pp. 41–2. But the *troc* does not preclude the use of money as the language for equalising exchanges – as the 'balancing instrument', in Oresme's phrase.

31   cf. the typology of towns outlined by Braudel, *The Mediterranean*, Vol. 1, pp. 312 ff.

32   Gascon, *Grand commerce*, passim; H. A. Lloyd, *The Rouen Campaign, 1590–1592: Politics, Warfare and the Early-Modern State* (London, 1973), pp. 1–3; E. E. Rich, 'Expansion as a concern of all Europe', in G. R. Potter (ed.), *The New Cambridge Modern History*, Vol. 1, *The Renaissance, 1493–1520* (London, 1957), pp. 457–8, 465–6; Andrews, *Spanish Caribbean*, p. 65; M. Trudel, *The Beginnings of New France, 1524–1663* (Toronto, 1973), pp. 1–54.

33   Imbart de La Tour, *Origines de la Réforme*, Vol. 1, p. 224; Morineau, 'La conjoncture', p. 906. Yet shortages within France did not prevent royal grants of licences to export grain to Italy: for example, *Catalogue des actes de François Iᵉʳ*, Vol. 1, nos 2798, 2873, 2921.

34   Spooner, *International Economy*, p. 266; Ladurie, 'Les masses profondes', p. 583; Morineau, 'La conjoncture', p. 993; Neveux, 'Déclin et reprise', p. 187; M. Baulant, 'Le prix des grains à Paris de 1431 à 1788', *Annales ESC*, vol. 23 (1968), p. 538.

35   Gascon, *Grand commerce*, pp. 613 ff., 945; P. Deyon, 'Variations de la production textile aux XVIᵉ et XVIIᵉ siècles: sources et premiers résultats', *Annales ESC*, vol. 18 (1963), p. 947; Morineau, 'La conjoncture', p. 925; Gascon, 'La France du mouvement', p. 270; H. Lapeyre, *Une Famille de marchands: les Ruiz* (Paris, 1955), pp. 601, 456.

36   Caster, *Commerce du pastel*, p. 383.

37   See below, p. 134.

38   Gascon, 'La France du mouvement', p. 330; Spooner, *International Economy*, p. 298; Braudel, *The Mediterranean*, p. 220; Benedict, *Rouen during the Wars of Religion*, pp. 229–34; E. Trocmé and M. Delafosse, *Le Commerce rochelais de la fin du XVᵉ siècle au début du XVIIᵉ* (Paris, 1953), p. 198.

39   F. Braudel, *Civilisation matérielle et capitalisme*, Vol. 3 (Paris, 1979), p. 287.

40   Below, pp. 100–1.

41   For example, Malestroit, below, p. 99; E. Le Roy Ladurie, *Histoire du climat depuis l'an mil* (Paris, 1967).

42   Pierre de Brantôme, *Oeuvres complètes*, ed. L. Lalanne, Vol. 4 (Paris, 1868), p. 335; J. Spengler, *Économie et population: les doctrines français avant 1800, de Budé à Condorcet* (Paris, 1954), pp. 21 ff.

43   Especially with Emmanuel Le Roy Ladurie and his followers: see also note 50 below.

44   Ladurie's estimate: 'Les masses profondes', pp. 559–61.

45   Thus Goubert, *Ancien régime*, p. 35.

46   In Normandy, at least: Bois, *Crise*, pp. 167, 224.

47   The foregoing draws especially upon Bois, *Crise*; Sivery, *Hainault*; Neveux, 'Déclin et reprise'; and L. Merle, *La Métairie et l'évolution agraire de la Gâtine poitevine de la fin du Moyen Age à la Révolution* (Paris, 1958).

48 ibid., pp. 202–4; Jacquart, *Crise rurale*, pp. 46–7; Ladurie, *Paysans de Languedoc*, Vol. 1, p. 290; cf. J. Jacquart, 'La rente foncière, indice conjoncturel?', *Revue historique*, vol. 253 (1975), pp. 363–4.

49 See above, pp. 32–4, and below, pp. 111–12.

50 Linked, in Ladurie's view, with technological stagnation, itself a function of the *mentalités* both of depressed peasants and of *rassembleurs des terres* (see *Paysans de Languedoc*, Vol. 1, p. 639; J. M. Pesez and E. Le Roy Ladurie, 'Le cas français', *Villages désertés et histoire économique (XIᵉ–XVIIIᵉ siècle)* (Paris, 1965), p. 234). A. Croix, 'La démographie du pays nantais au XVIᵉ siècle', *Annales de démographie historique* (1967), pp. 75–8, postulates a precise correlation between bad harvests and falls in rates of conception, and vice versa.

51 See the discussion by J. Heers, 'Les limites des méthodes statistiques pour les recherches de la démographie médiévale', *Annales de démographie historique* (1968), pp. 43–72.

52 Ordinance of Villers-Cotterets (1539), arts 51–3 (Isambert, *Recueil général*, Vol. 12, pp. 610–11); A. Vaquier, *Le premier registre paroissial de l'état-civil d'Ermont, 1558–1577* (Persan-Beaumont, 1962), pp. 1–2; Goubert, *Cent mille provinciaux*, p. 51.

53 cf., however, the demographic 'cycles' discerned by J. Dupâquier and E. Le Roy Ladurie, 'Quatre-vingt villages (XIIIᵉ–XVIIIᵉ siècles)', *Annales ESC*, vol. 24 (1969), pp. 424–33; and the conclusions reached by E. Baratier, *La Démographie provençale du XIIIᵉ au XVIᵉ siècle avec chiffres de comparaison pour le XVIIIᵉ siécle* (Paris, 1961), pp. 88–94.

54 cf. Ladurie's with Morineau's estimate: 'Les masses profondes', p. 561, and 'La conjoncture', p. 904.

55 In relation to the calculations that follow, cf. especially B. H. Slicher van Bath, 'Yield ratios, 810–1820', *A.A.G. Bijdragen*, vol. 10 (1963); Ladurie, 'Les masses profondes', pp. 569–75; Braudel, *The Mediterranean*, Vol. 1, pp. 420–7; F. Braudel, *Capitalism and Material Life*, Vol. 1 (English trans., London, 1967), pp. 79 ff.

56 cf. Morineau's 'conventional' figure of 750g per head per day ('La conjoncture', p. 978).

57 Assuming biennial crop-rotation in the south and triennial in the north.

58 An estimate based on Devèze, *Vie de la forêt*.

59 This figure assumes family units of five members, triennial crop-rotation, appropriation at the rate of 20 per cent of the produce and 10 per cent for maketing: cf. Jacquart, *Crise rurale*, p. 140, and Goubert, *Ancien régime*, p. 130. But cf., too, Morineau, 'La conjoncture', p. 980, where four-member households appear to be assumed; and on taxation cf. below, pp. 110–11.

60 Calculated from Bois, *Crise*, p. 140; Ladurie, *Paysans de Languedoc*, Vol. 1, pp. 240–1; and Jacquart, *Crise rurale*, p. 140; cf., too, G. Fourquin, *Les Campagnes de la région parisienne à la fin du Moyen Age* (Paris, 1964), pp. 516–27.

61 M. Baulant, 'Prix et salaires à Paris au XVIᵉ siècle: sources et résultats', *Annales ESC*, vol. 31 (1976), pp. 954–95.

62 Gascon, 'La France du mouvement', p. 397; Gascon, *Grand commerce*, pp. 348–50; R. Gascon, 'Immigration et croissance au XVIᵉ siècle: l'exemple de Lyon (1529–1563)', *Annales ESC*, vol. 25 (1970), pp. 988–1001; J. Nadal and E. Giralt, *La Population catalane de 1553 à 1717: l'immigration française* (Paris, 1960), pp. 78–113. Compare A. Croix, *Nantes et le pays nantais au XVIᵉ siècle: étude démographique* (Paris, 1974), p. 210; P. Tucoo-Chala, 'Un exemple d'essor urbain: Pau au XVIᵉ siècle', *Annales du Midi*, vol. 78 (1966), pp. 345–61. And compare, too, Braudel's claim that France 'was a vast emigration zone' (*Capitalism and Material Life*, Vol. 1, p. 29).

63 Zeller, *Institutions*, pp. 384–5; N. Z. Davis, *Society and Culture in Early-Modern*

France (London, 1975), pp. 17–64; J. Imbert, 'L'Église et l'état face au problème hospitalier au XVIe siècle', *Études Gabriel Le Bras*, vol. 1 (Paris, 1965), pp. 577–92; G. Procacci, *Classi sociali e monarchia assoluta nella Francia della prima meta del secolo XVI* (Turin, 1955), pp. 24–37.

64 Nicolas de Montand, *Le Miroir des françois* (1582), pp. 443, 454–5.

65 Baulant, 'Prix et salaires à Paris'; E. Le Roy Ladurie and P. Couperie, 'Le mouvement des loyers parisiens de la fin du Moyen Age au XVIIIe siècle', *Annales ESC*, vol. 25 (1970), pp. 1020–1; cf. the movements of rents and wages, often paid in kind, in rural Languedoc: Ladurie, *Paysans de Languedoc*, Vol. 1, pp. 280–91, 270.

66 *Les Paradoxes du seigneur de Malestroit* (Paris, 1578), p. 8.

67 Thireau, *Charles Du Moulin*, pp. 418–31, esp. p. 428.

68 *Discours de Jean Bodin sur le rehaussement . . . [et response] aux paradoxes de Monsieur de Malestroit* (Paris, 1578), p. 28. On the Malestroit–Bodin debate see especially P. Harsin, 'L'afflux des métaux précieux au XVIe siècle et la théorie de la monnaie chez les auteurs français', *Revue d'histoire économique et sociale* (1927), pp. 321–50.

69 Bodin, *République*, pp. 705–6, 876, 883, 877.

70 In the mid-1580s France was importing large quantities of Iberian salt to combat a disastrous domestic shortage; while, with grain prices climbing steeply at home, hundreds of French vessels were lading grain in the Baltic – apparently in order to carry it to Spain to exchange for the silver specie that flowed into the French western ports at that time (P. Dollinger, *The German Hansa* (London, 1964), pp. 349, 359; P. Jeannin, 'L'économie française au milieu du XVIe siècle et le marché russe', *Annales ESC*, vol. 9 (1954), p. 29; Lapeyre, *Les Ruiz*, p. 550; Braudel, *The Mediterranean*, vol. 1, pp. 586 ff.; Spooner, *International Economy*, pp. 164, 231).

71 Gascon, 'La France du mouvement', p. 270.

72 On these particular propositions cf. Braudel, *Civilisation matérielle et capitalisme*, Vol. 3, pp. 94, 248, arguing that in general Europe's late-medieval and early-modern trade routes 'encircle France at a fair distance, barely touching it', and that 'the mosaic [*sic*] of customs barriers is not a decisive problem in itself'.

73 J. Tanguy, *Le Commerce du port de Nantes au milieu du XVIe siècle* (Paris, 1956), p. 77; P. Dardel, 'Les relations maritimes et comerciales entre la France, notamment les ports de Rouen et du Havre, et les ports de la mer Baltique de 1497 à 1783', *Annales de Normandie*, vol. 19 (1969), p. 53; E. Coornaert, *Les Français et le commerce international à Anvers, fin du XVe–XVIe siècles*, 2 vols (Paris, 1961); Y. Renouard, 'Les hommes d'affaires français de la Renaissance', *Revue historique*, vol. 228 (1962), pp. 321–6; J. Meuvret, 'Manuels et traités à l'usage des négociants aux premières époques de l'âge moderne', *Etudes d'histoire moderne et contemporaine*, vol. 5 (1953), pp. 5–29; D. Richet, 'Une société commerciale Paris–Lyon dans la deuxième moitié du XVIe siècle', *Bulletin de la Société de l'Histoire de Paris et de l'Ile de France*, vol. 92 (1965), pp. 30–2; Gascon, *Grand commerce*, pp. 203 ff.

74 Consider, for example, the bases of Braudel's calculations (*The Mediterranean*, Vol. 1, p. 441; *Civilisation matérielle et capitalisme*, Vol. 2, pp. 186–7, and Vol. 3, pp. 254–68), and of Spooner's, *International Economy*, p. 310.

75 Seyssel, *Monarchie de France*, pp. 162, 200; L. Pannier and P. Meyer (eds), *Le Débat des hérauts d'armes* (Paris, 1877), pp. 27–9.

76 Picot, *Histoire des États-généraux*, Vol. 2, p. 255; C. W. Cole, *Colbert and a Century of French Mercantilism* (Hamden, Conn., 1964), pp. 16–18; Gascon, *Grand commerce*, pp. 713, 945; Smith, *Anti-Courtier Trend*, pp. 117–24, 154–6; L. Sozzi, 'La polémique anti-Italienne en France au XVIe siècle', *Accademia della scienze di Torino: atti*, vol. 106 (1972), pp. 99–190.

77 E. Coornaert, 'La politique économique de la France au début du règne de François Ier', *Annales de l'université de Paris*, vol. 8 (1933), pp. 414–27.

78 *Ordonnances des rois de France: règne de François Ier*, Vol. 2 (1517–20), pp. 531–4; ibid., Vol. 6 (1530–2), pp. 241–5; *Ordonnances des rois de France*, Vol. 21, pp. 166–72; cf. Imbart de La Tour, *Origines de la Réforme*, Vol. 1, pp. 330–1.

79 Notably by E. Levasseur, *Histoire des classes ouvrières et de l'industrie en France avant 1789*, 2 vols (Paris, 1901), Vol. 2, pp. 74–5, cf. pp. 125–6.

80 For example, *Ordonnances des rois de France*, Vol. 2, pp. 189–90 (1343), pp. 352–80 (1351); ibid., Vol. 5, pp. 499–502 (1372); ibid., Vol. 11, pp. 48–52 (1420); *Ordonnances des rois de France: règne de François Ier*, Vol. 6 (1530–2), pp. 166–7, 192–3; ibid., Vol. 7 (1533–5), pp. 200–2.

81 Fontanon, *Édicts et ordonnances*, Vol. 1, ff. 807, 825–6.

82 Coornaert, 'La politique économique', p. 416.

83 *Ordonnances des rois de France: règne de François Ier*, Vol. 1 (1515–16), pp. 474–7; ibid., Vol. 2 (1517–20), pp. 502–4, 469–71; ibid., Vol. 5 (1527–9), pp. 9–11, 280–3; ibid., Vol. 6 (1530–2), pp. 129–31, 203–6, 231–2; ibid., Vol. 7 (1533–5), pp. 199–200; Spooner, *International Economy*, pp. 121, 124 ff.

84 *Ordonnances des rois de France: règne de François Ier*, Vol. 6 (1530–2), pp. 269–70; ibid., Vol. 7 (1533–5), pp. 13–16; Fontanon, *Édicts et ordonnances*, Vol. 2, ff. 113, 114–25.

85 From 1500 to 1546 gold coins constituted on average two-thirds of the total annual coinage of the French royal mints. For the remainder of the century that average fell to 17 per cent of total issues (calculated from Spooner, *International Economy*, pp. 334–7).

86 Thus Spooner (ibid., p. 104), from whose work I derive most of the material upon which the foregoing paragraph is based; see also E. Szlechter, 'La monnaie en France au XVIe siècle', *Revue historique de droit français et étranger*, sér. 4, vol. 29 (1951), p. 509.

87 Spooner, *International Economy*, p. 106; Doucet, *Institutions*, Vol. 1, pp. 200–2.

88 Hotman, *Francogallia*, p. 476.

89 Spooner, *International Economy*, pp. 161, 163, 330.

90 cf. John II's introduction of the gold franc in 1360 (above, p. 87). The introduction of a silver coin, as the exact nominal equivalent of that gold coin, in the sixteenth-century silver-inflationary phase, is noteworthy.

91 Above, p. 99.

92 Gascon, 'La France du mouvement', pp. 326–7. Doubtless the rejection was influenced by Malestroit's critic Bodin, deputy for Vermandois at this assembly and a leading light in its deliberations (cf. below, p. 138). Yet Bodin had already recognised as a 'mark of sovereignty' that 'only the sovereign prince has power' over the 'value and weight of money' (*République*, p. 242).

93 Fontanon, *Édicts et ordonnances*, Vol. 2, pp. 173–9.

94 *Ordonnances des rois de France: règne de François Ier*, Vol. 3 (1521–3), pp. 18–20; ibid., Vol. 7 (1533–5), pp. 124–6; C. M. Cipolla, *European Culture and Overseas Expansion* (Harmondsworth, 1970), p. 69; Braudel, *The Mediterranean*, Vol. 1, p. 298.

95 Fontanon, *Édicts et ordonnances*, Vol. 4, pp. 663–6; on the relative advantages of small over larger ships in the sixteenth century, see Braudel, *The Mediterranean*, Vol. 1, pp. 299–312; on galleys, see J. F. Guilmartin, Jr, *Gunpowder and Galleys* (Cambridge, 1974), pp. 264–73.

96 *Ordonnances des rois de France: règne de François Ier*, Vol. 5 (1527–9), pp. 61–2; ibid., Vol. 7 (1533–5), pp. 51–3; Fontanon, *Édicts et ordonnances*, Vol. 1, ff. 747–8.

97 Gascon, *Grand commerce*, pp. 310–11; cf. above, p. 89, *Ordonnances des rois de France: règne de François Ier*, Vol. 2 (1517–20), pp. 1–3; ibid., Vol. 6 (1530–2), pp. 245–55; Fontanon, *Édicts et ordonnances*, Vol. 1, ff. 1042–5; G. d'Assailly, 'Des édits somptuaires', *Revue politique et parlementaire*, vol. 70 (1968), pp. 72–7.

98 Isambert, *Recueil général*, Vol. 12, pp. 672–4; Fontanon, *Édicts et ordonnances*, Vol. 1, ff. 975–6; cf. J. U. Nef, *Industry and Government in France and England, 1540–1640* (Ithaca, NY, 1957), p. 20.

99 There are 184 separate royal acts creating a total of 433 new fairs (i.e. three-, four- or six-monthly) and 138 weekly markets listed in Vol. 1 (1515–30) alone of the *Catalogue des actes de François Ier*. Although these grants, many of them made in response to applications from local seigneurs, are scarcely proof of a coherent royal policy in relation to commerce, they may nevertheless be taken to indicate how trade was thriving and how widespread was the urge to attract a share of it.

100 Fontanon, *Édicts et ordonnances*, Vol. 2, ff. 425–6, 469–78, 485–90.

101 The 'general *cahier*' of the Third Estate in Orléans on matters of 'merchandise' is printed in C. J. Meyer, *Des États-généraux et autres assemblées nationales*, 18 vols (Paris, 1788–9), Vol. 11, pp. 454–75; and in Lalourcé and Duval, *Recueil des cahiers généraux des trois ordres des États-généraux*, 6 vols (Paris, 1789), Vol. 1, pp. 427–47. Lalourcé and Duval also print (ibid., Vol. 2, pp. 327–55) the equivalent portion of the Third Estate *cahier* at Blois in 1576, which is not included by Meyer. See also Picot, *Histoire des Etats-généraux*, Vol. 2, pp. 252–5, and Vol. 3, pp. 31–3, 38; and cf. Gascon, 'La France du mouvement', p. 348.

102 L'Hôpital, *Oeuvres*, Vol. 1, pp. 375–411, 441–53, and Vol. 2, pp. 161–7; Picot, *Histoire des États-généraux*, Vol. 2, p. 311; Meyer, *Des États-généraux*, Vol. 13, pp. 182–211.

103 Ordinance of Roussillon (art. 38), of Orléans (arts 107, 138, 144), of Blois (arts 355–8) (Isambert, *Recueil général*, Vol. 14, pp. 90, 96–7, 459–60); Fontanon, *Édicts et ordonnances*, Vol. 1, f. 833; Nef, *Industry and Government*, p. 20.

104 In his unpublished 'Traité de la réformation de la justice' (*Oeuvres*, Vol. 4, p. 44): cf. above, p. 183, n. 24.

105 Article 147 of the ordinance of Orléans (Isambert, *Recueil général*, Vol. 14, p. 97) simply directed that ancient measures be used without fraud.

106 Picot, *Histoire des États-généraux*, Vol. 2, pp. 258–9, and Vol. 3, pp. 38–9; Lalourcé and Duval, *Recueil des cahiers généraux*, Vol. 2, p. 342; ordinance of Orléans (arts 98–9) and of Blois (art. 59) (Isambert, *Recueil général*, Vol. 14, pp. 88, 460–1).

107 L'Hôpital, *Oeuvres*, Vol. 1, pp. 356–7; cf. A. H. J. Greenidge, *Infamia: Its Place in Roman Public and Private Law* (Oxford, 1894), pp. 67, 131–2.

108 Doucet, *Institutions*, Vol. 1, p. 278; G. Bord, 'Recherches sur les origines des tribunaux de commerce: la bourse commune des marchands de Toulouse', *Mélanges de droit, d'histoire et d'économie offerts à Marcel Laborde-Lacoste* (Bordeaux, 1963), pp. 29–41; P. Logié, 'Le tribunal de commerce d'Amiens (1567–1967)', *Bulletin trimestriel de la Société des Antiquaires de Picardie*, vol. 52 (1967), pp. 29–43. *Tribunaux consulaires* were first formally created in Toulouse in 1549 and then in Rouen in 1557; but they multiplied greatly by virtue of the edicts of 1563 and 1566.

109 Fontanon, *Édicts et ordonnances*, Vol. 1, ff. 1091–6.

110 cf. Nef, *Industry and Government*, p. 15.

111 Fontanon, *Édicts et ordonnances*, Vol. 4, ff. 1373–9.

112 See below, p. 139.

113 Karcher, 'Assemblée des notables', pp. 122–35. For the commissioners' instruc- tions to 'receive the complaints of our poor people', see Hanotaux, *Origines de l'institution*, p. 194.

114 See above, pp. 82–3.

115 For instance, Fontanon, *Édicts et ordonnances*, Vol. 4, f. 1376.

116 See above, pp. 65–6.

117 See the estimate by Morineau, 'La conjoncture', p. 980, evidently assuming four members per household.

118 Baulant, 'Prix des grains', p. 538.
119 cf. above, pp. 96–7.
120 In Béziers in 1587–8 wheat sold at 4·17 *livres per setier* (66 litres in this district): see Ladurie, *Paysans de Languedoc*, Vol. 2, pp. 820–1.
121 See above, pp. 90, 97.
122 P. Ourliac and J. de Malafosse, *Histoire du droit privé*, Vol. 2, *Les Biens* (Paris, 1961); E. Meynial, 'Notes sur la formation de la théorie du domaine divisé (domaine directe et domaine utile) du XIIᵉ au XIVᵉ siècle dans les romanistes: étude de dogmatique juridique', *Mélanges Fitting*, vol. 2 (Paris, 1969), pp. 411–61; P. Tisset, 'Mythes et Réalités du droit écrit', *Etudes d'histoire du droit privé offertes à Pierre Petot* (Paris, 1958), pp. 554–6; P. Ourliac, 'Droit commun et commune opinion', *Studi clasice*, vol. 7 (1965), pp. 103–7. Compare J. Yver, 'L'état des études d'histoire du droit privé en France', *Revue historique de droit français et étranger*, sér. 4, vol. 45 (1967), pp. 708–11; F. Schulz, *Classical Roman Law* (Oxford, 1951), pp. 338–40; A. Rodger, *Owners and Neighbours in Roman Law* (Oxford, 1972), p. 1; F. A. Mann, 'Outlines of a history of expropriation', *The Law Quarterly Review*, vol. 75 (1959), pp. 188–219.
123 Schnapper, *Les Rentes*, pp. 50–7, et passim.
124 Quoted in Ourliac and de Malafosse, *Droit privé*, Vol. 2, p. 168.
125 Filhol, *Cristofle de Thou*, p. 272.
126 Schnapper, *Les Rentes*, p. 283.
127 Quoted in Thireau, *Charles Du Moulin*, p. 269, n. 368.
128 Though the uses of tithe records as an index to the yield of the land (cf. the estimates discussed above, p. 96, and works noted in note 55) are rightly questioned in J. Goy and E. Le Roy Ladurie (eds), *Les Fluctuations de la produit de la dîme: conjoncture décimale et domaniale de la fin du Moyen Age au XVIIIᵉ siècle* (Paris, 1972) – notably in the contributions by Frèche (pp. 214–44) and Morineau (pp. 320–33).
129 See above, pp. 95–6; also Bois, *Crise*, p. 233; R. Moulin, 'Transactions entre le seigneur et les habitants d'Espinouse et de Saint-Jeannet en 1527', *Annales de Haute-Provence*, vol. 38 (1965), p. 21.
130 J. B. Wood, *The Nobility of the Election of Bayeux, 1463–1666: Continuity through Change* (Princeton, NJ, 1980), p. 149.
131 Jacquart, *Crise rurale*, pp. 241–5; J. Estèbe, 'La bourgeoisie marchande et la terre à Toulouse au XVIᵉ siècle (1519–1560)', *Annales du Midi*, vol. 76 (1964), pp. 457–67; P. Raveau, *L'Agriculture et les classes paysannes: la transformation de la propriété dans le Haut Poitou au XVIᵉ siècle* (Paris, 1926), pp. 292–5; E. Le Roy Ladurie, 'Sur Montpellier et sa campagne aux XVIᵉ et XVIIᵉ siècles', *Annales ESC*, vol. 12 (1957), pp. 223–30; L. Le Clert, 'Les bourgeois de Troyes possédant fiefs en 1523', *Annuaire administratif, statistique et commercial du département de l'Aube*, année 68 (1894), pp. 17–38; cf. J.-M. Constant, 'Quelques problèmes de mobilité sociale et la vie matérielle chez les gentilshommes de Beauce aux XVIᵉ et XVIIᵉ siècles', *Acta poloniae historica*, vol. 36 (1977), pp. 83–94.
132 Jacquart, *Crise rurale*, pp. 232–40; Ladurie, *Paysans de Languedoc*, Vol. 1, p. 256.
133 P. Goubert, 'Le paysan et la terre: seigneurie, tenure, exploitation', in Braudel and Labrousse (eds), *Histoire économique et sociale de la France*, Vol. 2 (1970), p. 135.
134 See above, pp. 33–4.
135 Jacquart, *Crise rurale*, p. 167.
136 Monluc, *Commentaires*, p. 829.
137 Bercé, *Histoire des Croquants*, Vol. 2, p. 701.
138 Monluc, *Commentaires*, p. 483; Pillorget, *Mouvements insurrectionnels*, p. 242; G. Procacci, 'La Provence à la veille des guerres de religion: une période décisive, 1533–1545', *Revue d'histoire moderne et contemporaine*, vol. 5 (1958), pp. 256–7; S.-C. Gigon, *La Révolte de la gabelle en Guyenne (1548–1549)* (Paris, 1906), pp. 54,

230; Ladurie, 'Les masses profondes', pp. 846, 830; Bercé, *Histoire des Croquants*, Vol. 2, p. 701.

139 E. Le Roy Ladurie, *Carnival: A People's Uprising at Romans, 1579–1580* (London, 1980), pp. 331–2; Bercé, *Histoire des Croquants*, Vol. 2, p. 707.

140 cf. G. Fourquin, *The Anatomy of Popular Rebellion in the Middle Ages* (Oxford, 1978), p. 146.

141 Gigon, *Révolte de la gabelle*, p. 123; Bercé, *Histoire des Croquants*, Vol. 2, p. 707.

142 See above, pp. 29–30.

143 Bercé, *Histoire des Croquants*, Vol. 1, pp. 276–7; J. Lestrade, *Les Huguenots en Comminges* (Paris, 1900), pp. 204, 210–11; G. Post, *Studies in Medieval Legal Thought* (Princeton, NJ, 1964), pp. 39–50.

CHAPTER 5

1 On medieval heresy in general, see especially: M. D. Lambert, *Medieval Heresy: Popular Movements from Bogomil to Huss* (London, 1977); R. Morghen, 'Problèmes sur l'origine de l'hérésie au Moyen-Age', in J. Le Goff (ed.), *Hérésies et sociétés dans l'Europe pré-industrielle, 11ᵉ–18ᵉ siècles* (Paris, 1968), pp. 121–34; J. L. Nelson, 'Society, theodicy, and the origins of heresy: towards a re-assessment of the medieval evidence', *Church History*, vol. 9, ed. D. Baker (1972), pp. 65–77; A. Borst, *Les Cathares* (Paris, 1974), esp. p. 108.

2 N. Cohn, *The Pursuit of the Millennium* (London, 1970), p. 282; N. Cohn, *Europe's Inner Demons*, p. 251; K. Thomas, *Religion and the Decline of Magic* (London, 1971); H. R. Trevor-Roper, 'The European witch-craze of the sixteenth and seventeenth centuries', *Religion, the Reformation and Social Change* (London, 1967), pp. 90–192; R. Muchembled, 'Sorcellerie, culture populaire et Christianisme au XVIᵉ siècle', *Annales ESC*, vol. 28 (1973), p. 274. P. Bertin, 'Une affaire de sorcellerie dans un village d'Artois au XVIᵉ siècle', *Bulletin trimestriel de la Société Académique des Antiquaires de la Morinie*, vol. 18 (1957), p. 616, notes how in 1572, the year of the St Bartholomew's Day massacre, Charles IX was informed that his realm contained one hundred thousand witches.

3 See especially the contributions by L. Kolakowski and T. Manteuffel, in *Hérésies et sociétés* (above, n. 1), pp. 97–101; and G. Leff, *Heresy in the Middle Ages: The Relation of Heterodoxy to Dissent, c.1250–c.1450*, 2 vols (Manchester, 1967), Vol. 1, pp. 1–13.

4 Lambert, *Medieval Heresy*, p. 336.

5 Above, Chs 2 and 4.

6 M. Piton, 'L'idéal épiscopal selon les prédicateurs français de la fin du XVᵉ et du début du XVIᵉ siècle', *Revue d'histoire écclésiastique*, vol. 61 (1966), pp. 77–118, 393–423.

7 A fine example is the career of Vital de Thèbes: P. E. Ousset, 'Le clergé d'Aspet aux XVIᵉ et XVIIᵉ siècles', *Revue de Comminges*, vol. 68 (1955), pp. 49–69.

8 M. M. Edelstein, 'The social origins of the episcopacy in the reign of Francis I', *French Historical Studies*, vol. 8 (1974), pp. 371–92.

9 G. Le Bras, in A. Artonne *et al.* (eds), *Répertoire des statuts synodaux des diocèses de l'ancienne France* (Paris, 1969), pp. 5–7; Imbart de La Tour, *Origines de la Réforme*, Vol. 2 (Paris, 1946), p. 289, n. 1; F. Rapp, *L'Église et la vie religieuse en Occident à la fin du Moyen Age* (Paris, 1971), p. 213; M. Venard, 'Pour une sociologie du clergé au XVIᵉ siècle: recherche sur le recrutement sacerdotal dans la province d'Avignon', *Annales ESC*, vol. 23 (1968), p. 1015.

10 Will (1527) of Dame Jacquelyne de Laignes of Chaource, quoted in Galpern, *Religion of the People*, p. 25; F. Villard, 'Le livre de raison de Pierre Auneteau, vicaire de Saint-Jean-Baptiste de Châtellerault (1540–1552)', *Bulletin de la Société*

des Antiquaires de l'Ouest, sér. 4, vol. 7 (1964), pp. 428–30; A. Leroux, 'Livre de raison et registre de la famille de Pierre de Sainte-Feyre (1497–1553)', *Bulletin de la société scientifique, Historique et Archéologique de la Corrèze*, vol. 12 (1890), pp. 498–540.

11 See especially Delaruelle, *L'Église au temps du grand Schisme*, pt 2; L. Mâle, *L'Art religieux de la fin du Moyen Age en France* (Paris, 1925).

12 Rapp, *L'Église et la vie religieuse*, pp. 138, 144, 329; S. Ozment, *The Reformation in the Cities* (London, 1975), pp. 22–32.

13 Quoted in Adam, *Vie paroissiale*, p. 248.

14 See above, pp. 37–8.

15 Thomas à Kempis, *The Imitation of Christ* (London, 1910), pt 1, ch. 20 ('Of love of silence and to be alone').

16 Augustine, *Enarratio in Psalmum cxxx. 6*, in J.-P. Migne, *Patrologia Latina*, Vol. 37 (Paris, 1845), col. 1707. For remarks on Augustine's conception of the church as a social as well as a mystical body, and for references to his thought by leading Protestant reformers, see S. J. Grabowski, *The Church: An Introduction to the Theology of St Augustine* (London, 1957), pp. 171 ff., 205.

17 G. Baum *et al.* (eds), *Corpus Reformatorum*, Vol. 77 (Brunswick, Germany, 1870) (hereinafter cited as Calvin, *Opera*, Vol. 9), col. 748.

18 A Kempis, *Imitation of Christ*, pt 3, ch. 20 ('Against vain and secular knowledge').

19 For discussion of this designation of Lefèvre, see the famous essay by L. Febvre, 'The origins of the French Reformation: a badly put question?', in P. Burke (ed.), *A New Kind of History from the Writings of Lucien Febvre* (London, 1973), p. 54 and pp. 44–107 passim.

20 G. Bedouelle, *Lefèvre d'Étaples et l'intelligence des Écritures* (Geneva, 1976), pp. 99, 30–2, 40–6.

21 Quoted in E. F. Rice, Jr, 'Humanist Aristotelianism in France: Jacques Lefèvre d'Étaples and his circle', in A. H. T. Levi (ed.), *Humanism in France at the End of the Middle Ages and in the Early Renaissance* (Manchester, 1970), p. 141.

22 Quoted C. Partee, *Calvin and Classical Philosophy* (Leiden, 1977), p. 147; see also ibid., ch. 2 passim; and H. Dörries, 'Calvin und Lefèvre', *Zeitschrift für Kirchengeschichte*, vol. 44 (1925), pp. 544–81.

23 For Cusanus' statement of this position, see P. Sigmund, *Nicholas of Cusa and Medieval Political Thought* (Cambridge, Mass., 1963), pp. 164–5. For discussions by earlier thinkers of the representation principle in varying terms – notably, delegation, and plenitude of power, as distinct from 'aristocratic' embodiment – see G. de Lagarde, 'L'idée de représentation dans les œuvres de Guillaume d'Ockham', *Bulletin of the International Committee of Historical Sciences*, vol. 9 (1937), pp. 425–51; B. Tierney, *Foundations of the Conciliar Theory* (Cambridge, 1955), pp. 4, 34–5; J. Quillet, 'Universitas populi et représentation au XIVᵉ siècle', *Miscellanea mediaevalia*, vol. 8 (1971), pp. 186–201; M. Wilks, 'Corporation and representation in the *Defensor Pacis*', *Studia Gratiana*, vol. 14 (1972), pp. 253–92, esp. 277–8. Other features of Cusanus' thought are stimulatingly discussed in D. Koenigsberger, *Renaissance Man and Creative Thinking: A History of Concepts of Harmony, 1400–1700* (Hassocks, Sussex, 1979), pp. 100–147.

24 *Ordonnances des rois de France: règne de François Iᵉʳ*, Vol. 4 (1524–6), pp. 72–3; ibid., Vol. 6 (1530), pp. 135–6; ibid., Vol. 7 (1533–5), pp. 183–4; Haag, *France protestante*, Vol. 10, p. 1; Isambert, *Recueil général*, Vol. 12, no. 275, for the edict of June 1539.

25 Doucet, *Institutions*, Vol. 2, p. 732; J. Lecler, 'Qu'est-ce que les libertés de l'Église gallicane?', *Recherches de science religieuse*, vol. 23 (1933), pp. 385–410; R. Doucet, *Etude sur le gouvernement de François Iᵉʳ dans ses rapports avec le parlement de Paris*, pt 1 (Paris, 1921), pp. 102, 147; cf. Sutherland, *Huguenot Struggle for Recognition*, pp. 19–20.

26 S. Mours, *Le Protestantisme en France au XVIe siècle* (Paris, 1959), p. 45; G. Berthoud, 'Les ajournés du 25 janvier 1535', *Bibiothèque d'humanisme et Renaissance*, vol. 25 (1963), pp. 307–24; E. L. Eisenstein, 'L'avènement de l'imprimerie et la Réforme', *Annales ESC*, vol. 26 (1971), pp. 1355–82; R. H. Bainton, *Erasmus of Rotterdam* (London, 1972), pp. 214–15.

27 Imbart de La Tour, *Origines de la Réforme*, Vol. 3 (Paris, 1914), p. 474; E. Droz, 'Pierre de Vingle, l'imprimeur de Farel', *Aspects de la propagande religieuse* (Geneva, 1957), pp. 38–78. For French translations of the Bible published from c.1472 onwards, see W. J. van Eys, *Bibliographie des Bibles et des Nouveaux Testaments en langue française des XVe et XVIe siècles* (Geneva, 1900–1), pp. 1–44.

28 R. Harl, 'Les placards de 1534', *Aspects de la propagande religieuse*, p. 93; A. Tricard, 'La propagande évangélique en France: l'imprimeur Simon du Bois (1525–1534)', ibid., pp. 1–37; V. Carrière, 'Guillaume Farel, propagandiste de la Réforme', *Revue d'histoire de l'Église de France*, vol. 20 (1934), pp. 37–8; H.-J. Martin, 'Ce qu'on lisait à Paris au XVIe siècle', *Bibliothèque d'humanisme et Renaissance*, vol. 21 (1959), p. 230; H. Hauser, *Études sur la Réforme française* (Paris, 1909), pp. 86–7, 255 ff.; R. M. Kingdon, 'Patronage, piety and printing', *Festschrift for F. B. Artz* (Durham, NC, 1964), pp. 28–32. For arguments, and some evidence, that for a time after 1517 printers gave Protestants – especially in Germany – better service than they gave Catholic propagandists, see Eisenstein, *Printing Press as an Agent of Change*, Vol. 1, p. 354; A. G. Dickens, *The German Nation and Martin Luther* (London, 1976), pp. 108–15.

29 Imbart de La Tour, *Origines de la Réforme*, Vol. 3, pp. 534–62; M. A. Screech, *Rabelais* (London, 1980), p. 178; F. Wendel, *Calvin* (London, 1965), p. 145; E. Léonard, *A History of Protestantism: The Establishment* (London, 1967), p. 102.

30 G. R. Potter, *Zwingli* (Cambridge, 1976), p. 106; L. Febvre, *Au cœur religieux du XVIe siècle* (Paris, 1968), p. 262; Mours, *Protestantisme en France*, p. 71; E. Léonard, *Histoire générale du protestantisme: la Réformation* (Paris, 1961), p. 97; J. Crespin, *Histoire des martyrs*, ed. D. Benoit, Vol. 2 (Toulouse, 1887), p. 536.

31 P. F. Geisendorf (ed.), *Livre des habitants de Genève*, 2 vols (Geneva, 1957–63); R. Mandrou, 'Les français hors de France aux XVIe et XVIIe siècles, I – A Genève: le premier refuge protestant (1549–1560)', *Annales ESC*, vol. 14 (1959), pp. 662–6; cf. Ladurie, *Paysans de Languedoc*, Vol. 1, pp. 348–9.

32 R. M. Kingdon, *Geneva and the Coming of the Wars of Religion in France (1555–1563)* (Geneva, 1956), pp. 31–40.

33 With 2,150 churches by 1562, according to Coligny's famous estimate, apparently geared – it is not always noted – to the suggestion that 'the more churches that can be included in the number, the better' (see H. Meylan and A. Dufour (eds), *Correspondance de Theodore de Bèze*, Vol. 3 (1559–61) (Geneva, 1963), pp. 280–1.

34 Kingdon, *Geneva and the Coming*, p. 146.

35 E. Doumergue, *Jean Calvin, les hommes et les choses de son temps*, Vol. 7 (Lausanne, 1927), pp. 338, 313, 317.

36 P. Dèz, 'Les articles politiques de 1557 et les origines du régime synodal', *Bulletin de la Société de l'Histoire du Protestantisme Français*, vol. 103 (1957), pp. 1–9; Calvin, *Opera*, Vol. 9, col. 715; P. de Felice, 'Le synode national de 1559', *Bulletin de la Société de l'Histoire du Protestantisme Français*, vol. 105 (1959), p. 7.

37 Calvin, *Opera*, Vol. 9, pp. lviii–lix. In my view, the widely held opinion that this term refers to the 'message' brought by Calvin's emissaries, and so to a specially prepared draft confession for which he was responsible, is quite unfounded. For the 1559 Confession, ibid., cols 739–52.

38 J. Quick (ed.), *Synodicon in Gallia reformata* (London, 1692), Vol. 1, pp. xiii (art. 31), 5 (art. 26); cf. Calvin, *Opera*, Vol. 9, col. 750. The clause concerning 'common suffrage' is omitted by Haag, *France protestante*, Vol. 10, p. 40.

39 Quick, *Synodicon*, Vol. 1, p. xii (art. 25); cf. Calvin, *Opera*, Vol. 9, cols 748, 718.

40 Quoted in E. Léonard, 'La notion et le fait de l'Eglise dans la Réforme protestante', *Xe Congrés international des sciences historiques* (1955), vol. 4, pp. 107–8.

41 Quick, *Synodicon*, Vol. 1, p. xiii (art. 32); cf. Calvin, *Opera*, Vol. 9, col. 750.

42 Quoted in R. M. Kingdon, *Geneva and the Consolidation of the French Protestant Movement, 1564–72* (Geneva, 1967), p. 103; cf. Wendel, *Calvin*, p. 304.

43 See especially the fifth and sixth national synods (Paris 1565, and Vertueil 1567): Quick, *Synodicon*, Vol. 1, pp. 57–8, 75, 61, 65–6; cf. Haag, *France protestante*, Vol. 10, pp. 69, 77, 72–3, 75–6.

44 Quoted in Kingdon, *Geneva and the Consolidation*, p. 103; also ibid. for an account of the Morély and Ramus issues outlined below.

45 Bèze, *Correspondance*, Vol. 3, p. 73. The significance of the term 'concessus', repeated several times in this letter from Bèze to Bullinger, is indicated in Note 68 below.

46 Quoted in P. F. Geisendorf, *Théodore de Bèze* (Geneva, 1949), pp. 183, 173.

47 Calvin, *Opera*, Vol. 9, col. 763.

48 See N. M. Sutherland, 'The Huguenot struggle for recognition', *Proceedings of the Huguenot Society of London*, vol. 23 (1978), pp. 79–86.

49 Isambert, *Recueil général*, Vol. 14, pp. 124–7; Haag, *France protestante*, Vol. 10, pp. 48–52.

50 Bèze, *Correspondance*, Vol. 4, pp. 254–5; A. H. Guggenheim, 'Beza, Viret and the church of Nîmes: national leadership and local initiative in the outbreak of the wars of religion', *Bibliothèque d'humanisme et Renaissance*, vol. 37 (1975), pp. 33–47; Doumergue, *Jean Calvin*, Vol. 7, pp. 361–2.

51 Condé's move was itself, of course, part of a chain of events that included the previous month's massacre of Protestants at Vassy by Guise, and the latter's subsequent attempts to seize the political initiative *vis-à-vis* the regent and the king. For the material in the rest of this paragraph: Davis, *Society and Culture*, p. 167; G. Tholin, 'Documents relatifs aux guerres de religion, tirés des archives municipales d'Agen (juil. 1558–déc. 1595)', *Archives historiques du département de la Gironde*, vol. 29 (1894), pp. 20–1; A. H. Guggenheim, 'The Calvinist notables of Nîmes during the era of the religious wars', *The Sixteenth-Century Journal*, vol. 3 (1972), pp. 80–96; Galpern, *Religions of the People*, p. 168; Devic, *Histoire générale de Languedoc*, Vol. 12, 'Preuves', cols 601–4; Gascon, *Grand commerce*, p. 476; and, on Paris, D. Richet, 'Aspects socio-culturels des conflits religieux à Paris dans le seconde moitié du XVIe siècle', *Annales ESC*, vol. 32 (1977), p. 767.

52 Crespin, *Histoire des martyrs*, Vol. 3, p. 266; Tholin, 'Documents relatifs aux guerres de religion', pp. 24–5; Monluc, *Commentaires*, pp. 533, 577; Galpern, *Religions of the People*, pp. 169–71; Devic, *Histoire générale de Languedoc*, Vol. 12, 'Notes', p. 90, and 'Preuves', cols 607–22; E. Connac, 'Troubles de mai 1562 à Toulouse', *Annales du Midi*, vol. 3 (1891), pp. 310–39.

53 cf. the royal declaration of 14 July 1564: in towns that were seats of archbishops, bishops or *parlements*, 'the election of *prévôts des marchands*, mayor, *échevins* or other municipal *officiers* shall in future be doubled' (Isambert, *Recueil général*, Vol. 14, p. 172). In respect of Paris this was revoked within a month (ibid., p. 175).

54 F. Bonnardot, 'Essai historique sur le régime municipal d'Orléans, d'après les documents conservés aux archives de la ville (1389–1790)', *Mémoires de la Société Archéologique et Historique de l'Orléannais*, vol. 18 (1881), pp. 135–6; Gascon, *Grand commerce*, pp. 477–527.

55 Such a correlation is also observed by P. Benedict, 'The St Bartholomew's Massacre in the provinces', *The Historical Journal*, vol. 21 (1978), pp. 220–1.

56 Note, too, the removal of municipalities' jurisdiction over civil causes, by the ordinance of Moulins, 1566 (art. 71), above, p. 75.

57 J. M. Davies, 'Languedoc and its *gouverneur*: Henri de Montmorency-Damville, 1563–89', University of London unpublished PhD thesis, 1974, f. 175.

58 Whether the members of that assembly were to be nominated by diocesan assemblies is unclear. The position is ambiguously stated by L. Anquez, *Histoire des assemblées politiques des réformés de France, 1573–1622* (Paris, 1859), p. 9; and no such function is ascribed to diocesan assemblies in the Millau articles as printed in Haag, *France protestante*, Vol. 10, pp. 121–6. For the ordinary administrative divisions of Languedoc, including its dioceses and *généralités*, and the composition and roles of its municipal assemblies and provincial Estates, see P. Dognon, *Les Institutions politiques et administratives du pays de Languedoc, du XIIIe siècle aux guerres de religion* (Toulouse, 1895).

59 In relation to these conciliar arrangements, as to the councils of royal *gouverneurs*, the term 'fidélité' is evocative of considerations – clientage, alliance – such as are discussed above, pp. 36–7, cf. p. 79.

60 Haag, *France protestante*, Vol. 10, p. 118.

61 The *Reveille-matin* ('Edimbourg', 1574) consists of two dialogues, the first of which contains the proposals in question (pp. 143–57) and was evidently composed in 1573. The second refers to the Nîmes assembly of 1575, and cannot therefore have appeared before that year. In the second dialogue it is claimed that these proposals were discussed, and favourably received, at Nîmes. Haag (*France protestante*, Vol. 10, pp. 104–9) prints a version of them under the heading 'Fédération protestante', without date or author. I can find no evidence to support the remarkable contention that 'a great many of these proposals were accepted at Millau' (Salmon, *Society in Crisis*, p. 192).

62 Anquez, *Historie des assemblées politiques*, p. 3, n. 1.

63 See the account in Devic, *Histoire de Languedoc*, Vol. 12, cols 1112–38.

64 N. de Villegaignon, *Response* (1561), quoted in Yardeni, *Conscience nationale*, p. 101, n. 4.

65 T. de Bèze, *Du droit des magistrats*, ed. R. M. Kingdon (Geneva, 1971), pp. 45, 18. Huguenot political thought is discussed more fully below, pp. 153–5.

66 Romans, xiii, 1. For comment on how Protestants, and notably Bucer, interpreted this key Pauline precept, see Skinner, *Foundations of Modern Political Thought*, Vol. 2, pp. 204–6, 212–14.

67 H. A. Lloyd, 'Calvin and the duty of guardians to resist', *Journal of Ecclesiastical History*, vol. 32 (1981), pp. 65–7; P. Stein, 'Calvin and the duty of guardians to resist: a comment', ibid., pp. 69–70.

68 For comment on the principle of 'concession' in medieval legal doctrine, see W. Ullmann, *Medieval Political Thought* (Harmondsworth, 1975), pp. 55 ff. In Roman law the principle was especially relevant to the formation of groups that enjoyed corporate status as 'persons' in law only when this was conceded to them by higher authority: 'It is not conceded to people in general to form either societies or associations or similar bodies corporate: for these are ordered by laws, decrees of the Senate, and Imperial ordinances' (*Digest*, 3, 4, 1).

69 Below, p. 145.

70 Isambert, *Recueil général*, Vol. 14, pp. 280–302.

71 P. V. Palma Cayet, *Chronologie novenaire*, in C. B. Petitot (ed.), *Collection complète des mémoires relatifs à l'histoire de France*, sér. 1, vol. 38 (Paris, 1823), pp. 254–7.

72 Picot, *Histoire des États-généraux*, Vol. 2, esp. pp. 314–18, 385–6. In 1484, and again in 1561, there had been notable attempts to contrive control of the king's councillors by the Estates-General.

73 Picot, *Histoire des États-généraux*, Vol. 2, p. 356; Mayer, *Des États-généraux*, Vol. 13, pp. 212–315.

74 cf. Bodin, *République*, pp. 485–6, 254.

75 Picot, *Histoire des États-généraux*, Vol. 2, pp. 373, 493–5.

76 J. Russell Major, *The Deputies to the Estates-General in Renaissance France*

(Madison, Wis., 1960), pp. 138–9, 164–5; H. O. Evenett, *The Cardinal of Lorraine and the Council of Trent* (London, 1930), pp. 10–11; Harding, *Anatomy of a Power Élite*, pp. 34–6; Mousnier, *Vénalité des offices*, pp. 85, 42–3, 87–8.

77 But see above, pp. 93–4.

78 G. Lambert, *Histoire des guerres de religion en Provence (1530–98)* (Nyons, 1870; repr. 1972), Vol. 1, pp. 381–7; J. H. M. Salmon, 'The Paris Sixteen, 1584–94: the social analysis of a revolutionary movement', *Journal of Modern History*, vol. 44 (1972), pp. 547–51; F. Cromé, *Dialogue d'entre le maheustre et le manant*, ed. P. Ascoli (Geneva, 1977), p. 92; Drouot, *Mayenne*, Vol. 1, pp. 135–6, 91–4, 136–9; Devic, *Histoire générale de Languedoc*, Vol. 11, pp. 748–9; J. Loutchitsky (ed.), *Documents inédits pour servir à l'histoire de la Réforme et de la Ligue* (Paris, 1875), pp. 217 ff.

79 Salmon, 'Sixteen', pp. 544, 551–3; F. Bonnardot (ed.), *Registres des délibérations du bureau de la ville de Paris*, Vol. 9 (1586–1590) (Paris, 1902), pp. 121–4, 140.

80 cf. Bodin's phrase, above, p. 138.

81 E. Barnavie, 'Centralisation ou fédéralisme? Les relations entre Paris et les villes à l'époque de la Ligue (1585–1594)', *Revue historique*, vol. 259 (1978), pp. 343–4; the author hesitates to date this document firmly to 1588, to which year it nevertheless evidently belongs.

82 Quoted in Picot, *Histoire des États-généraux*, Vol. 3, p. 87.

83 For instance, Major, *The Deputies*, p. 21.

84 Taillandier, 'Assemblée des trois Estats de la prévosté de Paris, pour députer aux Estats-généraux de Bloys, 1588', *Bibliothèque de l'École des Chartes*, vol. 7 (1845–6), pp. 436–59.

85 Salmon, 'Sixteen', pp. 554 ff.; Ascoli, in Cromé, *Dialogue*, p. 111, n. 150; Devic, *Histoire générale de Languedoc*, Vol. 11, pp. 769–77; Lloyd, *Rouen Campaign*, pp. 127–9; Loutchitsky, *Documents*, pp. 232 ff.; Harding, *Anatomy of a Power Élite*, p. 91; H. Hours, 'Le "Conseil d'État" à Lyon pendant la Ligue: contribution à l'étude des gouverneurs de provinces', *Revue historique de droit français et étranger*, sér. 4, vol. 29 (1952), pp. 401–20; H. Drouot, 'Les conseils provinciaux de la Sainte-Union (1589–95)', *Annales du Midi*, vol. 65 (1953), pp. 421, 424; Drouot, *Mayenne*, Vol. 2, pp. 41 ff.

86 Richet ('Aspects socio-culturels', p. 779) stresses more emphatically than does Salmon the prominence of members of the legal fraternity among the Sixteen: they 'are, with the regular clergy and the *curés*, the motive force of radicalism'.

87 Drouout, *Mayenne*, Vol. 1, pp. 233–44, and Vol. 2, pp. 45–58; Maugis, *Histoire du parlement de Paris*, Vol. 2, p. 66; Salmon, 'Sixteen', pp. 557–61.

88 A. Magen, 'La ville d'Agen sous le sénéchalat de Pierre de Peyroneuc, seigneur de Saint-Chamarand (nov. 1588–janv. 1591)', *Comité des travaux historiques et scientifiques (Paris): Mémoires lus à la Sorbonne dans les séances extraordinaires du comité (etc.) d'histoire, philologie et sciences morales* (1865), pp. 510–14; F. Habasque, 'La domination de la reine de Navarre à Agen en 1585', *Bulletin historique et philologique du comité des travaux historiques* (1890), p. 247.

89 L. Raynal, *Histoire du Berry depuis les temps les plus anciens jusqu'en 1789* (Bourges, 1844–7), Vol. 4, p. 25; Yardeni, *Conscience nationale*, p. 246; Drouot, *Mayenne*, Vol. 1, pp. 338, 326, 438, 290; P. Deyon, *Amiens, capitale provinciale: étude sur la société urbaine au 17e siècle* (Paris, 1967), pp. 429–30.

90 Cromé, *Dialogue*, p. 124.

91 Drouot, *Mayenne*, Vol. 2, pp. 21–5.

92 Cromé, *Dialogue*, pp. 122–3, 133, 52, 189; cf. above, p. 45.

93 Haag, *France protestante*, Vol. 10, p. 228.

94 R. Mousnier, *L'Assassinat de Henri IV* (Paris, 1964), pp. 334–7.

CHAPTER 6

1 See in general: W. Ullmann, *A History of Political Thought: The Middle Ages* (London, 1970); W. Ullmann, *Law and Politics in the Middle Ages: An Introduction to the Sources of Medieval Political Ideas* (London, 1975); M. J. Wilks, *The Problem of Sovereignty in the Later Middle Ages* (Cambridge, 1963); J. Le Goff, *Pour un autre Moyen Age: temps, travail et culture en Occident* (Paris, 1977), p. 89.

2 *Digest*, 1, 4, 1 (the 'lex regia').

3 Kantorowicz, *King's Two Bodies*, pp. 121–2.

4 Aristotle, *Politics*, 1252ᵇ 30.

5 T. Renna, 'Aristotle and the French monarchy, 1260–1303', *Viator: Medieval and Renaissance Studies*, vol. 9 (1978), pp. 309–24.

6 See G. Post, 'Two notes on nationalism in the Middle Ages, II: *Rex imperator*', *Traditio*, vol. 9 (1953), pp. 296 ff.

7 'Quod omnes similiter tangit, ab omnibus comprobetur' (*Code*, 5, 59, 5).

8 H. de Lubac, *Exégèse médiévale*, Vol. 2(ii) (Paris, 1964), pp. 369–91; C. Trinkaus, *In Our Image and Likeness: Humanity and Divinity in Italian Humanist Thought*, Vol. 2 (London, 1970), pp. 563–78.

9 Gaguin to Ficino, quoted in R. Lebègue, 'Le Platonisme en France au XVIᵉ siècle', *Association Guillaume Budé, 3–9 septembre 1953: actes du congrès* (Paris, 1954), p. 334; A. Renaudet, *Préréforme et humanisme (1494–1517)* (Paris, 1953), pp. 78–87.

10 E. Garin, *L'Éducation de l'homme moderne* (Paris, 1968), p. 171; Rabelais, *Gargantua et Pantagruel*, I, x; Ullmann, *Law and Politics*, p. 88, n. 4; Kelley, *Foundations of Modern Historical Scholarship*, p. 73; Ourliac, 'Droit commun et commune opinion', *Studi clasice*, vol. 7 (1965), p. 105.

11 Thus Claude de Seyssel, *Monarchie de France* (p. 108), continuing to place cardinal emphasis upon the organological analogy.

12 H. A. W. Meyer, *The Epistle to the Romans*, 2 vols (Edinburgh, 1881–4).

13 B. Guenée and F. Lehoux, *Les Entrées royales françaises de 1328 à 1515* (Paris, 1968), pp. 9–29, 253–57; E. Konigson, 'La cité et le prince: premières entrées de Charles VIII (1484–1486)', in J. Jacquot (ed.), *Les Fêtes de la Renaissance*, Vol. 3 (Paris, 1975), pp. 64–5; M. McGowan, 'Form and themes in Henry II's entry into Rouen', *Renaissance Drama*, new ser., vol. 1 (1968), pp. 224–5; F. A. Yates, *Astraea: The Imperial Theme in the Sixteenth Century* (Harmondsworth, 1977), pp. 141–3, 149–72, esp. 162–4.

14 R. E. Giesey, *The Royal Funeral Ceremony in Renaissance France* (Geneva, 1960); Kantorowicz, *King's Two Bodies*, pp. 435–6; quoted by V.-L. Tapié, *France in the Age of Louis XIII and Richelieu* (London, 1974), p. 4.

15 M. P. Gilmore, *Argument from Roman Law in Political Thought, 1200–1600* (Cambridge, Mass., 1941), pp. 41–2. On jurists' not treating private and public law as 'separate spheres of legal thought', cf. G. Post, 'A Romano-canonical maxim: "Quod omnes tangit" in Bracton', *Traditio*, vol. 4 (1946), p. 246.

16 Pierre Rebuffi, *Commentaria in constitutiones seu ordinationes regias* (Lyon, 1613), f. 723.

17 See above, pp. 111–12.

18 Rebuffi, *Commentaria*, f. 723.

19 Notably that most influential of commentators Bartolus of Sassoferrato, in his commentary on the *Primam Digesti veteris partem*.

20 Thus the prevailing view among sixteenth-century jurists, contrary to that of their late-medieval predecessors.

21 See below, p. 165, for one jurist's vexing of the question.

22 See above, p. 150.

23 Charles du Moulin, *Commentarii in consuetudines parisiensis, prima pars*, quoted in Church, *Constitutional Thought*, pp. 182, n. 9, and p. 189, n. 34.
24 Chasseneux, *Catalogus*, ff. sig. *ij^ro, 40vo, 132ro, 284vo.
25 ibid., f. 148ro; Charles de Grassaille, *Regalium Franciae iura omnia* (Lyon, 1538), p. 166.
26 ibid., pp. 160–1; Thireau, *Charles Du Moulin*, p. 256.
27 Rebuffi, *Commentaria*, ff. 6, 10, 568.
28 Church, *Constitutional Thought*, pp. 105–6; Thireau, *Charles Du Moulin*, pp. 120–5.
29 Hotman, *Francogallia*, p. 513 and ch. 20 passim; cf. Bodin, *République*, p. 1027, explaining the excessive litigiousness of the French by reference to 'the multitude of laws', rather than of lawyers.
30 'Etienne Junius Brutus', *Vindiciae contra tyrannos*, ed. A. Jouanna *et al.* (Geneva, 1979), pp. 62, 228.
31 Hotman, *Francogallia*, p. 295.
32 Bèze, *Du Droit*, p. 9; *Vindiciae*, pp. 63, 102.
33 Hotman, *Francogallia*, p. 401; *Vindiciae*, p. 125.
34 ibid., pp. 136–41. Neither in Hotman's nor in Beza's tract – the two other main works of Huguenot political theory – do explicitly philosophical contentions figure so conspicuously as in this passage of the *Vindiciae*.
35 Hotman, *Francogallia*, p. 255; *Vindiciae*, p. 180. The argument from property was virtually ignored by Beza.
36 Hotman, *Francogallia*, pp. 250, 448; *Vindiciae*, pp. 157–60.
37 Hotman, *Francogallia*, pp. 230–3; *Vindiciae*, p. 104.
38 Hotman, *Francogallia*, p. 204; *Vindiciae*, p. 128; Bèze, *Du Droit*, p. 14.
39 Hotman, *Francogallia*, p. 416; *Vindiciae*, pp. 189–90.
40 Hotman, *Francogallia*, pp. 342–9.
41 ibid., pp. 154, 458 ff.; *Vindiciae*, pp. 134–48.
42 ibid., pp. 52–63; Bèze, *Du Droit*, pp. 18–19, 53–4.
43 Probably Philippe du Plessis-Mornay, though several candidates have been nominated; the pseudonym 'Junius Brutus' was plainly intended to allude to the ancient Roman whom Machiavelli, amongst others, had praised for 'destroying the kings and liberating his country' (*Discourses*, bk III, ch. ii (p. 403).
44 Hotman, *Francogallia*, pp. 292–5, cf. pp. 154–5.
45 Bèze, *Du Droit*, pp. 10, 64; cf. Aristotle, *Nicomachean Ethics*, 1094^a 1–1094^b 11, 1176^b ff., and *Politics*, 1328^a 22–1328^b 22. On Calvin's misgivings as to the uses of 'pagan philosophers' cf. above, p. 124.
46 *Vindiciae*, pp. 137, 130–1, 134, 158; cf. Aristotle, *Nicomachean Ethics*, 1179^b 4–1180^a 24, and *Politics*, 1311^a 4.
47 Hotman, *Francogallia*, pp. 343, 291, cf. p. 231 (identifying 'the people' with 'the orders' or 'the Estates').
48 *Vindiciae*, pp. 136, 131, 137, 220; cf. Hotman's recurrent insistence on the Ciceronian formula 'salus populi suprema lex', without linking it either with state or with sovereignty as such. For Bodin's position in this respect, see below, p. 160; and for a seventeenth-century variation of the formula, below, p. 171.
49 See above, p. 13.
50 *Vindiciae*, pp. 221–2.
51 ibid., p. 221; cf. Skinner, *Foundations of Modern Political Thought*, Vol. 2, pp. 332–3, holding that the argument of the *Vindiciae* is throughout for popular sovereignty.
52 Bèze, *Du Droit*, p. 44.
53 For instance, ibid., p. 19, where the contention also occurs that although the sovereign die 'the sovereignty remains entire'.
54 ibid., pp. 23, 20, 16, 55, 56, 48.

55 J. H. M. Salmon, 'Bodin and the monarchomachs', in H. Denzer (ed.), *Jean Bodin: Verhandlungen der internationalen Bodin Tagung in München* (Munich, 1973), pp. 359–78.

56 C. R. Baxter, 'Jean Bodin's daemon and his conversion to Judaism', in Denzer, *Jean Bodin*, p. 10.

57 cf., however, *République*, p. 152.

58 R. E. Giesey, 'Medieval jurisprudence in Bodin's conception of sovereignty', in Denzer, *Jean Bodin*, pp. 167–86; M. Reulos, 'Les sources juridiques de Bodin: textes, auteurs, pratique', in ibid., pp. 187–94.

59 cf., however, *République*, pp. 122, 158.

60 cf., however, ibid., pp. 436, 438, 445; and cf., too, Loyseau, below, p. 165.

61 *République*, pp. 5, 7.

62 ibid., p. 4.

63 ibid., pp. 1–2.

64 See W. J. Ong, *Ramus: Method and the Decay of Dialogue* (Cambridge, Mass., 1958), p. 307.

65 cf. Bodin's early disparagement of Aristotelian 'division' for political analysis, with his own resort to 'division' in criticising Aristotle himself (*République*, pp. 10, 78, 373).

66 That these were the parts of the definition that Bodin had initially in mind is abundantly clear from his subsequent discussion, despite his divergence from the strict requirement of his chosen method: cf. K. D. McCrae, 'Ramist tendencies in the thought of Jean Bodin', *Journal of the History of Ideas*, vol. 16 (1955), pp. 306–23.

67 It may be thought that Bodin intended no significant distinction between 'power' and 'sovereignty', and that the phrase 'puissance souveraine' was simply his French rendering of the familiar *summa potestas* which he himself employed for his definition in the Latin (1586) edition of the *République*. But the distinction is important, as I hope to show; and it is plainly implicit in his preference, in the definition, for the two-word phrase over the one word 'souveraineté' – a term long since available to political writers, and of which he himself was in any case to make much play (for instance, *République*, p. 122).

68 ibid., pp. 11, 14–15, 273, 1013, 1050; cf. below, p. 160.

69 ibid., p. 122.

70 ibid., p. 221.

71 See above, p. 151.

72 *République*, p. 69.

73 cf. ibid., pp. 302–3, for a further distinction between power by 'force' and power by 'law' and 'right'.

74 ibid., pp. 224–8, 521.

75 ibid., pp. 221, 142, 135, 155, 132, 214–15, 222–3, 216, 131, 161, 156–7, 152.

76 See below, p. 160.

77 *République*, p. 134.

78 ibid., pp. 122–3.

79 ibid., pp. 70, 162–3, 168, 242. For the earlier exposition by Du Moulin of the principle 'omnes subditi . . . sunt clientes et homines Regis', in opposition to the feudal principle that the king was not immediate lord of his vassal's vassal, see Church, *Constitutional Thought*, p. 190; also above, pp. 151–2.

80 *République*, pp. 392, 372–409, 228–31, 231–44.

81 For instance, G. H. Sabine, *A History of Political Theory* (London, 1937), p. 345: 'Bodin's statement of the principle of sovereignty is generally agreed to be the most important part of his political philosophy.'

82 For examples, see Wilks, *Problem of Sovereignty*, p. 169.

83 The earlier work of Bodin was his 'De jure imperio', unpublished and eventually

destroyed: see Bodin, *Method*, p. 173; the treatise was the Bartolist *De Imperio et jurisdictione* – see R. Derathé, 'La place de Jean Bodin dans l'histoire des théories de la souveraineté', in Denzer, *Jean Bodin*, p. 246. A list concerning the powers of the Emperor Frederick I was among the numerous *novellae* inserted by medieval jurists into the *Corpus Iuris civilis*: see J. H. Franklin, *Jean Bodin and the Rise of Absolutist Theory* (Cambridge, 1973), p. 25.

84 For instance of Bodin's use of 'état' in referring to forms of *république* and in other senses, see the opening of *République* VI, iv (pp. 937–8).

85 ibid., pp. 339, 270, 313, 332.

86 From Herodotus onwards, according to Bodin, doubtless with his own contemporaries, and notably Hotman, particularly in mind.

87 ibid., pp. 122, 266–7, 474–98, 500–2, 338–9.

88 ibid., pp. 137–8.

89 ibid., pp. 500–2.

90 See ibid., p. 156. According to Giesey ('Medieval jurisprudence', in Denzer, *Jean Bodin*, pp. 176–7), Bodin's marginal citations at this juncture include support for sovereign taxation-powers on grounds of 'eminent domain'. This is not apparent from the text itself; and it is scarcely to be inferred from Bodin's own handling of the references in question in subsequent editions of his work that he considered such grounds to be essential to his argument. On the contrary, he distinguished between 'lawful' and 'lordly' monarchy precisely on the grounds that under the former the subjects enjoyed 'property of their goods' (*République*, p. 273); cf., however, note 91 below.

91 ibid., p. 140; cf. pp. 576, 877. For the medieval jurisprudential claim concerning the royal right to assert 'eminent domain' over private property in circumstances of 'necessity', cf. G. Post, 'Plena Potestas and consent in medieval assemblies', *Traditio*, vol. 1 (1943), p. 375; see also the discussion of property above, pp. 111–12, for some connection between 'eminent domain' and *necessitas*. Such a connection is not, however, the main thrust of Bodin's argument here.

92 See Wilks, *Problem of Sovereignty*, pp. 217–19, finding in this principle the foundation of the doctrine of *raison d'état*.

93 *République*, bk III, ch. iv passim. It is noteworthy that Bodin evaded the question whether magisterial disobedience was permissible when the sovereign's commands did *in fact* contravene natural law.

94 ibid., pp. 419, 427.

95 ibid., bk IV, ch. i, esp. pp. 507, 529, 525.

96 ibid., bk VI, ch. vi passim: quoted phrases at pp. 1055, 1054, 1049, 1033; cf. also p. 280.

97 ibid., p. 1057.

98 For instance, Plato, *Republic*, s. 531, and *Laws*, 746ᵇ–747, 757; Aristotle, *Nicomachean Ethics*, 1131ᵃ 30–1132ᵇ 20.

99 For some indications of Platonic and neoplatonic influences, see M. Villey, 'La justice harmonique selon Bodin', in Denzer, *Jean Bodin*, pp. 69–86; and of Aristotelian influences H. Weber, 'Utilisation et critique de la *Politique* d'Aristote dans la *République* de Jean Bodin', in R. R. Bolgar (ed.), *Classical Influences on European Culture, AD 1500–1700* (Cambridge, 1976), pp. 305–14.

100 *République*, preface to Gui du Faur ('Io. Bodinus', etc.) [p. vi].

101 Pierre Grégoire (Gregory of Toulouse), *De Republica libri XXVI* (1586), quoted in Gierke, *Natural Law and the Theory of Society*, p. 235, n. 35.

102 Relevant quotations – from Grégoire, *De Republica*; François Grimaudet, *Opuscules politiques* (1580); Adam Blackwood, *Adversus Georgii Buchanani diologum* (1581); and Pierre de Belloy, *De l'autorité du roy* (1587) – may conveniently be found in Church, *Constitutional Thought*, pp. 246–66; cf. above, p. 152.

103 cf. above, pp. 147, 150–1, 154. The positions were particulary defended by the Nevers historian and jurist Coquille: see above, p. 16.
104 The significance of the law–force interrelation in Henry IV's gaining of the throne is stressed in Lloyd, *Rouen Campaign*, pp. 191–5.
105 *République*, p. 743.
106 i.e., by the 'Paulette' edict, 1604.
107 *Traité des seigneuries* (1608), *Cinq livres du droit des offices* (1609), and *Des ordres et simples dignités* (1610): hereinafter cited, by book, chapter and section number, as, respectively, *Seigneuries*, *Offices* and *Ordres*, from the collected edition of *Les Oeuvres de Maistre Charles Loyseau* (Lyon, 1701).
108 Loyseau, *Discours de l'abus de justices de village* (1603), p. 11.
109 H. A. Lloyd, 'The political thought of Charles Loyseau (1564–1610)', *European Studies Review*, vol. 11 (1981), pp. 53–82, stresses the coherence and interdependence of the arguments in Loyseau's treatises, and enlarges upon the discussion presented here.
110 *Ordres*, vi, 12.
111 For example, Loyseau's etymological remarks on 'état', 'seigneur' and 'roturier', at *Offices*, I, i, 27–9; *Seigneuries*, i, 21; *Ordres*, iv, 31–2.
112 ibid., viii, 23.
113 Loyseau, *Traité du déguerpissement et delaissement par hypothèque* (1597), 'Avant-propos'.
114 Aristotle, *Categories*, 2ᵃ 11–4ᵇ 19; cf. *Metaphysics*, 1028ᵃ 33–5. For a summary statement of the method, see *Posterior Analytics*, 96ᵇ 15 ff.; cf. above, p. 9.
115 *Offices*, I, i, 100–1.
116 ibid., I, i, 98ff.; *Seigneuries*, i, 25; *Ordres*, 'Avant-propos'.
117 *Seigneuries*, i. 23–4, 26, 28, 84.
118 cf. above, p. 111.
119 *Seigneuries*, i, 34, 26–7, 33, 82, 85–6.
120 ibid., ii, 8–9, 53, 4–5, 41, 6, 7, 11; ibid., iii, 5–41; ibid., iv, 17–18.
121 ibid., iv, 13–16; *Offices*, V, i, 40; ibid., II, ii, 15.
122 ibid., III, iv, passim.
123 ibid., II, viii, 8–11; ibid., IV, iii, 75, cf. IV, vii, 58–63.
124 *Seigneuries*, ii, 92; *Offices*, II, ii, 42.
125 Cicero, *De officiis*, I, xxv; cf. Dante, *De Monarchia*, i, 12 – 'Consules propter cives et rex propter gentem'. On the ruler as *tutor* see W. Ullmann, 'Juristic obstacles to the emergence of the concept of the state in the Middle Ages', *Annali di storia de diritto*, vol. 12–13 (1968–9), pp. 43–64. According to Ullmann, late-medieval and early-modern 'jurisprudential science' ossified owing to jurists' fidelity to such Roman law concepts, and their resistance to Aristotle – a generalisation that certainly will not accommodate Loyseau. The significance of the 'guardian' concept in Calvin's thought is noted above, p. 137.
126 *Offices*, II, ii, 21, and IV, vii, 8; cf. above, p. 149.
127 *Offices*, I, i, 118–20, and V, i, 32. The term 'proceeds' clearly invokes the neoplatonic concept of 'procession', of which the fullest account is that of Proclus, *The Elements of Theology*, ed. E. R. Dodds (Oxford, 1933), pp. 29–43.
128 i.e. *eudaimoniá* as discussed in the *Politics* and the *Nicomachean Ethics*: see especially the latter, at 1098ᵇ 32–4. Since Aristotle on the relative merits of 'action' and 'contemplation' has been variously interpreted, it is noteworthy that Loyseau's exact contemporary Althusius also considered the philosopher to have favoured the active as distinct from the contemplative life (see *Politica Methodica digesta of Johannes Althusius*, ed. C. J. Friedrich (Cambridge, Mass., 1932), p. lxxviii); cf. Bodin, *République*, p. 8, for Bodin's reading of Aristotle on 'the action of the intellect'.
129 *Offices*, I, vi, 10, and II, ii, 29.

130 *Seigneuries*, iii, 11–12.
131 See above, pp. 45–6.
132 Aristotle, *Metaphysics*, 1045^b ff., esp. 1049^b.
133 *Ordres*, i, 3, and viii, 15.
134 *Offices*, I, iii, 43, 73. Bodin, too, stressed the importance of 'provision' (*République*, p. 231).
135 *Ordres*, vii, 85, and vi, 66, 62, 65.
136 *Seigneuries*, x, 1, 43, 62.
137 See Gilmore, *Argument from Roman law*, p. 64.
138 See above, pp. 44, 150–1.
139 For the continuing dominance of 'Aristotelianism' in intellectual activity throughout the period under consideration, see C. B. Schmitt, 'Towards a reassessment of Renaissance Aristotelianism', *History of Science*, vol. 11 (1973), pp. 159–93; also L. W. B. Brockliss, 'Philosophy teaching in France, 1600–1740', *History of Universities*, vol. 1 (1981), pp. 131–68.
140 Above, p. 17.
141 Giesey, 'Medieval jurisprudence', in Denzer, *Jean Bodin*, p. 186.

EPILOGUE

1 The quotations from seventeenth-century writings in what follows may conveniently be found in W. F. Church, *Richelieu and Reason of State* (Princeton, NJ, 1972), pp. 222. 510, 191.

Bibliography

The *Bibliographie annuelle de l'histoire de France*, published in Paris by the Centre National de la Recherche Scientifique (CNRS), now lists each year over ten thousand titles of new books and articles, a significant proportion of them on topics in France's sixteenth-century history. The articles so listed are drawn from several hundred occasional collections and some eighteen hundred periodicals. These last include many local journals, a few examples of which are included in the following survey. Of necessity, this survey is highly selective. Limited for the most part to writings in English or in French, it aims to give some impression of what is available by way of secondary literature to the reader who wishes to embark upon further inquiry into topics over which the foregoing chapters have ranged. Although a degree of overlap is unavoidable, I have tried as far as possible not to repeat references already given in the notes, which should therefore be used in conjunction with what follows.

The major survey of historical writing in Europe from Petrarch to Burckhardt is still E. Fueter, *Geschichte der neuern Historiographie* (Munich and Berlin, 1911): French translation by E. Jeanmaire, as *Histoire de l'historiographie moderne* (Paris, 1914). Interestingly enough, Fueter also produced a *Geschichte des Europaischen Staatensystems von 1492 zu 1559* (Munich and Berlin, 1915). D. Hay, *Annalists and Historians: Western Historiography from the VIIIth to the XVIIIth Century* (London, 1977), is a helpful introductory essay, concentrating on Britain, France and Italy. Medieval historiography is studied by B. Lacroix, *L'Historien au Moyen Age* (Montreal, 1971): see the review of this work by R. W. Hanning, in *History and Theory*, Vol. 12 (1973), pp. 419–34. In this same field, a collection of papers edited by B. Guenée, *Le Métier d'historien au Moyen Age: études sur l'historiographie médiévale* (Paris, 1977), includes (pp. 233–300) a contribution by M. Schmidt-Chazan, 'Histoire et sentiment national chez Robert Gaguin'; while Guenée himself asks 'Y-a-t-il une historiographie médiévale?', *Revue historique*, Vol. 258 (1977), pp. 261–75. The idea of 'exemplar' history is discussed by G. H. Nadel, 'Philosophy of history before historicism', *History and Theory*, vol. 2 (1964), pp. 291–315. M. P. Gilmore, the distinguished author of *The World of Humanism* (New York, 1952), comments on Commynes and Guicciardini, and contrasts them with Bodin, in his 'Freedom and determinism in Renaissance historians', *Studies in the Renaissance*, Vol. 3 (1956), pp. 49–60. On Guicciardini and his notorious fellow-citizen, the best starting-point is F. Gilbert, *Machiavelli and Guicciardini: Politics and History in Sixteenth-Century Florence* (Princeton, NJ, 1965); but Machiavelli's use of the term 'lo stato' is re-examined with characteristic panache by J. H. Hexter, *The Vision of Politics on the Eve of the Reformation: More, Machiavelli and Seyssel* (New York, 1973). As for Commynes, who continues to attract a good deal of scholarly attention, J. Dufournet has published a set of *Études sur Philippe de Commynes* (Paris, 1975); and P. J. Archambault explores 'History as entropy in Commynes's *Mémoires*', *Symposium*, Vol. 27 (1973), pp. 5–18. Commynes, however, is not simply to be classified with the *rhétoriqueurs*, features of whose approach to history are considered by R. E. Asher, 'Myth, legend and history in Renaissance France', *Studi francesi*, Vol. 39 (1969), pp. 409–19. A distinguished student of the French Renaissance, Franco Simone, has discerned 'Une entreprise oubliée des humanistes français: de la prise de conscience historique du renouveau culturel à la naissance de la première histoire littéraire', in A. H. T. Levi (ed.), *Humanism in France at the End of the Middle Ages and in the Early Renaissance* (Manchester, 1970), pp. 106–31 – a collection that contains a number of important papers; while, in another collection presented to a leading Renaissance scholar, S. Kinser traces 'Ideas of temporal change and cultural process in France, 1470–1535', in A. Molho and J. A. Tedeschi (eds), *Renaissance Studies in Honor of Hans Baron* (Dekalb, Ill., 1971), pp. 703–56.

The idea that in the sixteenth century French scholars made a major contribution to the development of modern historical writing is of long standing: see, for instance. J. G. A. Pocock's chapter on 'The French prelude to modern historiography', in his *The Ancient Constitution and the Feudal Law* (Cambridge, 1957). But the outstanding work in this field, dealing particularly with the aspect which I have designated 'institutional' history, is D. R. Kelley, *Foundations of Modern Historical Scholarship: Language, Law and History in the French Renaissance* (New York, 1970); see also Kelley's article 'The rise of legal history of the Renaissance', *History and Theory*, vol. 9 (1970), pp. 173–94. Modern historians have not distributed their researches equally among their sixteenth-century French predecessors. Pasquier is discussed at length by G. Huppert, *The Idea of Perfect History: Historical Erudition and Historical Philosophy in Renaissance France* (Urbana, Ill., 1970), who, especially by analysing the celebrated sixteenth-century bibliographer La Croix du Maine's *Bibliothèque française* (Paris, 1584), argues strongly in favour of a connection between historical study and 'the professional tradition of the magisterial class'. Pasquier has also been examined by P. Bouteiller, 'Un historien du XIVe siècle: Estienne Pasquier', *Bibliothèque d'humanisme et Renaissance*, vol. 6 (1945), pp 357–92; his *Écrits politiques* and his *Lettres historiques pour les années 1556–94* are both edited by D. Thickett (Geneva, 1966), who has also published a study of *Estienne Pasquier (1529–1615): The Versatile Barrister of Sixteenth-Century France* (London, 1979). Huppert's book derives its title from La Popelinière, to whom its author devotes considerable space. On that same historian, G. W. Sypher discusses 'La Popelinière's *Histoire de France*: a case of historical objectivity and religious censorship', *Journal of the History of Ideas*, vol. 24 (1963), pp. 41–54; M. Yardeni assesses 'La conception de l'histoire dans l'œuvre de La Popelinière', *Revue d'histoire moderne et contemporaine*, vol. 11 (1964), pp. 109-26; and D. R. Kelley writes on 'History as a calling: the case of La Popelinière', in the Molho and Tedeschi *festschrift* for Hans Baron already mentioned. To Kelley we also owe a recent study of *François Hotman: A Revolutionary's Ordeal* (Princeton, NJ, 1973); and the same author's numerous articles in the related fields of historiography and legal and political philosophy include '*Fides historiae*: Charles Dumoulin and the Gallican view of history', *Traditio*, vol. 22 (1966), pp. 347–402. But for some account of du Haillan the searcher must still turn to P. Bonnefon, 'L'Historien du Haillan', *Revue d'histoire littéraire de la France*, vol. 15 (1908), pp. 642–96; and, for a recent impression of how de Thou laboured under harassment from interested parties, to H. R. Trevor-Roper's lecture *Queen Elizabeth's First Historian: William Camden and the Beginnings of English 'Civil History'* (London, 1971). S. Kinser, *The Works of Jacques-Auguste de Thou* (The Hague, 1966), is essentially a bibliographical study: see also A. Soman, 'The London edition of de Thou's *History*: a critique of some well-documented legends', *Renaissance Quarterly*, vol. 24 (1971), pp. 1–12. Bodin, of course, has been the subject of an immense literature, of which the most useful items in respect of his historiographical achievement are J. H. Franklin, *Jean Bodin and the Sixteenth-Century Revolution in the Methodology of Law and History* (New York, 1963), and the section devoted to papers on this theme in H. Denzer (ed.), *Jean Bodin: Verhandlungen der internationalen Bodin Tagung in München* (Munich, 1973).

An outline of subsequent developments is furnished in W. F. Church's essay, 'France', in O. Ranum (ed.), *National Consciousness, History and Political Culture* (Baltimore, Md, 1975), pp. 43–66. Ranum's own case-studies of a number of seventeenth-century historians, *Artisans of Glory: Writers and Historical Thought in Seventeenth-Century France* (Chapel Hill, NC, 1980), includes a refreshing account of Mézeray, on whom see also P. K. Leffler, 'From humanist to Enlightenment historiography: a case-study of François Eudes de Mézeray', *French Historical Studies*, vol. 10 (1977–8), pp. 416–38. While M. Tyvaert argues that these historians used a considerable range of source-materials ('Érudition et synthèse: les sources utilisées par les histoires générales de la France au XVIᵉ siècle', *Revue française d'histoire du livre*, vol. 5 (1974), pp. 249–66), the same author shows how they ascribed a similar range of virtues to their rulers: 'L'image du roi: légitimité et moralité royales dans les histoires de France au XVIIᵉ siècle', *Revue d'histoire moderne et contemporaine*, vol. 21 (1974), pp. 521–47. How the discipline has fared in more recent institutional circumstances is described by W. R. Keylor, *Academy and Community: The Foundation of the French Historical Profession* (Cambridge, Mass., 1975); and how French historians from Thierry onwards have approached, and how their successors ought to approach, the subject of the 'state' is discussed by B. Guenée, 'L'histoire de l'état en France à la fin du Moyen Age, vu par les historiens français depuis cent ans', *Revue historique*, vol. 232 (1964), pp. 331–60. As for the *Annalistes*, the fullest account of their development since the Second World War is provided by T. Stoianovich in his weightily documented *French Historical Method: The Annales Paradigm* (Ithaca, NY, 1976). But there is no substitute for reading the *Annaliste* leaders' own attempts to expound, and to refine, their tenets: notably, L. Febvre, *Combats pour l'histoire* (Paris, 1953), and F. Braudel, *Écrits sur l'histoire* (Paris, 1969). Questions of methodology have always been a major preoccupation of that school: the second volume of *Mélanges en l'honneur de Fernand Braudel* (Toulouse, 1973) is entirely devoted to such matters. Whatever reservations some Anglo-Saxon historians may continue to entertain about the effects of that preoccupation, it goes without saying that all students of current French historical writing must ponder Braudel's masterpiece, *The Mediterranean and the Mediterranean World in the Age of Philip II* (English trans.,

London, 1972–3) – just as he himself 'read and re-read' the work of Vidal de La Blache.

P. Pinchemel, *France: A Geographical Survey* (English trans., London, 1969), is a fine and instructive example of the French approach to geographical study. The contrast between this approach as developed by Vidal and that of the German 'anthropogeographical' school is heavily underscored by J. Ancel, *Géopolitique* (Paris, 1936); see also the essay by Vidal's pupil Albert Demangeon, 'Géographie politique', *Annales de géographie*, vol. 41 (1932), pp. 22–31. More recent attempts to define the 'region' in 'functional' as distinct from 'natural' geographical terms include E. Juillard, 'La région: essai de définition', *Annales de géographie*, vol. 71 (1962), pp. 483–99, and P. Léon, 'La région lyonnaise dans l'histoire économique et sociale de la France: une esquisse (XVIe–XXe siècles)', *Revue historique*, vol. 237 (1967), pp. 31–62. But debate continues over defining 'region', and 'community', too – the latter a question on which English readers may usefully consult A. Macfarlane, *Reconstructing Historical Communities* (Cambridge, 1977), as well as J. Blum, 'The internal structure and polity of the European village community from the fifteenth to the nineteenth century', *Journal of Modern History*, vol. 43 (1971), pp. 541–76. Meanwhile, however, the major pillars of French historical study continue to consist in socio-economic investigations of districts that have at least some historical claim to be treated as 'unities'. In respect of the period considered in this book, such investigations have proceeded throughout the present century. The most influential of recent *thèses* are E. Le Roy Ladurie, *Les Paysans de Languedoc* (Paris, 1966; abridged English trans., Urban, Ill., 1974), and J. Jacquart, *La Crise rurale en Ile-de-France, 1550–1670* (Paris, 1974). The results of their respective researches have been widely disseminated: Ladurie is a principal contributor to F. Braudel and E. Labrousse (eds), *Histoire économique et sociale de la France*, Vol. 1 (Paris, 1977), which also draws heavily upon the work of Jacquart, himself – with Ladurie once more – a contributor to G. Duby and A. Wallon (eds), *Histoire de la France rurale*, Vol. 2 (Paris, 1975). But to these *thèses* should now be added Guy Cabourdin's, a demographically oriented study of Lorraine, first completed in 1964 and published at last as *Terres et hommes en Lorraine* (Nancy, 1977); the Marxist-oriented work of Guy Bois on Normandy, published as *Crise du féodalisme: économie rurale et démographie en Normandie orientale du début du 14e siècle au milieu du 16e siècle* (Paris, 1976); and the work of J.-P. Gutton, who has added to his *thèse* on *La Société et les pauvres: l'exemple de la généralité de Lyon (1534–1789)* (Paris, 1971) two volumes that show a keener awareness than most of problems concerning the nature of 'community': *Villages du Lyonnais sous la monarchie, XVIe–XVIIIe siècles* (Lyon, 1978), and *La Sociabilité villageoise dans l'ancienne France: solidarités et voisinages du XVe au XVIIIe siècle* (Paris, 1979). Even so, older investigations in this genre retain much of their value, owing not least to the data that they contain. They include: H. Sée, *Les Classes rurales en Bretagne du XVIe siècle à la Révolution* (Paris, 1906); R. Latouche, *La Vie en bas-Quercy du quatorzième au dix-huitième siècle* (Paris, 1923); J. Régné, *La Vie économique et les classes sociales en Vivarais au lendemain de la guerre de Cent Ans* (Aubenas, 1926); and P. Raveau, *L'Agriculture et les classes paysannes: la transformation de la* *propriété dans la haute-Poitou au XVIe siècle* (Paris, 1926), together with the same author's *Essai sur la situation économique et l'état social en Poitou au XVIe siècle* (Paris, 1931). Two further *thèses* on the region adjacent to Paris in the period immediately prior to that studied by Jacquart are Y. Bézard, *La Vie rurale dans le sud de la région parisienne de 1450 à 1560* (Paris, 1929), and G. Fourquin, *Les Campagnes de la région parisienne à la fin du Moyen Âge (du début du XIIIe siècle au début du XVIe siècle)* (Paris, 1964) – a work which, like Jacquart's on the same region, contests a number of Bezard's judgements.

In general, sixteenth-century French urban history has been rather less well served by the thesis-writers. Notable exceptions, though markedly different from each other in focus, organisation and length, are: B. Chevalier, *Tours, ville royale (1356–1520): origine et développement d'une capitale à la fin du Moyen Age* (Louvain, 1975); R. Gascon's thousand-page study, *Grand commerce et vie urbaine au XVIe siècle: Lyon et ses marchands (environs de 1520–environs de 1580)* (Paris, 1971), which, in the manner approved by Braudel, pursues 'the problem' far beyond the confines of Lyon itself; and P. Benedict, *Rouen during the Wars of Religion* (Cambridge, 1981), a penetrating work that unfortunately appeared too late to be used in this book. In *Carnival: A People's Uprising at Romans, 1579–1580* (English trans., London, 1980) E. Le Roy Ladurie offers many insights into conditions of urban life, though his main concern is to analyse social conflicts. Ladurie will also contribute the third, as yet unpublished, volume (*La Ville classique*) to the five-volume *Histoire de la France urbaine* (Paris, 1980–) edited by G. Duby. Otherwise, the fortunes of particular towns may be traced in a number of notable studies. These include R. Boutruche *et al.*, *Bordeaux de 1453 à 1715* (Bordeaux, 1966), and P. Wolff, *Histoire de Toulouse* (Toulouse, 1961). They also include the series on town histories published in Toulouse, among them E. Baratier (ed.), *Histoire de Marseille* (1973); F. Lebrun (ed.), *Histoire d'Angers* (1974); J. Meyer (ed.), *Histoire de Rennes* (1971); and M. Mollat (ed.), *Histoire de l'Ile-de-France et de Paris* (1971). P. Dollinger, P. Wolff and B. Guenée (eds), *Bibliographie d'histoire des villes de France* (Paris, 1967), is a useful guide to publications in this field prior to that date. While the *Bibliographie annuelle* contains abundant evidence of the activity that persists at the local level, present-day academic historians have not matched the zeal with which earlier generations discussed municipal institutions and events. Examples of the latter in receding chronological sequence are: E. Delcambre, *Le Consulat de Puy en Velay des origines à 1610* (Le Puy, 1933); H. de Mazières, *Le Régime municipal en Berry des origines à 1789* (Paris, 1903); G. Testaud, *Des jurisdictions municipales en France des origines jusqu'à l'ordonnance de Moulins* (Paris, 1901); and F. Bonnardot, *Essai historique sur le régime municipal d'Orléans d'après les documents conservés aux archives de la ville (1389–1790)* (Orléans, 1881). Perhaps potential students of municipal constitutional affairs have been discouraged by attitudes of the modern school such as that expressed in J. Dhont, 'Petit-Dutaillis et les communes françaises', *Annales ESC*, vol. 7 (1952), pp. 378–84. However, M. Zarb has traced the *Histoire d'une autonomie communale: les privilèges de la ville de Marseille du Xe siècle à la Révolution* (Paris, 1961); summary accounts of 'Les municipalités en haute-Normandie' may be found in S. Deck's series of contributions to the *Annales* *de Normandie*, beginning in vol. 10 (1960), pp. 207–27; and H. de Carsalade du Pont examines *La Municipalité parisienne à l'époque de Henri IV* (Paris, 1971).

On the government of the kingdom in general, convenient introductions are F. Dumont and P.-C. Timbal, 'Gouvernés et gouvernants en France: périodes du Moyen Age et du XVIe siècle', *Anciens pays et assemblées d'États*, vol. 35 (Brussels, 1966), pp. 181–233, and J. H. Shennan, *Government and Society in France, 1461–1661* (London, 1969). D. Richet, *La France moderne: l'esprit des institutions* (Paris, 1973), is a stimulating short essay. Although R. Mousnier, *Les Institutions de la France sous la monarchie absolue*, 2 vols (Paris, 1974–80; Vol. 1 now available in English trans., Chicago, Ill., 1980), includes material on the sixteenth century, its concern is with the subsequent period, and it is powerfully informed by its author's ideas on social structure: see comment by R. Mettam, 'Two-dimensional history: Mousnier and the *ancien régime*', *History*, vol. 66 (1981), pp. 221–32. The standard work on France's sixteenth-century governmental institutions is still R. Doucet's *Les Institutions de la France au XVIe siècle*, 2 vols (Paris, 1948), though G. Zeller, *Les Institutions de la France au XVIe siècle* (Paris, 1948), is both briefer and more perceptive on certain topics. P. Imbart de La Tour, *Les Origines de la Réforme*, Vol. I, *La France moderne* (Paris, 1905), argued strongly that by the opening of the sixteenth century the French monarchy was well on the road towards 'absolutism'. A dogged opponent of such a view is the American historian J. Russell Major, whose ideas, developed in a number of works, are conveniently summarised in his 'The French Renaissance monarchy as seen through the Estates-General', *Studies in the Renaissance*, vol. 9 (1962), pp. 113–25. For a critique of, and yet another alternative to, Major's position, see B. Guenée, 'Espace et État dans la France du bas-Moyen Age', *Annales ESC*, vol. 23 (1968), pp. 744–58. Disagreement turns essentially upon the question how far the government of the French Renaissance kings exemplifies 'administrative centralisation'. It is unlikely to be resolved until far more is known in detail about how sixteenth-century royal administration actually worked – a subject that has again been relatively neglected amid the recent preoccupations of French historians. A distinguished exception is H. Michaud, whose *La Grande Chancellerie et les écritures royales au XVIe siècle* (Paris, 1967) contains a wealth of archival information and perceptive comment; see also her paper on 'L'entourage des grands officiers et les "cabinets" des secrétaires d'état au XVIe siècle' in the symposium *Origines et histoire des cabinets des ministres en France* (Hautes études médiévales et modernes, vol. 24: Geneva, 1975), which contains several other useful contributions on this theme. 'Personal and genealogical notices' on royal administrative personnel prior to the emergence of the *secrétaires d'état* are supplied by A. Lapeyre and R. Scheurer, *Les Notaires et secrétaires du roi sous les règnes de Louis XI, Charles VIII et Louis XII, 1461–1515*, 2 vols (Paris, 1978). Knowledge of a similar kind on the membership of the royal council at the beginning of the sixteenth century would be greatly enhanced by publication of M. Harsgor's *thèse* of 1972, 'Recherches sur le personnel du conseil du roi (1483–1515)'. Studies of the council and its development are badly needed. In relation to most of the sixteenth century R. Mousnier's volume, *Le Conseil du roi de Louis XII à la Révolution* (Paris, 1970), is disappointingly thin on its declared subject. On *officiers* and office-holding in general, however, Mousnier's magisterial study, *La Vénalité des offices sous Henry IV et Louis XIII*, 2nd edn (Paris, 1971), deals with that century much more fully than its title might suggest. A phase in the extension of office-selling is explored by C. Stocker, 'Public and private enterprise in the administration of a Renaissance monarchy: the first sales of offices in the *parlement* of Paris (1512–1524)', *The Sixteenth Century Journal*, vol. 9 (1978), pp. 4–29; and S. Mastellone relates the practice to aspects of ideological and social change in his *Venalità e machiavellismo in Francia (1572–1610): all' origine della mentalità politica borghese* (Florence, 1972). Instances of the cadres of provincial government are discussed by: A. Bossuat, *Le Bailliage royal de Montferrand (1425–1556)* (Paris, 1957); J. M. Schmittel, 'La prévôté de Mézières aux XVIe, XVIIe et XVIIIe siècles', *Études ardennaises*, année 3 (1958), pp. 35–46; and E. Appolis, 'Une "municipalité" intermédiaire en Languedoc: la sénéchaussée', *Anciens pays et assemblées d'États*, vol. 47 (1968), pp. 225–31. For government in Languedoc prior to the wars of religion, P. Dognon, *Les Institutions politiques et administratives du pays de Languedoc* (Toulouse, 1895), remains fundamental. As for the *gouverneurs*, the first book-length study of those controversial potentates is R. R. Harding's challenging and informative *Anatomy of a Power Élite: The Provincial Governors of Early Modern France* (New Haven, Conn., 1978).

On the administration of justice, J. H. Shennan surveys both the political and the judicial role of *The Parlement of Paris* (London, 1968) from its origins to the Revolution. Features of judicial procedure at the sovereign courts are considered in two substantial articles by B. Schnapper: 'La justice criminelle rendue par le parlement de Paris sous le règne de François Ier', *Revue historique de droit français et étranger*, vol. 52 (1974), pp. 252–84, and 'La répression pénale au XVIe siècle: l'exemple du parlement de Bordeaux (1510–1565)', *Recueil de mémoires et travaux publié par la société d'histoire du droit et des institutions des anciens pays de droit écrit*, vol. 8 (1971), pp. 1–54; see also the comparative study on an important aspect by J. H. Langbein, *Torture and the Law of Proof: Europe and England in the Ancien Régime* (Chicago, Ill., 1977). The reforming proposals of a bold and eccentric *avocat* at the Paris *parlement* are the subject of Y. Jeanclos, *Les Projets de réforme judiciaire de Raoul Spifame au XVIe siècle* (Geneva, 1977). French law as such is surveyed by F. Olivier-Martin, *Histoire du droit français des origines à la Révolution* (Paris, 1948). That distinguished legal historian's leading successor in the field, Gabriel Lepointe, has written a brief introductory *Histoire du droit public français* (Paris, 1957); and students of French private law have available the three-volume textbook by P. Ourliac and J. de Malafosse, *Histoire du droit privé* (Paris, 1961–9). The tortuous emergence of a conceptual distinction between these forms of law is examined at length by G. Chevrier, 'Remarques sur l'introduction et les vicissitudes de la distinction du "jus privatum" et du "jus publicum" dans les œuvres des anciens juristes français', *Archives de philosophie du droit*, nouv. sér., vol. 1 (1952), pp. 5–77. Much scholarship has been devoted to the study of France's customary laws. Important works by leading historians include E. Chênon, *Le 'Pays' de Berry et le 'détroit' de sa coutume* (Paris, 1916), and F. Olivier-Martin, *Histoire de la coutume de la prévôté et vicomté de Paris*, 2 vols (Paris, 1922–30) – the latter rich in quotations from the commentary of that doyen of sixteenth-century jurists, Du Moulin, whose career and work have at last received a full-scale assessment: J.-L. Thireau, *Charles Du Moulin (1500–1566): étude sur les sources, la méthode, les idées politiques et économiques d'un juriste de la Renaissance* (Geneva, 1980). R. Filhol, editor of *Le Vieux coutumier de Poitou* (Bourges, 1956), had also studied another important figure in the field of sixteenth-century judicial reform, *Le Premier président Christofle de Thou et la réformation des coutumes* (Paris, 1937). A useful brief review of how modern research has modified notions of France's division between the 'Germanic' legal tradition of the north and the 'Roman' tradition of the Midi is presented by J. Yver, 'L'état des études d'histoire du droit privé en France', *Revue historique de droit français et étranger*, sér. 4, année 45 (1967), pp. 708–11. The previous volume of the same periodical contains (p. 695) a summary of G. Chevrier's paper, 'La pénétration du droit romain dans quelques pays de coutumes du Centre et de l'Est (Berry-Nivernais, Champagne, Bourgogne ducale) du XIVᵉ à la fin du XVIIIᵉ siècle'. The significance of the sixteenth-century redaction in relation to local usages and juridical 'Gallicanism' is considered by V. P. Mortari, *Diritto romano e dirito nazionale in Francia nel secolo XVI* (Milan, 1962); while the continuance of seigneurial justice in territories adjacent to the capital itself is examined by P. Lemercier, *Les Justices seigneuriales de la région parisienne de 1580 à 1789* (Paris, 1933).

On royal finance, although M. Wolfe, *The Fiscal System of Renaissance France* (New Haven, Conn., 1972), is a valuable guide, current impressions of the volume of royal revenues still owe a great deal to J. J. Clamageran's *Histoire de l'impôt en France*, 3 vols (Paris, 1867–76). Clamageran's conclusions may often be suspect, but the subject is daunting. A. Guéry, 'Les finances de la monarchie française sous l'ancien régime', *Annales ESC*, vol. 33 (1978), pp. 216–39, reviews the sources, but offers disappointingly little by way of fresh data on the sixteenth century. For its closing decades, however, hopes are raised by the announcement of a forthcoming work by R. J. Bonney. Meanwhile, studies of documents relating to budgets in particular years are provided by: R. Doucet, *L'État des finances de 1523* (Paris, 1923); R. Doucet, *L'État des finances de 1567* (Paris, 1929); and H. Michaud, 'L'Ordonnancement des dépenses et le budget de la monarchie, 1587–1589', *Annuaire-bulletin de la société de l'histoire de France* (1970–1), pp. 87–150. On the *bureaux des finances*, the somewhat dated studies of E. Everat, *Le Bureau des finances de Riom de 1551 à 1790* (Riom, 1900), and J. Vannier, *Essai sur le bureau des finances de la généralité de Rouen, 1551–1790* (Rouen, 1927), have more recently been joined by G. Delaume, *Le Bureau des finances de la généralité de Paris* (Paris, 1966). Responses in the *pays d'états* to royal tax-demands are illustrated in J. Gay, 'Les exigences de la fiscalité royale en Bourgogne dans la seconde moitié du XVIᵉ siècle (1547–72)', *Revue historique de droit français et étranger*, sér. 4, année 44 (1966), pp. 172–4. Gay is also a contributor to the set of papers on the financial role of the provincial Estates, in *Études sur l'histoire des assemblées d'États: publication de la section française de la Commission Internationale pour l'Histoire des Assemblées d'États et du Centre International d'Études d'Histoire Comparée du Droit de la Faculté de Droit et des Sciences Économiques de Paris* (Paris, 1966), pp. 95–222. Tax administration and its political and social significance in another of the *pays d'états* are investigated for the entire sixteenth century by L. Scott van Doren in two articles: 'War taxation, institutional change and social conflict in provincial France: the royal *taille* in Dauphiné, 1494–1559', *Proceedings of the American Philosophical Society*, vol. 121 (1977), pp. 70–96; and 'Civil war and the foundations of fiscal absolutism: the royal *taille* in Dauphiné, 1560 –1610', *Proceedings of the 3rd Annual Meeting of the Western Society for French History, Denver, December 4–6 1975* (1976), pp. 35–53.

The leading historian of sixteenth-century French representative assemblies is J. Russell Major. Sixteen years after reviewing the available archival and printed materials in his 'French representative assemblies: research opportunities and research published', *Studies in Medieval and Renaissance History*, vol. 1 (1964), pp. 183–219, he has added his detailed account of provincial Estates, *Representative Government in Early Modern France* (New Haven, Conn. 1980), to his earlier works on *Representative Institutions in Renaissance France, 1429–1559* (Madison, Wis., 1960) and *The Deputies to the Estates-General in Renaissance France* (Madison, Wis., 1960). Major's numerous articles in this field include 'The assembly at Paris in the summer of 1575', *Studia gratiana*, vol. 15 (1972), pp. 699–715, and 'The payment of the deputies to the French national assemblies, 1484–1627', *Journal of Modern History*, vol. 27 (1955), pp. 217–30. On those deputies, an attempt at a sociological analysis of data presented by Major is J.-J. Hermandiquer, 'Sociologie des États-généraux de 1483 à 1651', *Annales ESC*, vol. 16 (1961), pp. 355–8. A comment on the relation between the deputies and their constituents is provided by O. Ulph, 'The mandate system and representation to the Estates-General under the old system', *Journal of Modern History*, vol. 23 (1951), pp. 225–31; and another, on the same theme, by C. Soule, 'Les pouvoirs des députés aux États-généraux de France', *Anciens pays et assemblées d'États*, vol. 37 (1965), pp. 61–82. Although Soule has attempted a broad survey of *Les Etats-généraux de France, 1302–1789: étude historique comparative et doctrinale* (Heule, 1968), the only full treatment of this subject remains G. Picot's four-volume *Histoire des États-généraux* (Paris, 1872), still valuable for its documentation even though changed historical perspectives have rendered questionable Picot's view of what the assemblies achieved.

The contention that 'estates' or 'orders' convey a description not merely of certain legal and political institutions, but also of how early-modern French society was 'stratified' through and through, has been stoutly maintained by Roland Mousnier of the Sorbonne. A critic both of Marxist and of *Annaliste* approaches to sociological analysis, Mousnier has expounded his ideas in numerous essays, the most accessible of which is his *Social Hierarchies* (English trans., London, 1973). Those ideas in turn have been widely and sharply criticised, notably by P. Goubert, 'L'ancienne société d'ordres: verbiage ou réalité?', *Colloque franco-suisse d'histoire économique et sociale* (Geneva, 1969), and by A. Arriaza, 'Mousnier, Barber and the "society of orders"', *Past & Present*, no. 89 (1980), pp. 39–57. Significantly enough, Mousnier was not a participant in the symposium *Ordres et classes: colloque d'histoire sociale, Saint-Cloud, 24–25 mai 1967* (Paris, 1973), which yielded stimulating papers, notably by Goubert and J. Le Goff. The Sorbonne professor's progress as an interpreter of French society is traced by E. Rotelli, 'La structure sociale dans l'itinéraire historique de Roland Mousnier', *Revue d'histoire économique et sociale*, vol. 51 (1973), pp. 145–82. Like the *Annalistes*, he, too, has come to stress the importance of the family as the key group in that society; the former devoted an entire issue of their periodical to 'Famille et société', *annales ESC*, vol. 27 (1972), pp. 799–1234. On this topic, the pioneer work of P. Ariès, *L'Enfant et la vie familiale sous l'ancien régime* (Paris, 1960: English trans., *Centuries of Childhood*, London, 1962), has been followed by J. L. Flandrin, *Familles: parenté, maison, sexualité dans l'ancienne société* (Paris, 1976: English trans., Cambridge, 1980); see also the same author's *Amours paysannes, 16ᵉ–19ᵉ siècles* (Paris, 1975). To these socio-psychological studies should be added the drier but at least as significant works on inheritance practices noted above (p. 178, n. 37), and the demographic indications interpreted in P. Laslett (ed.), *Household and Family in Past Time: Comparative Studies in the Size and Structure of the Domestic Group over the Last Three Centuries in England, France, Serbia, Japan and Colonial North America* (Cambridge, 1972).

It has been suggested that the *Annalistes* turned rather belatedly to the subject of the family, despite the emphasis upon *psychologie* and *sensibilité* laid by their founder Febvre, whose view of the 'psychological instability of sixteenth-century men' is criticised in J. Frappier, 'Sur Lucien Febvre et son interprétation psychologique du XVIᵉ siècle', *Mélanges d'histoire littéraire (XVIᵉ–XVIIᵉ siècles) offerts à Raymond Lebègue* (Paris, 1969), pp. 19–31. Their recognition of the subject's importance stemmed from their mounting concern with historical demography, a field in which French scholars have been major methodological pioneers – chief among them Louis Henry, author, with M. Fleury, of that 'famous little manual' *Des Registres paroissiaux à l'histoire de la population: manuel de dépouillement et d'exploitation de l'état-civil ancien* (Paris, 1956). The *Revue d'histoire économique et sociale*, vol. 39 (1961), pp. 510–32 and 538–40, contains summaries of and comment upon works by other leading figures in this field: M. Reinhard, A. Armengaud, J. Dupâquier and E. Baratier, the first three of whom have essayed an *Histoire générale de la population mondiale* (Paris, 1968). Even so, information on France's sixteenth-century population remains fragmentary: as much is apparent from the survey by the prominent demographic historian and critic of Mousnier, P. Goubert, of 'Recent theories and research in French population between 1500 and 1700', in D. V. Glass and D. E. C. Eversley (eds), *Population in History: Essays in Historical Demography* (London, 1965), pp. 457–73. However, both demographic and sixteenth-century considerations have always loomed large in the thinking of that indefatigable *Annaliste* figure E. Le Roy Ladurie, whose contribution with J. M. Pesez – 'Le cas français: vue d'ensemble' – to the volume *Villages désertés et histoire économique, XIᵉ–XVIIIᵉ siècles* (Paris, 1965), pp. 127–252, is important. Mousnier himself introduces the demographically oriented study of M. Couturier, *Recherches sur les structures sociales de Châteaudun (1525–1789)* (Paris, 1969); and Dupâquier comments at length on another significant study specifically of a sixteenth-century urban region, 'Statistique et démographie historique: reflexions sur l'ouvrage d'A. Croix, *Nantes et le pays nantais au XVIᵉ siècle*',

Annales ESC, vol. 30 (1975), pp. 394–401. Finally, the *Annales de démographie historique*, published from 1965 onwards by the Société de Démographie Historique, include numerous chronologically and thematically wide-ranging studies that encompass the sixteenth century. Among such articles may be noted. A. Fierro, 'La population du Dauphiné au XIVe au XXe siècle' (1978, pp. 355–417), and J.-P. Poussou, 'Les mouvements migratoires en France et à partir de la France de la fin du XVe siècle au début du XIXe siècle' (1970, pp. 11–78).

The recent prominence of quantitative demographic inquiry is linked with the concern of modern social historians to probe the behaviour and *mentalités* of groups below the level of the ruling élites. Among the most insightful of such historians is N. Z. Davis, eight of whose sensitive and amply documented essays, on subjects that include the poor, crowd violence and – especially – women, are collected in her *Society and Culture in Early Modern France* (London, 1975). Yet, while this concern has greatly broadened and enriched historical understanding, its pursuit has perhaps facilitated a survival of long-standing assumptions about the condition of the nobility. These assumptions include the view that in the course of the sixteenth and early seventeenth centuries a 'crisis' occurred in the economic fortunes of established noble families, who were challenged and to some extent displaced by a rival 'new' nobility of quasi-*bourgeois* origins, the *noblesse de robe*. F. Billacois, 'La crise de la noblesse européenne (1550–1650): une mise au point', *Revue d'histoire moderne et contemporaine*, vol. 23 (1976), pp. 258–77, notes some grounds for resisting such assumptions which, in the case of France, are strongly questioned in two recent works by young American researchers: J. Dewald, *The Formation of a Provincial Nobility: The Magistrates of the Parlement of Rouen, 1499–1610* (Princeton, NJ, 1980), and J. B. Wood, *The Nobility of the Élection of Bayeux, 1463–1666: Continuity through Change* (Princeton, NJ, 1980). See also the articles by Wood, 'The decline of the nobility in sixteenth and early seventeenth-century France: myth or reality?', *Journal of Modern History*, vol. 38 (1976), and by W. A. Weary, 'The house of La Tremoille, fifteenth through eighteenth centuries: change and adaptation in a French noble family', *Journal of Modern History*, vol. 39 (1977) – both instances of that periodical's remarkable practice of making available in photocopied form contributions which have received its editorial blessing, but are not printed in the pages of its issues. How *robins* rose to achieve high rank is the concern of D. Richet's paper 'Élite et noblesse: la formation des grands serviteurs de l'État (fin XVIe–début XVIIe siècle)', *Acta Poloniae historica*, vol. 36 (1977), pp. 47–63. How noble status was acquired by commoners purchasing lands to which it seemed to be attached is examined in J. R. Bloch, *L'Anoblissement en France au temps de François Ier* (Paris, 1934); and examples of how noble status was proved are discussed by M. Nortier, 'Maintenues de la noblesse de 1473 à 1528', *Cahiers Léopold Delisle*, vol. 9 (1960), pp. 5–27, and by J. Durand de Saint-Front, 'La recherche de la noblesse de l'élection de Valognes en 1523', *Revue du département de la Manche*, vol. 10 (1968), pp. 187–216, 238–89. By no means all such commoner-purchasers gained the status in question, as J.-M. Constant shows in his 'Quelques problèmes de mobilité sociale et la vie matérielle chez les gentilshommes de Beauce aux XVIe et XVIIe siècles', *Acta*

Poloniae historica, vol. 36 (1977), pp. 83–94. In any case, as A. Jouanna has illustrated in several articles together with her *Ordre social: mythes et réalités dans la France du XVIe siècle* (Paris, 1977), 'nobility' in early-modern French society involved a host of ethical and related elements, and is not to be reduced to considerations merely of legal proofs and conditions of material life.

Nevertheless, conditions of material life remain central to twentieth-century historians' investigations of that society. Price-movements continue to be charted, and their interpretation re-examined. Recent contributions in this field are D. Richet, 'Causes of inflation in France in the XVIth century: problems of measurement and interpretation', *Journal of European Economic History*, vol. 4 (1975), pp. 707–15, and J. Day and G. Bois, '"Crise du féodalisme" et conjoncture des prix à la fin du Moyen Age', *Annales ESC*, vol. 34 (1979), pp. 305–24. But among other relevant topics into which *Annaliste* historians, Ladurie well to the fore, have launched ambitious inquiries are climate, nutrition, disease, together with that key issue, the level of agricultural production. Examples of such continuing inquiries are: M. Baulant and E. Le Roy Ladurie, 'Une synthèse provisoire: les vendanges du XVe au XIXe siècle', *Annales ESC*, vol. 33 (1978), pp. 763–71; the set of papers on 'Histoire de la consommation: contribution à l'histoire de la consommation alimentaire du XIVe au XIXe siècle', *Annales ESC*, vol. 30 (1975), pp. 402–632; E. Le Roy Ladurie, 'Un concept: l'unification microbienne du monde (XIVe–XVIIe siècles)', *Revue suisse d'histoire*, vol. 23 (1973), pp. 627–96; and J. Goy and E. Le Roy Ladurie (eds), *Les Fluctuations de la produit de la dîme: conjoncture décimale et domaniale de la fin du Moyen Age au XVIIIe siècle* (Paris, 1972). And yet, for all the breadth of vision and methodological ingenuity that such inquiries exhibit, what has not emerged hitherto is a satisfactory overview of the sixteenth-century 'French economy'. Despite its undoubted value, the first volume of the *Histoire économique et sociale de la France*, already cited (above, p. 211), is not such a work. All too promptly, *Annaliste* dialectical proficiency reduces projected synthesis to fresh thesis and antithesis. As much is apparent in that volume from Ladurie's account of the peasantry, weighed down by debates and excursions; from Gascon's contribution on towns and trade, unbalanced by its author's familiarity with the Lyon case; and even from Morineau's searching and stimulating attempt to establish 'les conjonctures' in his concluding chapter. Thus, the economic affairs of the kingdom as a whole remain in effect uncharted. Even so, meticulous local and regional studies multiply apace, often focusing upon particular topics highlighted long since by M. Bloch in his extremely influential *French Rural Economy: An Essay in Its Basic Characteristics*, first published half a century ago (English trans., London, 1966). These topics include the engrossing of lands whether by seigneurs or by townsmen, proprietors' use of share-cropping leases, and how far such developments undermined rural social structures and prepared the way for agrarian capitalism or retarded its emergence. In respect of these and related questions, see: M.-T. Lorcin, *Les Campagnes de la région lyonnaise aux XIVe et XVe siècles* (Paris, 1974); G. Sicard, *Le Métayage dans le Midi toulousain à la fin du Moyen Age* (Toulouse, 1956); L. Merle, *La Métairie et l'évolution agraire de la Gâtine poitevine de la fin du Moyen Age à la Révolution* (Paris, 1958); M. Simonot-Bouillot, 'La

métairie et le métayer dans le sud du Châtillonais du XVIᵉ au XVIIIᵉ siècle',
Annales de Bourgogne, vol. 34 (1962), pp. 217–51; J. L. Goldsmith, 'Agricultural specialization and stagnation in early-modern Auvergne', *Agricultural history*, vol. 47 (1973), pp. 216–34; and two articles by J.-M. Constant, 'Gestion et revenus d'un grand domain d'après les comptes de la baronnie d'Auneau aux XVIᵉ et XVIIᵉ siècles', *Revue d'histoire économique et sociale*, vol. 50 (1972), pp. 165–202, and 'La propriété et le problème de la constitution des fermes sur les censives en Beauce aux XVIᵉ et XVIIᵉ siècles', *Revue historique*, vol. 249 (1973), pp. 353–76. Constant's articles are based on his unpublished *thèse*, 'Nobles et paysans en Beauce aux XVIᵉ et XVIIᵉ siècles', which is reviewed by J.-L. Bourgeon in *Revue historique*, vol. 262 (1979), pp. 271–9.

On commerce and industry, the prolific Pierre Chaunu, historian of Seville's Atlantic trade and of so much more, reviews Gascon's *Grand commerce* (cf. above, p. 212) in his 'Lyon des confins: réflexions sur l'économie d'échange au sommet du XVIᵉ siècle', *Revue d'histoire économique et sociale*, vol. 50 (1972), pp. 145–64. For France's Iberian trade, A. Girard, *Le Commerce français à Seville et Cadix au temps des Habsbourg: contribution à l'étude du commerce étranger en Espagne aux XVIᵉ et XVIIᵉ siècles* (Paris, 1932), remains useful. Two articles by C. Douyère on 'Les marchands étrangers à Rouen au XVIᵉ siècle (vers 1520–vers 1580): assimilation ou ségrégation?', drawn from her *thèse* on that subject, have appeared in *Revue des sociétés savantes de haute-Normandie*, no. 69 (1973), pp. 23–61, and no. 76 (1974), pp. 27–61. France's cloth industry and trade in textiles continue to attract considerable attention. Recent contributions include: P. Wolff, 'Esquisse d'une histoire de la draperie en Languedoc du XIIᵉ au début du XVIIᵉ siècle', in a set of conference-papers on *Produzione, commercio e consumo dei panni di lana, nei secoli XII–XVIII* (Florence, 1976), pp. 435–62; P. Deyon, 'La concurrence internationale des manufactures lainières aux XVIᵉ et XVIIᵉ siècles', *Annales ESC*, vol. 27 (1972), pp. 20–32; and R. Deslimon, 'Structures d'un marché de draperie dans le Languedoc au milieu du XVIᵉ siècle', *Annales ESC*, vol. 30 (1975), pp. 1414–46. How cloth was manufactured is examined by F. Concato, 'La technique drapière en Normandie à la fin du Moyen Age, XIVᵉ–XVᵉ siècles', *Annales de Normandie*, année 25 (1975), pp. 75–98. Far less material is available on other industrial activities in France, though on technology in general the distinguished historian of this subject Bertrand Gille has edited, for the 'Encyclopédie de la Pléiade', a *Histoire des techniques* (Paris, 1978); see also the same author's *Les Ingénieurs de la Renaissance* (Paris, 1964). However, a number of papers on *Mines et métallurgie (XIIᵉ–XVIᵉ siècles)* were delivered at the 98th Congrès National des Sociétés Savantes, held appropriately at Saint-Étienne in 1973, and published as vol. 1 (Paris, 1975) of the transactions of its Section de Philologie et d'Histoire jusqu'à 1610.

Although the interaction of 'economy' and 'society' has held a dominant position in modern French historical thinking, recent work has tended to seek in 'popular culture', as distinct from material affairs, a key to the character of social relationships, and to emphasise in particular the significance of popular religious beliefs, associations and ritual behaviour. A pioneer in this field, as in others, was Lucien Febvre, whose *Le Problème de l'incroyance au XVIᵉ siècle: la religion de Rabelais* (Paris, 1942), though generalising too freely from literary evidence and straining its case on the impossibility of atheism for sixteenth-century people, has stimulated much subsequent study. Folklorists abound; early-modern popular literature has its scholarly interpreters – see, for instance, G. Bollème, *La Bibliothèque bleue: la littérature populaire en France du XVIᵉ au XIXᵉ siècle* (Paris, 1971). Witchcraft has excited a perhaps excessive degree of interest; two recent articles on this theme are R. Muchembled, 'Sorcellerie, culture populaire et christianisme au XVIᵉ siècle, principalement en Flandre et en Artois', *Annales ESC*, vol. 28 (1973), pp. 264–84, and A. Soman, 'Les procès de sorcellerie au parlement de Paris (1565–1640)', *Annales ESC*, vol. 32 (1977), pp. 790–814. In more orthodox vein, the writings of E. Delaruelle are among the most rewarding investigations of late-medieval and early-modern religious sentiment. In addition to indications already given in the notes, see his *La Piété populaire au Moyen Age* (Turin, 1975), and his stimulating paper 'Observations sur le baroque religieux de 1500 à 1650', *Actes des journées internationales d'étude du baroque, Montauban, 1963* (Toulouse, 1965), pp. 95–106. John Bossy provides convenient introductions to and elaborations upon the work of his fellow-researchers in his review-article 'Holiness and society', *Past & Present*, no. 75 (1977), pp. 119–37, and in his 'The Counter-Reformation and the people of Catholic Europe', *Past & Present*, no. 47 (1970), pp. 51–70. Like Bossy in the latter paper, M. Venard illustrates the insistence of the post-Tridentine church upon parochial at the expense of confraternal practices in his 'Les confréries de penitents à la fin du XVIᵉ siècle dans la province ecclésiastique d'Avignon', *Cahiers d'histoire publiés par les universités de Clermont, Lyon, Grenoble*, vol. 9 (1964), pp. 83–4; Vernard's *thèse*, on *L'Église d'Avignon au XVIᵉ siècle*, is reviewed by D. Julia in *Revue d'histoire de l'Eglise de France*, vol. 64 (1978), pp. 168–76.

Papers of the international conference held in Trent to mark the quatercentenary of the famous Council, and published as *Il Concilio di Trento e la riforma tridentina* (Rome, 1965), include (pp. 383–400) M. François, 'La réception du Concile de Trente en France sous Henri III' – a subject also discussed by R. M. Kingdon, 'Some French reactions to the Council of Trent', *Church History* (1964), pp. 149–56. The origins and development of the much-discussed but never definitively enumerated liberties of the Gallican church in relation to both Pope and king are traced by J. Lecler, 'Qu'est-ce que les libertés de l'église gallicane?', *Recherches de science religieuse*, vol. 23 (1933), pp. 385–410, 542–68; see also W. J. Bouwsma, 'Gallicanism and the nature of Christendom', in the Molho and Tedeschi (eds) *festschrift* for Hans Baron, *Renaissance Studies* (above, p. 209), pp. 809–30. That the French king already had *de facto* control of episcopal appointments prior to the agreement struck in Bologna is argued by R. J. Knecht, 'The Concordat of 1516: a reassessment', *University of Birmingham Historical Journal*, vol. 9 (1963), pp. 16–32. Yet chapters were capable of stout resistance to royal nominations, as F. Villard shows in his 'L'élection de Claude de Tonnerre à l'évêché de Poitiers (19 août–23 septembre 1507)', *Bulletin de la Société des Antiquaires de l'Ouest et des Musées de Poitiers*, sér. 4, vol. 10 (1970), pp. 469–80. M. M. Edelstein analyses 'The social origins of the episcopacy in the reign of France I', *French Historical Studies*, vol. 8 (1974), pp. 371–92; and J. Lestocquoy assesses 'Les évêques français au milieu du XVIe siècle', *Revue d'histoire de l'Église de France*, vol. 45 (1959), pp. 25–40. Their worldly involvements are illustrated by H. Dubief, 'Les opérations commerciales de Louis Guillart, évêque de Tournai, puis de Chartres, en 1524', *Revue du Nord*, vol. 43 (1961), pp. 149–54; and the relatively slow reaction of bishops and other ecclesiastical dignitaries in south-western France to the early challenge of the Protestant Reformation is indicated by G. Hubrecht, 'Le concile provincial de Bordeaux de 1528', in *Études d'histoire du droit canonique dédiées à Gabriel Le Bras* (Paris, 1965), vol. 1, pp. 169–78 – a *festschrift*, containing a number of important contributions, for the doyen of French canon law historians and co-founder of the periodical *Archives de sociologie religieuse*.

J. Le Goff (ed.), *Hérésies et sociétés dans l'Europe pré-industrielle, 11e–18e siècles* (Paris, 1968), is an invaluable collection of papers on unorthodox religious beliefs and practices, and their transmission. A convenient introduction to the coming of the Protestant Reformation is J. Delumeau, *Naissance et affirmation de la Réforme* (Paris, 1965), though the dramatic significance of the movement's impact with its attendant forces is nowhere better conveyed than in A. G. Dickens, *Reformation and Society in Sixteenth-Century Europe* (London, 1966). E. G. Léonard has written the standard *Histoire générale du protestantisme*, Vol. 1, *La Réformation*, and Vol. 2, *L'Établissement* (Paris, 1961: the English translations of this work, ed. H. H. Rowley, contain extensive bibliographical indications); see the review by P. Chaunu, 'Réforme et église au XVIe siècle', *Revue historique*, vol. 227 (1962), pp. 361–76. In a famous essay, L. Febvre diagnosed 'Une question mal posée: les origines de la Réforme française et le problème général de la Réforme', *Revue historique*, vol. 161 (1929), pp. 1–73. The question nevertheless continues to prompt various kinds of answer; see, for instance: J. Carbonnier, 'De l'idée que le protestantisme s'est faite de ses rapports avec le catharisme, ou des adoptions d'ancêtres en l'histoire', *Bulletin de la Société de l'Histoire du Protestantisme français*, année 101 (1955), pp. 72–87; M. Mousseaux, 'Des origines françaises de la Réforme', in the same periodical, année 107 (1961), pp. 146–65; and J. Solé, 'Les origines de la Réforme: protestantisme, eschatologie et anabaptisme', *Annales ESC*, vol. 28 (1973), pp. 1123–30. So, too, has the role of Lefèvre d'Etaples, upon assessments of which Febvre made tart comments: see R. Stauffer, 'Lefèvre d'Étaples, artisan ou spectateur de la Réforme', *Bulletin de la Société de l'Histoire du Protestantisme français*, année 113 (1967), pp. 405–23; but the fullest investigation of Lefèvre's thought is now G. Bedouelle, *Lefèvre d'Étaples et l'intelligence des Écritures* (Geneva, 1976).

Again in the wake of Febvre, the importance of Strasbourg in relation to the early French Reformation is examined in several contributions to the valuable collection of papers edited by G. Livet and F. Rapp, *Strasbourg au cœur religieux de XVIe siècle* (Strasbourg, 1977). Turning to the social composition of the movement, Léonard and S. Mours, in *Le Protestantisme en France au XVIe siècle* (Paris, 1958), were alike satisfied that its adherents came from all levels of society. Pointers to how their general conclusions may have to be revised are contained in: R. A. Mentzer, 'Heresy suspects in Languedoc prior to 1560: observations on their social and occupational status', *Bibliothèque d'humanisme et Renaissance*, vol. 39 (1977), pp. 561–8; and D. Nicholls,

'Social change and early Protestantism in France: Normandy, 1520–62', *European Studies Review*, vol. 10 (1980), pp. 279–308. The distinctive role of women in the movement has attracted considerable attention, from N. Z. Davis (see her volume of essays, above, p. 218), from J.-J. Hermandiquer ('Les femmes dans la Réforme en Dauphiné', *Bulletin philologique et historique du Comité des Travaux Historiques et Scientifiques* (1959), pp. 381–97), and from several contributors to *Archiv für Reformationsgeschichte*, vol. 63 (1972), pp. 141 ff. Moreover, women historians have recently been strongly to the fore in investigating French Protestantism during the religious wars. They include: A. H. Guggenheim, in articles (noted above, p. 199) drawn from her unpublished thesis, 'Calvinism and the political élite of sixteenth-century Nîmes'; J. Davies, 'Persecution and Protestantism: Toulouse, 1562–75', *The Historical Journal*, vol. 22 (1979), pp. 31–52; J. Garrisson-Estèbe, whose newly published *thèse, Protestants du Midi* (Toulouse, 1980) – a work that regrettably reached me after completion of this book – makes superb use of consistory records to illuminate Protestantism as a social phenomenon; and N. M. Sutherland, whose *The Huguenot Struggle for Recognition* (New Haven, Conn., 1980) focuses upon the formation of royal policy in relation to the 'religious' edicts. From among the many discussions of the term 'Huguenot', the suggestions recorded by C. de Grandmaison, 'Origines et étymologie françaises du mot Huguenot', *Bulletin de la Société de l'Histoire du Protestantisme Français*, année 51 (1902), pp. 7–13, are noteworthy. Even more so is M. Reulos' view of the organisation and corporate nature of the reformed churches in relation to legal concepts: see his 'Synodes, assemblées politiques des Réformés français, et théorie des États', *Anciens pays et assemblées d'États*, vol. 24 (1962), pp. 95–111; and the same author's 'Les sources du droit ecclésiastique des églises réformées de France au XVIe et XVIIe siècles: Écriture et discipline', in vol. 1, pp. 343–52, of the Gabriel Le Bras *festschrift* already mentioned (above, p. 222). The failure of those churches, or at least of their leaders, to gain a political accommodation in 1561 is examined by D. Nugent, *Ecumenism in the Age of the Reformation: The Colloquy of Poissy* (Cambridge, Mass., 1974); the quatercentenary of the massacre that befell them eleven years later is marked by a wide-ranging collection of papers, *Actes du colloque l'Amiral de Coligny et son temps* (Paris, 1974); and the political ideas of their most fervent opponents thereafter are discussed by F. J. Baumgartner, *Radical Reactionaries: The Political Thought of the French Catholic League* (Geneva, 1975).

The classic study of sixteenth-century political thought is P. Mesnard, *L'Essor de la philosophie politique au XVIe siècle* (Paris, 1936). Q. Skinner, *The Foundations of Modern Political Thought* (Cambridge, 1978), has been widely acclaimed as an outstanding survey of political ideologies from Dante to Bodin, and contains extensive bibliographies of primary and secondary sources. Still more recent – again too late for its perceptive readings to be used for this present book – is N. Keohane, *Philosophy and the State in France: From the Renaissance to the Enlightenment* (Princeton, NJ, 1980). The standard study of sixteenth-century French ideas concerning royal authority and the subjects' rights on the evidence of the writings of the legists is W. F. Church, *Constitutional Thought in Sixteenth-Century France* (Cambridge,

Mass., 1941). An acquaintance with Roman and medieval legal conceptions is essential to an understanding of those writers; here, W. Ullmann, *Law and Politics in the Middle Ages: An Introduction to the Sources of Medieval Political Ideas* (London, 1975), is an invaluable guide. Important essays by the distinguished American scholar Gaines Post are collected in his *Studies in Medieval Legal Thought: Public Law and the State, 1100–1322* (Princeton, NJ, 1963). In his '*Vera philosophia*: the philosophical significance of Renaissance jurisprudence', *Journal of the History of Philosophy*, vol. 14 (1976), pp. 267–79, D. R. Kelley shows how Renaissance jurists thought of themselves as practitioners of the highest form of philosophy. Apart from the legal tradition, other philosophical influences that informed sixteenth-century French thought may be explored in: *Platon et Aristote à la Renaissance: 16ᵉ colloque international de Tours, 1973* (*De Pétrarque à Descartes*, Vol. 32) (Paris, 1976), which has contributions by C. B. Schmitt and M. Reulos on the place of Aristotle and of Plato in university teaching; D. O. McNeil, *Guillaume Budé and Humanism in the Reign of Francis I* (Geneva, 1975); W. J. Ong, *Ramus: Method and the Decay of Dialogue* (Cambridge, Mass., 1958); I. Zanta, *La Renaissance du stoïcisme au XVIᵉ siècle* (Paris, 1914); D. P. Walker, 'The *Priscia Theologia* in France', *Journal of the Warburg and Courtauld Institutes*, vol. 17 (1954), pp. 204–59; and F. A. Yates, *The French Academies of the Sixteenth Century* (London, 1967). Turning to the French monarchy, there is a depressing lack of modern works on the leading early sixteenth-century jurists Rebuffi, Chasseneux and Grassaille; the best introduction to them remains that provided by Church in his *Constitutional Thought*, already noted. However, R. E. Giesey examines 'The juristic basis of dynastic right to the French throne', *Transactions of the American Philosophical Society*, vol. 51, pt 5 (1961), pp. 3–47, as well as the principal Huguenot opponents of monarchical authority in his 'The monarchomach triumvirs: Hotman, Beza and Mornay', *Bibliothèque d'humanisme et Renaissance*, vol. 32 (1970), pp. 41–56. A. d'Andrea and P. D. Stewart have edited another major Huguenot polemic against Italian influences upon French affairs, Innocent Gentillet's *Discours contre Machiavel* (Florence, 1974), on which see also C. E. Rathé, 'Innocent Gentillet and the first "Anti-Machiavel"', *Bibliothèque d'humanisme et Renaissance*, vol. 27 (1965), pp. 186–225. The Huguenot position in relation to contract theory figures in H. Höpfl and M. P. Thompson's re-examination of 'The history of contract as a motif in political thought', *American Historical Review*, vol. 84 (1979), pp. 915–44. A detailed study of earlier Huguenot political thought is V. de Caprariis, *Propaganda e pensiero politico in Francia durante le guerre di religione*, Vol. 1, *1559–1572* (Naples, 1959); while R. Linder discusses *The Political Ideas of Pierre Viret* (Geneva, 1964), pastor in Nîmes at the opening of the 1560s. From the extensive literature on Bodin, J. H. Franklin, *Jean Bodin and the Rise of Absolutist Theory* (Cambridge, 1973), deserves particular mention. Franklin is also one of the numerous contributors to the distinguished symposium edited by Denzer (above, p. 210); and more recent work on Bodin includes P. L. Rose, 'The *politique* and the prophet: Bodin and the Catholic League, 1589–1594', *The Historical Journal*, vol. 21 (1978), pp. 783–808.

The standard political history of France is still the *Histoire de France illustrée* edited at the beginning of the present century by E. Lavisse; the sixteenth century is covered in Vol. V, pts 1 and 2, by H. Lemonnier (Paris, 1903–4), and Vol. VI, pt 1, by J.-H. Mariéjol (Paris, 1911). Since these historians' day the focus of French historical scholarship has shifted away from the study of men and events. However, the leader of the famous descent into Italy is the subject of Y. Labande-Mailfert, *Charles VIII et son milieu (1470–1498): la jeunesse au pouvoir* (Paris, 1975); and A. Denis has re-examined *Charles VIII et les Italiens: histoire et mythe* (Geneva, 1979). A major biographical treatment of Francis I will shortly appear, by R. J. Knecht who has published foretastes of his views in a number of shorter pieces. They include his Historical Association pamphlet, *Francis I and Absolute Monarchy* (London, 1969), where Knecht takes issue with Major's interpretation of the monarchy as essentially consultative; and the same author's 'Francis I: prince and patron of the northern Renaissance', in A. G. Dickens (ed.), *The Courts of Europe: Politics, Patronage and Royalty, 1400–1800* (London, 1977). The imperial ideology in France, a tradition that informed King Francis's rivalry with Charles V, is examined by G. Zeller, 'Les rois de France, candidats à l'Empire', *Revue historique*, vol. 173 (1934), pp. 273–311, 497–534, and by F. A. Yates in the course of the essays that constitute her *Astraea: The Imperial Theme in the Sixteenth Century* (London, 1975). The magnificent encounter between Francis and his other rival, Henry VIII of England, is described by J. G. Russell, *The Field of the Cloth of Gold* (London, 1969). Studies of individual administrators and diplomats who rose to high royal office, and thereby to high ecclesiastical office as well, are: A. Buisson, *Le Chancelier Antoine Duprat* (Paris, 1935); M. François, *Le Cardinal de Tournon, homme d'état, mécène et humaniste (1489–1562)* (Paris, 1951); and G. Baguenault de Puchesse, *Jean de Morvillier, évêque d'Orléans, Garde des Sceaux de France, 1506–77* (Paris, 1869). Portentous mid-century diplomatic negotiations are considered by C. Thellier, 'Après la paix du Cateau-Cambrésis de 1559: négociations engagées pour fixer les limites entre les possessions espagnoles et françaises au nord et à l'est de la France', *Anciens pays et assemblées d'États*, vol. 48 (1969), pp. 77–91. Although L. Romier's judgements on France's political condition at the outset of the religious wars, and especially on the Queen Mother, have since been challenged, his *Le Royaume de Catherine de Médicis*, 2 vols (Paris, 1922), contains much of value. So, too, does J. W. Thompson, *The Wars of Religion in France, 1559–76* (London, 1958), though a detailed and up-to-date account of the wars, combining narrative with analysis, has now been supplied by J. H. M. Salmon, *Society in Crisis: France in the Sixteenth Century* (London, 1975). N. M. Sutherland has made a number of important contributions to knowledge of particular political episodes; her articles include 'Calvinism and the conspiracy of Amboise', *History*, vol. 47 (1962), pp. 111–38, and, most recently, 'The assassination of François duc de Guise, February 1563', *The Historical Journal*, vol. 24 (1981), pp. 279–95. In her 'Catherine de Medici: the legend of the wicked Italian queen', *The Sixteenth Century Journal*, vol. 9 (1978), pp. 45–56, she traces how interested and biased writers have denigrated the Queen Mother, who is now the subject of a major study by a leading historian of ecclesiastical affairs, I. Cloulas, *Catherine de Médicis* (Paris, 1979). Another queen, more reputable than Catherine in religion and more fortunate in her offspring, is portrayed by N. L. Roelker, *Queen of Navarre: Jeanne d'Albret, 1528–1572* (Cambridge, Mass., 1968). There is no satisfactory study of the last of the Valois kings, on whom the *Bibliothèque d'humanisme et Renaissance*, vol. 40 (1978), prints two relevant articles, by R. J. Sealy ('The *Palace Academy* of Henry III', pp. 61–83) and by E. H. Dickerman ('Henry III of France, student of *The Prince*', pp. 281–8). Dickerman is also the author of a study of two important later sixteenth-century politicians and administrators, the one a *surintendant des finances* and a chancellor, the other a highly influential *secrétaire d'état*: *Bellièvre and Villeroy: Power in France under Henry III and Henry IV* (Providence, RI, 1971).

Older works focusing on the leaders of the opposing factions in the religious wars include J. Delaborde's *Gaspard de Coligny, amiral de France*, 3 vols (Paris, 1879–82), and H. Forneron, *Les Ducs de Guise et leur époque*, 2 vols (Paris, 1877). By and large historians have dealt more generously with the former and his associates than with the latter. J. Shimizu has produced a recent assessment of the principal victim of the *Saint-Barthélemy*: *Conflict of Loyalties: Politics and Religion in the Career of Gaspard de Coligny, Admiral of France, 1519–1572* (Geneva, 1970). But conflicting loyalties in the case of the Guises damagingly involve their association with international Catholicism, and with Spain. In this connection, J. de Croze, *Les Guise, les Valois et Philippe II*, 2 vols (Paris, 1866), is still worth consulting for its materials; much more recently, N. M. Sutherland has brought a wide political perspective to bear upon *The Massacre of St Bartholomew and the European Conflict, 1559 to 1572* (London, 1972). On political manœuvring in the 1580s, De Lamar Jensen has written a lively account of Spanish machinations in his *Diplomacy and Dogmatism: Bernardino de Mendoza and the French Catholic League* (Cambridge, Mass., 1964); for criticisms of this work, see the review-article by Sutherland, in *History*, vol. 51 (1966), pp. 323–31. Finally on matters of political biography, the multi-fascicule *Dictionnaire de biographie française*, launched in 1933, has now reached the letter G; it remains to be seen how the Guises will fare at its contributors' hands.

The best textbook in English on the sixteenth century in general is H. G. Koenigsberger and G. L. Mosse, *Europe in the Sixteenth Century* (London, 1968). In French, a still more wide-ranging and methodologically ambitious survey is M. Morineau, *Le XVIᵉ siècle* (Paris, 1973). Although to compile a bibliography of the state would require a volume in its own right, attention may be drawn in conclusion to the following three works, the authors of which each approaches the problem from a particular standpoint. The distinguished American historian of medieval government in France, J. R. Strayer, writes *On the Medieval Origins of the Modern State* (Princeton, NJ, 1970). The third of the three essays in the English philosopher M. Oakeshott's *On Human Conduct* (Oxford, 1975) considers 'that ambiguous human relationship commonly called a modern European state'. And the concept of the state in European political thought from the sixteenth century onwards is discussed from the standpoint of a student of political science by K. H. F. Dyson, *The State Tradition in Western Europe* (Oxford, 1980) – a volume that contains an extensive bibliography.

Index